SCOTT FORESMAN ENGLISH

ON TARGET

TEACHER'S EDITION

2

INTERMEDIATE

Second Edition

James E. Purpura
Teachers College, Columbia University

Diane Pinkley
Teachers College, Columbia University

Teacher's Edition revised by Randee Falk

Longman

I dedicate this book to the memory of two wonderful parents, Josephine Mercurio Purpura and Michael F. Purpura. JP

I dedicate this book to Georgie, Adrian, José, and Montse, and Jennifer, with appreciation and love. DP

Acknowledgments

We are especially grateful to James R. Herbolich of ESADE Idiomas in Barcelona and to Stephen Gudgel of the Institute of North American Studies in Barcelona for their insightful comments and support throughout this project. A sincere word of thanks to Laura Le Dréan and Joanne Dresner at Pearson Education for believing in us. Thanks to Steve Albanese for being there whenever we needed you.

Reviewers and Piloters

Our thanks to the following reviewers and piloters whose comments and suggestions were of great value in the development of the second edition of *Scott Foresman English*.

Angie Alcocer, Maria Alvarado School, Lima, Peru; **Walter A. Alvarez Barreto,** Santa Teresita School, Lima, Peru; **Chuck Anderson,** Athenée Français, Tokyo, Japan; **Paula Banks Al-Saihati,** Dhahran Ahliyya Schools, Saudi Arabia; **Lourdes Betancourt,** English Resource Center, Caracas, Venezuela; **Elba de Buenafama,** School Hipocampitos, Los Teques-Caracas, Venezuela; **Alexandra Espinoza Cascante,** Instituto Universal de Idiomas, San José, Costa Rica; **Orquídea Flores/Romelia Pérez,** Colegio Nuestra Señora de la Paz, Puerto La Cruz, Venezuela; **Brigite Fonseca,** Colegio Bom Jesus, Joinville, Santa Catarina, Brazil; **Edmundo Gallardo,** Universidad de Occidente, Culiacán, Sin., Mexico; **Ana María García,** Instituto Tecnológico de Estudios Superiores de Monterrey, Mexico; **Victor A. García,** Universidad de Occidente, Culiacán, Sin., Mexico; **Irma K. Ghosn,** Lebanese American University, Byblos, Lebanon; **Carmina González Molina,** Instituto Cultural, A.C., Mexico City, Mexico; **Lucero González Mendieta,** Universidad de Occidente, Culiacán, Sin., Mexico; **Luz Ma. González,** Universidad de Occidente, Culiacán, Sin., Mexico; **Gloria I. Gutiérrez Vera,** Colegio Regiomontano Country, Monterrey, Mexico; **Tatiana Hernández Gaubil,** Colegio Madre del Divino Pastor, San José, Costa Rica; **Madeleine Hudders,** University of Puerto Rico, San Juan, Puerto Rico; **Denise Khoury,** Notre Dame de Louaize School, Lebanon; **Jerome D. Klena,** Nihon Gaigo Senmon Gakko, Tokyo, Japan; **Jane Lyon Lee,** Chungang University, Seoul, Korea; **Francisco J. Martínez,** Instituto La Salle Preparatoria, León, Mexico; **Javier Murillo,** Universidad de Occidente, Culiacán, Sin., Mexico; **Jorge Obregón Aragón,** Universidad de Occidente, Culiacán, Sin., Mexico; **Paula Sánchez Cortés,** Centro de Idiomas, ENSE de N.L., Monterrey, Mexico; **Nitzie de Stanley/Mireya Miramare,** IFISA, Puerto La Cruz, Venezuela; **Erick Soriano Moreno,** Universidad de Occidente, Culiacán, Sin., Mexico; **Elizabeth Vélez,** Colegio San Agustín, Cabo Rojo, Puerto Rico; **Diana Yupanqui Alvarez,** San Antonio de Mujeres School, Lima, Peru

On Target 2 Teacher's Edition, Second Edition

Copyright © 2000, 1991 by Addison Wesley Longman, Inc.
A Pearson Education Company
All rights reserved.
No part of this publication may be reproduced, stored in a retrieval system, or transmitted in any form or by any means, electronic, mechanical, photocopying, recording, or otherwise, without the prior permission of the publisher. Exception: The Placement, Mid-Book, and End-of-Book Tests (pages TExviii–TExxii) and the Vocabulary Expansion Activities (pages T140–T151) may be duplicated for classroom use without formal permission.

Pearson Education, 10 Bank Street, White Plains, NY 10606

Editorial directors: Allen Ascher, Louise Jennewine
Acquisitions editor: Bill Preston
Director of design and production: Rhea Banker
Development editors: Barbara Barysh, Marilyn Hochman
Production manager: Alana Zdinak
Production supervisor: Liza Pleva
Executive managing editor: Linda Moser
Senior production editor: Virgina Bernard
Production editor: Lynn Contrucci
Director of manufacturing: Patrice Fraccio
Senior manufacturing buyer: Edith Pullman
Photo research: Quarasan and Aerin Csigay
Cover design: Charles Yuen
Text design and composition: Quarasan
Photo and illustration credits: See page ii.

ISBN: 0-201-66415-1

2 3 4 5 6 7 8 9 10—WC—05

CONTENTS

Introduction to *Scott Foresman English, Second Edition*

This new edition of *Scott Foresman English* is a theme-based, integrated skills series for secondary and adult students. It is a unique and flexible program with multiple entry levels. The components can be used together as a comprehensive eight-level course or individually as separate mini-courses. The series consists of:

On Your Mark 1 and 2	INTRODUCTORY
In Contact 1 and 2	BEGINNING
On Target 1 and 2	INTERMEDIATE
In Charge 1 and 2	ADVANCED

Key Features of the First Edition

The second edition of *Scott Foresman English* maintains and builds on the key features of the successful and popular first edition.

- **An integrated syllabus** presents the communication skills—listening, speaking, reading, writing—together with functions, notions, and grammar.

- **Thematic units** teach English through a variety of high-interest topics and content.

- **A learner-centered approach** makes students active participants in every lesson by activating their prior knowledge of the topics and encouraging them to share and express their personal experience, ideas, and opinions in English.

- **The development of critical thinking skills** such as classifying, sequencing, making inferences, and drawing conclusions helps students learn more effectively and retain learned material longer.

- **The application of learning strategies** such as applying prior knowledge, scanning for specific information, skimming for main ideas, and getting meaning from context helps students take responsibility for their own learning and become more effective, independent learners.

New Features of the Second Edition

The second edition incorporates many ideas and improvements suggested by teachers from around the world.

- **Revised and updated content** includes new conversations, listening activities, and readings.

- **Summary of skills** charts highlight the new unit organization and identify and summarize key language skills, strategies, and topics in each unit.

- **Grammar presentations and practice** allow students to focus on form, meaning, and use. Many new and revised grammar presentations provide clear explanations and examples. New exercises and activities offer a balance of controlled and communicative practice.

- **Learning strategies** are now highlighted in all levels with the symbol ➡. Many new strategies have been added to promote effective, independent learning and academic success.

- **Review sections** have been added every three units to recycle and reinforce grammar focus and key vocabulary.

- **Teacher's Editions** are easier to use, with unit objectives, listening scripts, and answers to exercises clearly identified and highlighted.

- **Achievement tests** allow teachers and students to assess their progress after each unit.

- **The audio program** is now available in two formats: audiocassettes and audio CDs.

Components of the Program

Each level of *Scott Foresman English*, Second Edition, contains these components.

Student Book

Each Student Book contains twelve thematic units. A new Summary of Skills chart following the Contents highlights and summarizes the important language skills, strategies, and teaching points in each unit. New review material following Units 3, 6, 9, and 12 reinforces key vocabulary and grammar points. Additional material includes a Starting Out section (providing a brief introduction to the course), an irregular verb list, an International Phonetic Alphabet (IPA) chart, a unit-by-unit vocabulary list, and an index.

Workbook

The Workbook provides further practice and reinforcement of vocabulary and grammar, as well as additional interactive speaking activities and listening tasks. A self-test page (Check Your Knowledge) at the end of each unit allows students to assess their own progress.

Teacher's Edition

The Teacher's Edition contains full-size, full-color reproductions of the Student Book pages opposite complete teaching suggestions for the Student Book and references to corresponding Workbook practice exercises. Answers to all Student Book exercises are now highlighted in boxes on the corresponding Teacher's Edition pages. Listening scripts to all Student Book and Workbook exercises, along with the Workbook Answer Key, follow the Student Book pages. Each Teacher's Edition unit ends with suggestions for evaluating language and communication skills. The Teacher's Edition also includes Placement, Mid-Book, and End-of-Book Tests, information on basic teaching techniques, and a Scope and Sequence chart. *On Target 1* and *2* also provide Vocabulary Expansion Activities. These reproducible blackline masters provide additional vocabulary enrichment work.

Audio Program

All material appearing on the audio program is indicated in the Student Book and Workbook pages with the symbol 🎧. The audio program is available in two formats, audiocassettes and audio CDs. Both contain conversation models as well as materials for the Warm Up, Listen, and Pronunciation sections in the Student Book and selected listening exercises in the Workbook.

Achievement Tests

The new Achievement Tests provide an additional option for evaluation. The Achievement Test book contains tests for all twelve units and an answer key.

Introduction to *On Target*

About the Authors

James E. Purpura is currently Assistant Professor of Linguistics and Education in the TESOL and Applied Linguistics programs at Teachers College, Columbia University, in New York City. He holds a Ph.D. in TESL/Applied Linguistics from the University of California at Los Angeles.

Dr. Purpura worked at the Institute of North American Studies, Barcelona, Spain, from 1982 to 1990, first as an instructor, then as Director of Courses. In addition, he has taught in France, Iran, Saudi Arabia, and Kuwait. He has also worked as a curriculum specialist in Iran, Saudi Arabia, and San Diego, California, and was involved in curriculum development at Kuwait University. His scholarly publications appear in *Language Learning*, *Language Testing*, and *Issues in Applied Linguistics*.

Diane Pinkley is the Director of the TC TESOL Certificate Program at Teachers College, Columbia University, in New York City. She holds a B.A. from Avila College, Kansas City, Missouri, and an M.A. in English language and literature from the University of Michigan. She is currently pursuing studies leading to an Ed.D. in TESOL at Teachers College, Columbia University.

Ms. Pinkley worked as Curriculum Coordinator at the Michigan Language Center in Ann Arbor, Michigan, as well as instructor and Director of Courses at the Institute of North American Studies in Barcelona, Spain. She has taught American and British literature and American culture, and all levels of EFL/ESL.

A Student Book Unit

In response to teachers' feedback on the first edition, the unit organization of the new edition has been restructured for greater clarity and ease of use. Each unit is divided into four distinct sections, each identified with a different color, which highlight the pedagogic features and language skills.

GETTING STARTED

This unit opening section consists of three parts.

Warm Up

Warm Up activates students' prior knowledge of the unit theme. It introduces the theme by means of a short listening passage. Interactive activities follow to get students talking about how the theme relates to their knowledge, feelings, and life experiences.

Figure It Out

Figure It Out presents the new language in a functional context in the form of a conversation, mini-reading, or questionnaire. Students begin to acquire the language before they analyze it in the Grammar section. Comprehension questions check understanding. A Vocabulary Check exercise helps students discover the meaning of the target vocabulary from context. This exercise is indicated in the Student Book with the symbol ☑.

Talk About It

Talk About It provides students with the opportunity to practice one or more aspects of the target language in a controlled context. This is an intermediary step between cue dependency and real production.

GRAMMAR

This section presents the target grammar of the unit. Grammar presentations and practice focus on structure, meaning, and usage, and are designed to encourage students to analyze the language by means of inductive and deductive reasoning. A variety of exercises gives students the opportunity to practice language structure individually and in pairs or groups. Check Your Understanding exercises allow students to test their understanding of specific situations in which particular tenses and other grammar points are used. These exercises are indicated with the symbol ☑. A culminating Express Yourself activity allows students to use the language communicatively in personalized contexts. This activity is indicated with the symbol 🔀.

LISTENING and SPEAKING

This third section integrates listening and speaking strategies, skills, and activities.

Listen

The Before You Listen activities focus on anticipating meaning and applying prior knowledge to the listening task. These prelistening activities are followed by strategies such as listening for details, making inferences, and organizing information. These strategies are indicated with the symbol ➡.

Pronunciation

This section provides practice in perceiving and producing the phonology of English (sounds, intonation, stress, reduction, etc.).

Speak Out

Speak Out activities develop fluency as the students share information, opinions, and experiences. In addition, each unit focuses on at least one discussion strategy, which is indicated with the symbol ➡.

READING and WRITING

This final section integrates reading and writing strategies, skills, and activities.

Read About It

Read About It contains high-interest readings that reflect and extend the unit themes. Prereading exercises (Before You Read) focus on applying students' prior knowledge. Reading strategies such as scanning, understanding sequence, and getting meaning from context are presented and then checked in comprehension exercises. These strategies are indicated with the symbol ➡.

Think About It

Think About It presents activities that offer students further opportunities to apply strategies and share personal knowledge and experience related to the readings in open-ended, creative ways.

Write

This section focuses on specific writing tasks—such as writing a topic sentence, narrowing a topic, using supporting details—that prepare students to write with confidence in English.

Write About It

Write About It tasks, consistent with the unit themes, are purposeful and communicative because students are writing for a real audience of their peers. A new, culminating Check Your Writing exercise applies the important writing process steps of peer feedback and revision. These exercises are indicated with the symbol ☑.

A Teacher's Edition Unit

Each unit in the Teacher's Edition starts with a list of unit objectives. These objectives are followed by complete teaching information for each section of the Student Book unit.

The teaching information contains suggestions for previewing and presenting material, language and cultural notes, and a rich variety of optional extension activities, including ideas for discussion topics, vocabulary enrichment, spelling, games and competitions, and research projects. These optional activities add flexibility to the course length, depending on how few or how many of the optional activities are used.

- The **Preview** section gives suggestions for introducing content and for developing the target language. During the Preview, you will want to encourage students to say as much as they can about the content or theme. Model correct usage, but remember that the objective here is to get students involved and to give them the language they need to express their ideas.

- The **Presentation** section provides effective, step-by-step suggestions for presenting the lesson, using clear, practical teaching methods.

- A variety of **Options** provides flexibility so that you can adapt the lesson to the needs of your class and offer additional activities for reinforcement and enrichment.

- The **Evaluation** section at the end of each unit contains suggestions for four different ways to evaluate your students' progress. See pages TExi–TExii for more information.

- **Workbook links** suggest points at which the corresponding material in the Workbook may be assigned, indicated with the symbol [Link] .

- **Language Notes** explain colloquial English, foreign words, idiomatic expressions, and provide additional information about usage.

Presenting a Unit

GETTING STARTED

Warm Up

Each unit in *On Target* opens with a Warm Up section that both introduces students to the theme of the unit and involves them in the theme. It typically consists of a listening passage to which students must respond and one or more interactive exercises in which they talk about the unit theme.

Preview suggestions include the introduction of the target language through the use of pictures, realia, mime, and Total Physical Response (TPR) (see page TExiii). Depending on students' abilities, you may wish to skip this section and have the students learn the language directly from the recording and the Student Book pages.

In general, all the target language appears in the Warm Up and Figure It Out sections. These sections have been carefully designed so that students can discover the meaning of the new language through the pictures and context. Because of this, you should begin the presentation of each unit by reading the unit title and the Warm Up section with the class. Encourage students to say as much as they can about the pictures and text. Model any language they need. Use the Preview suggestions to clarify or for reinforcement or review.

Play the recording and have students complete the corresponding exercises. Use the procedures outlined in Listen on page TEix.

Figure It Out

This section demonstrates the use of the new language in functional situations.

There are several ways to present this section to students. You will want to choose the method that best suits your classroom and your method of teaching.

Whatever method you use, first have students comment on the pictures and predict what the section is about. Using prior knowledge and anticipating meaning are valuable comprehension tools.

Most of the units contain conversations. In presenting them, you can emphasize listening and aural comprehension by reading the conversations aloud as students listen with their books closed. For each listening, you will want to set up a comprehension task. For some classes, ask a simple factual question and tell students to listen for the answer. For more advanced students, you should set more difficult tasks, such as inferring where the speakers are, what their relationship is, etc. You may find it valuable to have students read the comprehension questions before they listen.

Next, read the conversations again as students follow along in their books. If necessary, a few yes/no questions will help students focus on meaning.

Then have students work in pairs or groups to read the conversations aloud. They might also answer the comprehension questions and do the meaning-from-context exercise at this time.

Finally, ask for volunteers to perform the conversations for the class. Encourage students to adapt or add to the conversations by introducing new topics or adding additional speakers as their level of proficiency permits. Simple props will make performing the conversations fun and meaningful.

For units that contain mini-readings or questionnaires, see Read About It on page TEx for ideas and suggestions.

Presenting Vocabulary

Active and Receptive Vocabulary

On Target includes both active and receptive vocabulary. The active vocabulary has been selected for its usefulness and frequency of occurrence in real communication. A list of the active vocabulary for each unit is included in Unit Vocabulary at the back of the Student Book (see page 132). In addition, receptive vocabulary appears throughout the unit. Students are not expected to learn these non-target words. Instead, they should learn to develop a tolerance for ambiguity with respect to unknown vocabulary. As long as they can complete the activities, understanding every word is not necessary. Students should be encouraged not to use dictionaries but to try to make intelligent guesses about meaning based on the use of context, cognates, word families, and other strategies.

Introducing Vocabulary

Every opportunity should be taken to involve students in the learning process. Introduce vocabulary through pictures, realia, or TPR (see page TExiii). Encourage students to provide synonyms, antonyms, examples, or simple definitions. Many English words are similar in form and meaning to words in other languages. Students should be trained to recognize these cognates (and cautioned on the dangers of false cognates).

Help students understand and use the techniques of paraphrasing and circumlocution to elicit and communicate new, unfamiliar vocabulary—for example, to say "the thing you cut bread with" for *knife*, or "go behind (someone)" for *follow*. As often as possible, help them understand meaning through the use of word associations. For example, the meaning of many verbs can be demonstrated through the use of different complements—e.g., *run out of gas* on the highway, *run out of money* at the store, *run out of eggs* while making a cake.

Finally, encourage students to use only monolingual dictionaries. Bilingual dictionaries force students to see English in terms of their own language instead of as a distinct tool for communication. Translation should be used only as a last resort.

Vocabulary Notebooks

Encourage students to keep notebooks of new vocabulary, to include both the words they learn in the Student Book and words they want to know in order to express their own ideas. Have students make up sentences to illustrate the meaning of the new words. This can be done individually or in pairs or groups. Write the best examples on the board for students to copy into their notebooks. If students group the words by meaning and function, at the end of the year they will have their own personal dictionaries. (You may want to collect and check the notebooks periodically to make sure that students' example sentences are correct.)

Talk About It

This mini-dialogue presents a series of connected conversational cues (a discourse chain) that trains students to relate roles, functions, and language possibilities. Have students work in pairs to read the situation and identify the roles; for example, in Unit 1 the situation involves a discussion of different ways that students can make progress in learning a language, and the roles are two students who are asking each other about their progress in learning English. Assign or let students choose roles. Have them read the functions (printed in small type) and the mini-dialogue aloud. Answer any questions about vocabulary or grammar. Then focus attention on the exercise cues; in Unit 1, these cues consist of items on a Language-Learning Awareness Questionnaire (see Student Book, pages 1–3). Do one example with a student or ask a pair to do one example as a model. Then have the pairs work together to complete the exercise. Encourage students to add examples.

GRAMMAR

In this section, students are given a brief grammatical description of the target language and are asked to apply those rules (deductive reasoning), or they are given a number of examples and are asked to use the examples to formulate rules (inductive reasoning).

This presentation is followed by exercises designed to accomplish one of two purposes: to train students to use the language accurately and to encourage them to use it fluently. The exercises designed for accuracy can be done by the students independently, in class or as homework; however, you will probably find it preferable to have students complete them in pairs or small groups. In this way, students can help each other form the correct answers. Check Your Understanding exercises follow to allow students to test their understanding of the specific situations in which the particular points are used. These exercises are done individually and then students are encouraged to check their answers with a partner. The Express Yourself exercises should be done in pairs to promote fluency and proper use of new vocabulary. Cooperative learning and peer correction are invaluable in developing both accuracy and fluency.

LISTENING and SPEAKING

Listen

The listening selections on the audio program provide practice in understanding ordinary English discourse. Each listening section begins with Before You Listen prelistening questions, which establish the context and help students activate and share prior knowledge. The prelistening questions are followed by the presentation of a specific listening strategy, highlighted with ➡. You will want students to answer the prelistening questions, to comment on any pictures, charts, etc., and to discuss the strategy before you play the recording or read the selection aloud. Always remind students that they don't have to understand every word of the selection in order to do the exercise.

The first time you play the recording or read the selection aloud, have students listen with their books closed. Set a purpose for listening by asking a simple, factual question and having students listen for the answer. When they answer the question, have them tell you anything else they can remember about what they heard.

Have students open their books and reread the directions. Play the recording or read the selection again and tell them to listen for the specific information the exercise asks for. According to students' ability, you can have them mark the exercise at this time or during a third listening.

After students have written their answers, play the recording or read the selection again for students to check their work.

Pronunciation

To communicate understandably, a speaker must pronounce individual sounds correctly and use the patterns of word stress, intonation contours, and rhythms that are characteristic of a language. The listener, too, must participate actively, using his or her knowledge of those elements to derive meaning. Good pronunciation evolves only gradually. However, students should be encouraged from the start to listen carefully to the way English sounds are produced and to attempt the pronunciation of all of them.

A book alone cannot teach pronunciation; it can only serve as a guide. It is your voice and the voices on the recordings that must provide the models for the class. Speakers on radio and TV, recordings, and class visitors who are native speakers can provide additional models. Good models, consistent patterns, and ample opportunity to listen and speak are essential for developing good pronunciation.

On Target focuses on perceiving and producing such aspects of English phonology as plural and past tense endings, word and sentence stress, intonation, reduction, and elision. Most students will not be able to produce such things as intonation and stress with perfect accuracy. Concentrate instead on their hearing and understanding these aspects of English.

Have students read the explanation and make any predictions about the target sound. Play the recording or read the examples several times while students listen. Remember that they must be able to perceive a sound before they can produce it. Next, play the recording or repeat each word or sentence first for the class, then for groups, and finally individuals to repeat. Then have students complete the exercises and formulate the rule if required.

You will find it valuable to have students work in pairs or groups to read the examples to each other. This gives additional, needed practice in forming the sounds correctly.

Speak Out

Begin by setting up a situation in which the target discussion strategy highlighted with ➡ would be used. For example, if the strategy focuses on persuading, you might ask students how late they are allowed to stay out on weekday evenings and how they would try to get permission from their parents to stay out later. Elicit examples from the class and/or refer them to the strategy presentation box in the Student Book. Have one or more pairs of students use the expressions in a conversation based on your example.

Divide students into pairs or groups according to the activity and have them read the directions. Answer any questions they have. For some units, you may wish to model a conversation for the class or have students do so. Then have students complete the activity. Monitor the groups, but do not interrupt for correction. Instead, take note of repeated errors for later reteaching or review.

Encourage students to use the language in the strategy boxes as much as possible, inside and out of class. The purpose of this activity is to help students gain confidence in their oral performance. The constant reinforcement of this language will result in greater fluency.

Read About It

The reading selection in Read About It extends the theme of the unit and provides the opportunity for improving reading strategies and critical thinking skills. The section opens with Before You Read prereading questions, which introduce the content and help students recall prior knowledge of the subject. Commenting on any illustrations along with using such reading strategies as skimming and scanning further preview the selection. In most units, the prereading questions are followed by specific reading strategies (highlighted with ➡) aimed at helping students focus their attention on reading for specific information, examples, or main ideas. In other units, reading strategies immediately follow the reading selections and focus on guessing meaning from context and making inferences.

Most reading done for information or pleasure is silent reading, so students should read the selections silently. Encourage them to read without dictionaries. Stopping to look up unknown words interrupts the flow of reading and makes it more likely that students read word for word rather than for general meaning. In addition, the selections have all been carefully written to enable students to use cognates and to understand meaning from context.

The reading may be assigned as homework, but you will probably find it more beneficial to have students read in class. Set a time limit to encourage them to keep reading without stopping at each unknown word. Watch to make sure they are not relying on their dictionaries.

Think About It

A final Think About It section presents challenging, creative activities related to the reading. Some exercises check comprehension, the ability to get meaning from context, and other reading skills. These exercises can be completed in pairs or small groups. Other open-ended activities offer students further opportunities to develop critical thinking skills and share personal knowledge and experience in imaginative ways.

Write

In the Write sections, specific elements of paragraph writing are presented—such as identifying what makes a good paragraph, narrowing a topic, writing a topic sentence, adding supporting details, and writing a concluding sentence—along with other important academic writing skills and forms

such as summarizing and writing instructions. The presentations are immediately followed by one or more exercises that allow students to apply and practice the target elements or skills.

Write About It

Write About It tasks are purposeful and communicative. Students write for a real purpose related to the unit theme and for a real audience of their peers

On Target also incorporates key elements of the writing process to help students brainstorm and organize ideas, write their first drafts, and then edit and revise their paragraphs. The new Check Your Writing exercises at the end of each unit focus students' attention on key points from the unit and help them edit and revise their drafts, applying the important writing process steps of peer feedback and revision. The following steps highlight and summarize key aspects of the writing process. Depending on your teaching objectives and classroom situation, you may follow these steps as guidelines for using the writing process more extensively and comprehensively.

1. Prewriting

Prewriting includes the important strategies of brainstorming, focusing, and organizing information. These strategies help students to generate, select, and organize ideas so that they can write a first draft of a paragraph about a specific topic.

In **brainstorming**, students make a list of as many ideas about a particular topic as they can. The purpose of brainstorming is to generate and explore lots of possible ideas. Students should not worry at this point whether or not their ideas are good or bad but should just write them down.

Once students have a list of possible ideas, they can then focus on choosing the best, most useful ideas for inclusion in a paragraph. In **focusing**, students should keep the ideas that relate to the topic they will write about and eliminate ideas that do not.

After students choose the ideas they want to write about, they are ready to organize them in a paragraph. Each Write section focuses on a specific element—such as writing topic sentences, narrowing a topic, or writing supporting sentences—for **organizing** ideas in a paragraph. These sections have been expanded and improved in the new edition to include more examples and models of the target elements.

Most students find it beneficial to do some or all prewriting with a partner because this enables them to invent and generate more new ideas from each other's ideas.

2. First Draft

Many students do not realize that good writing is usually the result of many revisions or drafts. Knowing that they will write more than one draft allows students to focus on different aspects of their writing in each draft. As students write their first drafts, they should concentrate on composition, not mechanics (such as grammar, spelling, and punctuation). Have them work with partners to write good topic sentences. Remind them that every supporting sentence should amplify the topic sentence and that the sentences should be in a logical order. Assure them that good writers revise several times.

3. Revision

Revising includes making such changes as adding new information, deleting nonessential information, and arranging the information in the best order. Editing for mechanics—to check grammar and proofread for correct spelling and punctuation—is a final step of revision. Students should understand that you expect correct grammar, spelling, and punctuation in the final copy, but that revision of these comes last in the writing process.

Peer editing is an effective tool for second-language writers. Have students exchange papers with a partner and read the partner's paper for interest and accuracy of content. Do they understand what the other person is trying to say? Do they have any questions they would like answered to make the passage clearer? Do they see anything that is out of place or irrelevant? The new, culminating Check Your Writing exercises can help students focus their attention on these and other questions. After peer editing, have students work independently to improve their drafts. Partners can then get back together to discuss the improvements and to work on mechanics. You may wish to have partners sign each other's final drafts. This gives each person a stake in the other's success.

4. Correction

When correcting students' writing, concentrate on paragraph structure and ideas over grammar, punctuation, and spelling. You might use one color pencil to comment on content and another to mark errors in mechanics.

Student compositions will probably contain many mechanical errors. For this reason, you may wish to concentrate only on one aspect in a particular composition. For example, if a student is having difficulty with English punctuation, you might mark only the punctuation errors. Or you may wish to mark only the errors in the target language of the unit.

However you do it, be sure to let students know that you and the rest of the class are interested in what they have to say by providing some means of presenting their work.

5. Presenting

All writing should be done with an audience in mind. Public acceptance of the writer's product validates both the writer and the writing process. Therefore, you should arrange to have students present their writing to the class—*if they so wish*.

Following are some suggestions for presenting:

- Have students read their articles or paragraphs aloud to a group or to the class.
- Display the papers on a bulletin board.
- Place a number of samples from an assignment in a notebook to be shared by interested members of the class.

Using these elements of paragraph writing for the writing process makes students confident writers, providing them with both a blueprint and the tools for constructing paragraphs.

Remember that good readers often become good writers. By providing a variety of English language materials for students to read (magazines and newspapers as well as books, fiction as well as nonfiction), you will be increasing their understanding of writing in English.

Evaluation

The second edition of *On Target* offers a new supplementary test booklet for each level, containing an individual achievement test for each unit. These new achievement tests complement and expand on the three other ways of evaluating students' progress provided in the first edition: a self-test of vocabulary and grammar, a dictation for aural comprehension and writing, and a check of oral proficiency.

Achievement Tests

The new Achievement Test booklet for each level contains tests for all twelve units. Each unit test measures students' progress in grammar, vocabulary, pronunciation, reading, and writing. There are separate scales for different parts of the test, so you can test all or selective skills, depending on your teaching objectives.

Self-Test

Each unit in the Workbook ends with a self-test called Check Your Knowledge, allowing students to assess their own progress. Encourage students to complete these tests without looking back at their student books. Although you may want to have students complete the tests in class so that you can record their scores, the tests are best treated as a learning experience. Students are interested in their own progress and will take responsibility for review if they know that their mistakes here will not be held against them in their final grades.

Dictation

Dictation can be a valuable diagnostic tool. By careful correction, you can discover which areas need reteaching or review. For example, if students consistently drop the third person singular simple present tense ending, you will want to do additional practice on hearing, saying, and spelling that ending. Information on giving and correcting dictations can be found on page TExv.

Evaluating Oral Communication Skills

Oral communication has one primary goal—to get the message across as clearly as possible. The ability to communicate orally in a second or foreign language involves a complex set of competencies or abilities, each of which may develop at its own pace. We define oral communication skills in terms of five competencies. See the Oral Communication Skills Assessment Scale.

Oral assessment can make students anxious, so use strategies that help students feel safe. Engaging in small talk before the beginning of an oral exam—for example, asking students how they are or talking about the weather and other simple topics—can help students feel more relaxed and at ease. You can also make students feel more comfortable by using clear directions and procedures so that they know what to expect.

You may choose to assess students individually or to have them work in pairs or small groups, depending on your objectives. (For example, if you want to assess students' ability to manage a discussion, you need to have students interacting in small groups.) Audio- or videotaping students during oral exams is an effective tool for learning and assessment. This allows you to listen several times and score what you observe. Audio- or videotaping also gives you the option of involving students in self- or peer assessment—that is, students can listen/observe and evaluate themselves or each other.

However you conduct oral assessment, introduce students gradually to the criteria of correctness so that they understand the objectives and know how to improve. In the beginning, assess only one or two of the following abilities. Gradually add more. Use the number scale in the box to rate the abilities. You can modify the scale to meet your specific needs.

Oral Communication Skills Assessment Scale

| 3 = excellent | 1 = fair |
| 2 = good | 0 = poor |

1. **COMMUNICATIVE EFFECTIVENESS**
   Using language to convey ideas
   3 2 1 0

2. **GRAMMATICAL ACCURACY**
   Using grammar forms and vocabulary correctly
   3 2 1 0

3. **GRAMMATICAL APPROPRIATENESS**
   Using appropriate forms in context (with appropriate formality, politeness)
   3 2 1 0

4. **INTELLIGIBILITY**
   Using accurate pronunciation and intonation
   3 2 1 0

5. **INTERACTIVE EFFECTIVENESS**
   Using strategies to keep communication going
   3 2 1 0

Vocabulary Expansion Activities

The twelve reproducible, supplementary activities (one for each unit in the student book) provide students with additional tools for becoming independent learners by increasing their active and receptive vocabularies. They present vocabulary-building skills such as recognizing prefixes and suffixes, understanding noun compounds, and inferring extended meanings. Topics of other activities include idioms, empty verbs (*take, have, break*, etc.), phrasal verbs, and other specific difficulties of English vocabulary.

The language presented in each activity has always been introduced in the corresponding Student Book unit. A good time to present the activity is after students have completed the unit. Students should be familiar with the language and can apply strategies for getting meaning from context to help them understand the target skill or topic in each activity. As students complete each activity, encourage them to think of as many additional examples of the specific topic as possible. Answers to the vocabulary expansion activities appear at the end of the teaching notes for each unit.

Teaching Techniques

Using Realia

The use of realia in the classroom will motivate students and make them realize the relevance of their language study. Realia includes anything from the real world: native speakers, radio and TV programs, films, records and tapes, printed materials such as brochures, tickets, schedules, ads, maps, menus, and objects such as food, clothing, toy vehicles and furniture, photos and other pictures. *On Target* incorporates the use of realia in the introduction of vocabulary and in many of the Options.

Total Physical Response

Total Physical Response (TPR), developed by James J. Asher, plays an important role in developing language skills. This technique relieves the pressure on students to speak before they are ready to do so, allowing students to respond without fear or hesitation. TPR is especially helpful at the early stages of learning, when students might not be capable of producing a verbal response. In fact, research shows that many students go through a "silent period" before they begin to speak. During this time they require intense listening practice to help them acquire the language. TPR is ideal for learners at this stage.

To begin, give a command or series of commands while performing the actions with the students. For example, *Stand up. Sit down. Open your book. Close your book. Stand up. Sit down.* Repeat, modeling the actions with the whole class or individual rows or groups. Then give the commands again, this time waiting a second or two to see if students respond correctly. If students cannot follow the directions, model the actions again until they are able to respond.

Next, give the commands without modeling the actions. Be sure to vary the order to make sure everyone understands and is not just doing a memorized series of actions. As vocabulary builds, one of the best ways to check understanding is to give a humorous or unexpected command: *Stand on your chair. Sit under the table.*

When students are able to follow your commands without confusion or delay, have individual students give commands to the class, to a small group, or to a partner. Encourage them not to use their hands or give other visual clues. At this point, do not stop students to correct pronunciation as long as they are being understood.

Once students understand basic commands, you can use TPR to build vocabulary. Provide pictures or props for each student. Give such commands as *Point to the bus. Point to the car. Show me the taxi.* Gradually add the target vocabulary: *Point to the plane. Point to the pilot. Show me the airport.*

TPR techniques can also be used to clarify verb tenses and question/answer patterns. For example, give a student a command: *Peter, go to the window.* As the student is doing so, model *Peter is going to the window. What's he doing? He's going to the window.* For past tense, simply wait until the student arrives and say, *Peter went to the window. What did he do? He went to the window.*

Once you and your students are used to using these techniques, you will find them well suited not only for introducing and practicing new language but also as a quick change of pace after sedentary practice. Give a series of quick commands to vary the routine and to let students move around. Everyone will feel better after a break.

Working in Pairs and Groups

Most of the language practice and skill development activities in *On Target* can be done in pairs or in groups of three or four. There are many advantages to having students work in pairs or groups.

Student involvement and participation are maximized. Each student gets the opportunity to speak many times during each class. In addition, each student practices all the examples in an exercise instead of eight or ten students each practicing one example.

Students are able to collaborate on answers and rehearse them before speaking in front of the whole class. The pair or group is responsible for each member's participation. Students can confirm their knowledge or learn from their partners or groups. Anxiety is reduced, which increases success.

Face-to-face interaction simulates real-life social contact, encouraging the use of eye contact, proper intonation, emotional tone, rejoinders, exclamations, etc., which are difficult when reciting in front of the class.

Forming the Groups

You will want to give each student in the class the opportunity to work with as many different partners or groups as possible during the term or year. You might assign partners and/or groups at the beginning of each week or even at the beginning of each class. You can do this in a variety of ways. The simplest is just to have students sitting next to or in front of and behind each other work together. You can put two to four slips of paper numbered 1, two to four slips numbered 2, etc., in a bag for the students to draw from. (The 1s work together, the 2s work together, etc.) Or you can put the names of half the students in the bag for the other half to draw from. Sometimes you may want to have students choose their own partners or groups.

No matter how you assign the groups, you will want one member of each group to act as leader. It is the group leader's task to keep the group working smoothly and talking in English. The reader should take any necessary notes and report any conclusions to the class. At first you may want to choose those students who have greater English fluency for this position, but it is important that every student be given the opportunity to act as a group leader.

Procedures

Always make sure everyone understands what to do. Have students read the instructions and any examples or models. They can do this silently or by reading aloud to each other. To encourage effective reading of the directions, set a time limit. Then have students close their books and tell each other what they are supposed to do. Answer any questions the pairs or groups have.

Always read the example, or model one of the items with a student. If you like, you can then ask for volunteers to do the next item as an additional model for the class.

Establish a time limit. This will help keep

students on task. Most activities in *On Target* can be completed in no more than five minutes. Longer activities can have a longer time limit, but don't let students continue beyond their ability to speak English.

As students are talking, walk around the class and monitor as many groups as possible. Encourage students to speak only in English. Answer questions and provide any language they need. Students will make mistakes, but don't interrupt for error correction. Students should feel free to express themselves however they can. Repeated errors should be noted for later reteaching and review.

Remind students that error correction is the learner's responsibility as well as the teacher's. Encourage them to recognize their own mistakes. Peer- and self-correction are valuable tools in learning because students feel less pressure than they do from teacher correction. Train students to help each other give the correct answers before you step in to help. You might give them copies of the Assessment Scale on page TExii to help them evaluate themselves and each other. Keeping a record of their performance in each unit will help them assess their progress.

Conclude the activity by having a few pairs do parts of the activity for the class or by having the group leader report the group's conclusions.

Remember that this kind of practice gives all students the chance to use their new language often. This extended listening and speaking time will greatly improve their confidence and ability.

Pair or group work can result in a noisy classroom, but remember—it's the sound of students communicating in English!

Games and Activities

Games

The value of using games in the classroom lies not only in the fact that they are refreshing and fun, but also in that they are real situations in which language is used for a purpose. Many kinds of games can be effectively adapted for language learning. Childhood games such as "Twenty Questions," "Bingo," and "Battleships" are good choices, as are games adapted from TV such as "Jeopardy" and "Hollywood Squares." Commercial card games and board games are another rich source. The imaginative teacher will see that some basic board games can be used to reinforce or review language functions, grammar, and vocabulary. "Snakes and Ladders" is one example.

In this game, students must decide if sentences are grammatically correct (if the

focus is grammar) or if vocabulary words are correctly used in context (if the focus is vocabulary). They do this in order to reach the FINISH on the board first and win. Students take turns playing in groups of four. Each group has a copy of the board. One student in each group begins by throwing a die or spinning a number wheel. The student moves a marker along the board according to the number on the die or wheel. In each free space on the board, there is a sentence to test grammar or vocabulary. The student playing must decide, with *no* help from the other players, whether the sentence in the space is correct or not. If the sentence is correct and is identified as correct, the student stays on that space. If the sentence is incorrect and is identified as incorrect, the student must correct it. If the student makes a mistake, he

Snakes and Ladders

START 1	He made me to wash the car! 14	If I were you, I would apologize. 15	16	28	I wish I have green eyes. 29
Do you —— know what UFO means? 2	Mary insisted on going with them. 13			27	If I had known I would have called you! 30
Can you tell me what is the time? 3	12	The thief must have came in the window. 17	I wish they has left a phone number! 26		31
	11	By the time the police arrived, the thief already went. 18		25	She expected him do a good job. 32
5	Have you gone to the store still? 10	19		24	I must have left my wallet at home. 33
I've already finished my homework. 6	9	20	23		I don't think you ought to have done that! 34
The olives were pick when they were ripe. 7	8	21	22		**FINISH** 35

or she must move back two spaces. The other players in the group determine if the student playing is correct in his or her decision. If the group cannot agree, the teacher acts as a referee and gives the final answer. Also on the board are drawings of snakes and ladders. If the player lands on a snake, he or she must "slide" down the snake to its tail, thereby losing spaces. If the player lands on the ladder, he or she "climbs" the ladder to the top, thereby gaining spaces on the way to the FINISH.

Surveys

Having students survey each other provides real language practice. Students enjoy surveys because they find out new information about their classmates and because they can compare their own lives and attitudes with those of their peers.

Begin a survey by having students tell you the questions they want answered about a topic. Write the questions on the board. You need one question for each student to ask. Have each student ask every other student his or her question and record the answers. (If your class is large, have students do the survey in groups with one member of each group asking the same question.)

Next, have each student summarize his or her results and write them on the board. You may wish to have students make a graph of the class's responses.

Finally, talk about the answers. Were any of them surprising? Which questions was the class evenly divided about? Were there any that everyone answered the same?

Interactive Dictations

Dictations are an excellent means for students to gain proficiency in aural comprehension and writing, especially when normal stress, intonation, and speed are used. Dictations can also be valuable diagnostic tools. By careful correction, you can discover which language skills need reteaching or review.

In interactive dictations, students not only write down a dictated item but also contribute to the dictation in some original way as well. For example, if you are dictating a few sentences describing a room, students can draw the room after they have taken down the dictation. Or, if you are dictating some sentences from a mystery story, students can predict what might happen next after each sentence. Or, if you are dictating a short conversation, students can write more original dialogue to continue the conversation. The key element in these dictations is the learner's opportunity to personalize the dictation by contributing original information.

Dictations can be corrected by the teacher, but peer correcting allows learners the opportunity to identify their own problem areas and interact together.

Tests

Placement Test

On Target was designed for learners who have had approximately 140 to 360 hours of instruction in English. However, you may have students whose level you are unsure of. These guidelines and the Placement Test on page TExviii will help you place those students in the appropriate level of *Scott Foresman English*.

Guidelines for Testing

Try to make the testing conditions as relaxed as possible. Remember that a test is almost certainly viewed by the student as a threatening experience. You will want to do everything possible to lessen the tension. Smile. Aim for a conversational approach.

First, ask basic questions. Find out the student's name, address, occupation, and favorite subject in school. Ask about the student's hobbies, what the student did yesterday, what the student will do after school, how long the student has lived in your city, etc. If the student cannot answer these questions, he or she should begin with *In Contact*, Level 1. If the student answers appropriately, go on to the Placement Test on page TExviii.

A student who answers fewer than six of the questions in the test on page TExviii correctly should take the Placement Test in *In Contact*, Level 2. A student who answers fewer than ten questions correctly should begin with *On Target*, Level 1. A student who answers between ten and twenty questions correctly should begin with *On Target*, Level 2. If a student answers more than twenty questions with no difficulty, you will want to continue with the Placement Test in *In Charge*.

Procedures for Testing

Make a copy of the test for every student. Go over the test with the students. For the Listening section, play the recording or read the audioscript aloud two or more times. Then allow sufficient time for students to complete the test. *Note:* The Listening section for the Placement test appears before Unit 1 on the Student Book audiocassette and CD.

Listening Audioscript

Jack: Hi, Jane. What've you got there?

Jane: Hi, Jack. It's a letter from my cousin Bonnie.

Jack: Oh, really? What's she been doing?

Jane: Really amazing things! She sent me this letter from Africa. She's been there for over a month.

Jack: Wow! What's she been doing there?

Jane: She's been taking photographs of wild animals for *Discoveries Magazine*. She says that after she finishes her job there, she's going to go to Alaska to take more pictures.

Jack: Wow! What a change! I must say, though, that I like cold weather better than hot weather. I'd love to go to Alaska.

Jane: Well, Jack, if you'd saved your money instead of buying a new car, you'd be able to go there.

Jack: Well, I could have saved it, but I wanted that car!

Jane: Do you still have it? I don't see you driving it these days.

Jack: Of course I still have it. Right now it's at the garage. It's being fixed.

TExvi

Mid-Book Test

Procedures for Testing

Make a copy of the Mid-Book Test on pages TExix–TExx for every student; then follow the procedures for the Placement Test. *Note:* The Listening section for the Mid-Book Test appears after Unit 6 on the Student Book audiocassette and CD.

Listening Audioscript

Greg: Can you believe it? I just found out I've won an all-expense-paid trip to Hawaii!

Bill: How did you manage to do *that*?

Greg: I entered a contest and I won! I might not be able to go to Hawaii, though.

Bill: Why not?

Greg: Well, according to the contest rules, I may have to go at a certain time—in the month of June. But I still have some final exams then.

Bill: If I were you, Greg, I'd try to take the exams early, so I could go to Hawaii. Going on a great trip is more important than exams!

Greg: Missing these exams would mean I couldn't graduate! I'll talk to my teachers to see if I can take them early, though.

Bill: Wow, Hawaii! Just think, if you hadn't entered that contest, you wouldn't have won the trip. It isn't a trip for two people, is it? I'd be happy to go with you!

Greg: Sorry, Bill. It's only for one person. Dream on!

Answers

A. 1. F; Greg won a trip to Hawaii. 2. T 3. T
   4. F; Bill suggests taking the exams early.
   5. F; The trip is for only one person.
B. *Answers will vary. Follow the **Correction** instructions on page TExi.*
C. 1. b 2. c 3. d 4. a 5. c
D. 1. had (already) played 2. doing 3. Have, finished 4. had, worked 5. would have made 6. must have broken
E. *Answers will vary. Follow the **Correction** instructions on page TExi.*

Because many of the answers in this test will vary, use your own judgment in determining the number of points for each correct answer.

End-of-Book Test

Procedures for Testing

Make a copy of the End-of-Book Test on pages TExxi–TExxii for every student; then follow the procedures for the Placement Test. *Note:* The Listening section for the End-of-Book test appears after Unit 12 on the Student Book audiocassette and CD.

Listening Audioscript

Customer: Waiter!

Waiter: Yes, Madam?

Customer: Could I move to another table? The sun coming in the window is bothering me.

Waiter: Certainly, Madam. Please follow me to table 18.

Customer: Thank you. Oh, I've changed my mind about what I ordered for lunch, too. I want tomato soup instead of vegetable soup, and I want chocolate ice cream instead of pie for dessert.

Waiter: Very well, Madam. Tomato soup and chocolate ice cream.

Customer: And tell that man at the next table to put out that cigarette! I don't want to smell smoke while I eat!

Waiter: Yes, Madam.

Customer: And don't you have any clean glasses? Look! My water glass has spots on it. And the flower on this table is completely dead!

Waiter: Terribly sorry, Madam. I'll bring you a new glass and a fresh flower right away.

Customer: Well, hurry up! I haven't got all day, you know. And where in the world is my lunch?

Waiter: I'll bring it right away.

Customer: What took you so long? And look! There's a fly in my soup!

Waiter: Don't worry, Madam. I won't charge you a penny more for it! Have a nice lunch now.

Answers

A. 1. b 2. c 3. a
B. 1. The sun was bothering her. She changed her mind about what she ordered for lunch. She didn't want the man near her to smoke. Her glass had water spots on it. The flower on the table was dead. She didn't think the waiter brought her lunch fast enough. There was a fly in her soup. 2. She had tomato soup and chocolate ice cream. 3. He said he wouldn't charge a penny more for the fly in her soup. 4. *Answers will vary. Follow the **Correction** instructions on page TExi.*
C. *Answers will vary, but the students should use a different past modal phrase in each sentence, for example, "A picture might have fallen off the wall." Follow the **Correction** instructions on page TExi.*
D. *Answers will vary. Follow the **Correction** instructions on page TExi.*
E. *Answers may vary slightly* 1. Have all the rooms painted. 2. Have all the pictures hung. 3. Get someone to install a new carpet. 4. Have some trees planted.
F. 1. had never met 2. to hand over 3. must have had 4. leaving 5. wishes

Because many of the answers in this test will vary, use your own judgment in determining the number of points for each correct answer.

Placement Test

A. Listen to the conversation. Answer the questions.

1. Where is Jane's cousin Bonnie? _____

2. What is her job? _____

3. Where is she going next? _____

4. Who likes cold weather? _____

5. Did Jack save his money for a vacation? _____

6. What did Jack buy? _____

7. Does he still have it? _____

8. What is Jack having done? _____

B. Write the correct form of the verb on the line.

1. Steve really enjoys **(play)** _____ basketball.

2. By the time the police arrived, the thief **(escape)** _____.

3. Paul isn't at work yet. I guess that he **(miss)** _____ his train to the city.

4. I wish that I **(study)** _____ for my driving test more. Now I have to take it again next week.

5. You still **(finish, neg.)** _____ your homework! Get busy right now!

6. Ms. Jackson refused **(let)** _____ her children attend the concert.

7. Carmen said that her new boss **(have)** _____ a lot of problems with the employees lately.

8. They have to tear down that new building because they **(build, neg.)** _____ it correctly.

9. I'm not sure that Judy **(be able to)** _____ come with us to the concert next week. I think that she has other plans.

10. I **(collect)** _____ coins for over twenty years. I really enjoy working on my collection!

C. Write **may**, **might**, **must**, **may have**, **might have**, or **must have** and the correct form of the verb on the line.

1. Did you hear that loud noise? There **(be)** _____ an accident at the corner.

2. Gerardo **(go)** _____ to California on vacation, but he's not sure.

3. Tim isn't here today. He **(be)** _____ on vacation.

4. The boss is late today. He **(miss)** _____ his train.

D. Write the following sentences again. Use the new subjects.

1. People grow apples all over the world.

   Apples _____.

2. Someone is fixing my computer.

   My computer _____.

3. No one invited Eric to the party.

   Eric _____.

4. Someone stole my car.

   My car _____.

Mid-Book Test (Units 1–6)

🎧 **A.** Read the sentences and then listen to the conversation. Circle **T** if the sentence is true and **F** if the sentence is false. If the sentence is false, correct it.

1. T   F   Greg won a trip to Italy.

_____

2. T   F   Greg entered a contest to win the trip.

_____

3. T   F   Greg might not be able to go because of exams.

_____

4. T   F   Bill suggests taking the exams next semester.

_____

5. T   F   The trip includes all family members.

_____

B. What do you think Greg should do?

_____

_____

_____

C. Circle the letter of the correct word for each sentence.

1. You know, you really should _____ your old car and buy a new one!
   a. take advantage of   **c.** go along with
   b. get rid of   **d.** put off

2. Marge is really _____ her summer vacation. She is going to visit her children in California.
   a. insisting on   **c.** looking forward to
   b. proposing   **d.** subscribing to

3. Our landlord is very _____ about the rules in our apartment building. We can't make any noise at all.
   a. valuable   **c.** gifted
   b. fake   **d.** strict

4. Is smoking permitted in this building? What is the office _____?
   a. policy   **c.** trait
   b. prodigy   **d.** strategy

5. First my son wanted to go to a university close to home, and now he wants to go somewhere far away. I wish he would stop _____.
   a. avoiding the issue   **c.** changing his mind
   b. being underhanded   **d.** making his mark

D. Write the correct form of the verb on the line. Use the negative when necessary.

1. By the time Midori Goto was ten, she **(play)** _____ with the New York Philharmonic Orchestra.

2. I know my room's a mess. I put off **(do)** _____ the cleaning as long as I can!

3. **(Finish)** _____ you _____ all your homework for tomorrow yet?

4. How long **(work)** _____ you _____ there before the company went out of business?

5. If we had known you were going to be in town, we **(make)** _____ other plans!

6. Look! There's water all over the floor! The pipes under the sink **(must/break)** _____

E. You are at a very expensive health camp for the summer. There are many rules and regulations about diet, exercise, health classes, and activities that the camp instructors and staff force you to follow. Write a short note to a friend explaining what they make you do at the camp.

_____

_____

_____

_____

_____

_____

_____

End-of-Book Test (Units 7–12)

🎧 **A.** Listen to the conversation and circle the letter of the word that describes the tone the speaker used.

1. The customer's tone was

    a. informative   **b.** complaining   **c.** humorous

2. The waiter's tone during the conversation was

    a. persuasive   **b.** aggressive   **c.** patient

3. The waiter's tone at the end of the conversation was

    a. sarcastic   **b.** complaining   **c.** helpful

🎧 **B.** Listen again and fill in the chart.

1. What problems did the customer mention?
2. What did the customer have for lunch?
3. What did the waiter say to the customer at the end?
4. What would you have done if you had been the waiter?

C. You were sleeping in your bed when you heard a loud crashing noise downstairs. Speculate about what caused the noise. Use a different modal in each sentence.

1. _____

2. _____

3. _____

D. You have a local reputation as a good cook, and the community center has asked you to explain how to make that delicious fruit salad you often serve. Write your instructions for the community cookbook below. Use the passive voice.

_____

_____

_____

_____

E. Antonio wants to have his house redecorated and his yard fixed up. He is writing a list of what he plans to have done. Using the cues in parentheses, finish his list.

1. _____ (all the rooms / paint)

2. _____ (picture / hang)

3. _____ (new carpet / install)

4. _____ (trees / plants)

F. Complete the soap opera commercial with the correct verb forms.

Today, on the soap opera *Romance World*, many exciting things happen. Kimberly tells Alan she wishes she **(1. never / meet)** _____ him. Andrea forces Ted **(2. hand over)** _____ their father's secret will. Kent realizes that Wanda **(3. must / have)** _____ something to do with the disappearance of Randy, his beloved son. Julia insists on **(4. leave)** _____ school to live in New York. And the biggest shock of all! Why does Roberto confess to Francesca that he **(5. wish)** _____ she would marry his brother instead? Find out at noon on Channel 3!

SCOTT FORESMAN ENGLISH

ON TARGET

2

INTERMEDIATE

Second Edition

James E. Purpura
Teachers College, Columbia University

Diane Pinkley
Teachers College, Columbia University

Photos: p. vii, PhotoDisc, Inc.; p. 1, PhotoDisc, Inc.; p. 7, Corbis/Digital Stock; p. 11, Corbis/Bob Krist; p. 28, PhotoDisc, Inc.; p. 33, Robin Sachs/PhotoEdit; p. 34, (m) UPI/Corbis-Bettman; (b) Hola!; p. 36, (t) Don Hunstein/Sony Classical; (b) Linda Creighton, *US News and World Report*; p. 40, (t) Carmontelle, Luis Carrogis. Leopold Mozart and his Children. Watercolor 1763–64. Musee de la Ville de Paris, Musee Carnavalet, Paris, France. Giraudon/Art Resource, NY; (b) Bettman; p. 41, Okoniewski/Liaison Agency, Inc.; p. 43, (l) PhotoDisc, Inc.; (c) Kevin Peterson/PhotoDisc, Inc.; (r) Barbara Penoyar/PhotoDisc, Inc.; p. 48, PhotoDisc, Inc.; p. 58, Rob Crandall/Stock Boston/PNI; p. 61, Courtesy Indiana Division of Tourism and Film Development; p. 62, PhotoDisc, Inc.; p. 67, (t) Corbis/Bettman-UPI; (bl) Culver Pictures; (br) Gregory Pace/Sygma Photo News; p. 70, Corbis/David Turnley; p. 72, Brown Brothers; p. 73, Brown Brothers; p. 75, Lawrence Migdale/Stock Boston/PNI; p. 78, British Museum; p. 79, PhotoDisc, Inc.; p. 80, PhotoDisc, Inc.; p. 82, Brown Brothers; p. 88, (t, m) Loren Alexander McIntyre; p. 90, Richard Cash/PhotoEdit; p. 92, The Royal Collection; p. 93, Corbis/Hulton-Deutsch Collection; p. 97, (t) PhotoDisc, Inc.; (b) AP/Wide World Photos; p. 99, AP/Wide World Photos; p. 103, Fritz-Henle Photo Researchers; p. 104, (t) Courtesy of Life Magazine ©1947; (m) Copyright, 2000, Malcolm S. Kirk/Peter Arnold, Inc.; p. 105, PhotoDisc, Inc.; p. 110, ©Leonard Lee Rue III/Animals Animals/Earth Scenes; p. 111, PhotoDisc, Inc.; p. 117, ©Corbis/Matthew McKee/Eye Ubiquitous; p. 118, Peter Pearson/Tony Stone Images; p. 119, PhotoDisc, Inc.; p. 123, PhotoDisc, Inc.; p. 124, UNICEF; p. 125, UNICEF.

Illustrations: Susan Blubaugh p. 24; Joe Boddy pp. 18, 45; Tom Brocker p. 8; Eldon Doty pp. 20, 108; Al Hering p. 107; Tim Jones p. 76; Ben Mahan pp. 5, 55, 120 (t); Paul Meisel pp. 85, 113; Matt Mellit p. 89; John O'Brien p. 65, ©1999 John O'Brien, from cartoonbank.com. All rights reserved. Joseph Rogers p. 75; Larry Ross p. 66; Margaret Sanilippo pp. 53, 54, 114; S. D. Schindler pp. viii, 50, 51; George Ulrich pp. 15, 22, 35, 49, 69, 120 (b), 121; Randy Verougstraete pp. 12, 13, 21.

Cover photos: Gotham Studio/Jan Cobb (dartboard); Jim Barber/The Stock Rep (keyboard); ©1999 Jim Westphalen (type).

CONTENTS

SUMMARY OF SKILLS

Theme	Grammar	Listening and Speaking	Reading and Writing
Unit 1 **Making Progress** Page 1	Present Perfect Tense; *Already, Yet, Still*	**Listening:** Sound Off ➤ Listening for Distinctions **Pronunciation:** Consonant Clusters with *–ed* Endings **Speaking:** A Universal Language ➤ Summarizing	**Reading:** The Human Brain ➤ Identifying Main Ideas **Writing:** A Letter of Inquiry
Unit 2 **Whodunit?** Page 11	Degrees of Certainty: Modal Auxiliaries	**Listening:** What's on TV? ➤ Listening for Details **Pronunciation:** Stress on Two-Syllable Words **Speaking:** What's Your Future? ➤ Expressing Certainty and Uncertainty	**Reading:** The Meeting ➤ Confirming Predictions **Writing:** A Narrative
Unit 3 **Because I Told You To!** Page 21	Orders, Requests, Permission, Persuasion, Advice *Make, Have, Let*	**Listening:** It's in the Tone ➤ Listening for Tone **Pronunciation:** Contrastive Stress **Speaking:** Asking for Permission ➤ Using Formal and Informal Language	**Reading:** Roles in Human Society ➤ Recognizing Definitions and Examples **Writing:** A Letter of Application

Review (Units 1–3)

Theme	Grammar	Listening and Speaking	Reading and Writing
Unit 4 **Child's Play** Page 33	Past Perfect Tense; Past Perfect Progressive Tense	**Listening:** A Child Prodigy ➤ Identifying Causes and Results **Pronunciation:** Using Intonation to Ask a Yes/No Question **Speaking:** Solving a Problem ➤ Confirming Understanding	**Reading:** Mozart: Child Prodigy ➤ Understanding Paragraph Structure **Writing:** Coherence
Unit 5 **The Real You?** Page 43	Gerunds; Verbs Followed by Infinitives/ Gerunds	**Listening:** Our Many Faces ➤ Taking Notes **Pronunciation:** Reducing *of* **Speaking:** Pet Peeves ➤ Discussing Feelings	**Reading:** Your Personality in the Palm of Your Hand? ➤ Using Graphics **Writing:** A Personal Letter
Unit 6 **If I Had My Way** Page 53	Talking About Unreal Situations: The Second Conditional; Asking for and Giving Advice	**Listening:** Workplace Changes ➤ Listening to Summarize **Pronunciation:** Rhythm **Speaking:** What Would You Do? ➤ Encouraging and Discouraging	**Reading:** Utopias: Nowhere Lands ➤ Getting Meaning from Context **Writing:** An Analysis

Review (Units 4–6)

STARTING OUT

OBJECTIVES

- To exchange personal information
- To ask about course objectives and policies
- To use classroom language
- To foster a productive classroom atmosphere

Note: This unit provides a brief introduction to the course and reviews some common question patterns and expressions. Keep the activities moving quickly. Spend no more than one or two class sessions on this unit. If students do not have their books on the first day of class, write the activities on the board.

You may wish to read Introducing Vocabulary, page TEviii, and Working in Pairs and Groups, page TExiii, before proceeding with the lesson.

Getting to Know You

Preview

Focus attention on the photograph. Have students work in pairs, in small groups, or as a class to describe the photograph. Elicit as much vocabulary as possible, including **course** (subject, class). Then have students read the introduction.

Presentation

❶ Have students read the instructions. Ask them what questions they would ask for **b. nationality/hometown.** (Where are you from? What's your hometown?) Then divide the class into groups of three or more to complete the exercise. You might suggest that students write down their questions and the responses. Circulate to assist students, as necessary. Review the answers as a class. (*Answers will vary.*)

❷ Have students find new partners to complete the exercise. Remind them to refer to the questions and the responses they wrote down for Exercise 1.

Option: Have students work in pairs or groups to brainstorm as many questions as they can for the categories in Exercise 1. Which group can come up with the most questions?

Option: You may wish to add categories students can ask each other about—for example, free-time activities, astrological sign, and favorite movie star or singer. Ask students for additional suggestions.

Option: For homework, have students write paragraphs about the classmates they interviewed in Exercise 1.

Option: Have each student write his or her name on a slip of paper. Collect the slips and distribute them so that no one has his or her own name. Have students stand up. Then have them, one by one, try to find the person whose name they have without asking, "Is your name (Maria)?" Instead, they should ask questions such as "Does your name begin with an *M*? Do you have a middle name?" When a student finds the correct person, he or she should sit down. Continue until everyone is seated.

❸ Focus attention on the diagram. Introduce or review the words for the shapes. Introduce **influence** by asking, *What person has influenced, or changed, your life?* You might want to mention a person who has influenced your life and explain how. Then have students read the instructions and fill in the diagram. (*Answers will vary.*)

Getting to Know You

As you speak English in this class, you will see that you can learn new information about your classmates and your teacher as well as share your own thoughts with them. Begin your new course in English by getting to know more about your classmates.

 Work in groups of three or more. Find out about your partners by asking as many questions as possible. Use the categories and the words in the box to help you make questions.

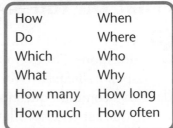

How	When
Do	Where
Which	Who
What	Why
How many	How long
How much	How often

a. name
b. nationality/hometown
c. address
d. age
e. family

f. job/school
g. education
h. English
i. skills
j. hobbies

2 Find a partner from another group. Tell your partner what you learned about the people in your group.

3 Look at the diagram. In the bigger rectangle, write the name of a person you love very much. In the smaller rectangle, write the name of a person who has influenced your life in important ways. On the line, write the year you felt the happiest in your life. In the square, write the names of your best friends. In the triangle, write one of your goals in life. In the circle, write three adjectives that describe your personality.

4 Work with a partner. Show your diagram to your partner. Ask and answer questions about each other's diagrams.

Getting the Facts

5 When we begin a new class, we need to "get the facts" about the class. Look at the cues and ask your teacher questions. Take notes on a sheet of paper.

    a. number of units to finish   **d.** date of final exam

    b. number of exams   **e.** grading policy

    c. number of compositions   **f.** homework policy

What Do You Say?

6 When we don't understand something in class, we ask questions. For example, we could say, "How do you spell *technique?*" Work with a partner. Write at least five common questions students ask in class. Share your list with the class.

7 In class we ask questions, give opinions, clarify, correct, and ask for the floor (permission to talk). Work with a partner. Look at each situation and write a short conversation on the lines. When you finish, read your conversation to another group.

Situation		**Conversation**
		Ask for clarification.
1. You don't understand something the teacher has just said.	**A:**	*Did you get what the teacher said?*
		Clarify.
	B:	*Yeah, he said the paper is due tomorrow.*
		Correct politely.
2. Someone said, "I ate kitchen in the chicken."	**A:**	_____
		Accept correction.
	B:	_____
		Ask for opinion.
3. Find out what someone thinks of a book he or she has read.	**A:**	_____
		Give opinion.
	B:	_____
		Agree.
4. Someone says that living in an English-speaking country is the only way to learn English.	**A:**	_____
		Disagree politely.
	B:	_____
		Interrupt and ask for floor.
5. One of your partners is talking too much and you have an important point to add.	**A:**	_____
		Turn over the floor.
	B:	_____

④ Encourage students to include as much detail as possible, but make sure they feel comfortable sharing their information. (*Answers will vary.*)

Getting the Facts

Presentation

⑤ Introduce or review **getting the facts** (getting the necessary information) and **policy** (procedure, plan, course of action). Then have students read the directions. You may wish to have them work in pairs or in small groups to write out the questions before they interview you. Encourage students to take notes as you answer.

Answers

Answers will vary somewhat. Possible answers: **a.** How many units will we finish? **b.** How many exams will we have? **c.** How many compositions will we write? **d.** What is the date of the final exam? **e.** What is your grading policy? **f.** How much homework will we have?

What Do You Say?

Presentation

⑥ Have students read the instructions and brainstorm common classroom questions. [*Examples*: What does (policy) mean? Would you repeat that, please? Could you speak a little more slowly? What do we have to do for homework? Could you please give another example?] List the questions on the board.

⑦ Have pairs of students create conversations. Ask students to read their conversations to the class. (*Answers will vary.*)

☸ Option: Provide a large assortment of pictures of objects, places, and activities. Each student should choose two—one that shows something he or she likes and one that shows something he or she dislikes. Have students explain to a group or to the class why they like or dislike the content of each picture.

☸ Option: Use this technique to keep students interested and involved during review of vocabulary, language possibilities, grammar points, and so on. Draw a mountain peak on the board. Draw an equal number of lines for "rest stops" on each side of the mountain. Divide the class into two teams. Tell them that they can consult with team members to answer questions you will ask them. For example, to review language possibilities, you might ask, *What do you say to a classmate when you don't understand something she just said?* (*Possible answer:* Excuse me. Could you please repeat what you just said?) Have the teams take turns answering your questions. For each correct answer, draw an X on the team's next rest stop up the mountain. For an incorrect answer, erase that team's highest X. The first team to reach the top of the mountain wins.

MAKING PROGRESS

OBJECTIVES

- To talk about language learning
- To analyze one's own learning strategies
- To use the present perfect tense
- To use the adverbs **already, still,** and **yet**
- To listen for details
- To pronounce final consonant clusters with **–ed/–d** endings
- To summarize
- To identify main ideas
- To figure out the meanings of words from the context
- To write a letter of inquiry, considering format, content, and organization
- To use word maps

GETTING STARTED

Warm Up

Preview

Note: As a general preteaching procedure, elicit from students as many vocabulary words as possible. Have students model or define the words they know for the class. If none of the students are familiar with a word, present the word as new. For more information on introducing vocabulary, see page TEviii.

- Elicit or present **characteristics** by asking students to name things that good dancers (tennis players, computer operators) have in common. You might want to get them started by suggesting such characteristics as discipline, focus, and interest.

- Elicit or present **to make progress** by discussing students' hobbies and pastimes. Ask, *What do you do in your spare time? How long have you been taking dancing lessons (playing tennis, working on a computer)?* After a number of students have responded, ask, *Are you getting better? How do you know that you are making progress?*

Presentation

❶ Have students work independently to write their lists. Then have them discuss their lists as a class. Do they all agree on the characteristics of successful students?

 Workbook: Practice 1

Option: Have students work in pairs or small groups to compare the characteristics of good students and good teachers. Students will probably agree that although good teachers and good students have different roles, they share many characteristics.

❷ Have students read the directions. Play the recording or read the audioscript aloud two or more times. Remind students that they do not have to understand every word in order to answer the question.

Audioscript: The audioscript for Exercise 2 appears on page T152.

Answers
a. yes **b.** yes **c.** no

Figure It Out

Preview

- Discuss things students have learned to do independently to check their understanding of **awareness, basics, on (your) own, memorize, participate,** and **resources.** Have them talk about how they learned the basics (the information that everything else is based on), what resources they used (books, TV shows, computer programs, and so on), and how they became aware of those resources. Ask whether they think it's easier to learn something on their own or by participating in a class.

- Tell students that they are going to complete a questionnaire about their own language-learning habits and **strategies.** As a preliminary activity, ask them to list things they feel they can already do well in English and things they would like to do better.

(Figure It Out continues on page T2.)

MAKING PROGRESS

GETTING STARTED

Warm Up

1 What are the characteristics of a successful student? Make a list.

2 When we improve, we say that we are "making progress." Listen to the conversations. Are the people making progress? Circle *Yes* or *No*.

    a. Yes No   **b.** Yes No   **c.** Yes No

Figure It Out

3 People learn languages in many ways. Some learn best from reading and writing, others from listening and speaking. Fill out the questionnaire and find out how you think you learn best.

Your Language-Learning Awareness

Your Previous Learning Experience: How Far Have You Come?

1. How many languages have you studied? _____

2. List the languages you know in order, from best to least.

    _____

(continued on next page)

3. Have you ever learned a language on your own?   *yes*   *no*

   If so, how did you learn it? Circle the letters. If you used other methods, write them on the line.

   a. I watched TV or listened to the radio.
   b. I talked with native speakers in person.
   c. I studied from a textbook.
   d. I read newspapers, magazines, or information on the Internet.
   e. _____

Your Language Activities and Skills: Where Are You Now?

4. You are now studying English in a class. Circle the letters of your favorite activities. If you have any other favorites, write them on the lines.

   a. Listening to dialogues on tape   a. Listening to classmates' conversations
   b. Talking with a partner   b. Participating in class discussions
   c. Reading silently   c. Memorizing new words and expressions
   d. Doing grammar exercises   d. Writing compositions
   e. _____   e. _____

5. Which statement or statements best describe your feelings about your skills in English? Circle the letter(s) or write your statement on the line.

   a. I've already learned the basics of spoken English; now I need to learn to read better and faster.

   b. I've come a long way with my speaking, but now I need to learn to write better in English.

   c. I've learned a lot of grammar, but I still haven't learned all the words I need to get my ideas across clearly.

   d. I don't have any trouble reading English, but I want to understand people better when they talk to me.

   e. _____

How Can You Make More Progress?

6. A. Have you taken advantage of resources for learning English in your community? If you have tried the activity, check *Already;* if you have not tried it, check *Not Yet.*

   Have you …   *Already*   *Not Yet*

   a. listened for the words in English songs?   _____   _____
   b. chatted in English on the Internet?   _____   _____
   c. read an English language magazine?   _____   _____
   d. written a postcard or letter in English?   _____   _____

   a. listened to English radio programs?   _____   _____
   b. spoken with friends in English?   _____   _____
   c. read an English language newspaper?   _____   _____
   d. written a diary or journal in English?   _____   _____

   a. watched TV programs in English?   _____   _____
   b. joined an English language club?   _____   _____
   c. read a short story or novel in English?   _____   _____
   d. written a poem or story in English?   _____   _____

   B. Which of these strategies have helped you the most? Circle the letter(s).

7. A. Count all the **a**'s, **b**'s, **c**'s, and **d**'s you circled in the questionnaire.

   a's total = _____   **b**'s total = _____   **c**'s total = _____   **d**'s total = _____

(continued on next page)

(Figure It Out continues from page T1.)

Presentation

❸ Have students read the directions silently. Then have them skim the questionnaire on pages 1–3 and note the four main sections: "Your Previous Learning Experience: How Far Have You Come?" "Your Language Activities and Skills: Where Are You Now?" "How Can You Make More Progress?" and "Your Language-Learning Needs: How Do You Expect to Use Your English?" Have students complete the entire questionnaire independently in class or for homework.

🌐 **Option:** For 7A, be sure students understand that they are to go back to the beginning of the questionnaire and count all of the **a**'s, **b**'s, **c**'s, and **d**'s they marked. Then ask students how they prefer to learn English. Is it through listening, speaking, reading, or writing? Point out that we learn languages by using all these skills, but some of us find certain skills easier and more useful than others. Have students fill out the questionnaire independently, section by section. After each of the four sections is completed, have them share their answers with a partner, in a small group, or as a class.

🌐 **Option:** After students have completed and discussed each section, have a pair of students take a poll of the class. One student should ask the questions, and the other should write the answers on the board. For the first section, have the pair of students poll those who have learned languages independently to find out the most popular methods (3a–e). For the second section, have the pair poll the class for the most popular kinds of activities (4a–e) and the most commonly expressed needs (5a–e). For the third section, have the pair poll the class for the most popular learning resources (6B).

(Figure It Out continues on page T3.)

Unit 1

T2

⚙ **Option:** Before students complete the last section of the questionnaire, you might have them work with partners and summarize what they have found out about their own learning styles.

After students have completed the last section, have them discuss their answers to question 10 in pairs, in small groups, or as a class. Have them tell whether their preferred skills are consistent with their needs. Have them also discuss what they can do if their preferred skills are not consistent with their needs and, more generally, how they can apply what they've learned from the questionnaire to their own language-learning experiences.

☑ ❹ **Vocabulary Check** Have students read the directions and complete the matching exercise. Review the answers as a class.

Answers
1. e 2. f 3. a 4. d 5. g 6. c 7. h 8. b

 Workbook: Practice 2

⚙ **Option:** You may want to have students keep Vocabulary Notebooks (see page TEviii.)

- Students may write down new vocabulary and expressions from the Student Book and from class discussions. They can also make up sentences to illustrate the meaning of new words and expressions.

- Another way to use Vocabulary Notebooks to build and review vocabulary is to make **word maps.** This strategy helps students organize and show relationships among terms and new information. The Vocabulary Expansion activity for this unit (see page T140) discusses word maps and presents an example. You may prefer to do the activity at this time.

Talk About It

⚙ **Option:** You may prefer to postpone this activity until after the grammar presentation (page 4) if you feel your students need extra help with the present perfect tense.

Presentation

Note: The purpose of this activity is to develop fluency. Students should be encouraged to speak without fear of interruption for error correction. If you notice persistent errors, write them down for later reteaching or review.

❺ Arrange students in pairs. Have them read the directions silently. Ask one pair of students to read the example conversation aloud for the class. Then, have students complete the activity. Direct them to item 6A on page 2 and have them use the items listed there as cues. Encourage them to ask questions about other learning activities as well.

⚙ **Option:** Have students write out their dialogues from Talk About It independently in class or for homework.

 Workbook: Practice 3

B. The letter(s) with the highest count represent(s) your probable learning style.

   a. You prefer to learn through listening.
   b. You tend to learn better through speaking.
   c. You prefer to learn through reading.
   d. You learn better through writing.

If you wrote answers for **e**'s, think about how this reflects your language-learning style. Which skills do you prefer? Check the box(es).

☐ listening   ☐ speaking   ☐ reading   ☐ writing

Your Language-Learning Needs: How Do You Expect to Use Your English?

8. Why are you studying English? Circle the letter(s). If you have other reasons, write them on the line.

   a. To travel to an English-speaking country

   b. To get a job that requires English language skills

   c. To take college courses that use English language textbooks

   d. To live in an English-speaking country

   e. _____

9. Given your responses to question 8, which of the following skills is most important for you? Write numbers from 1 (most important) to 6 (least important) in the boxes.

   ☐ listening   ☐ speaking   ☐ reading   ☐ writing   ☐ grammar   ☐ vocabulary

10. Compare your answer in question 7B with the skills you ranked 1 and 2 in question 9. Are the skills you prefer consistent with the ones you need most?

✓ **④ Vocabulary Check** The words and expressions on the left are from the previous questionnaire. Match them with the correct meanings on the right.

_____ **1.** characteristics	**a.**	to make a lot of progress
_____ **2.** on your own	**b.**	ways to do something, methods
_____ **3.** to come a long way	**c.**	to use
_____ **4.** to memorize	**d.**	to learn from memory
_____ **5.** to get across	**e.**	qualities of a person or thing
_____ **6.** to take advantage of	**f.**	without anyone else
_____ **7.** resource	**g.**	to communicate
_____ **8.** strategies	**h.**	something that can be used for help

Talk About It

⑤ With a partner, take turns asking and answering questions about your progress in English. Use questionnaire item 6 for help.

Ask about progress.
A: Have you memorized all the irregular verbs yet?

Explain progress.
B: No, I still haven't memorized them all, but I've learned a lot of them.

Ask about progress.
A: Have you read any novels in your English class yet?

Explain progress.
B: We've already read some poems, but we haven't read a novel yet.

GRAMMAR

The Present Perfect Tense: *Already, Yet, Still*

The present perfect tense (*have/has* + past participle) is used to talk about actions that happened at an indefinite time in the past, but that have importance in the present. When we refer to a definite time in the past, we use the simple past tense.

> **A:** **Have** you ever **studied** Chinese? *(any time from the past to the present)*
>
> **B:** Yes, I **took** a course last year. *(specific time in the past)*
>
> Common time expressions with the present perfect tense:
>
> | ever | never | always | before | so far | up to now | by now | since |

Already, yet, and *still* are three more expressions of indefinite time used with the present perfect tense.

> **A:** What **has** the new principal **accomplished so far**?
>
> **B:** She promised to hire ten teachers in three years, and she**'s already hired** seven.
>
> **A:** She also promised to put new computers in the classrooms. **Has** she **done** that **yet**?
>
> **B:** Well, I'm sorry to say she **hasn't done** that **yet**, and she **still hasn't lowered** tuition. But I'm sure she will. She's the best principal we**'ve ever had**.

 1 **Check Your Understanding** Use the conversation above to figure out the meanings and uses of *already, still,* and *yet* in the present perfect tense. Circle the answer or answers in each statement.

  a. Already   Still   Yet   usually occurs in affirmative sentences.

  b. Already   Still   Yet   usually occurs in negative sentences.

  c. Already   Still   Yet   usually occurs in questions.

  d. Already   Still   Yet   means the person has finished earlier than expected.

  e. Already   Still   Yet   means the person has not finished.

2 Hiroko and Carlos are talking about one of their classes. Write the correct form of the verb on the line. Use the negative when necessary.

HIROKO: Hi, Carlos. How are you getting along in history class?

CARLOS: Well, I don't know. There sure is a lot of reading. I (**1. finish, still**) _still haven't finished_ all the books on the reading list. I'm getting worried.

HIROKO: I know. I'm having a hard time keeping up, too. I (**2. begin, still**) _____ some of the books, either.

CARLOS: And what about the book report? (**3. you, do, yet**) _____ it _____ ?

GRAMMAR

The Present Perfect Tense:
Already, Yet, Still

Preview

To help students understand the difference between the present perfect tense and the past tense, write the following sentences on the board.

They <u>have gone</u> to many basketball games.
I <u>went</u> to many basketball games last year.
She <u>went</u> to a basketball game yesterday.

Point out that the first sentence uses the present perfect tense; the second and third sentences use the past tense. Ask, *What is the difference in time between the first sentence and the next two sentences?* (In the first sentence, the action happened at an indefinite or non-specific time in the past; in the second and third sentences, the action happened at a specific time in the past.)

Presentation

Have students read the grammar explanations and the example conversations independently in class or for homework.

Ⓩ **Option:** Review irregular past participles with students. Verbs used in this section include **begin**, **buy**, **choose**, **do**, **meet**, **pay**, **read**, **see**, **sing**, **take**, and **write**.

Ⓩ **Option:** Ask students to find the word **accomplished** in the example conversation and figure out its meaning from the context (achieved, done). Have them check their answers in a dictionary.

☑ ❶ **Check Your Understanding** Have students read the directions silently. Then have them complete the activity in pairs or in small groups. Review the answers as a class.

> **Answers**
> a. Already b. Still, Yet c. Yet d. Already
> e. Yet

Ⓩ **Option:** Ask students to make sentences about changes that have and haven't happened in their own school, using the present perfect tense with **already**, **yet**, and **still**. You may want to write the sentences on the board for students to copy into their notebooks.

Ⓩ **Option:** Elicit sentences with each of the time expressions in the first grammar box. Make sure students know that **never = not + ever**, that **so far** and **up to now** have the same meaning, and that **since** means "after a time."

Ⓩ **Option:** Point out that **already**, **still**, and **yet** occur in different positions in a sentence. Elicit these positions based on the conversation in the box (**already**—before past participle; **yet**—end of question or sentence it occurs in; **still**—before **have/has**). Tell students that **already** can also occur at the end of a sentence (She's hired seven already).

❷ Have students read the directions silently. Then have them complete the activity independently. Review the answers as a class.

> **Answers**
> 1. still haven't finished 2. still haven't begun
> 3. Have you done ... yet 4. still haven't
> written 5. have already done 6. haven't
> read ... yet

Ⓩ **Option:** You might want to have pairs of students practice the completed conversation in Exercise 2.

❸ Have students read the directions silently. Direct them to the example. Then have pairs complete the exercise. For the completed actions (those marked *done*), encourage students to make up sentences that indicate when the actions were completed.

Answers
a. Have you filled out your application yet? I've already filled it out. I did that last week. b. Have you seen the campus yet? No, I haven't seen it yet. *or* No, I still haven't seen it. c. Have you asked your teacher to write a letter of recommendation yet? Yes, I've already asked my teacher to write a letter of recommendation. I asked her three weeks ago. d. Have you gotten an acceptance letter yet? Yes, I've already gotten an acceptance letter. I got one last month. e. Have you chosen your courses yet? No, I still haven't chosen them. *or* No, I haven't chosen them yet. f. Have you bought your textbooks yet? No, I still haven't bought them. *or* No, I haven't bought them yet. g. Have you met your roommate yet? No, I still haven't met my roommate. *or* No, I haven't met my roommate yet. h. Have you paid your tuition yet? Yes, I've already paid it. I paid it two months ago.

🌐 **Option:** If necessary, explain that in the United States, high school students who want to go to college must usually take tests, get letters of recommendations from their teachers, and send in applications to one or more schools. Often, they visit the college campuses (grounds and buildings). If a college accepts them, they get an acceptance letter. Before they start school, they usually choose their courses, and if they are going to live in a dormitory, they find out who their roommate(s) will be.

❹ Have students work in pairs. Encourage them to use **already**, **still**, and **yet** in their sentences. Review the answers as a class.

🌐 **Option:** Write the following groups of words on the board or make a copy of them for each student. Have students work independently or in pairs to put the words in the right order to form sentences. Review the sentences as a class.

1. new/she/?/yet/hired/has/teachers (Has she hired new teachers yet?)
2. a/accomplished/they/./already/lot/have (They have already accomplished a lot.)
3. hasn't/her/sent in/still/./application/she (She still hasn't sent in her application.)
4. tuition/?/reduced/they/have/yet/costs (Have they reduced tuition costs yet?)
5. received/acceptance/already/he's/letter/./an (He's already received an acceptance letter.)
6. still/joined/club/./English-language/an/haven't/I (I still haven't joined an English-language club.)

Note: Already can be placed at the end of sentences 2 and 5.

☑ ❺ **Check Your Understanding** Have students complete the activity independently. You might want to suggest that they write out possible responses for each situation first. For example, for the first item a student could write "I have already done research at the library."

Answers
Present perfect tense: giving an update on a class project or describing preparations for a party

Simple present tense: showing someone how to write a letter or telling about one's learning style

Future tense: discussing plans for next year

 Workbook: Practices 4, 5, 6, 7

❻ **Express Yourself** This activity is communicative and interactive. It connects the grammar point—in this case, use of the present perfect tense—to students' lives.

🌐 **Option:** Write the headings "simple past tense" and "present perfect tense" on the board. Have the class suggest time expressions that can be used with the present perfect tense (ever, since, for two years) and time expressions that can be used with the simple past tense (yesterday afternoon, last year, a week ago). Write the expressions in the appropriate columns on the board. Then elicit a sentence with each time expression, and write the sentences in the appropriate columns.

T5

HIROKO: I finished reading the book last week, but
I **(4. write, still)** _____
the report.

CARLOS: Well, you **(5. do, already)**
_____ a lot more than I have.
I **(6. read, yet)** _____ the book
_____ .

HIROKO: Don't worry. You'll finish everything in time.
You always do.

3 Gina is getting ready to begin college next week. Lisa
wants to know what Gina has to do. Work with a
partner. Take the roles of Gina and Lisa and ask and
answer questions, following the example.

Example:

  LISA: Have you filled out your application yet?

 GINA: Of course, I've already filled it out. I did that
three months ago.

done **a.** fill out the application

_____ **b.** see the campus

done **c.** ask teacher to write a letter of recommendation

done **d.** get an acceptance letter

_____ **e.** choose your courses

_____ **f.** buy your textbooks

_____ **g.** meet your roommate

done **h.** pay your tuition

4 With a partner, discuss what you *have* and *haven't done* in your English
class so far. Take turns making sentences.

  a. write a postcard   **e.** sing a song

  b. do a role play   **f.** learn to write business letters

  c. read a poem   **g.** take a quiz

  d. see a video   **h.** idea of your own

5 **Check Your Understanding** Check the situations in which you
are likely to use the present perfect tense with *already, still*, and *yet*.
Compare your answers with a partner's.

☐ Giving your teacher an update on your class project

☐ Showing a friend how to write a college application letter

☐ Describing your preparations for a party

☐ Telling someone about your learning style

☐ Explaining your vacation plans for next year

6 **Express Yourself** With your partner, choose one of the situations you
checked. Imagine yourselves in the situation and write a dialogue. When
you finish, read your dialogue to another group.

LISTENING and SPEAKING

Listen: Sound Off

1 **Before You Listen** What strategies do you use to remember important information? Check the appropriate box.

	Always	Sometimes	Never
a. I "see" it on the page in my mind.	☐	☐	☐
b. I write it down several times.	☐	☐	☐
c. I associate it with things I already know.	☐	☐	☐
d. I repeat it aloud or in my mind.	☐	☐	☐
e. I use movement or rhythm to help me remember.	☐	☐	☐
f. I underline or highlight in my book.	☐	☐	☐
g. I imagine situations I can use it in.	☐	☐	☐

h. Your own idea: _____

 Listening for Distinctions When a speaker discusses differences between items (in categorizing, for example), it is important to listen carefully for the characteristics that make each item different from the other(s).

 2 Today's guest on the talk show, *Sound Off,* is going to talk about different learning styles. Read the chart. Then listen to the program and complete the chart.

Learning Styles	How Learners Learn	What Learners Do
1. Visual	*through their eyes*	**a.** *notice details around them* **b.** _____
2. Tactile		**a.** _____ **b.** _____
3. Auditory		**a.** _____ **b.** _____
4. Kinesthetic		**a.** _____ **b.** _____

3 Work with a partner. Look at your charts and answer the questions.

  a. Which learning style best describes you? Why?

  b. Can you think of other characteristics that describe your learning style?

  c. How can an awareness of your learning style help you learn English?

LISTENING and SPEAKING

Listen: Sound Off

Presentation

❶ Before You Listen Tell students to think about how they learn new information, for example, vocabulary, grammar, and pronunciation. Then have them read the directions and complete the activity. Review the responses as a class. (*Answers will vary.*)

➡ **Listening for Distinctions** This is the first of several learning strategies that appear in every unit. The purpose of these strategies is to help students learn more effectively and independently.

Have students read the strategy. Point out that this strategy is a special form of listening for details, used when two or more things are being compared and contrasted.

🎧 **❷** Read the directions with the class. Then play the recording or read the audioscript aloud two or more times for students to complete the exercise. Have students listen again to check their work, if necessary.

Audioscript: The audioscript for Exercise 2 appears on page T152.

Answers

Possible answers: **1.** through their eyes; notice details around them; "see" things in their minds **2.** through touching or manipulating; are good with machines and physical procedures; often have to hold something while they listen or read **3.** through hearing; use rhythm and sound to help them remember things and memorize easily **4.** through movement; take things (such as machines) apart and put them back together; use movement and rhythmic routines to help them remember

---

❸ Have students complete the activity with partners. Then review the responses as a class. (*Answers will vary.*)

🌐 **Option:** Poll the class to find out how many students fit each learning style. Have students with each learning style discuss how they might better use their style to learn English.

🌐 **Option:** Write the following list of functions on the board for students to copy. Play the recording for Exercise 2 or read the audioscript again and have students check the functions that are used. Ask them to give an example of each function used.

- ☑ introducing someone
- ☑ asking for an opinion
- ☑ giving an opinion
- ☑ giving reasons for an opinion
- ☐ convincing
- ☑ agreeing
- ☐ disagreeing
- ☑ generalizing

🔗 *Workbook: Practice 8*

Pronunciation

Preview

- Write the regular verbs **ask**, **help**, **perform**, and **turn** on the board for students to copy. Ask students to say each word aloud to themselves and to underline the final consonants (**sk, lp, rm, rn**). Introduce the term **consonant cluster** and point out that a consonant cluster consists of two or three consonant sounds that are pronounced together.

- Write the past tense forms of the four verbs on the board (**asked, helped, performed, turned**) and have students repeat the words after you. Elicit that the past tense ending is pronounced /t/ with the verbs ending in **k** and **p** and /d/ with the verbs ending in **m** and **n**.

Presentation

Read the pronunciation explanation with the class. Focus attention on the words in the box and their final sounds. You may wish to have students work in pairs to list other words that have the same final sounds as **reduced** and **learned**.

❹ Have students work in pairs to complete the exercise.

🎧 ❺ Play the recording or read the dialogue aloud twice and have students check their predictions. Then review the answers as a class. You might want to have students write the answers on the board.

> **Answers**
> A: /n/, /nd/; B: /k/, /kt/; A: /b/, /bd/;
> B: /k/, /kt/; A: /č/, /čt/

❻ Have the pairs work together to read the dialogue.

 Workbook: Practice 9

Speak Out

Preview

- Discuss the meanings of **artificial** and **natural**. Ask students to discuss what an artificial language might be.

- Ask students to summarize what they found out about their language-learning needs and preferences in the questionnaire on pages 1–3. Introduce or review **summarize** (to give the main points).

Presentation

➡ **Summarizing** Have students read the strategy and the expressions in the box.

Have students read the explanation, look at the photograph, and read the captions.

Note: The purpose of this activity is to develop fluency. Students should be encouraged to speak without fear of interruption for error correction. If you notice persistent errors, write them down for later reteaching or review.

Pronunciation

Consonant Clusters with *–ed* Endings

When the *–ed/–d* ending of regular past tense verbs is pronounced /t/ or /d/, we often pronounce two or three consonant sounds together. This is called a consonant cluster.

reduce	reduced	learn	learned	laugh	laughed
/rədus/	/rədu**st**/	/lɜn/	/lɜ**nd**/	/læf/	/læ**ft**/

 4 Work with a partner. Predict the final sound(s) of the underlined letters. Write your predictions within the slash marks. The first one is done for you. (See the IPA chart on Student Book page 131.)

A: I didn't jo<u>in</u> a conversation club. Have you jo<u>ined</u> one yet?
/n/   /nd/

B: No, and I didn't che<u>ck</u> out any library books. Have you che<u>cked</u> any out yet?
/ /   / /

A: No, and I didn't subscri<u>be</u> to a magazine. Have you subscri<u>bed</u> to any yet?
/ /   / /

B: No, and I didn't ta<u>lk</u> to any English tourists. Have you ta<u>lked</u> to any yet?
/ /   / /

A: No, and I didn't wa<u>tch</u> any films in English. Have you wa<u>tched</u> one yet?
/ /   / /

 5 Listen to the dialogue and check your predictions.

6 Practice reading the dialogue, focusing on consonant clusters.

Speak Out

STRATEGY **Summarizing** In discussions, it is important to be able to summarize the main ideas in a brief form. When you summarize, use expressions to show that you are focusing on the most important information.

To sum up, ...	Up to now, we've agreed that ...	In short, ...
In summary, ...	We've concluded that ...	Overall, ...

Some people think that world communication would be easier with an artificial universal language. One well-known artificial language is Esperanto, developed by Ludwig Zamenhof of Poland.

**La astronauto,
per speciala instrumento,
fotografas la lunon.**

(An astronaut photographs the moon with a special instrument.)

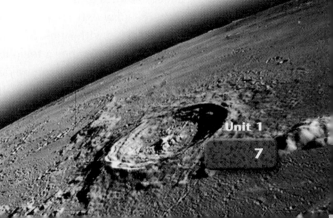

7 Work in small groups. Discuss the advantages and disadvantages of adopting a natural or an artificial language as a common means of world communication. One person in your group will take notes.

8 Now, one member of your group will summarize the group's results for the class. Do the groups agree or disagree? Use the expressions on page 7 for summarizing.

READING and WRITING

Read About It

1 **Before You Read** How much do you know about the human brain? Write **T** if you think the statement is true and **F** if you think the statement is false.

_____ **a.** The human brain weighs about 6.6 pounds (3 kilos).

_____ **b.** Different parts of the brain have different functions.

_____ **c.** Damage to the brain cannot cause loss of speech.

STRATEGY **Identifying Main Ideas** You understand more when you can identify the main idea expressed in each paragraph of a text. The main idea is often found in the first sentence. However, it can be anywhere in the paragraph, and sometimes it is implied.

The Human Brain

The brain is the most complicated organ in our bodies. Our thinking, remembering, and communicating abilities originate in this small mass. It is difficult to imagine that this small gray
5 organ, which weighs less than 2.2 pounds (1 kilo), is so important, but scientists have shown that the human brain is the most complex organ of the body.

Scientists have not been able to solve all the
10 mysteries of the brain. They still have not discovered exactly how learning takes place. However, they have made some progress. They have found that certain parts of the brain are responsible for different aspects of learning,
15 memory, and language.

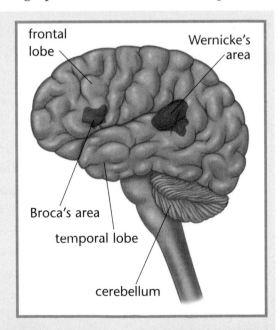

frontal lobe
Wernicke's area
Broca's area
temporal lobe
cerebellum

Recent studies indicate that the two halves of the brain—the right hemisphere and the left hemisphere—play extremely important roles in learning and communicating. The left hemisphere deals with rules, lists of information, and short-term memory. Short-term memory is what we use to remember a telephone number long enough to call someone after we look it up.
20 In contrast, the right hemisphere deals with feelings, colors, and long-term memory. Long-term memory is what we use when we drive a car each day or remember how to get to work.

❼ Have students read the directions. Make sure they understand what an artificial language, such as Esperanto, is. Allow them time to discuss the advantages and disadvantages of both a natural and an artificial language. Be sure that one student in each group takes notes.

❽ Have one student in each group summarize the group's discussion for the class. Be sure the student focuses on the main ideas and uses one or more of the expressions in the box on page 7.

Option: You might want to tell students more about Esperanto. Ludwig Zamenhof began creating Esperanto while he was a teenager. He based his language on Indo-European root words. The grammar has only 16 rules, and each of the 28 letters in the alphabet stands for only one sound. Today, several million people can speak Esperanto. More than 600 schools teach it to 20,000 students a year. Around 7,500 books have been written in Esperanto, including translations from about 65 other languages.

Option: Some students may want to look in the library or on the Internet for information on Esperanto or another artificial language (Volaphk, Ido, Interglossa, Interlingua, Solresol, and so on) and its inventors. Have them summarize their findings for the class.

Option: Have students work in groups to invent a simple artificial language. They can base their languages on features of their own language, English, or any other languages they may know. Have each group prepare a poster showing the special features of its language and some sample sentences. Display the posters and ask the groups to explain their languages to the class.

 Workbook: Practice 10

READING and WRITING

Read About It

Presentation

❶ Before You Read Have students work independently or in pairs to complete the activity. Tell students that they will check their answers after they've read the article.

> **Answers**
> Explanations for false answers are provided. **a.** F; The human brain weighs less than 2.2 pounds (1 kilo). **b.** T **c.** F; Our communicating abilities originate in the brain, so damage to the brain (Broca's area) affects language production.

➡ **Identifying Main Ideas** Have students read the strategy. Tell them that the strategy is especially useful when reading complex or difficult material. Encourage them to identify the main idea of each paragraph as they read the article. Have students read the article independently in class or for homework. Encourage them to read it without using dictionaries. If they read in class, you may want to set a time limit.

❷ Have students reread the article, this time underlining or highlighting the sentence (or sentences) that expresses the main idea of each paragraph. Discuss the answers as a class, looking at one paragraph at a time. Encourage students to justify their answers.

Answers
Answers may vary somewhat. Possible answers:
Paragraph 1: The brain is the most complicated organ in our bodies. (sentence 1)
Paragraph 2: Scientists have not been able to solve all the mysteries of the brain. However, they have made some progress. (sentences 1 and 3)
Paragraph 3: Recent studies indicate that that the two halves of the brain—the right hemisphere and the left hemisphere—play extremely important roles in learning and communicating. (sentence 1)
Paragraph 4: Scientists now know that certain aspects of language are housed in different areas of the brain. If these areas are damaged, language production and comprehension are affected. (sentences 1 and 2)

❸ Have students write the definitions individually or in pairs. Discuss the definitions as a class.

Answers
a. to begin, come from **b.** to happen **c.** to be involved in or responsible for **d.** to be located in **e.** a division or section **f.** to put two things together

🌀 **Option:** To check students' understanding of the article, write the following questions on the board or ask them orally.

1. What abilities originate in the brain? (abilities to think, remember, and communicate)

2. What are the two major parts of the brain? (the right hemisphere and the left hemisphere)

3. What do the left and the right hemisphere each deal with? (The left hemisphere deals with rules, lists of information, and short-term memory; the right hemisphere deals with feelings, colors, and long-term memory.)

4. Why are scientists interested in learning about brain damage? (Studies of people with brain damage show where in the brain different aspects of language are housed.)

Think About It

❹ Have students discuss the question in pairs, in small groups, or as a class. Encourage them to think about short-term memory versus long-term memory.

❺ If necessary, have students refer to the questionnaire on pages 1–3 and their answers to Listening and Speaking exercises 1 and 3 on page 6. Have students share their responses in pairs, small groups, or as a class.

🌀 **Option:** Have students write comprehension questions of their own about the article. Have them exchange questions with a partner and answer their partner's questions.

🌀 **Option:** Have students find out more information about these or other areas of the brain. Students can work in groups and report their findings to the class.

Write: A Letter of Inquiry

Presentation

Have students read the explanation silently. You might want to discuss with students the different kinds of formal letters they have written.

❻ –❼ Have students circle the letters of the elements they would include in a letter of inquiry. Then have them figure out the order in which the elements would appear. Finally, have them compare their ideas with the letter shown on page 10.

Answers
Answers may vary. Possible answers: h, d, c, a, f

🌀 **Option:** Ask students to discuss why each item listed should or should not be included in a letter of inquiry.

25 Scientists now know that certain aspects of language are housed in different areas of the brain. If these areas are damaged, language production and comprehension are affected. A person with damage in Broca's area, in the frontal lobe, can still understand language but has great difficulty producing it. A person with damage in Wernicke's area, in the temporal lobe, can speak easily and fluently, but cannot attach correct meanings to words or put them in correct order. As research continues, scientists will identify more connections between language and the brain in their search to understand what it is that makes us uniquely human.

2 One way to remember main ideas is to underline or highlight them as you read. Underline or highlight the main ideas in the reading. Check your answers with the class.

3 Use the context to guess the meanings of the following words. Do not use a dictionary. Write your definitions on a piece of paper.

    a. to originate (line 3)   **c.** to deal with (line 20)   **e.** lobe (line 24)
    b. to take place (line 11)   **d.** to be housed in (line 22) **f.** to attach (line 26)

Think About It

4 Do you have a good memory? What kinds of things do you remember?

5 Now that you have thought about your learning strategies and learning styles, describe the kind of learner you are.

Write: A Letter of Inquiry

When you write a formal letter asking for information, you are writing a letter of inquiry. Letters of this type are frequently sent to colleges and universities, businesses, and other institutions.

6 You just saw an ad for computer courses at Harrison College, and you would like more information. Circle the letters of what you would probably do in your letter of inquiry.

    a. request list of courses _____
    b. ask for teachers' names _____
    c. request an application _____
    d. mention your past computer courses _____
    e. ask about teachers' education _____
    f. ask about tuition _____
    g. tell about your family _____
    h. give reason for writing _____

7 How would you order the ideas in your letter? Write the numbers on the lines above, beginning with 1 for your first idea.

1525 Woodmont Avenue
Arnold, PA 00268
February 21, 2000

Harrison College
Office of Admissions
200 College Avenue
Lake City, New York 01005
Dear Sir or Madam:

I am writing to obtain information about computer courses at Harrison College. I have already taken two computer courses and would like to continue my studies.

Could you please send me a list of courses, information about tuition, and an application form?

I look forward to hearing from you soon.

Sincerely,

Diane M. Jackson

Diane M. Jackson

8 A formal letter contains several parts. Find these parts and write the letters on the letter of inquiry above.

a. the return address

b. the inside address

c. the greeting

d. the body

e. the closing

f. the signature

Write About It

9 You want to take a course at Davis Community Center. Decide what you want to study. Then write a letter of inquiry.

New at Davis Community Center!

Six-Week Courses	Twelve-Week Courses
Drawing	French Cooking
Oil Painting	Photography
Ceramics	Bonsai
Weaving	Surfing the Net
Jewelry Making	Designing Web Pages

For more information, write to:
Office of Admissions
Davis Community Center
200 Walnut Avenue • Davis, New York 01012

10 **Check Your Writing** Exchange papers with a partner. Use the questions below to give feedback to your partner. When you get your paper back, revise as necessary.

- Does the letter include all the parts of a formal letter of inquiry?
- Is it clear what the writer is asking for?
- Are the ideas ordered in a logical way?
- Is the language accurate?

⑧ Have students complete the task independently. Then have them work in pairs to check their answers.

Answers

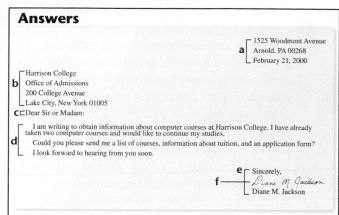

a ⌐ 1525 Woodmont Avenue
    Arnold, PA 00268
    ⌐ February 21, 2000

b ⌐ Harrison College
    Office of Admissions
    200 College Avenue
    Lake City, New York 01005

c ⌐ Dear Sir or Madam:

d I am writing to obtain information about computer courses at Harrison College. I have already taken two computer courses and would like to continue my studies.

Could you please send me a list of courses, information about tuition, and an application form?

I look forward to hearing from you soon.

e ⌐ Sincerely,

f *Diane M Jackson*
    Diane M. Jackson

Write About It

Presentation

⑨ Have students read the directions silently. Remind them to use what they learned in Exercises 6–8 about the format, content, and organization of letters of inquiry. Encourage them to follow the model on page 10 and also to use their own ideas. (*Letters will vary.*)

Cultural Note: Community centers are neighborhood organizations that have recreational and educational activities.

☑ **⑩ Check Your Writing** Point out that feedback tells us what is clear to our readers and what is not clear. Suggest to students that they use the feedback to help them revise their writing. You might want to have students give written feedback. Tell them to be as specific as possible and to give suggestions for improvement.

 Workbook: Practice 11

Option: You may want students to compare and contrast the styles and conventions of business letters in their countries with those in the United States. Have them bring in sample letters from their countries to show to the class. What similarities and differences are there in the format, content, organization, and language (form of expression)?

Vocabulary Expansion: Using word maps
See page T140. (*Answers will vary.*) Note that the last unit objective refers to the Vocabulary Expansion activity.

EVALUATION

See page TExi.

Unit 1 Achievement Test

Self-Check See Check Your Knowledge, page 8 of the Workbook.

Dictation Dictate the following sentences to your students. For more information on dictation, see page TExv.

1. Gina has chosen her courses for the fall and has already bought the books that she needs.

2. Scientists have solved many mysteries of the brain, but they still have not discovered exactly how learning takes place.

Dictate the following sentences to your students and have them complete the sentences with their own ideas. Then have them work in pairs or small groups to compare their answers.

3. I've visited quite a few interesting places, but I haven't gone to _____ yet.

4. I've already seen several good films this year, but I still haven't seen _____.

5. I've already done many interesting things in my life. For example, I've _____ and I've also _____.

Communication Skills

1. Ask individuals to summarize what they found out about their own learning styles. How do they think this information will help them study in the future? As they answer, pay attention to their use of learning styles and skills vocabulary.

2. Ask students to tell about things they have already accomplished in their lives and things they haven't done yet but would like to do in the future. Pay attention to their use of the present perfect tense with **yet**, **already**, and **still**.

WHODUNIT?

OBJECTIVES

- To talk about mysteries and detective stories
- To speculate
- To make deductions
- To use **may, might,** and **could** to express possibility
- To use **must** and **have to** to express near certainty that something is true
- To use **can't** to express near certainty that something is impossible
- To listen for details
- To use stress to differentiate the noun function from the verb function of a word
- To express certainty and uncertainty
- To make and confirm or modify predictions while reading
- To understand the elements of a narrative
- To write a narrative
- To classify descriptive adjectives

GETTING STARTED

Warm Up

Preview

- Ask students about the kinds of books they like to read. Elicit as many kinds as possible (love stories, mysteries, plays, Westerns, poetry, adventure novels, science fiction, biographies, autobiographies, comics, short stories). Encourage students to give examples.

- Elicit or present **robbery.** Have students discuss robberies they have heard or read about.

Presentation

❶ Write the word **whodunit** on the board, and have students analyze it to figure out why it is used with mysteries.

Language Note: Whodunit is a noun made up of **who** + **dun** (i.e., **done**) + **it**. The word literally asks, "who committed the crime?" and is used to refer to mystery, detective, and crime stories. The grammatically correct form, **who** + **did** + **it,** is not used as a word.

❷ Have students work in pairs to list famous writers of mystery and detective stories. To help them, put the initials of some writers they know on the board. Accept writers of various languages, but encourage students to think of English-language writers (Sir Arthur Conan Doyle, Agatha Christie, Dashiell Hammett, Dorothy Sayers, and so on). You might also ask them to name some famous fictional detectives—from books, TV, or film (Sherlock Holmes, Columbo, Micky Spillane, Hercule Poirot, Starsky and Hutch, Miss Marple, Sam Spade, and so on). As a class, discuss the kinds of crimes the writers write about.

🌐 **Option:** Have students work in pairs or in groups to brainstorm all the words they associate with detective and mystery stories (detective, private eye, gun, shoot, police, crime, kill, victim, fingerprints, spy, murder, witness, and so on). Have students make word maps using the words they brainstormed.

🎧 ❸ Have students read the directions. Play the recording or read the audioscript aloud twice. Allow students time to label the floor plan and draw the path. Have them work in pairs to compare their answers. Then have them listen again to check their work. Review the answers as a class. You might want to draw the blank floor plan on the board for one student to complete as the class gives the answers.

Audioscript: The audioscript for Exercise 3 appears on page T152.

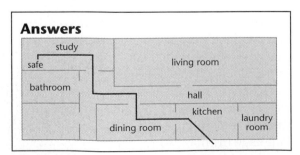

Answers

 Workbook: Practice 1

GETTING STARTED

Warm Up

1 Mysteries and detective stories are popular because the reader has to put together all the pieces to understand the final picture. We often call this kind of story a "whodunit." Can you guess why?

2 Work with a partner. List some famous mystery and detective story writers. What kinds of crimes do they write about?

3 Are you a good detective? Listen to two thieves committing a robbery. Write the names of the rooms. (The thieves don't mention every room.) Draw their path on the floor plan.

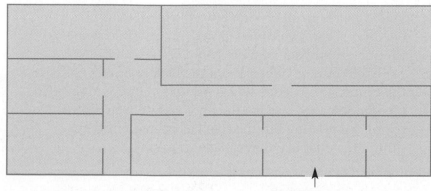

You are here.

Figure It Out

The crime you heard being committed was reported to the police.
Detective Leeds and his assistant, Ms. Scott, are investigating it.

Police Report

Crime: Cash, jewels, and papers taken from safe

Victim: Portia Powell, 64, widow

Time of crime: Between 11:00 p.m. and 7:30 a.m., October 9, 1999

Possible Suspects	Possible Motives
Paul Powell, son	Recent fight with mother about money
Penny Powell, daughter	Mother didn't like fiancé
Howard Forbes, daughter's fiancé	Out of work; Portia against marriage
Ms. Butler, housekeeper	Recently fired because of missing silverware
Laura Lane, lawyer	Portia refused to pay bills for legal services
Sara Shaw, accountant	Possible illegal use of bank account

A. DETECTIVE LEEDS: So, Mrs. Green, you live next door to the victim, Portia Powell.

    MRS. GREEN: Yes, I do. And I always thought something terrible might happen to her—always
5   bragging about her cars and her valuable jewels and …

    MS. SCOTT: Did she keep her jewelry in the house?

    MRS. GREEN: Yes, in the safe with all her important papers. Since her husband died, she's kept a lot of
10   cash in there, too. She locked it up so her son, Paul, couldn't get it.

    DETECTIVE LEEDS: Why didn't she just put it in the bank?

    MRS. GREEN: Well, according to the housekeeper, Portia thought her accountant was stealing from her bank account!

15 **B. DETECTIVE LEEDS:** Well, I talked to all of Mrs. Powell's family and neighbors, and I've come up with six possible suspects. Right now, any one of them could be the thief.

    MS. SCOTT: I checked out the house. From the look of things, the thief must be someone who's pretty familiar with it.
20   No windows are broken, the door hasn't been forced open, and nothing but the safe has been disturbed. I think the thief may have a key.

Figure It Out

Preview

- If possible, display pictures to elicit or present **accountant**, **assistant**, **fiancé**, **housekeeper**, and **lawyer**. Have students name people they know who have each role or occupation.

- Elicit or present **bank account**, **suspect** (noun), **motive**, **to brag**, **to commit**, **to disturb**, **to fire**, **to force** (open), and **to lock**. Tell the story of a crime—if possible, bring in a relevant newspaper article and photo—using the target vocabulary with as much explanation as is needed. You may want to use synonyms or draw figures on the board for clarification. Ask if any students are familiar with other similar crimes. If so, have them tell the stories. Help them with any vocabulary they need to express their ideas.

Presentation

Have students read the introductory sentences. Instructions for presenting the conversations appear on page TEvii.

Option: Make a copy of the police report. Cut and paste two possible suspects and their motives on each of three cards. Divide the class into three groups and give each group one of the cards. Allow time for the groups to study their information. Then form groups of three with one member from each of the previous groups. Have the members of each group tell each other what they know about the suspects. Students may want to take notes as they listen. Who does each group think committed the crime?

Focus attention on the police report. Have students read the report to answer the following questions.

1. What time did the crime take place? (between 11 p.m. and 7:30 a.m. on October 9, 1999)

2. What was the crime? (Cash, jewels, and papers were taken from a safe)

3. How old is Portia Powell? (64)

4. Did Portia Powell have a husband? (Yes, but he died.)

5. Are Mrs. Powell's children suspects? Why? (Yes. Her son recently had a fight with her about money, and she didn't like her daughter's fiancé.)

6. Why are Mrs. Powell's housekeeper, lawyer, and accountant suspects? (Her housekeeper was recently fired because of missing silverware; her lawyer was probably upset because Mrs. Powell refused to pay her; her accountant was possibly stealing from her bank account.)

Read the conversations on pages 12 and 13 aloud as students follow along silently. You can also have students read the conversations independently in class or for homework. After the initial presentation of the conversation, have students answer the following questions, as a class or in groups, to check their understanding.

1. How many suspects did Detective Leeds come up with? (six)

2. Does the criminal probably know Portia Powell? Why do you think so? (Yes. No windows or doors were broken or forced open.)

3. What was in Portia Powell's safe? (jewels, important papers, and cash)

4. Why didn't Portia Powell keep her money in the bank? (She thought her accountant was stealing money from her bank account.)

5. Who does Detective Leeds think is the criminal? (the son, Paul)

6. Who do you think the criminal is? (*Answers will vary.*)

Have students read the conversations aloud in groups of three.

☑ ❹ **Vocabulary Check** Have students complete the exercise individually in class or for homework. Review the answers as a class.

> **Answers**
> 1. f 2. c 3. d 4. a 5. e 6. g 7. h 8. b

 Option: Have students close their books. Call on students to retell each conversation from memory.

 Option: Have students work independently, in pairs, or in groups to list TV shows or movies that deal with mysteries or detectives. Have them report their lists to the class. You might want to have them rate the shows by assigning a number of stars to each: ***** = excellent; **** = very good; *** = OK; ** = not very good/boring; * = terrible. Have students compare their lists and ratings and discuss why they rated each show as they did.

> **Link** *Workbook: Practice 2*

 Option: Read the following sentences aloud to students as a dictation. Then tell students that these sentences describe a crime. Have them number the sentences in the order in which they think the actions happened. Have pairs or groups of students compare their sequences and justify them. Accept any order students can justify.

1. Someone heard a noise and asked who was there.
2. Someone opened a window.
3. Someone began to fight with a woman and killed her.
4. Someone walked down the hall.
5. Someone opened a door.

Talk About It

 Option: You may prefer to postpone this activity until after the grammar presentation (page 14) if you feel students need extra help with modal auxiliaries that express degrees of certainty. You also might direct students to Workbook Practice 4 for help in understanding the modals.

Presentation

Note: The purpose of this activity is to develop fluency. Students should be encouraged to speak without fear of interruption for error correction. If you notice persistent errors, write them down for later reteaching or review.

❺ Have students work in pairs. Ask them to read the directions. Then have a pair of students read the example conversation aloud. Have students complete the activity. Tell them to talk about each of the suspects, using information from the police report and the conversations on pages 12 and 13.

 Option: Brainstorm with students additional people who could be suspects in the Powell case. Give each person a name, a family, a relationship to Mrs. Powell, and a motive. Write the names and motives on the board. Have students continue the activity with these new suspects.

> **Link** *Workbook: Practice 3*

 Option: Have students work in pairs or small groups. Have them think of favorite mysteries they have read, have seen on TV or in the movies, or have heard about in real life. Have them talk about the suspects in each case. You may want to have the pairs or groups describe the mysteries to the rest of the class.

DETECTIVE LEEDS:	Yeah. It might be anyone on the list. Personally, I think it may be the son, Paul.
MS. SCOTT:	Why do you think it might be him?
DETECTIVE LEEDS:	Well, it appears that he recently had an argument with his mother—a big one according to the neighbors. Over money, they think.
MS. SCOTT:	Hmmm. He might have a lot of bills to pay, or he could owe money to someone.
DETECTIVE LEEDS:	You might be right. Let's check it out.

25

30

 4 **Vocabulary Check** The words on the left are from the police report and the conversations. Match them with the meanings on the right.

_____ **1.** illegal (police report)   **a.** a place to keep money or jewelry
_____ **2.** victim (line 2)   **b.** about
_____ **3.** valuable (line 5)   **c.** person taken advantage of
_____ **4.** safe (line 8).   **d.** worth a lot of money
_____ **5.** to come up with (line 16)   **e.** to find; to figure out
_____ **6.** suspects (line 16)   **f.** against the law
_____ **7.** to check out (line 18)   **g.** people thought to be involved in a crime
_____ **8.** over (line 28)   **h.** to investigate

Talk About It

 5 Work with a partner. You are detectives working on the Powell case. Take turns asking about the possible suspects in the police report.

Speculate about possible suspect.
A: I think Mrs. Powell's daughter Penny might be the thief.

Ask for reason.
B: Why do you think it's Penny?

Give possible motive and make deduction.
A: Her mother doesn't really like her boyfriend. Penny must be pretty upset about that.

Agree to reasoning and mention other suspect.
B: That could be the motive, but the lawyer may be the thief, too.

Degrees of Certainty: Modal Auxiliaries

When we talk about events or situations that are possible in the present or future, we use the modal auxiliaries *may*, *might*, or *could*. In questions, *may* and *might* usually follow the phrase *Do you think ... ?* To speculate about choices, we use *could*.

> **SCOTT:** So what have you come up with?
>
> **LEEDS:** I'm not sure. It **may be** Howard Forbes. He sure needs the money and he's been acting very nervous.
>
> **SCOTT:** **Do you think** he **might leave** town?
>
> **LEEDS:** I doubt it. He doesn't have any money.
>
> **SCOTT:** Who else **could** it **be**?
>
> **LEEDS:** Well, it **could be** Ms. Butler. She worked for the Powells for thirty-five years, and she's furious because Mrs. Powell just fired her.

1 Mr. and Mrs. Loubet are worried about their daughter's vacation, so they're giving her some advice. On a piece of paper, write the reasons for their advice.

Example:

Don't walk around without a map. *You could get lost.*

a. Don't carry a lot of cash.
b. Don't eat any strange food.
c. Don't talk to strangers.
d. Don't leave your tickets in your hotel room.
e. Don't swim right after you eat.
f. Don't take only shorts and T-shirts.
g. Don't leave the hotel without your passport.

When we know most of the facts and draw a logical conclusion, we use *must* or *have to*. This means we are almost certain that something is true. When we are almost certain that something is impossible, we use *can't*.

> **LEEDS:** So you think Ms. Butler is the thief?
>
> **SCOTT:** Well, it **can't be** Laura Lane. She didn't even know the safe was behind the picture. I think it **has to be** Ms. Butler. She's the only one who could get to the safe.
>
> **LEEDS:** You're probably right. It **must be** her.

GRAMMAR

Degrees of Certainty: Modal Auxiliaries

Preview

- To review modal auxiliaries, write the following pairs of sentences on the board.

   There is life on other planets in the universe.
   There might be life on other planets in the universe.

   Penny and Howard are on their way to the Bahamas now.
   Penny and Howard could be on their way to the Bahamas now.

   Ask students to tell which words are different in each pair (**is/might be** and **are/could be**). Then ask them to tell how the sentences in each pair differ in meaning. (The first sentence in each pair states something as certain; the last sentence in each pair states something as possible.) Elicit that the modal auxiliaries **might** and **could** are used to say that something is possible.

- Below the second pair of sentences, write the following pair.

   Penny is on her way to the Bahamas now.
   Penny could be on her way to the Bahamas now.

   Ask students to look at the last four sentences together and explain how modals are different from verbs. (They do not change form to agree with the subject.) Make sure students understand that a modal is followed by a verb in the base form.

Presentation

Have students read the explanation and the example conversation in the box. Make sure students understand that when expressing possibility, **may**, **might**, and **could** mean about the same thing. If students are aware that **could** is the past form of the ability

modal **can**, you might point out that here **could** does not have past meaning but is used to talk about the present and future.

❶ Have students read the directions and complete the activity. Then have them compare answers in pairs, small groups, or as a class.

> **Answers**
> Answers will vary. Possible answers:
> a. You could/might/may lose it.
> b. You could/may/might get sick.
> c. They could/might/may be dangerous.
> d. Someone could/might/may steal them.
> e. You could/might/may get sick.
> f. You could/might/may get cold.
> g. You could/might/may need it.

✪ **Option:** Have students work in pairs to think of more advice to give the Loubet's daughter—about language, long-distance telephone calls, letters home, and so on. Have pairs share their advice with the class or in a group. Make sure the pairs state reasons for each piece of advice they give. You may want to have the pairs make up short conversations between the Loubets and their daughter and present them to the class.

✪ **Option:** Have students work in groups to brainstorm other situations in which they would use **might**, **may**, and **could**. Then have the groups make up short conversations based on some of the situations they brainstormed. Encourage them to include some questions with **Do you think ... ?** Have the groups share their conversations with the rest of the class.

Have students read the next explanation and the example conversation in the box. Make sure students understand that **can't** expresses near certainty—but near certainty that something is false, rather than near certainty that something is true.

✪ **Option:** Have students work in groups to brainstorm other situations in which they would use **must**, **have to**, and **can't**. Have them make up short conversations based on these situations, and then have them share their conversations with the rest of the class.

T14

☑ ❷ **Check Your Understanding** Have students complete the activity independently. Review the answers as a class.

Answers

Mrs. Butler must/has to be the thief because she's the only one who could get to the safe.

Sara Shaw could be the thief because Mrs. Powell thought she was stealing from her bank account.

Laura Lane can't be the thief because she didn't even know the safe was behind the picture.

❸ Have students read the directions and then complete the activity. Review the answers as a class. You might want to have students skim the conversation first before they complete it.

Answers

1. might 2. can't 3. might 4. might
5. might 6. must 7. might 8. must

❹ Have students read the directions and then complete the activity independently in class or for homework. Remind students to use the modals **might**, **may**, **must**, or **could** in their sentences. (*Answers will vary.*)

☑ **②** **Check Your Understanding** Based on the information about the theft so far, how certain are you about Laura Lane, Sara Shaw, and Ms. Butler? Complete the chart with the name of each suspect and your reason.

Someone *is* the thief.
_____ *must/has to be* the thief because _____.
_____ *could be* the thief because _____.
_____ *can't be* the thief because _____.
The neighbor *isn't* the thief.

③ Sue is talking to Bob about her boss. Complete the conversation with *might*, *must*, or *can't*.

Bob: What's the matter, Sue?

Sue: Mr. Fox hasn't arrived yet. He's always on time for work.

Bob: Don't worry. He **(1.)** _____ be in a traffic jam.

Sue: No, that **(2.)** _____ be it. His car is at the mechanic's.

Bob: Then he **(3.)** _____ be on the subway.

Sue: Oh, come on. He never takes the subway!

Bob: Did you try calling him? He **(4.)** _____ be sick.

Sue: He was fine yesterday, just a little nervous.

Bob: Nervous about what?

Sue: The accountants discovered that a huge sum of money is missing. It **(5.)** _____ be as much as a million dollars!

Bob: What? There **(6.)** _____ be a mistake! Check the computer!

Sue: We did. The money is gone.

Bob: Do you think we **(7.)** _____ have a thief in the office?

Sue: Hey, wait a minute. The money is missing … and Mr. Fox is missing. Are you thinking what I'm thinking?

Bob: Yes! Fox **(8.)** _____ be on a plane with the million dollars!

④ Optimists look at the positive, and pessimists look at the negative. Read each sentence on the top of page 16. Then write two conclusions, one from the optimist's (+) perspective, and one from the pessimist's (–).

Example:

Tom has lost his appetite, and he spends all his time looking
out the window and sighing.

(+) *He must be in love!*   (−) *He must be sick.*

  a. George doesn't earn a lot of money, but he's driving a new car.

  b. You see a man leaving a package at your neighbor's house.

  c. You were supposed to meet Mary for lunch, but she hasn't shown up.

  d. You usually see the same woman at the bus stop in the morning,
but she isn't there this morning.

  e. Your friend said she'd be home tonight, but no one answers the phone.

5 Compare your sentences with a partner's. Which responses do you agree
with? Are you an optimist or a pessimist?

6 **Check Your Understanding** In which situations are you likely to use
might, may, could, or *must*? Compare your answers with a partner's.

  ☐ Talking about tomorrow's weather
  ☐ Speculating about who the killer is in the novel you're reading
  ☐ Describing a suspect to the police
  ☐ Talking about career possibilities with a counselor
  ☐ Offering reasons for a friend's late arrival

7 **Express Yourself** With a partner, choose one of the situations you
checked above. Imagine yourselves in the situation and write a dialogue.

LISTENING and SPEAKING

Listen: What's on TV?

1 **Before You Listen** What words do you associate with the word *mystery?*
Make a list on a sheet of paper. Share your ideas with the class.

STRATEGY **Listening for Details** When you need to get specific facts and information,
you listen for details such as a specific time, place, number, or name.

2 Listen to a commercial for *Midnight Mystery Theater,* a popular TV
show. Complete the chart. Then tell how you think the story will end.

Midnight Mystery Theater

Tonight's Episode Title: _____

Channel: _____ **Time:** _____

Main Actor: _____ **Main Actress:** _____

Plot Summary: _____

Possible End of Story: _____

5 Have partners compare their two responses to each situation, and have them discuss whether they think they're optimists or pessimists. Then have students share their responses to the situations and their conclusions about themselves with the class.

☑ **6 Check Your Understanding** Have students read the directions and then complete the activity independently in class or for homework.

> **Answers**
> Answers will vary. The modals would probably be used in all the situations except the one describing a suspect to the police. Ask students to explain their responses.

7 Express Yourself This activity gives students a chance to use modals in the situations they determine are appropriate. Ask each pair to share its dialogue with the class.

 Workbook: Practices 4, 5, 6, 7, 8

Option: Have students bring in photographs of themselves as babies or young children. Display the photos or pass them around. Have students guess who they are.

LISTENING and SPEAKING

Listen: What's on TV?

Presentation

1 Before You Listen Have students write their lists independently in class or for homework. To get them started, you might suggest a few words, for example, **detective, murder, suspects, plot, victim, murderer, motive** and **solution**.

Have students work in pairs or groups to compare lists. Each group should compile a list to share with the class. You might write the class's composite list on the board. If students have vocabulary notebooks, have them copy the words into their notebooks.

➡ **Listening for Details** Have students read the strategy. Have them name situations in which it is important to listen for details (listening to announcements of bus, train, and airplane arrivals and departures; listening to messages on a telephone answering machine; listening to a teacher's explanation about what will be on the next test; listening to weather reports and sports scores, and so on).

🎧 **2** Have students read the directions. Then focus their attention on the chart. Present or review **midnight, episode,** and **plot.** Play the recording or read the audioscript aloud twice. Give students time to fill in the chart and to write a possible ending to the story. Then have them work in pairs to compare their answers. Let them listen again to check their work. Ask individuals to share their story endings with the rest of the class. Alternatively, have students share their endings in groups and have each group choose a favorite ending and present it for the class.

Audioscript: The audioscript for Exercise 2 appears on page T153.

> **Answers**
> "The Victim"; Channel 5; 12:00 (midnight); Peter Carleton; Joan Young; When a wife becomes mysteriously sick, she suspects that her husband and his beautiful assistant are trying to kill her. (*Answers will vary.*)

 Workbook: Practice 9

T16

Unit 2

Pronunciation

Preview

Write **record** on the board and ask how many syllables it has (two). Then write the following conversation on the board and read it aloud.

A: I really like that album.

B: Do you want to record it?

Ask students to tell which syllable in **record** is accented, or receives the primary word stress (the second). Then write A's response on the board and read it aloud.

A: No, but I'd like to listen to it again. Can I borrow the record this weekend?

Ask students to tell which syllable of **record** is accented in this sentence (the first).

Presentation

Have students read the explanation and the examples in the box independently in class or for homework.

❸ Have students read the directions and the questions. Read the explanation and the examples in the box aloud. Have students answer the questions as a class. Point out that the two uses of **suspect** are similar to the two uses of **record**. (**Suspect** is used as both a noun and a verb and has a different pronunciation for each form of the word.)

> **Answers**
> second syllable; first syllable

🎧 ❹ Play the recording or read the audioscript aloud twice for students to circle their answers. Have them listen again to check their work.

Audioscript: The audioscript for Exercise 4 appears on page T153.

> **Answers**
> a. progress b. progress c. suspect
> d. suspect e. convict f. convict g. record
> h. record i. present j. present

❺ Have students say the words with a partner. The partner should identify each word as a noun or a verb. If necessary,

do this activity as a class before students do it in pairs.

 Option: Have students work in small groups. Have them write a sentence for each word. Then have them take turns saying the sentences aloud.

Link *Workbook: Practice 10*

Speak Out

Preview

Introduce or review any necessary vocabulary from the list of cues in the box.

Presentation

➡ **Expressing Certainty and Uncertainty**

Focus students' attention on the language for expressing certainty and uncertainty. Ask individuals if they think they will continue to study English after they finish this class. Encourage them to use the language for expressing certainty and uncertainty in their answers.

Note: The purpose of this activity is to develop fluency. Students should be encouraged to discuss their opinions without fear of interruption for error correction. If you notice persistent errors, write them down for later reteaching or review.

❻ Have students read the directions and the example. If necessary, use the second and third lines of the example to point out the difference between uncertainty (I'm not sure) and certainty about something negative (I'm never going to get married). Then have students complete the activity in small groups. Encourage them to use the language for expressing certainty and uncertainty.

Link *Workbook: Practice 11*

 Option: Some students may enjoy working in pairs or groups to make up their own mysteries. Encourage them to use the language for expressing certainty and uncertainty. Then have them present their mysteries to the class.

Pronunciation

3 Look at the examples in the box. When "suspect" is used as a verb, on which syllable is the primary word stress? When it is used as a noun, which syllable is the stress on?

4 Listen to the conversation. Circle the word you hear.

	Noun	Verb		Noun	Verb
a.	progress	progress	**f.**	convict	convict
b.	progress	progress	**g.**	record	record
c.	suspect	suspect	**h.**	record	record
d.	suspect	suspect	**i.**	present	present
e.	convict	convict	**j.**	present	present

5 With a partner, take turns pronouncing the words. Make sure that your partner hears the word you want to say.

Speak Out

STRATEGY ▶ **Expressing Certainty and Uncertainty** To show the degree of certainty you have about a topic, you can use certain words and expressions.

Expressing Certainty	Expressing Uncertainty
I'm sure that ...	I'm not at all sure that ...
... will most likely ...	It's possible that ...
I'll definitely ...	I might/may/could ...

6 Work in a small group. How certain are you about your future? Ask and answer questions using the cues. Use the language for expressing certainty and uncertainty.

Example:

A: Do you think you'll ever get married?
B: Well, I'm not sure. I might if I meet the right person.
A: Not me. I'm never going to get married.

a. get married
b. have only one occupation
c. have children
d. become rich or famous
e. live to be very old

f. invent something
g. live in another country
h. appear on television
i. learn more languages
j. idea of your own

Read About It

1 **Before You Read**

a. What helps you choose a book to read? The title? The cover? The thickness? The price? The author? Someone's recommendation? List the criteria in order of importance to you.

b. What types of books do you like to read—love stories, science fiction, biography, whodunit, autobiography, poetry, or nonfiction?

c. Classify the following titles into the categories of books above.

A History of Rome	*Turkey: Land of Dreams*
Beautiful but Dead	*In Love at Carnival*
Elvis: The King Lives On	*Spies at Midnight*
Again a Broken Heart	*War on Planet Dorn*
Collected Short Poems	*Laser Killers of the 21st Century*

 STRATEGY **Confirming Predictions** When you read, you interact with the text by making predictions. As you read on, you confirm or modify your ideas.

2 The story "The Meeting" contains examples of some of the interactions you can have with a text. Answer the questions as you read.

The Meeting

Jessica was furious. She was still the company president,[1] and when she called a meeting for 10:00, she meant exactly 10:00. "Where *is* everybody?" she asked aloud.[2]

Suddenly, the door to the secretary's office opened. "Well, at
5 least *one* person's coming," thought Jessica, as she picked up her papers for the meeting. Steps came closer and closer. Jessica looked up.[3] "Oh, it's you," she said in a cold voice. "What do you want?" Then she raised her hand to her throat as she realized what was happening.[4]

10 "To watch you die, Jessica!" Jessica heard her name and the shot at the same time. Her name, echoing again and again, was the last thing she ever heard.

After the police left later that afternoon,[5] the office staff had a meeting. Morrison, the accountant, broke the silence.[6] "Shall I be
15 the first to say it? OK! I'm glad she's dead!"

[1] Why do you think Jessica was furious?

[2] What can you guess about Jessica's personality so far?

[3] What do you think Jessica will say?

[4] What do you think the person might do?

[5] Why were the police there?

[6] What do you think he might say?

READING and WRITING

Read About It

Presentation

❶ **Before You Read** Make sure students understand **criteria** before they begin the activity. Have them complete **a** independently in class or for homework. Then have individuals share their answers with the class. What is the most popular **criterion**?

Have students read **b** independently in class or for homework. Review **fiction** and **nonfiction**. Take a class survey to find out which type of book is the most popular.

Have students work independently, in pairs, or in groups to classify the titles in **c**. Make sure students understand the vocabulary in the titles before they complete the activity.

Answers

Love stories: *Again a Broken Heart; In Love at Carnival*

Science fiction: *War on Planet Dorn; Laser Killers of the 21st Century*

Biography: *Elvis: The King Lives On*

Whodunit: *Beautiful but Dead; Spies at Midnight*

Poetry: *Collected Short Poems*

Nonfiction: *A History of Rome; Turkey: Land of Dreams*

➡ **Confirming Predictions** Have students read the strategy. Ask students to tell whether they are aware of using this strategy. Point out that by using this strategy readers pay closer attention to what they are reading. As they develop ideas about what comes next, they become more focused on their reading—whether their predictions are confirmed or modified.

❷ Have students read "The Meeting" independently in class or for homework. Make sure they understand that they are to answer the interaction questions as they read. Have students work in pairs to compare their answers, and then have the class discuss the answers. Make sure students understand that most questions can't be answered with certainty at this point. The story is incomplete. Point out that if students were to read the complete story, they would confirm some of their predictions and modify others.

❸ Have students read the directions and work independently or in pairs to complete the activity.

> **Answers**
> Answers will vary. Possible answers:
> **a.** sound of a gun **b.** employees **c.** to say something when no one has been talking **d.** reason for doing something **e.** give someone a better job **f.** to say loudly and with force **g.** (too) energetic, doing what will be good for oneself without concern for others **h.** be certain **i.** to remain at an event one doesn't want to be at

Think About It

Presentation

❹ ❺ Have students answer the discussion questions in pairs, in small groups, or as a class. Ask individuals to share their answers with the class. Make sure they give reasons for their responses. Emphasize that there are no right or wrong answers.

☸ **Option:** Have students work in pairs or groups to write an ending to "The Meeting." First, they should probably decide who the killer is and what his or her motives were. Have the pairs or groups share their endings. You might want to post them on the bulletin board.

☸ **Option:** Have students reread "The Meeting" in preparation for a dramatization of the story. Assign the roles—or have the students choose the roles—of Jessica, Morrison, Maria, and Derek. Have students think about their characters as they reread the story. How old is the character? What is his or her personality? How does he or she talk? How does he or she walk? Have groups of four present their dramatizations to the class. For large classes, you may wish to add characters, for example, Martínez, Angela, and other staff members. Before doing the dramatizations, students will need to decide who killed Jessica. If they did the preceding option, they can use an ending written by a group member.

Write: A Narrative

(*See page 20.*)

Presentation

Have students read the explanation and the narrative independently in class or for homework. Encourage them to speculate on the ending of the mystery after they read "Describing the events." Encourage their comments on the ending of the story.

❻ Have students answer the question (**Answer: b**), and then have them discuss how the story uses this organization. What time word is used in the story to connect events? (then)

❼ Have students work in pairs to select the details for both readings. Then have them compare their answers as a class. (*Answers will vary.*)

"How can you say that?" said Jessica's assistant, Maria. "The police might think you killed her!"

"Well, dear, someone did! And many of us had a motive. Even you, Maria!" Morrison replied.

20 "That's right, Maria," Derek, an advertising manager, agreed.[7] "We all know she wasn't going to promote you. Angela was going to get the better position, not you."

"You actually think I could kill someone over something like that? You must be joking!" exclaimed Maria. "And what about you, Derek?
25 Jessica took that big advertising account away from you and gave it to the new man, Martinez. He'll have your job someday. You'll see!"[8]

"That kind of talk isn't necessary, Maria. Control yourself!" said Morrison.[9] "I'm sure Martinez tried hard to get that account. We all know how hardworking he is."

30 "He's aggressive all right, and very ambitious," added Derek. "I'm convinced he'll do anything to become the president of the company someday."[10]

"Did you notice how many times he met with Jessica last week?" asked Maria. "When I asked him what was going on, he said it was
35 just something about the account."[11]

"Well," commented Derek as he calmly arranged his papers, "at least we're never going to have to sit through any more meetings with Jessica."

[7] What do you think Maria's motive could be?

[8] Why do you think Maria said this?

[9] What does Morrison's remark suggest about Maria's personality?

[10] Who does Derek think is guilty? How does he suggest this?

[11] What do you know about Martinez's personality? Why do you think he met with Jessica so often?

3 Use the context to guess the meanings of the words and expressions. Write your definitions on a piece of paper.

a. shot (line 11)
b. staff (line 13)
c. to break the silence (line 14)
d. motive (line 18)
e. to promote (line 21)
f. to exclaim (line 24)
g. aggressive (line 30)
h. be convinced (line 31)
i. to sit through (line 37)

Think About It

4 Who do you think the killer might be? Why? How did you reach your conclusion?

5 Describe the personalities of Jessica's coworkers. Do you think you would enjoy working with any of these people?

Write: A Narrative

A narrative is a story. A good narrative sets the scene, describes the events, and provides an ending. When we write a narrative, we want the reader to feel close to the scene and events. To do this and to make the story real, we use details about people, place, time, sounds, feelings, conversations, and actions.

Setting the scene It was a clear autumn night. The moon was out, and there was a light wind. I decided to walk home after the movie.

Describing the events I got to my apartment building and unlocked the door. I walked to the elevator and pushed the button. When the doors opened, I saw a tall blond man standing inside. He walked past me quickly without saying a word. I didn't think anything about it until the elevator stopped on my floor. That's when I noticed blood on the door and a large pool of blood on the floor. The door opened and I walked out. I walked slowly down the hall toward my apartment. Then I heard the elevator doors open again. Someone was walking toward me! I was so frightened I couldn't move. I just stood there in front of Mrs. Manz's apartment.

Ending the story Then someone touched my arm. I must have jumped a foot! It was Mrs. Manz. "You didn't step in the tomato sauce, did you?" she said. "I was carrying a big jar of my sister's homemade tomato sauce when the elevator stopped suddenly, and I dropped it. What a mess! I just went down to the basement to get something to clean it up with."

6 How do you organize the events in a narrative? Circle the correct answer.

    a. In the order of importance (rank order)

    b. In the order they occur in time (chronological order)

    c. In the order in which they are located (spatial order)

7 Good narratives include many details to make the story real. With a partner, find examples of these details in "The Meeting" and the story above.

    a. the place   **c.** the weather   **e.** the actions

    b. the time   **d.** the people   **f.** the sounds

Write About It

8 Think of something that happened to you recently. It can be something *funny, sad, exciting, embarrassing,* or *frightening.* Use this word to focus your paragraph. Write a narrative about what happened. Organize your ideas and use time words to connect them.

9 **Check Your Writing** Exchange your story with a partner. Use the checklist below to give feedback to your partner.

> • Does the narrative set the scene, tell the events, and have an ending?
> • Which details help bring the reader close to the story?
> • Are there any places where more detail is needed?

Write About It

Preview

- Have the class brainstorm a list of time expressions to use to connect ideas in a narrative (then, first, later, next, at the same time, meanwhile, finally, and so on).

- Have students discuss what makes a story effective. Write their ideas on the board. (a clear description of the scene, clearly described and organized events, details that make the story seem real, interesting, realistic people, interesting/real-sounding conversations; an interesting ending)

Presentation

8 Have students write their stories. Review what makes a story effective (see Preview section).

9 **Check Your Writing** Have partners give each other feedback, using the checklist and the ideas discussed in class. Have students share their revised stories with the class. Collect them and post them on a bulletin board.

 Workbook: Practice 12

Vocabulary Expansion: Descriptive adjectives See page T141.

Answers
Answers will vary. Possible answers: **A. 1.** Age: young, middle aged, old **2.** Height: tall, medium height, short **3.** Weight/body type: well-built, chubby, thin, large, overweight, small, little, scrawny, big, heavy-set **4.** Hair: dark, black, blonde, curly, gray, long, red, straight, brown, short, bald **5.** Facial characteristics: double chin, chubby, scar

EVALUATION

See page TExi.

Unit 2 Achievement Test

Self-Check See **Check Your Knowledge,** page 16 of the Workbook.

Dictation Have students number their sheets of paper from 1 to 10. Dictate sentences 1, 3, 5, 7, and 9. Have students write original sentences for 2, 4, 6, 8, and 10. For more information on dictation, see page TExv.

1. It was a dark and stormy night.
2. (another sentence describing the setting)
3. The tall man on the corner looked very suspicious.
4. (another sentence describing the man)
5. Suddenly, police cars with flashing lights and screaming sirens appeared.
6. (a sentence describing the man's reaction)
7. An angry, older man got out of the back of a police car and pointed at the man.
8. (a sentence telling what the man said)
9. The man threw a knife to the ground and ran away.
10. (a sentence telling what the older man did next)

Have students write endings to the story.

Communication Skills

1. Show a series of pictures that tell the story of a crime or mystery. Have students tell the stories. As they speak, listen for the correct use of key vocabulary and the modals of possibility and certainty.

2. Have each student speculate/make predictions about the following topics. Pay attention to their use of modals.

- Possible weather forecast for the weekend
- Possible vacation plans next summer
- Who might win the Nobel Peace Prize or an Academy Award
- Whom the student might marry, how many children he or she might have

BECAUSE I TOLD YOU TO!

OBJECTIVES

- To talk about orders, requests, permission, persuasion, and advice
- To talk about authority and social roles
- To use verb + object + (*to*) + verb
- To listen for tone
- To hear and use contrastive stress
- To use formal and informal language to ask for, grant, and deny permission
- To recognize definitions and examples
- To write a letter of application

GETTING STARTED

Warm Up

Preview

- Write **Because I told you to!** on the board and have students think of people who might use this expression, for example, parents when speaking to children. Ask students whom *they* might use the expression with, for example, children and friends. Finally, ask them to brainstorm situations in which a parent might say, "Because I told you to!"

Language Note: Because I told you to! is used by a person in authority who expects the listener to obey without an explanation of why. It's used most often by parents when speaking to children.

- Have students list people in their lives who have some authority over them and people whom they have some authority over.

- As a preliminary to a discussion of roles, elicit or present **acquaintance**, **manager**, **colleague**, **landlord**, **tenant**, **citizen**, and **client**. Ask students to name real-life examples.

Presentation

❶ Have students read the activity. Focus their attention on the pictures. Point out that the red-haired man in each picture is the same man but that in each picture he is playing a different role. Ask the students to identify his role in each picture. (1, military officer; 2, a father; 3, a citizen/customer waiting in line) Then ask who has the authority role in each picture. (in pictures 1 and 2, the red haired man.) For picture 3, elicit that the person who probably has the authority role—a clerk—is not shown. Have students write their lists individually and then share them in groups or as a class.

 ❷ Have students read the instructions. Make sure they understand each of the roles listed. Play the recording or read the conversations aloud at least twice. Remind students that they do not have to understand every word in order to complete the activity. Then have students work in pairs to compare their answers. Have them listen again to check their answers.

Audioscript: The audioscript for Exercise 2 appears on page T153.

> **Answers**
> **1.** e **2.** g **3.** d **4.** b

Option: Have students listen again to tell whom the woman is talking to in each conversation. Have them identify the words that indicate the roles.

Link *Workbook: Practice 1*

Figure It Out

Preview

- Have students work in pairs, in groups, or as a class to brainstorm verbs they associate with power or authority. (*Possible verbs*: force, make, expect, allow, tell, order, want)

(*Figure It Out continues on page T22.*)

GETTING STARTED

Warm Up

1 In one day a person plays many roles, depending on where he or she is. For example, the same person can be a father or husband, a boss or employee, a patient with his doctor, a friend with a neighbor, and a good citizen who registers to vote. How many roles do you have in one day? List them.

2 According to the role we are in, we are expected to behave in certain ways. Listen to the conversations. One woman is playing several roles. Write the number of the conversation on the line next to her role.

_____ **a.** tenant   _____ **d.** employer   _____ **g.** citizen

_____ **b.** daughter   _____ **e.** patient   _____ **h.** client

_____ **c.** police officer _____ **f.** wife   _____ **i.** mother

Figure It Out

PAUL:	Hi, Jake! I haven't seen you in ages! What's new?
JAKE:	Oh, not much. So, how do you like your new job?
PAUL:	I love it! I'm really happy I decided to change jobs. My new boss is great!
JAKE:	Tell me about it.
PAUL:	What can I say? She's the best boss I've ever had. First of all, she lets us choose our own hours. So now I start work at ten and leave at six. I miss all the rush hour traffic that way.

5

10	**JAKE:**	Lucky you. Mr. Rachet still makes us come in at eight and stay until at least five. We've tried to persuade him not to be so inflexible, but he refuses to listen. He says the personnel department makes the rules, and we have to follow them.
15	**PAUL:**	Does he still force you to work a lot of extra hours?
	JAKE:	Well, he doesn't exactly force us, but he expects us to do it.
20	**PAUL:**	Yeah, well, my new boss sometimes asks us to work overtime, too, but she always pays us for it. She's got a great sense of humor, and she listens to us and appreciates our ideas. In fact, she encourages her employees to give her ideas for improving the company.
25	**JAKE:**	No kidding. Mr. Rachet has never allowed us to contribute any of our own ideas. He just wants us to do exactly as he says. It's very frustrating.
30	**PAUL:**	Listen, why don't you let me ask my boss if we have an opening? I think she'd appreciate a hard worker like you. And I know I can convince her to give you an interview.
	JAKE:	That's great! When can I meet her?
	PAUL:	You already know her—I'm working for my wife now!

3 Answer the questions.

a. In your country, are employees free to express their own opinions and give suggestions to their bosses? Is this a good idea? Why or why not?

b. Do you think it is a good idea for husbands and wives to work together in the same office? Why or why not?

4 **Vocabulary Check** Match the words on the left with their meanings on the right.

_____	**1.** rush hour (line 8)	**a.**	to give
_____	**2.** inflexible (line 12)	**b.**	to show approval and support
_____	**3.** to expect (line 18)	**c.**	to permit
_____	**4.** to appreciate (line 23)	**d.**	position; job
_____	**5.** to encourage (line 24)	**e.**	disappointing
_____	**6.** to allow (line 26)	**f.**	to understand the value of
_____	**7.** to contribute (line 27)	**g.**	to persuade; to make a person agree
_____	**8.** frustrating (line 29)	**h.**	to think something will happen
_____	**9.** opening (line 31)	**i.**	time when many people are trying to get to or from work
_____	**10.** to convince (line 32)	**j.**	not wanting to change

(Figure It Out continued from page T21.)

⊛ **Option:** Have students create word maps for **power/authority**. Write **power/authority** on the board and draw a circle around it. Then draw a branch from **power/authority**, write **force**, and circle it. Elicit other words from students and do the same. Allow students to finish this word map in pairs. Have them share their word maps with other pairs and with the class. You might list the following question words on the board to help them think of items: *Who? What? When? Where? Why? How?*

- Discuss a work situation to elicit or present **personnel department, sense of humor, (to work) overtime, rush hour,** and **(job) opening**.

- Have students look at and talk about the pictures on page 22. Who are the bosses? What kinds of personalities do these two bosses seem to have? How do the employees seem to feel? You might ask students to try to guess what the people are talking about.

Presentation

Read the conversation on pages 21 and 22 aloud as students listen. You can also have students read the conversation silently in class or at home. After the initial presentation of the conversation, have students answer the following questions, as a class or in groups, to check comprehension.

1. How does Paul like his new job? (He loves it.)

2. Why doesn't Jake like his job? (He doesn't like the way his boss manages.)

3. What is Jake's boss like? (He's too inflexible; he expects Jake to work overtime; he doesn't allow his employees to contribute their own ideas.)

4. What is Paul's boss like? (She lets the employees choose their own hours; she pays them for working overtime; she has a great sense of humor; she encourages

the employees to give her ideas for improving the company.)

5. What other role does Paul's boss play in his life? (She's his wife.)

Have students read the conversation aloud in pairs. You may want to assign to each student a part to practice before class to encourage fluency.

⊛ **Option:** Have students close their books. Ask individuals to retell the conversation from memory. Write the following key expressions and words on the board to guide them: seen in ages, new job, great boss, inflexible boss, work hours, overtime, sense of humor, contribute ideas, job opening, wife.

❸ Have students read and think about the questions. Students can then discuss their responses in small groups or as a class. (*Answers will vary.*)

☑ ❹ **Vocabulary Check** Have students complete the exercise individually in class or for homework. Ask individuals to share their answers with the class.

Answers
1. i 2. j 3. h 4. f 5. b 6. c 7. a
8. e 9. d 10. g

 Workbook: Practice 2

⊛ **Option:** Remind students that **time** is used in many expressions. Have students work independently or in pairs to figure out what the following expressions mean: **overtime** (time past the normal amount), **work full time** (work a full day every day of the work week—usually 35 to 40 hours), **work part time** (work less than full time), **time off** (time not at work), **on time** (not late), **in time** (soon enough), **time is up** (no more time), **save/waste time** (use time well/not use time well). Have students use the expressions in sentences. If they are keeping vocabulary notebooks, have them add the expressions and sentences to their notebooks.

Talk About It

⊕ **Option:** You may prefer to postpone this activity until after the grammar presentation (page 23) if you feel students need extra help with expressing orders, requests, permission, and so on. You might also direct students to Workbook Practice 4.

Preview

List these occupations on the board: *typist, mail clerk, receptionist, accountant, manager, secretary, salesperson, janitor.* Then write the following definitions on the board or dictate them to the class.

1. a person who works with records of money that is earned and spent
2. a person who cleans a building
3. a person who distributes letters and packages
4. a person who sells a company's products
5. a person who is in charge of employees
6. a person who types letters and reports
7. a person who greets people who come to a company and gives them information
8. a person who organizes his or her boss's work, answers the phone, corresponds with customers, and so on.

Have students match the definitions with the occupations listed.

Presentation

Note: The purpose of this activity is to develop fluency. Students should be encouraged to speak without fear of interruption for error correction. If you notice persistent errors, write them down for later reteaching or review.

➎ Have students work in pairs. Have them read the instructions and the conversation. Then have them complete the activity. Each pair can take the roles of *all* the workers, or pairs can concentrate on asking and answering questions between two occupations of their choice. Have pairs present their dialogues to the class. Encourage students to talk about orders and requests, as in the example.

⊕ **Option:** Write or have students write additional occupations to continue the activity.

T23

You might have each pair think of an occupation and present their conversation to the other students, who must then figure out the occupation.

⊕ **Option:** Tell students to imagine that one of the workers listed, for example, the mail clerk, was suddenly promoted to chief executive. Ask partners to create conversations with this mail clerk as the new boss. Have them present their dialogues to the class or in groups. How has the focus of the conversation changed?

 Workbook: Practice 3

GRAMMAR

Orders, Requests, Permission, Persuasion, Advice

Presentation

Have students read the grammar explanation and the examples independently in class or for homework. Review the grammar explanation and the examples with the class. Ask students to think of additional examples for the verbs shown, using the same workplace context.

Have students find the two negative sentences. Ask students to specify the position of **not** in each of the negative sentences. (The second sentence in the box has **not** before the infinitive **to make**. The fourth sentence in the box has **didn't** before the main verb **allow**.

➊ Have students complete the exercise independently and compare answers. Then discuss the answers as a class, having students explain the differences in meaning.

Answers
a. D b. D

☑ ➋ **Check Your Understanding** Have students complete the exercise independently. Then discuss the answers as a class, having students explain the differences in meaning.

Answers
1. b 2. a 3. c 4. d

Talk About It

5 The company you work for has a new chief executive. You and your colleagues are discussing the changes she has made. With a partner, ask and answer questions. Ask the people in the box.

secretary	mail clerk
accountant	receptionist
typist	manager
janitor	salesperson

Ask about request.

A: What did the new boss tell you to do?

Report request.

B: She asked me to tell all our clients that they have to pay now or face legal action.

Express surprise.

A: You're kidding me!

Report order.

B: No, and that's not all! She also told me not to use the phone for personal calls.

GRAMMAR

Orders, Requests, Permission, Persuasion, Advice

Verbs that are followed by a noun phrase (NP) and an infinitive (*to* + verb) are often used to express orders, requests, permission, persuasion, and advice.

> Mr. Smith **told the secretary to type** a letter. (*order*)
>
> He also **warned her not to make** personal phone calls at work. (*order*)
>
> The secretary **asked Mr. Smith to give** her a day off. (*request*)
>
> Mr. Smith **didn't allow her to take** a day off. (*permission*)
>
> Instead, he **persuaded his secretary to work** on Saturday. (*persuasion*)

1 Read the pairs of sentences. Do they have the same (S) meaning or different (D) meanings? Circle **S** or **D**. Compare your answers with a partner's.

  a. She asked to leave.
     She asked her secretary to leave.   **S**   **D**

  b. She didn't promise to be at the meeting.
     She promised not to be at the meeting.   **S**   **D**

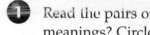 **2** **Check Your Understanding** Match each sentence with the correct meaning.

   ____ **1.** I told him not to eat so much.

   ____ **2.** I didn't tell him to eat so much.

      a. I didn't say anything about food to him, and he ate too much.

      b. I saw that he was eating too much, and I asked him to stop.

_____ **3.** They asked us not to go to the beach.

_____ **4.** They didn't ask us to go to the beach.

    c. They didn't want us to go to the beach, so they said, "Will you please stay home?"

    d. They went to the beach, but they didn't invite us.

Some verbs are followed by a noun phrase (NP) and the base form of the verb alone.

Make, Have, Let

He **made his secretary work** overtime.	(*order, persuasion*)
He **had her type** more letters.	(*request, persuasion*)
He **didn't let her take** any time off.	(*permission*)

3 Complete the dialogue with the correct form of the verb in parentheses. Add an appropriate noun phrase.

Tom: You're too strict with the kids, Anna. You make **(1. study)** _them study_ too much. You ought to let **(2. enjoy)** _____ their childhood!

Anna: And you're too easy with them. You never tell **(3. do)** _____ anything. You allow **(4. watch)** _____ too much TV. You should encourage **(5. read)** _____ more. We should expect **(6. do)** _____ their best in everything.

Tom: But are you really helping? When you force **(7. do)** _____ so much, they get frustrated. You want **(8. study)** _____ all day, and **(9. help)** _____ around the house, and **(10. be)** _____ polite. It's too much to expect. Experts advise parents **(11. push, *neg.*)** _____ their children too hard.

Anna: Tom, did your parents teach **(12. think)** _____ like that?

4 Review the dialogue you just completed and answer the questions.

a. Which verbs are followed by *to*?

_____

b. Which verbs are NOT followed by *to*?

_____

c. Change the sentence, "Anna asked Tom to change his ways."

to a question: _____

to a negative: _____

to a negative infinitive: _____

Make; Have; Let

Preview

- Have students read the grammar explanation and the examples. Make sure students understand how these verbs are similar to and different from the verbs on page 23. (They express similar functions; the verb that follows the noun phrase is in the base form—it doesn't have **to**.) Ask students to think of additional examples for the verbs shown.

- Introduce **obligation** (something you are *made* to do) and **privilege** (something someone *lets* you do).

✪ **Option:** Have students work in pairs or small groups to discuss their personal *obligations* and *privileges*. Have one person in each group make lists for all the functions. Are some students' privileges other students' obligations? You may wish to discuss as a class.

Presentation

❸ Have students complete the exercise independently and then check their answers in pairs.

> **Answers**
> 1. them study 2. them enjoy 3. them to do 4. them to watch 5. them to read 6. them to do 7. them to do 8. them to study 9. to help 10. to be 11. not to push 12. you to think

❹ After students answer the questions, review the answers as a class. Focus attention on the two negative sentences in item **c**. Have students discuss how the two sentences differ in meaning.

> **Answers**
> **a.** tell, allow, encourage, expect, force, want, advise, teach **b.** make, let **c.** Did Anna ask Tom to change his ways? Anna didn't ask Tom to change his ways. Anna never asked Tom to change. Anna asked Tom not to change his ways. Anna asked Tom to stay the same.

✪ **Option:** Write additional sentences like the ones in item **c** in Exercise 4 on the board. Have students change each sentence to a negative and then to a negative infinitive. Have students work in pairs to think about how the two negative sentences differ in meaning. Then encourage them to explain their answers in groups or to the rest of the class.

✪ **Option:** Have students work in small groups to discuss how they think children should be raised and why they think so. Encourage them to look at the dialogue in Exercise 3 for help in expressing their ideas. Have one person in each group write down the group's ideas. If the members of the group disagree, have them present both opinions. Have the groups share their ideas with the rest of the class.

5 Have students complete the chart independently or in pairs. Check answers as a class.

Answers

Answers may vary slightly.

Order: have, make, tell, warn, force

Request: advise, invite, ask, would like

Permission: allow, let, permit

Persuasion: convince, encourage, persuade

Option: Ask students to remember pieces of advice that members of their families gave them at one time or another. Have them make a list. Encourage students to focus on important or interesting advice. Have them write paragraphs about their families' advice, using the ideas in the list. Have students work with partners to make sure that their paragraphs are easy to understand and that their sentences are grammatically correct. Ask several students to read their paragraphs to the class. Alternatively, tell students not to write their names on their paragraphs, and when they've finished, display the paragraphs on a bulletin board. Have the class read the paragraphs and figure out to whom each belongs.

6 Have students read the title of the newspaper article and predict what it will be about. Remind them that newspaper articles answer these questions: *Who? What? When? Where?* and *How?* Have them read to find out who found something, what he found, how he found it, when he found it, where it came from, and what happened as a result. Then have students complete the activity independently, in pairs, or small groups. Make sure they pay attention to the pronouns.

Answers

(See Unit 7 for additional information on reported speech.)

Answers may vary somewhat. Possible answers: **a.** What did his wife want him to do? His wife wanted him to take a trip to the Caribbean. **b.** What would his mother like him to do? His mother would like him to buy a nice house in the country. **c.** What did his brother tell him to do? His brother told him to buy the boat he's always wanted. **d.** What did his landlord encourage him to do? His landlord encouraged him to pay the rent a year in advance. **e.** What did his grandmother expect him to do? His grandmother expected him to donate some money to the senior citizens' club. **f.** What did his neighbor remind him to do? His neighbor reminded him to pay back the money he had lent him. **g.** What did his friend advise him to do? His friend advised him not to listen to anybody, to do what he wanted. **h.** What did the truck driver ask him to do? The truck driver asked him to share the reward with him since he had made it possible.

---

7 Express Yourself This activity gives students a chance to use requests, permission, and persuasion in an appropriate situation. Ask pairs to present their dialogue to the class.

 Workbook: Practices 4, 5, 6, 7

5 These are common verbs that are followed by an NP and an infinitive or a base verb. Write each verb in the correct category in the chart. Some verbs can go in more than one category.

advise	make	let	warn	encourage
convince	tell	invite	ask	persuade
have	allow	permit	force	would like

Order	Request	Permission	Persuasion

6 Read the article about Tom Adams. With a partner, ask and answer what people told Tom to do. Use the words in bold type as cues.

BANK GIVES REWARD

While Tom Adams was walking home from work last night, he found a bag that had fallen out of a bank truck. The bag contained over $20 million in cash and checks. Mr. Adams returned the bag to the bank. Delighted bank officials gave him a $50,000 reward.

Example:

"Put the money in the bank," his father **advised**.

A: What did his father advise him to do with the money?
B: He advised him to put it in the bank.

a. "I want us to take a trip to the Caribbean," said his wife.
b. "I'd like a nice house in the country," said his mother.
c. "Buy that boat you've always wanted," his brother **told** him.
d. "Pay the rent a year in advance," **encouraged** his landlord.
e. "I **expect** you to donate some money to the senior citizens' club," said his grandmother.
f. "Pay back the money I lent you," **reminded** his neighbor.
g. "Don't listen to anybody. Do what you want," his friend **advised**.
h. The truck driver **asked**, "Will you share the reward since I made it possible?"

7 **Express Yourself** Work with a partner. One plays the role of a parent (mother or father) and the other the child. Imagine a situation in which the child is making a request, the parent is denying permission, and the child is trying to persuade the parent to change his or her mind. Write a dialogue.

Listen: It's in the Tone

1 **Before You Listen** Who gives you advice? Do you listen to other people when they give you advice? Who do you give advice to?

STRATEGY **Listening for Tone** You can understand more when you focus on the speaker's tone of voice in addition to the words used. The speaker's tone tells what he or she really means and how he or she is feeling. Listening for tone also helps you understand how to respond appropriately.

2 Listen to the conversations and identify the tone of the first speaker in each one. Check the box in the correct column.

	Worried	Angry	Uncertain	Persuasive	Roles
a.	☐	☐	☐	☐	_____
b.	☐	☐	☐	☐	_____
c.	☐	☐	☐	☐	_____
d.	☐	☐	☐	☐	_____
e.	☐	☐	☐	☐	_____
f.	☐	☐	☐	☐	_____

3 Listen to the conversations again and identify the probable roles of the first speaker in each one. Complete the chart. Compare your ideas with a partner's.

Pronunciation

Contrastive Stress

Function words are usually unstressed, but they can be stressed to make a contrast.

A: And what about Pat? You asked her to help out, right?

B: No, I didn't ask **her**, I asked **him**.

	Stressed	Unstressed
him	/hɪm/	/ɪm/
her	/hɝ/	/ɝ/
them	/ðɛm/	/əm/

4 Predict the pronunciation of *him, her,* and *them*. If the word is stressed, underline it.

A: Are you sure you want Jeff to do the dishes?

B: Yes. I want <u>him</u> to do <u>them</u> this time. Paula did them last time.

LISTENING and SPEAKING

Listen: It's in the Tone

Presentation

❶ Before You Listen Have students answer the questions in pairs or in small groups. Encourage students to think of as many examples as possible. Ask them to explain when they listen to other people's advice. Have them share their ideas with the class.

➡ **Listening for Tone** Have students read the strategy. Ask them what kinds of feelings speakers can convey through tone. (*Examples:* anger, concern and worry, certainty or uncertainty, sarcasm, happiness) Have students think of situations in which they used tone to understand what someone was really saying and feeling.

🎧 **❷** Have students read the instructions and the column headings. Play the recording or read the audioscript aloud twice for students to check the correct boxes. Have students work in pairs to compare answers.

Audioscript: The audioscript for Exercises 2 and 3 appears on page T153.

> **Answers**
> **a.** angry **b.** persuasive **c.** worried
> **d.** angry **e.** uncertain **f.** persuasive

🎧 **❸** Play the recording or read the audioscript again so that students can complete the final column of the chart. After partners have compared ideas, discuss the answers to Exercises 2 and 3 as a class.

> **Answers**
> Answers may vary somewhat. Possible answers: **a.** father **b.** friend **c.** wife **d.** friend **e.** wife **f.** husband

Option: Have students work in groups to write short conversations in which speakers use some of the tones listed in the chart. Then have the groups present the conversations for the class, trying to convey their meanings through tone of voice as well as through the words used.

 Workbook: Practice 8

Pronunciation

Presentation

Have students read the explanation independently. Explain that function words include pronouns, articles, prepositions, and so on. Have students work in pairs to read the example conversation, stressing the words in dark type. (You may need to model the conversation.)

❹ Have students read the sentences and predict the stress in the pronunciation of **him**, **her**, and **them**.

Audioscript: The audioscript for Exercises 4 and 5 (pages 26 and 27) appears on page T154.

> **Answers**
> A: Are you sure you want Jeff to do the dishes?
> B: Yes, I want <u>him</u> to do <u>them</u> this time. Paula did them last time.
> A: Then, what do you want <u>her</u> to do?
> B: I want <u>her</u> to watch the baby.
> A: You know … I think you're nicer to <u>her</u> than to <u>him.</u>
> B: I am not. I'm nice to <u>them</u> both. They both have to learn to help around the house.

Option: Have students work in pairs to predict the stressed words. Have them practice the conversation aloud, switching roles to hear each other.

❺ Play the recording or read the dialogue aloud as students check their predictions. Have students practice the dialogue again in the same pairs as Exercise 4. Tell them to stress only the pronouns they've underlined. Then call on several pairs to read the dialogue to the class, and have the other students listen for the placement of stress.

Workbook: Practice 9

Speak Out

Presentation

➡ **Using Formal and Informal Language**
Have students read the strategy. Review the language for asking for, granting, and denying permission. (Note that the expressions under Granting Permission and Denying Permission are not aligned with particular expressions under Asking for Permission. They are possibilities.)

Next, write **borrow a pen** on the board. Have students tell you how they would ask their boss for permission to borrow a pen. How would they ask a friend?

Then, write **formal** and **informal** on the board. Have students make a list of people with whom they would use formal language in asking for permission and a list of people with whom they would use informal language.

Note: The purpose of this activity is to develop fluency. Students should be encouraged to speak without fear of interruption for error correction. If you notice persistent errors, write them down for later reteaching or review.

❻ Have students read the instructions, the example, and the list of roles. Have them think of situations for asking for permission. For example, the brother could ask the sister for a ride to the movies. Write the students' ideas on the board as cues. Help them think of other cues, if necessary. Remind them to use the list of ideas in the box.

Have students create conversations for each pair of roles. Encourage them to use the appropriate level of language for asking for, granting, and denying permission. When students finish, you might ask several pairs to perform some of their conversations for the class.

Workbook: Practice 10

READING and WRITING

Read About It

Presentation

❶ Before You Read Have students read the quote and discuss it in pairs or small groups. Ask individuals to share their ideas with the class.

T27

A: Then, what do you want her to do?

B: I want her to watch the baby.

A: You know … I think you're nicer to her than to him.

B: I am not. I'm nice to them both. They both have to learn to help around the house.

 5 Now listen to the dialogue and check your predictions. Then, with a partner, practice reading the dialogue, focusing on contrastive stress.

Speak Out

 Using Formal and Informal Language In speaking, it is important to be aware of the appropriate level of formality, for example, when asking for permission. You usually use more formal language when you speak to parents, older people, or employers. Use informal language when you are with coworkers, siblings, or friends.

	Asking for Permission	Granting Permission	Denying Permission
Formal Language	Could I possibly … Would you mind if … May I please …	Of course you may. By all means. Certainly.	Well, I prefer that you didn't. I prefer not.
Informal Language	Is it OK if I … Do you care if … How about if I …	Sure, no problem. No, go ahead. OK by me.	Not right now. Sorry, but … No way.

6 With a partner, ask for, grant, or deny permission for something. Choose roles from the box.

Example:

STUDENT: Professor Hiller, could I possibly get a copy of that paper you mentioned in your lecture? I'd really appreciate it.

PROFESSOR: By all means. Stop by my office on Thursday.

brother/sister	doctor/nurse	classmate/classmate
teacher/student	citizen/police officer	colleague/colleague
doctor/patient	landlord/tenant	employee/boss

READING and WRITING

Read About It

 1 **Before You Read** The English poet John Donne (1572–1631) said, "No man is an island." What do you think this means? Share your ideas with the class.

Unit 3

Recognizing Definitions and Examples Writers often use definitions and examples to clarify meaning. When you read, pay attention to words and expressions that signal a definition or an example in the text.

Definition	Example
... is ...	Take ... as an example.
... is defined as ...	For instance, ...
... is called ...	That is, ...
We can label ... as ...	In particular, ...

Roles in Human Society

Human beings are creatures of society. They take part in a complex social system which expects them to perform certain **roles**. Social scientists affirm that without roles, society could not function.

5　　To be successful, members of society need to know how others expect them to act so that they can act, or not act, in those ways. Let us take student life at a university as an example. When new students arrive, they do not yet know what their appropriate roles are. That is, they do not know what their roommates,
10　teachers, or advisers want them to do. To help them adapt quickly and correctly, authorities make them attend an orientation program. They learn the expected behavior for college students. We can label this their **prescribed role**.

In addition to the prescribed role, social scientists talk about the **subjective role**. For our college students, this means the expectations that each one has about what appropriate
15　behavior at a university is. In order to perform, he or she must know or find out what others' roles are and then look at his or her own perceptions in relationship to them.

When members of a society clearly perceive the rules of that society, and when their subjective roles are similar to their prescribed roles, they normally act in the ways that society expects them to. That is, they do and say what is considered correct. The actual performance of
20　a role, with its specific behavior, is called the **enacted role**. Our college students, if they have similar prescribed and subjective roles, will probably obey university rules and interact with their professors as students and with their roommates as friends. Their behavior will fall into the range of acceptable college student behavior.

Social scientists say that in order to protect itself and make sure that its members perform
25　their roles, society encourages those members to judge others' behavior as acceptable or unacceptable. For our college students, this means that they will have no conflicts or problems as long as they act like most college students. Then they will receive **positive sanctions** or rewards, such as good grades for studying hard. But if they decide to act very differently from their prescribed role, they will receive **negative sanctions** or punishments, such as failing
30　grades or expulsion from school. In this way, the university protects its own continuing social system. And in this way, according to social scientists, people in society at large maintain and protect the human need for interaction through roles in society.

➡ **Recognizing Definitions and Examples**
Have students read the explanation and the
expressions in the box (the Definitions and
the Examples). Then have students read the
article on page 28 independently in class or
for homework. If students read in class, you
may want to set a time limit.

❷ Have students read the directions and then complete the activities. Have them review the answers in small groups.

> **Answers**
> Answers will vary slightly. Possible answers: **roles:** behaviors a society expects its members to perform, so society can function **prescribed role:** the expected behavior **subjective role:** what an individual thinks is the expected behavior **enacted role:** the actual performance of a role **positive sanctions:** rewards **negative sanctions:** punishments

❸ Have students complete the activity independently. Review the answers as a class.

> **Answers**
> 1. b 2. d 3. f 4. g 5. e 6. c 7. a

Think About It

Presentation

❹ ❺ Have students discuss the questions as a class. If desired, have them first discuss the questions in pairs or small groups. Make sure they give their reasons. Ask them to develop their reasons with examples.

Option: Have students read the article again and then in small groups or as a class summarize each paragraph.

Option: You might want to have students discuss the rest of the famous passage from Donne's "Devotions" in groups or as a class. Write the passage, from Meditation 17, on the board or make a copy for each student. Help students with difficult words, and make sure they understand the meaning of the passage.

… No man is an island, entire of itself; every man is a piece of the continent, a part of the main. If a clod be washed away by the sea, Europe is the less, as well as if a promontory were, as well as if a manor of thy friend's or of thine own were. Any man's death diminishes me because I am involved in mankind, and therefore never send to know for whom the bell tolls, it tolls for thee.

Option: Encourage students to think of other famous sayings about people's relationships to society, either in English or in their own language. If necessary, list examples on the board. Students might need to research, using the Internet or the library.

All for one and one for all.   (*A. Dumas*)
United we stand, divided we fall.
                              (*G. P. Morris*)
A house divided against itself cannot stand.
          (*The New Testament, Mark 3:25*)

Have students discuss the meanings of the sayings.

Write: A Letter of Application

Preview

Have students discuss the characteristics of a business letter. Ask, *What kind of business letter did you write in Unit 1?* (a letter of inquiry) *Is a business letter formal or informal?* (formal) *Why is it formal?* (The letter is usually about a serious topic; the writer usually doesn't know the recipient or doesn't know the recipient well.)

Cultural Note: Often, people applying for a job send in their resume, which gives their education and work experience, and a brief cover letter "introducing" the resume.

Presentation

❻ Have students read the instructions and then complete the exercise independently.

> **Answers**
> a, b, c, e, g

❼ Have students read the letter on page 30 and work in pairs to compare their answers. Then ask individuals to share their answers with the class. (*Answers will vary.*)

2 Work with a partner. On a sheet of paper, write definitions for the six terms in bold type in the article.

3 Match the words on the left with their meanings on the right.

_____ **1.** to affirm (line 3)   **a.** in general
_____ **2.** to function (line 4)   **b.** to say is true
_____ **3.** to adapt (line 10)   **c.** removal from
_____ **4.** to label (line 12)   **d.** to work
_____ **5.** to perceive (line 17)   **e.** to understand
_____ **6.** expulsion (line 30)   **f.** to adjust; to change
_____ **7.** at large (line 31)   **g.** to call; to name

Think About It

4 Why are roles important in society?

5 Do you think schools should have positive and negative sanctions for students? Why or why not?

Write: A Letter of Application

When looking for a job, you need to write a formal letter called a letter of application. This type of letter includes all the conventions of a formal business letter as well as important information about the writer's qualifications for the job.

6 Imagine a friend told you about an opening for a computer programmer. You want to write a letter to apply for the job. What would you write in your letter? Put an **X** next to the items you would include. Write a question mark (?) if you are not sure.

_____ **a.** ask for an interview
_____ **b.** talk about your education
_____ **c.** talk about your past jobs
_____ **d.** talk about your family
_____ **e.** describe your present job
_____ **f.** ask for an application form
_____ **g.** give your reason for writing
_____ **h.** talk about the salary

7 Read the letter on page 30. Did the writer include all the items you checked in Exercise 6? Did she include anything you didn't check? If so, what?

148 Shady Road
Pittsburgh, PA 15069
September 23, 1999

Diane M. Datris
Vice-President
Mercurio Computers
1364 Kenneth Avenue
Kensington, PA 15068

Dear Ms. Datris:

Mr. Jonathan Chen encouraged me to write to you about an opening in your company for a computer programmer. I believe I am well qualified for this position. I have both educational qualifications and work experience in computer programming.

After completing a two-year course in computer programming at Tarentum Community College, I got a job as a programmer at Natrona Computer Works. During the three years I worked there, I wrote many programs. For the past year, I have worked at Arnold Bank, where I write programs as well as teach other employees to use computers. In addition to my computer experience, I speak Spanish and Chinese.

I would very much like to talk with you about the position, and would be available to discuss my credentials at your earliest convenience. You may contact me at 555-2649. I look forward to hearing from you soon.

Yours sincerely,

Freida Jackson
Freida Jackson

8 Review Freida Jackson's letter and answer the questions.

a. In a letter of application, which paragraph contains this information?
   1. introduction and reason for writing
   2. description of education and experience
   3. request for information or action

b. How many addresses are there in a formal business letter? Whose address is first? Second?

c. How do we say "hello" and "good-bye" in a formal business letter?

Write About It

9 Choose a job that you would like to apply for from the want ads in a local newspaper. Write a letter of application. Use Freida's letter as a model.

10 **Check Your Writing** Exchange papers with a partner. Use the questions below to give feedback to your partner. When you get your paper back, revise as necessary.

   • Does the letter include all the parts of a formal business letter?
   • Does each paragraph in the letter have a clear purpose?
   • Will the reader know what to do?

❽ Have students read the instructions and then answer the questions independently. Then have them review the answers in small groups or as a class.

> **Answers**
> **a. 1.** first paragraph **2.** second paragraph **3.** third paragraph **b.** two addresses. The address of the person who is sending the letter is first. The address of the person who will be receiving the letter is second.
> **c.** "hello": Dear, "good-bye": Sincerely yours.

Write About It

Presentation

❾ Remind students to use the information in Exercises 7 and 8 as they write their letters. Tell students that they can apply for any job they want but that they should make sure the information in the letter is appropriate for the job.

☑ **❿ Check Your Writing** Have pairs of students exchange their first drafts and use the questions to help them give each other feedback. After they revise their first drafts, have them write their final drafts.

 Workbook: Practice 11

Vocabulary Expansion: Using a dictionary
See page T142.

> **Answers**
> Answers for Parts A and B will vary, depending on the dictionary used. The answers given here were derived from *Merriam Webster's Collegiate Dictionary*, Tenth Edition, © 1999.
> **A.** Circled: a, b, c, d, e, f
> **B. 1.** Guide words: permeation • Perseid; **permit** has two entries: noun, verb.
> **2.** n. = noun; v. = verb; adv. = adverb; adj. = adjective; pron. = pronoun; prep. = preposition; conj. = conjunction; interj. = interjection.
> **Permit** can be used as both a verb and a noun.
> **3.** pér•mit (n), 3
> per•mít (v), 3
> **4.** Information will vary.

EVALUATION

See page TExi.

Unit 3 Achievement Test

Self-Check See **Check Your Knowledge,** page 24 of the Workbook.

Dictation Dictate the following questions. Then have students answer each one. For more information on dictation, see page TExv.

1. When you were two years old, what did your mother **make** you do?
2. When you were ten years old, what did your teacher **expect** you to do?
3. When you visited your grandparents, what did they **let** you do?
4. What has a friend **persuaded** you to do recently?

Dictate the following sentences. Have students write a logical question for each.

5. Anita made Susan type the report again. (Why did Anita make Susan type her report again?)
6. The coach forced Bill to run two miles. (Was Bill able to run the two miles?)
7. Joan encouraged her husband to take a trip. (Did her husband take the trip?)
8. They allowed John to stay up late and watch TV. (What did John watch?)

Have students work in pairs or groups to compare their questions. Are their questions logical?

Communication Skills

1. Ask students to describe the qualities of a good boss and a bad boss. What does this person want/encourage/expect/force/advise/warn/tell the employees to do? Listen for correct descriptive vocabulary and verbs.

2. Have students talk about their childhoods or their work/school situations, explaining their responsibilities and privileges. Pay attention to the language for reporting orders, requests, permission, and persuasion/advice.

Review Units 1–3

Unit review exercises can be assigned as homework or done in class. You can use them in different ways.

- Give the review exercises as a quiz. Have students work alone and submit their answers to you.

- Give the review exercises as you would other exercises in the book. Have students work alone and then compare answers with a partner.

- Have students work alone and then review answers as a class. Have selected students write their answers on the board. Then correct any errors as a class.

❶ Have students read the instructions and then complete the exercise. For general notes on the simple past and present perfect tenses, refer students to Unit 1, page 4.

Answers
1. have … been; 've … been 2. tried
3. weren't; were not 4. was; 've been; have been 5. Did … buy; Have … bought 6. did
7. haven't finished 8. borrowed 9. 've already gotten; have already gotten 10. was

❷ Have students read the instructions and then complete the exercise. For general notes on the present perfect with **already**, **still**, and **yet**, refer students to Unit 1, page 4.

Answers
Answers may vary. **a.** Maria hasn't made her bed yet. **b.** The taxi has not come yet. **c.** Linda has already done her grocery shopping. **d.** Ali has not started his term paper yet. **e.** Eva has already packed her bags.

❸ Have students read the instructions and then complete the exercise. For general notes on the modal auxiliaries **may**, **might**, and **could**, refer students to Unit 2, page 14.

Answers
Answers will vary. Possible answers:
1. might/may enjoy 2. might/may/could show 3. might/may/could … suggest
4. might/may prefer 5. could/might/may find

1 Complete the conversation with the simple past or present perfect tense. Use the negative when necessary.

PAT: Hey, Kate. How **(1. be)** _____ you _____?
I **(2. try)** _____ to call you last night, but you
(3. be) _____ at home.

KATE: Hi, Pat. I know. I **(4. be)** _____ really busy getting ready for my trip to Brazil.

PAT: So you are really going! **(5. buy)** _____ you _____ your plane ticket yet?

KATE: Yes, I **(6. do)** _____ that last week. But I still
(7. finish) _____ shopping for the trip.

PAT: Don't take too much—you won't have room for souvenirs.

KATE: That's why I just **(8. borrow)** _____ a big suitcase from Jane.

PAT: Well, do you need a ride to the consulate to get your visa?

KATE: Actually, I **(9. get, already)** _____ my visa, but thanks for offering. That **(10. be)** _____ thoughtful of you!

PAT: Hey, I want a nice present from Brazil.

2 Write sentences using the present perfect tense and *already, still,* or *yet.*

a. It is 11:30 a.m. Maria's bed is not made.

_____

b. Bill called a taxi. He is waiting outside his house with a suitcase.

_____

c. It is 7:30 a.m. Linda's grocery shopping is done.

_____

d. Ali's term paper is due tomorrow. He's thinking about starting it.

_____

e. Eva's going to Moscow today. She packed her bags last night.

_____

3 Complete the passage with *may, might,* or *could* and one of the verbs in the box.

enjoy	show
find	suggest
prefer	expect

   There are many aptitude tests that help people decide which jobs and careers they **(1.)** _____ pursuing. These tests identify likes, dislikes, and abilities that people have. An aptitude test **(2.)** _____ that a certain person has athletic or mechanical skills. A counselor **(3.)** _____ then _____ that he or she **(4.)** _____ to work with objects, machines, and tools. In other words, this person **(5.)** _____ satisfaction in a job as a coach, factory-line worker, or carpenter.

4 Complete the conversations with *might*, *must*, or *can't*.

1. **A:** Look at that man over there! He _____ be the new coach.
   B: He _____ be. The new coach is a woman.
2. **A:** I think Anne _____ win the chess match.
   B: Well, she _____ be good if she's playing Mr. Zappa.
3. **A:** We think we _____ go to the ballet on Sunday.
   B: It _____ be on Sunday! The theater is closed on Sundays.
   A: Well, the fourteenth _____ be a Saturday, then.

5 Rewrite the sentences but keep the same meaning. Use verbs that express orders, requests, permission, persuasion, and advice.

a. The boss said that the secretary had to stay late.

   _____

b. Jerry requested that we keep our voices down.

   _____

c. The babysitter gave permission. The kids stayed up until 9:00 p.m.

   _____

d. The doctor explained that she had to get more exercise.

   _____

e. John asked Mary if she wanted to go to lunch.

   _____

Vocabulary Review

Use the words in the list to complete the sentences.

1. Employers who are _____ and unwilling to change often lose good employees.
2. That Julia! She can _____ the best excuses for not having her work!
3. Some people use effective _____ to help them learn a language.
4. I truly _____ all your help on this project. Thank you again.
5. The boss is going to _____ Harry. Now he'll be a manager!
6. Our abilities to think, remember, and communicate _____ in the brain.
7. It is better to acknowledge a _____ rather than ignore it.
8. I left my wallet at home. Can you lend me some _____?
9. Language learners often use gestures to _____ their meaning.
10. The _____ described the men who stole her car to the police.

appreciate	inflexible
cash	victim
get across	come up with
conflict	promote
originate	strategies

❹ Have students read the instructions and then complete the exercise. For general notes on the modal auxiliaries **might**, **must**, and **can't**, refer students to Unit 2, page 14.

Answers
1. A: must; B: can't 2. A: might; B: must
3. A: might; B: can't; A: must

❺ Have students read the instructions and then complete the exercise. For general notes on verbs that express orders, requests, permission, persuasion, and advice, refer students to Unit 3, pages 23–24. For a list of the verbs, refer them to Exercise 5, page 25.

Answers
Answers may vary. **a.** The boss told the secretary to stay late. **b.** Jerry asked us to keep our voices down. **c.** The babysitter allowed the kids to stay up until 9:00 p.m. **d.** The doctor told her to get more exercise.
e. John invited Mary to go to lunch.

Vocabulary Review

Have students read the instructions and then complete the exercise.

Answers
1. inflexible 2. come up with 3. strategies
4. appreciate 5. promote 6. originate
7. conflict 8. cash 9. get across 10. victim

CHILD'S PLAY

OBJECTIVES

- To talk about child prodigies, intelligence, and creativity
- To use the past perfect and the past perfect progressive tenses
- To identify causes and results
- To use intonation to ask a yes/no question
- To confirm understanding
- To understand paragraph coherence
- To write a letter asking for information
- To use a dictionary for pronunciation, spelling, and etymology

GETTING STARTED

Warm Up

Preview

- Have students work in groups to list the three school subjects they think are the hardest and the three they think are the easiest. What other activities do they find hard or easy: playing a sport? playing a musical instrument? Have them report to the class. Do they all agree? You might want to compile lists on the board of the subjects students named as hard and easy.

- Use students' list of difficult subjects to elicit or present **field, level, exceptionally**, and **remarkable**. Explain that some remarkable children perform at exceptionally high levels in these difficult fields. We call these children **child prodigies**. Ask students whether they have heard of any famous child prodigies. What do they know about them? Then review students' list of easy subjects. Explain that the expression **child's play** is used to refer to something that is very easy to do.

- Introduce the idea of measurement and grading scales. Ask students what numbers indicate a high, or **superior**, grade. Then ask what numbers indicate a medium, or **average**, grade. Ask them to name the ways their performance is measured in this class (through tests, oral work, written work, and so on). On the board, write the following concepts: knowledge of vocabulary, attention span, good judgment, and ability to reason. Make sure students understand these concepts. Ask them if these concepts are important to use in an English class.

Presentation

Have students read the introductory paragraph. Ask someone to explain the difference between "child's play" and "child prodigy." Point out that some people find some things easy to do that other people find difficult to do. Point out then that child's play is not limited to child prodigies. Ask students to give examples of things they think are child's play.

❶ Have students read the questions independently. Discuss the answers as a class. Elicit as many characteristics of intelligence as possible.

✪ **Option:** Review with students other expressions in English that mean "easy": **it's a breeze; it's like taking candy from a baby; it's smooth sailing; it's a snap; it's a piece of cake**, and so on.

🎧 ❷ Have students read the information and instructions. Then play the recording or read the audioscript aloud two or more times for students to circle their answers.

Audioscript: The audioscript for Exercise 2 appears on page T154.

> **Answers**
> **a.** 1916 **b.** 100 **c.** 120–139

 Workbook: Practice 1

✪ **Option:** Ask students to name other kinds of tests they have taken—aptitude tests, achievement or progress tests, English proficiency tests, personality tests, driving tests, and so on. What does each kind of test measure? What kinds of scores are given? Do students think standardized tests are fair? Accurate?

GETTING STARTED

Warm Up

For most people, learning a subject like math or a skill like playing the piano is difficult. But for a few people, it's so easy we say it's "child's play." It's even more remarkable when these people are children. Exceptionally intelligent or talented children who perform at very high levels are called "child prodigies."

1 It is clear that prodigies have high intelligence, but experts do not agree on the qualities that make up intelligence. Is it the ability to learn languages, solve complicated math problems, or perhaps build a motor? What do you think intelligence is?

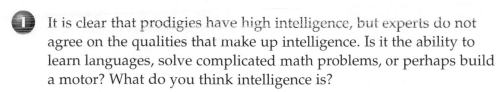

2 One of the best-known tests of intelligence is the Stanford–Binet Test, popularly known as the "I.Q." (Intelligence Quotient) Test. Listen to a talk about this test and circle the answers.

    a. The Stanford–Binet Test has been used since   1960   1973   1916.

    b. Normal or average intelligence corresponds to 100   101   110.

    c. Superior intelligence ranges from   110–120 120–139 129–159.

Figure It Out

3 Form three groups. Read only your group's text. Then, with your group, identify the most important information in the text.

John Stuart Mill, philosopher

    A. People all over the world have always admired child prodigies, such as the philosopher John Stuart Mill, who learned Greek at age three and Latin at age eight, and the composer Wolfgang Amadeus Mozart, who wrote his first opera at age twelve. Over the years, prodigies
5 have been identified in the fields of music, math, chess, and foreign languages. Today's prodigies have talent in those fields and in related ones, such as computer program design and video art. Almost all child prodigies are best in one field. These children need teachers who recognize their abilities and challenge them.

Bobby Fischer, chess champion

10 **B.** Bobby Fischer was born in Chicago in 1943. By the time he was six years old, his sister had taught him how to play chess. Soon he began to concentrate on chess instead of other childhood interests. Bobby played chess all through school, and by 1958 he had won the first of many U.S. championships. In the same year, he became the
15 youngest player ever recognized by the International Chess Federation. By the next year, Bobby had dropped out of high school and, at the age of fifteen, had published his first book on chess. Many tournaments and titles later, he became the world chess champion in 1972.

Diego Alonso, musician

20 **C.** Diego Alonso was born in Spain in 1983. Diego showed a love of music at a very early age, and by the time he was five, he had earned the title "the Spanish Mozart." By the time he was six, experts had measured his I.Q. at 190, almost twice the I.Q. of a normal adult. Diego and his family moved to the United States,
25 so Diego could study at a special school for gifted children. There, unlike most prodigies who concentrate on one field, he has shown interest and the ability to perform well in a number of different subjects in addition to music. Diego's parents and teachers have high hopes for this exceptional child.

4 Now form new groups of three students, with one student from each of the original groups. Cover the texts and tell each other the most important information. Fill in the chart.

Child Prodigies
Common fields of interests:
Educational needs:
Prodigies from history:
Modern-day prodigies:

Figure It Out

Preview

- Remind the class that prodigies are children with remarkable abilities or intelligence. Ask students to name as many adjectives as they can to describe a child prodigy (**smart**, **intelligent**, **exceptional**, and so on). If necessary, introduce **gifted** and **talented**. Ask students about some of the achievements of gifted or talented children. Point out that these children often learn to speak **foreign** languages, win **tournaments** of various kinds, **publish** books or music, and so on. Elicit as many ideas as possible.

- Ask if anyone can tell what a **philosopher** studies. (A philosopher studies the basic truths and principles of the universe.) Ask students to name some philosophers. (*Possibilities*: Plato, Rousseau, Nietzsche)

Presentation

❸ Have students read the instructions. Form the groups, and have each group read its text.

❹ Have students read the instructions and look at the chart. Answer any questions. Then have students form new groups. Have the students in each group summarize the texts for one another and then fill in the chart together. Have students check their answers by comparing them with the information in the texts.

Answers

Common fields of interest: music, math, chess, foreign languages, computer program design, video art

Educational needs: support of teachers who recognize their abilities and who challenge them

Prodigies from history: John Stuart Mill, Wolfgang Amadeus Mozart

Modern-day prodigies: Bobby Fischer, Diego Alonso

Option: As an alternative, you might read text **A** aloud while students take notes. Have them fill in the first two sections of the chart. Then have them form pairs. One student reads each of the remaining texts aloud so that the other can take notes. Have them fill in the rest of the chart.

☑ ❺ **Vocabulary Check** Have students complete the activity individually. Then review the answers as a class.

> **Answers**
> 1. d 2. f 3. e 4. a 5. c 6. b

 Option: Vocabulary Notebooks Follow the instructions on page TEviii.

 Option: Bring in or have a student bring in a chess set. Tell students what the pieces are called in English (king, queen, knight, rook or castle, bishop, pawn). If any students know how to play, ask them to demonstrate.

 Option: Bring in or have students bring in articles about prodigies—for example, articles from encyclopedias, magazines, or newspapers. Divide the class into groups, and give each group an article. Have one member of the group read the article and then relate its contents to the rest of the group. Encourage the other group members to ask as many questions as possible to get all the details.

 Option: Have interested students research, in the library or on the Internet, one of the prodigies mentioned so far in the unit or another prodigy of their choice. Have them report their findings to the class.

Link *Workbook: Practice 2*

Talk About It

 Option: You may prefer to postpone this activity until after the grammar presentation (page 35) if you feel your students need extra help with the past perfect tense.

Presentation

Note: The purpose of this activity is to develop fluency. Students should be encouraged to speak without fear of interruption for error correction. If you notice persistent errors, write them down for later reteaching or review.

❻ Have students work in pairs to read the instructions. Ask a pair of students to read the example conversation aloud for the rest of the class. Then have students complete the activity. Have each pair do all the examples, switching roles after

T35

they have done half, and/or ask a different pair of students to perform each interview for the class.

Option: Have students think of additional people who could be interviewed.

 Workbook: Practice 3

GRAMMAR

The Past Perfect Tense

Preview

• To focus attention on time relationships, write the following two pairs of sentences on the board. To help students, you might draw two time lines, one with the dates in the first two sentences, the other with the dates in the last two sentences.

Peter Alexander's sixth birthday was in May 1945.
He learned to play chess in June 1945.

Bobby Fischer's sixth birthday was in 1949.
He learned to play chess in 1948.

Ask, *Did Peter Alexander know how to play chess on his sixth birthday? (No.) Which happened first—he had his sixth birthday or he learned to play chess? (He had his sixth birthday.) Did Bobby Fischer know how to play chess on his sixth birthday? (Yes.) Which happened first—he had his sixth birthday or he learned to play chess? (He learned to play chess.)*

• Write the following sentences on the board. Ask pairs of students to compare the underlined verbs and explain when the past and the past perfect tenses are used. (We use the past tense to tell about something that happened in the past; we use past perfect tense to show that one action happened before another.)

When Peter Alexander turned six, he <u>learned</u> to play chess.

When Bobby Fischer turned six, he <u>had learned</u> to play chess.

(*The Past Perfect Tense section continues on page T36.*)

5 **Vocabulary Check** Match the words on the left with their meanings.

_____ **1.** to admire (line 1)   **a.** to leave; to quit

_____ **2.** field (line 5)   **b.** unusual

_____ **3.** to challenge (line 9)   **c.** big plans for success

_____ **4.** to drop out (line 16)   **d.** to think highly of

_____ **5.** high hopes (line 29)   **e.** to encourage effort or interest

_____ **6.** exceptional (line 29)   **f.** area of study

Talk About It

6 A reporter is researching an article on child prodigies. He is interviewing prodigies about their achievements as children. With a partner, take turns being the reporter and the prodigy. Use the model and your imagination.

> Name achievement and ask for confirmation.
>
> **A:** I understand that as a child you showed a lot of promise as a musician. Is that right?
>
> Confirm and give details.
>
> **B:** Yes, and by the way, by the time I was eight years old, I had already learned to play six instruments.

a. a musician

b. a computer expert

c. a child movie star

d. a dancer

e. a writer

f. a mathematician

g. a chess player

h. a linguist

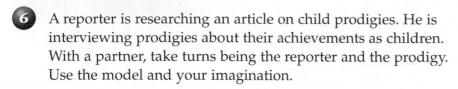

GRAMMAR

The Past Perfect Tense

We can use the simple past to talk about two actions in the past. However, to show that a past action happened before another past action or before a specific time in the past, we use the past perfect tense (*had* + past participle). We often use this tense with time words such as *when, by the time, already, after, before, never,* and *ever*.

> When John Stuart Mill was three, he **had** already **learned** Greek.
>
> By the time he turned eight, he **had** also **mastered** Latin.

1 Read the article about Midori. Underline the verbs in the past perfect tense.

When Midori Goto was four years old, she began studying the violin. By the time she was six, she had already played in concerts, and by the time she was ten, she had soloed with the New York Philharmonic Orchestra. Before her fifteenth birthday, she had even recorded her first album.

Midori Goto, violinist

2 What did Midori do first? Number each pair of actions 1 and 2.

a. _____ Midori played her first concerts.
_____ Midori had her sixth birthday.
b. _____ Midori soloed with the Philharmonic.
_____ Midori had her tenth birthday.
c. _____ Midori recorded her first album.
_____ Midori had her fifteenth birthday.

The Past Perfect Progressive Tense

We use the past perfect progressive tense (*had* + *been* + verb *–ing*) to talk about an action that was happening before or up to a specific time in the past.

> Midori **had been playing** the violin for eleven years when she recorded her first album.

3 Read the article about Mac Randall. Underline the verbs in the past perfect progressive tense.

Mac Randall had been reading for two years when he wrote his first story at the age of four. At that time, he had already been typing for a year. In fact, Mac had been writing fiction for a long time when he heard of John Lennon's death. This sad event made him turn his attention to music—at the age of eight.

Mac Randall, writer and composer

4 Now check the sentences that are true.

_____ **a.** Mac was writing before he started reading.
_____ **b.** Mac was reading before he started writing.
_____ **c.** Mac began typing before he was three.
_____ **d.** Mac began typing after he was three.
_____ **e.** Mac was writing before Lennon's death.
_____ **f.** Mac started writing after Lennon's death.

(Continued from page T35.)

Presentation

Have students read the grammar explanation and the examples on page 35 independently in class or for homework. Ask students to tell what they had learned by age six. Encourage them to use both affirmative and negative sentences. Write their answers on the board.

By age six, I had already learned to swim.

When I was six I hadn't learned to ride a bike yet.

❶ Have students read the article and complete the task independently. Have students check their answers in pairs.

Answers
1. had (already) played 2. had soloed
3. had (even) recorded

---

❷ Have students use the information in the article to complete the exercise. Have students check their answers in pairs.

Answers
a. 1, 2 b. 1, 2 c. 1, 2

 Option: Point out to students that with the time expressions **before**, **when**, and **by the time**, the past perfect tense occurs in the main clause, whereas with the time expression **after**, the past perfect tense occurs in the time clause. To help students understand this, write a pair of sentences, such as the following ones, on the board.

He <u>had learned</u> to play chess <u>before</u> he <u>turned</u> six.

He <u>turned</u> six <u>after</u> he <u>had learned</u> to play chess.

 Option: Have students work in pairs or small groups to make up an exercise similar to Exercise 2 about Bobby Fischer. They can do research at the library or on the Internet. Let them exchange their exercises with other pairs or groups and answer the questions.

Link *Workbook: Practices 4, 5*

The Past Perfect Progressive Tense

Presentation

Have students read the grammar explanation and the example independently in class or for homework.

❸ Have students read the article and complete the task independently. Have them check their answers in pairs.

Answers
had been reading, had (already) been typing, had been writing

---

❹ Have students use the information in the article to complete the exercise. Have them check their answers in pairs.

Answers
Sentences **b**, **d**, and **e** are true.

---

❺ Focus students' attention on the picture. Do students recognize the young actress? Have students complete the exercise independently. Review the answers as a class.

> **Answers**
> **a.** By the time she was four, she had shown a talent for dancing and had entered a dancing school. **b.** Before she made a musical, she had been appearing in short films for Educational Pictures. **c.** She had won the Oscar before she got a raise. **d.** Answers will vary.

❻ If necessary, go over question formation in the past perfect and past perfect progressive tenses. You might also suggest that students look closely at questions **a** through **c** in Exercise 5. Encourage them to use the past perfect and past perfect progressive tenses in questions. When students have finished, have them answer each other's questions.

☸ **Option:** Have students research Shirley Temple's life after her movie career ended, or tell them about it. (In 1969, she was a U.S. representative to the United Nations. In 1974, she was appointed U.S. ambassador to Ghana. In 1976, she was named chief of protocol in the U.S. Department of State. In 1989, she was named ambassador to Czechoslovakia.)

☸ **Option:** Have students list the events in their lives in a format similar to that shown in the resume in Exercise 5. Have them talk with a partner or the class about things they had accomplished by certain birthdays.

☸ **Option:** Write this calendar on the board or make a copy of it for each student.

Monday, December 18
pack bags—done
confirm reservations—to do

Tuesday, December 19
iron shirts—done
pick up dry cleaning—to do

Wednesday, December 20
renew passport—done
clean house—to do

Thursday, December 21
water lawn—to do
pick up tickets—done

Friday, December 22
buy traveler's checks—done
get a haircut—done

Saturday, December 23
catch 10:55 a.m. flight—done

Explain that John had had many things to do before he could go on his vacation. He had written everything down on his calendar, but he had been unable to get everything done before he left. Have the students work in pairs to tell what John had and hadn't accomplished by the dates on his calendar. (*Example:* By Monday, John had already packed his bags, but he still hadn't confirmed his reservations.)

☑ ❼ **Check Your Understanding** Have students complete the activity independently in class or for homework. Review the answers as a class.

> **Answers**
> Answers will vary. The only situation in which the past perfect and past perfect progressive tenses are not likely to be used is when interviewing a person about future career plans.

❽ **Express Yourself** This activity gives students a chance to use the past perfect tenses in situations they determine appropriate. Ask each pair to perform its dialogue for the class.

☸ **Option:** To practice time expressions with the past perfect and past perfect progressive tenses, ask students to write sentences using each of the time expressions introduced on page 35.

 Workbook: Practices 6, 7, 8

LISTENING and SPEAKING

Listen: A Child Prodigy

Presentation

❶ **Before You Listen** Have students write their lists independently. After pairs have compared answers, you might want to have them share their ideas with the class. (*Answers will vary.*)

T37

5 Shirley Temple was a famous American actress in the 1930s. Read her resume and answer the questions.

1928	Born in Los Angeles, California
1930	Shows talent for dancing
1931	Enters a dancing school
1932–1933	Appears in short films for Educational Pictures
1934	Receives contract from Fox movie company Makes first full-length musical and other movies Wins special Oscar award as "outstanding personality of 1934"
1935–1938	Is the most popular Hollywood star Gets a raise to $10,000 a week Recieves more fan mail than Greta Garbo Is photographed more often than President Roosevelt
1940s	Loses popularity in films
1945	Publishes autobiography, *My Young Life*

Shirley Temple, actress

    a. What had Shirley accomplished by the time she was four?

    b. What had she been doing before she made a musical?

    c. Had she won the Oscar award before or after she got a raise?

    d. Why do you think she wrote her autobiography?

6 On a sheet of paper, write three more questions about Shirley Temple. Give the questions to a partner to answer in writing.

7 **Check Your Understanding** Check the situations in which you are likely to use the past perfect or the past perfect progressive tense.

    ☐ Reporting a robbery to the police

    ☐ Telling a friend about a dream you had

    ☐ Describing your actions at a car accident before help arrived

    ☐ Interviewing a person about his or her career plans

    ☐ Describing your childhood achievements

8 **Express Yourself** With a partner, choose one of the situations you checked. Imagine yourselves in the situation and write a dialogue.

LISTENING and SPEAKING

Listen: A Child Prodigy

1 **Before You Listen** What are the advantages and disadvantages of being a child prodigy? Make a list. Compare your list with a partner's.

STRATEGY **Identifying Causes and Results** When you listen, it is important to understand the relationship between a cause and its result. To do this, listen for words and expressions such as *because, so, as, since, due to, if ... then,* and *as a result.*

2 Listen to the conversation about Dan, a child prodigy, and try to identify causes and results. Decide if the statements are **T** (true) or **F** (false).

_____ **a.** At first, Dan did well in school due to his high I.Q.

_____ **b.** Dan is losing his intelligence little by little.

_____ **c.** Because Dan isn't interested in school anymore, he dropped out.

_____ **d.** Since Mrs. Roberts expects him to excel, Dan is giving up.

_____ **e.** Dan had learned how to use a computer by the time he was five.

_____ **f.** The doctor thinks that Dan's behavior will change as he grows.

_____ **g.** Since Dan wants to be like the other kids, he doesn't want anyone to know he's a prodigy.

3 Work with a partner. Do you agree with the doctor's advice? Why or why not?

Pronunciation

Using Intonation to Ask a Yes/No Question

In spoken English, we can change a sentence into a yes/no question simply by using rising intonation. We use this pattern to confirm what someone said or to express surprise or disbelief.

He'd worked there a MONTH. *(Rising–Falling Intonation: Statement—This is what he said.)*

He'd worked there a MONTH? *(Rising: Confirmation—Is this what you said?)*

He'd worked there a MONTH? *(Rising: Surprise—Really? He told me a year.)*

---

4 Predict the intonation patterns. Write a question mark (?) on the line for rising intonation and a period (.) for rising–falling intonation.

A: You mean you don't recognize Steveland Morris's music **(1.)** _____

B: Steveland Morris **(2.)** _____

A: That's Stevie Wonder's real name **(3.)** _____

B: No kidding **(4.)** _____ He's won several Grammy awards **(5.)** _____

A: Yeah, and he was one of Motown's child prodigies **(6.)** _____ By the age of 13, he'd already had his first Motown hit **(7.)** _____

B: He was only thirteen **(8.)** _____

A: Yeah, and he was blind too **(9.)** _____

B: Blind **(10.)** _____ Wow, that's incredible **(11.)** _____

5 Listen to the dialogue and check your predictions. With a partner, practice reading the dialogue, focusing on intonation patterns.

➡ **Identifying Causes and Results** Have students read the strategy. Present or elicit a few sentences with some of the words and expressions given in the strategy. (Because his parents thought he was gifted, they sent him to a special school. His parents thought he was gifted, so they sent him to a special school.) Have students identify the cause and the result in each sentence.

 ❷ Have students read the instructions. Then play the recording or read the audioscript aloud two or more times for the students to write their answers. Let them listen again to check their answers, if necessary. Review the answers as a class.

Audioscript: The audioscript for Exercise 2 appears on page T154.

> **Answers**
> a. T b. F c. F d. T e. T f. T g. T

❸ Have students summarize the doctor's advice and then discuss it. Encourage them to use some cause-and-effect words in explaining their answers. Have students share their ideas as a class.

Option: Vocabulary Notebooks Follow the instructions on page TEviii.

Link **Workbook: Practice 9**

Pronunciation

Preview

- Write the following conversation on the board.

  A: That wasn't his first time in Florida.

  B: Really? Had he gone before?

  Say the sentence and the questions. Exaggerate the rising–falling intonation in the sentence and the rising intonation in the questions. Ask, *Which has a rising intonation—the sentence or the questions?* (the questions) *Which has a rising–falling intonation?* (the sentence) Repeat the conversation if necessary. Then, as you say each line of the conversation again, have students repeat it.

- Write the following conversation on the board and read it for the class to repeat.

  A: That wasn't his first time in Florida.

  B: You mean he'd gone before?

  Point out that in this conversation, a yes/no question is asked by using rising intonation with normal sentence word order. Explain that we often use this form of question when we want to show surprise or to confirm something we think we already know.

Pronunciation Note: We usually use rising intonation with yes/no questions and rising–falling intonation with information questions. Rising–falling intonation is also used in affirmative statements.

Presentation

Have students read the explanation silently. Then have them work with partners and practice saying the example sentences. Encourage the pairs to make up additional examples.

❹ Have students read the instructions. Encourage them to say the sentences aloud to predict the intonation patterns. Then have them write a question mark or a period.

 ❺ Play the recording or read the audioscript aloud for students to check their answers. Then divide the class into pairs to practice reading the dialogue. Have several pairs take turns reading the dialogue to the class.

Audioscript: The audioscript for Exercise 5 appears on page T154.

> **Answers**
> 1. question mark 2. question mark 3. period
> 4. period 5. question mark 6. period
> 7. period 8. question mark 9. period
> 10. question mark 11. period

Link **Workbook: Practice 10**

Speak Out

Presentation

➡ **Confirming Understanding** Have students read the strategy and the examples in the box. Point out that the sentences in the second and third columns can be used to respond to questions, such as those in the first column, or used on their own. Remind students that confirming questions, as in the Pronunciation section, can also be used to confirm understanding.

To practice using some of the language in the box, write this math problem on the board: (5 + 2 − 3) x 6= 24. Start explaining how you got the answer. *First, I added five and two and got seven. Then I subtracted three from seven and got four. Do you understand so far?* Pause and elicit one of the expressions for indicating understanding. Finish explaining the problem. Ask, *Do you understand?* to elicit another expression.

Note: The purpose of this activity is to develop fluency. Students should speak without fear of interruption for error correction. If you notice persistent errors, write them down for later reteaching or review.

❻ Have students read the directions. Give them a few minutes to figure out the answers. Then divide the class into pairs or groups to explain how they arrived at their answers. Monitor the groups to be sure they are using the language for asking for and indicating understanding.

Answers
a. 2 **b.** 33 (Each time you double the number that is added: 2 + 1 = 3, 3 + 2 = 5, 5 + 4 = 9, 9 + 8 = 17; 17 + 16 = 33.)
c. 4 and 5

 Workbook: Practice 11

READING and WRITING

Read About It

Presentation

❶ Before You Read Have students answer question **a** and share their ideas with the class. Then have students fill in the chart in **b,** either in class or for homework. As a class, have them compare their ideas.

Option: Have students scan the article on page 40 to answer these questions.

1. When was Mozart born? (1756)
2. Where was he born? (Salzburg, Austria)
3. What was his father's name? (Leopold Mozart)
4. Who were some famous people Mozart played for? (Empress Maria Theresa, Emperor Francis I)
5. What were the titles of some of his operas? (*The Marriage of Figaro, Don Giovanni, Cosi Fan Tutte,* and *The Magic Flute*)
6. How old was he when he died? (35)

➡ **Understanding Paragraph Structure** Have students read the strategy. Explain how the strategy will help them: If, as they read a paragraph, they think about which sentence expresses the main idea and how the other sentences support the main idea, they'll have a better sense of what the paragraph means and of how it relates to other paragraphs.

Speak Out

STRATEGY **Confirming Understanding** In conversation, you check to see if listeners understand what you are saying. You also show that you understand or don't understand what the other speakers mean.

Asking for Understanding	Indicating Understanding	Indicating Lack of Understanding
Do you see what I mean?	Oh, I see what you mean.	I'm not sure I get it.
Am I making myself clear?	OK, that makes sense.	I don't think I understand.
Are you following me?	Now I get it!	I'm totally lost.

6 Intelligence tests often contain items like the ones below. Choose one of the items. Explain to a partner or group how to figure out the answer. Use the expressions for checking understanding.

a. A rule of arithmetic applies to the numbers in the box: two numbers in any line can be added to produce the third number. What is the missing number? _____

6	2	4
2		0
4	0	4

b. What number comes after 17 in this series? 2 3 5 9 17 _____

c. Which two of these shapes are mirror images? _____

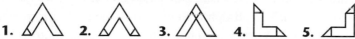

1.　2.　3.　4.　5.

READING and WRITING

Read About It

1 **Before You Read**

a. What kind of music do you enjoy? Give examples of singers, groups, and composers that you like.

b. Before you look at the article on page 40, complete the chart about Mozart.

What I know about Mozart:
What I think I know about Mozart:
What I'd like to learn about Mozart:

STRATEGY **Understanding Paragraph Structure** The paragraphs in a text are organized through the use of topic sentences that present the main ideas, supporting sentences that give more specific details about the main ideas, and concluding sentences that bring to an end the ideas in a paragraph. Understanding paragraph structure helps your overall comprehension of a text.

Mozart: Child Prodigy

Wolfgang Amadeus Mozart is considered one of the greatest musical child prodigies who ever lived. He was born in 1756, in Salzburg, Austria, where his father, Leopold Mozart, was a violinist and
5 composer. Both his father and mother encouraged him and his sister Maria Anna to study music, and both children played the harpsichord. Mozart also became a violin virtuoso as well as a composer. In fact, by the time he was five, he had composed
10 several minuets. Everyone quickly agreed that he was a genius.

Wolfgang Amadeus Mozart as a child, with father and sister

When it became apparent that both Mozart and his sister were musical child prodigies, their father took them on concert tours. In 1762, Mozart and his sister played for the Empress Maria
15 Theresa, the Emperor Francis I, and the court in Vienna. While touring, Mozart continued to compose music. When he played in Paris in 1764, he had already published four sonatas for the clavier and violin. By 1765, he had composed his first symphony, and by the time he was twelve, he had composed an opera. Leopold was proud of the universal admiration his children's talents aroused.

20 During his adult life, Mozart had a series of financial problems. As a result, he moved from city to city looking for positions. He worked in Milan, Salzburg, and Paris before he arrived in Vienna, where his concerts for the Emperor Joseph II were a great success. Mozart remained in Vienna from 1781 to 1787. While there, he wrote the opera *The Marriage of Figaro*, one of his greatest works, along with many piano concertos and string quartets. But soon Mozart's
25 character and his revolutionary ideas made him unpopular. Although such works as his exquisite opera *Don Giovanni* were successful, he went into debt and continued to have financial problems for the rest of his life.

During Mozart's last, difficult years, he composed some of the most beautiful music anyone has ever written. In addition to his last three symphonies, composed in seven weeks in 1788, he
30 wrote two operas, *Cosi Fan Tutte* in 1790 and *The Magic Flute* in 1791. Also in 1791, Mozart began to compose a requiem. He had been ill for some time, and he began to think the requiem was for himself. Mozart died in Vienna on December 5 of that year, still trying to complete the piece.

Scene from the opera *Don Giovanni*

35 At the time of his death at age thirty-five, Mozart had created 626 works, including nearly 50 symphonies, 20 operas, and 23 piano concertos. Still very poor, he was given a cheap funeral at Saint Stephen's Cathedral near the city of Vienna.

40 Mozart, one of the world's greatest musical prodigies, now lies buried in an unmarked grave at Saint Marx Cemetery, but his music continues to live on.

Have students read the text silently, either in class or for homework. If students read in class, you might set a time limit. You might want to have them read first for comprehension and then again to identify the topic, supporting, and concluding sentences of each paragraph. (Point out to students that not every paragraph in the article is organized through the use of a topic sentence, supporting sentences, and a concluding sentence.)

When students have finished, have them look back at the chart they filled out on page 39. Was their information correct? Did they find out what they wanted to know?

Option: Have students go back to the readings in Units 1 and 3 and analyze the paragraph structure. Which paragraphs have a topic sentence? Which paragraphs have a concluding sentence? In what ways do the supporting sentences support the main idea expressed in the topic sentence?

Option: Have interested students use the library or the Internet to find out more about Mozart. Have them report their findings to the class.

❷ Have students answer the questions independently. Review the answers as a class.

> **Answers**
> Answers may vary. **a.** By the age of six, he had learned to play the harpsichord and the violin. He had also composed several minuets. **b.** *The Marriage of Figaro, Don Giovanni, Cosi Fan Tutte, The Magic Flute* **c.** He had financial problems; his character and ideas made him unpopular; he became ill.

❸ Be sure that students understand that in order to complete the task, they only need to classify the words. They do not need to know, for example, what a minuet sounds like.

> **Answers**
> **Musicians:** composer, violinist, virtuoso
> **Musical Instruments:** clavier, harpsichord, violin
> **Musical Compositions:** minuet, opera, piano concerto, requiem, sonata, string quartet, symphony

❹ Have students complete the activity with a partner. Discuss the answers as a class.

> **Answers**
> Paragraphs 1–3 are organized through the use of a topic sentence, supporting sentences, and a concluding sentence. The first sentence of each of these paragraphs is the topic sentence; the last sentence is the concluding sentence. (Note that for paragraph 2, the first two sentences form the topic sentence.)

Think About It

Presentation

❺–❻ Have students discuss the questions as a class. You might want to have them freewrite their responses first.

Option: Have each student bring in a list of five musicians (or singers or composers) along with five songs (or compositions) they are famous for. Have students work in small groups to make two lists: one of the musicians and the other of their songs or compositions. Then have students work in small groups to quiz each other. Which group could match the most musicians with their compositions? You might want to have the students organize all the information on a poster or chart to put up in the classroom.

Option: Bring in recordings of Mozart's music to play for the class. You might play an example of an aria, a minuet, a piano concerto, a sonata, and so on. You might also play a videotape of one of Mozart's operas, either sung in English or with English subtitles.

Write: Coherence

Preview

* Write the following on the board.

  By the time Shirley Temple was six years old, <u>she</u> had already won an award. <u>However</u>, <u>she</u> remained popular for only about six years. <u>After that</u>, <u>her</u> films lost popularity.

  Ask students to tell how the underlined words are important in the paragraph. (The pronouns **she** and **her** refer to the proper noun *Shirley Temple;* we use them to avoid repeating *Shirley Temple.* **However** in the second sentence begins a contrasting idea to the idea in the first sentence. **After that** establishes the time sequence between the idea expressed in the third sentence and the idea expressed in the second sentence.)

* Help students think of other logical connectors that show contrast (**but, in contrast, nevertheless, on the other hand**) and sequence (**then, next, later**). You might also want to elicit some connectors that show example (**for instance, for example**), result (**so, therefore, as a result**), and reason (**for this reason, because of this**).

Presentation

Have students read the explanation. Tell students that when a paragraph is coherent, it is easier for readers to see how its main idea and supporting details are related. Point out that logical connectors used *within* paragraphs can also be used *between* paragraphs to make a reading coherent.

2 Answer the following questions.

    a. Why is Mozart considered a child prodigy?

    b. What are some of Mozart's most important works?

    c. Why was Mozart not successful in his last years?

3 Put these words from the article in the appropriate categories.

clavier	minuet	requiem	symphony	virtuoso
composer	opera	sonata	violin	
harpsichord	piano concerto	string quartet	violinist	

Musicians	Musical Instruments	Musical Compositions

4 Work with a partner. Look again at each paragraph in the article on page 40. Which paragraphs are organized through the use of a topic sentence, supporting sentences, and a concluding sentence? For those paragraphs, draw one line under the topic sentence and two lines under the concluding sentence.

Think About It

5 Many people of genius, especially musicians and artists, are not understood or appreciated in their own time. Why do you think this is so? Can you think of any such people?

6 Who are some famous musicians or composers from your own country? What works are they famous for?

Write: Coherence

When writing paragraphs, it is important to arrange sentences in a logical order and to connect them in a clear and meaningful way. To do this, we use pronouns, we repeat key words, and we link ideas with logical connectors. These devices help the sentences in a paragraph hold together and read smoothly, or have coherence.

7 Following are eight paragraphs that can be rearranged into two letters about getting a student loan. For each letter, put the paragraphs in the correct order.

Letter 1: **1.** ____ **2.** ____ **3.** ____ **4.** ____
Letter 2: **1.** ____ **2.** ____ **3.** ____ **4.** ____

   a. As you requested at the meeting, I am sending you a completed application form and copies of my earnings for the past year as well as information about the school I am going to attend.

   b. I would like to thank you for taking the time to meet with me on January 7. I am happy that you think I will be able to receive a student loan.

   c. However, in order to attend this school, I will need approximately $10,000 for the two-year period. Therefore, I would like to make an appointment with you to discuss my chances of getting a loan. Would it be possible for me to come in on Monday, January 7, at 10:00 a.m.?

   d. I look forward to meeting with you soon.

   e. Again, I appreciate the time you have taken to give me information about student loans, and I look forward to hearing from you.

   f. I am interested in applying for a college loan. I have been working as a cook for the past five years. I really like this line of work, and I am now ready to make it my career. As a result, I would like to study to become a professional chef.

   g. If you need any other information, please call me at (312) 555-5404, and I will send it to you as soon as I can.

   h. With this goal in mind, I have decided that I would like to attend The International School of Cuisines in Lyon, France. It is a two-year program at one of the best cooking schools in Europe. I am certain that I will easily get a job when I graduate.

8 With a partner, list the words and ideas that made it possible for you to order the paragraphs.

Write About It

9 You are interested in attending one of the following schools. Write a letter asking for information. Follow the format of the formal letter in Unit 3, page 30.

The International School of Cuisines   *Bread Loaf Writer's Conference*
The Julliard School of Music   *New Mexico School of Engineering*
National Dog Training Academy   *Harvard Law School*

 10 **Check Your Writing** Exchange letters with a partner. Use the questions below to give feedback. When you get your paper back, revise as necessary.

- Does the letter include all the parts of a formal letter?
- Is the purpose of the letter clear?
- Does the writer use appropriate devices to make the letter coherent? Explain.
- Are the verbs all correct?

❼ Have students read the directions and work independently or in pairs to organize the paragraphs into two letters. Have them use logical connectors as a guide. Refer them to Units 1 and 3 for the order of information in a business letter.

> **Answers**
> **Letter 1: 1.** f **2.** h **3.** c **4.** d
> **Letter 2: 1.** b **2.** a **3.** g **4.** e

❽ Have students complete the exercise with a partner. Discuss the answers as a class.

> **Answers**
> Answers will vary. Possible answers:
> **Letter 1: h.** With this goal in mind, …
> **c.** However, … this school …
> **Letter 2: a.** As you requested at the meeting, … **g.** If you need any other information … **e.** I appreciate the time you have taken to give me information …

Write About It

Presentation

❾ Have students use the appropriate information and format for their letters. (*Answers will vary.*)

☑ **❿ Check Your Writing** Have pairs of students exchange their first drafts and use the questions to give feedback on both the information and format. Then have them write their final drafts.

⊕ **Option:** Have students exchange their letters with partners and write letters in response.

 Workbook: Practice 12

Vocabulary Expansion: More about using a dictionary See page T143. (*Answers will vary, depending on dictionary.*)

> # EVALUATION
>
> See page TExi.
>
> **Unit 4 Achievement Test**
>
> **Self-Check** See **Check Your Knowledge**, page 32 of the Workbook.

Dictation Dictate the following incomplete sentences to your students and have the students complete the sentences. For more information on dictation, see page TExv.

1. One of the child prodigies I learned about in this unit is _____. By the time this prodigy was _____ old, _____ had _____.
2. Child prodigies are often identified in the fields of chess, _____, _____, and _____.
3. One test of intelligence is the _____. Average intelligence on the scale corresponds to the number _____.
4. Write the number that comes after the last one in this series: 0, 3, 4, 7, 8, 11, _____.

Dictate the following sentences to your students and have them complete the sentences with their own ideas. Then have them work in pairs or small groups to compare their answers.

5. By the time I was six years old, I had already _____.
6. My friend had _____ by the time I got there.
7. I'd been _____ for ages when I found out.
8. It was really fun! I'd never _____ before.

Communication Skills

1. Ask individuals to explain to the class how to solve some kind of problem, for example, a math problem or a visual puzzle. Alternatively, you might ask them to carry out some fairly complicated procedure, for example, how to assemble an appliance or cook a meal. Tell them that, as they explain, they should check to make sure their classmates are understanding their explanation. Pay attention to their use of language for confirming understanding.

2. Ask students to tell you about things they had already accomplished in their lives before they started to learn English. As they speak, pay attention to their use of the past perfect tense.

THE REAL YOU?

OBJECTIVES

- To talk about personality traits and ways to analyze personality
- To use gerunds
- To distinguish between verbs taking gerunds and verbs taking infinitives
- To take notes
- To hear and pronounce the reduction of **of**
- To discuss feelings
- To understand diagrams, drawings, and charts accompanying a text
- To write a personal letter
- To categorize compound adjectives that describe personalities

GETTING STARTED

Warm Up

Preview

Lead a discussion about **personality**. Ask, *What are some words for **personality** traits— that is, characteristics that are part of people's personalities?* (*Examples:* friendly, quiet, serious, outgoing, and optimistic) *Do you know the different **aspects** of your personality? Do you think you have a good sense of your own personality? Of your friends' personalities? Do you think it would be helpful to understand your own personality better? How could you find out more about yourself? How can you **analyze** your personality?*

Presentation

❶ Have students read the information and think about the question. Then discuss their responses in groups or as a class. If students have difficulty thinking of answers, you might write some answers on the board, for example, using astrology, graphology, numerology, palm reading, I Ching, and tarot cards. Include scientific disciplines such as psychology and psychiatry. Elicit or present explanations of terms that might be unfamiliar to some students.

Option: Write on the board **psychology**, **astrology**, **graphology**, and **numerology**. What feature is the same for all these words? (the suffix –**logy**) Ask students to figure out what the suffix means. (the study of something) Then ask students to try to figure out the definitions of the words. Help them analyze the first part of each word. (**psych–** = the mind; **astr–** = star; **graph–** = a writing; **numer–** = number)

Option: Have students work independently, in pairs, or in groups to make lists of as many scientific disciplines, such as astronomy, and as many nonscientific disciplines, such as astrology, as they can. Have students share their lists with the class. Ask, *Why are some disciplines considered scientific and others nonscientific?*

❷ Have students read the instructions. Make sure they understand all the vocabulary. Then play the recording or read the audioscript aloud two or more times. Make sure students have enough time to write in their answers. Have them work in pairs to compare their answers and then listen again to check their work. Review the answers as a class.

Audioscript: The audioscript for Exercise 2 appears on page T154.

Answers
Answers may vary. quiet: B; outgoing: R; optimistic: Y; don't often show anger: B, Y; control what they say: B; confident: R; express opinions easily: R; like to be alone: B; easygoing: Y; gentle: B

❸ Have students read and then answer the questions. Have them share their answers in groups or as a class.

(Exercise 3 Option appears on page T44.)

GETTING STARTED

Warm Up

1 People try to find out about their personalities in different ways, such as filling out questionnaires or reading horoscopes. What other ways can you think of?

2 Do the colors we prefer tell us anything about our personalities? Listen to the talk and match the colors red, blue, and yellow with their corresponding traits. Write **R** (red), **B** (blue), or **Y** (yellow) on the line. Some traits have more than one corresponding color.

_____ quiet   _____ confident

_____ outgoing   _____ express opinions easily

_____ optimistic   _____ like to be alone

_____ don't often show anger   _____ easygoing

_____ control what they say   _____ gentle

3 Which of the three colors do you prefer? Do you have any of the personality traits you marked for that color? Which ones?

Figure It Out

4 Complete the following personality questionnaire. Circle only one letter for each question.

All About *You*

1. What do you most look forward to doing?
- a. making friends
- b. discovering who I am
- c. having a happy home life
- d. getting a high-paying job

2. Do you have a hard time expressing your feelings?
- a. sometimes
- b. often
- c. usually
- d. never

3. What do you miss not having the most?
- a. more time to go out and have fun
- b. more time to learn new things
- c. more time to stay home and relax
- d. more time to get ahead

4. Which risk would you consider taking?
- a. participating in a dangerous sport
- b. investing money in the stock market
- c. defending a controversial issue
- d. opening up my own business

5. What do you put off doing the most?
- a. paying bills
- b. phoning friends
- c. writing letters
- d. taking care of my health

6. What can you easily imagine yourself doing?
- a. falling in love
- b. living in the country
- c. buying a larger home
- d. changing my career

7. Do you insist on having your own way at work or at home?
- a. often
- b. seldom
- c. sometimes
- d. almost always

8. What are you most often criticized for doing?
- a. talking too much
- b. not giving opinions
- c. not paying attention
- d. interrupting

9. Do you avoid accepting reponsibility for your actions?
- a. sometimes
- b. often
- c. infrequently
- d. never

10. What do you enjoy doing the most?
- a. going to a barbecue with friends
- b. hiking alone in the mountains
- c. spending time gardening
- d. eating out in a first-class restaurant

5 Which letter did you circle the most times? Read the personality description for that letter. Then tell a partner whether you agree with the description. Why or why not?

a. You are an outgoing and generous person with a good sense of humor. Sometimes you care too much about what others think of you.

b. You are an independent person who is cultured, artistic, and sensitive. Often you feel very shy.

c. You are a reliable, idealistic person who is very family oriented. Occasionally you feel bored and lonesome.

d. You are a very ambitious, responsible, and well-organized person. Sometimes you are too competitive.

(Exercise 3 continued from page T43.)

Option: Have students survey the class to find out how many students prefer each of the three colors and how many students feel their personality is similar to the personality described for people with their color preference. Ask, *Do you think color analysis works well?*

 Workbook: Practice 1

Figure It Out

Preview

- Elicit or present the vocabulary for personality traits in Exercise 5. To do this, you might want to display pictures of people who exhibit these traits and have students make up a name for each person and describe each person's personality. For example, a student might say, "This is Tom. He's very *competitive*. He always wants to win." Supply any vocabulary students need.

- You may want to elicit or clarify what **investing money in the stock market** means. If necessary, clarify **controversial issue** by giving examples of controversial issues and eliciting others from students.

Presentation

❹ Have students read the instructions for the questionnaire independently. Then have them read and complete the questionnaire independently in class or for homework. Remind students to choose only one answer—the most appropriate one—for each question.

❺ Have students read the directions and then complete the activity. After the pairs have discussed their results, have them share their reactions with the rest of the class. Who agrees with the results? Why? Who doesn't agree with them? Why?

Option: Instead of having students complete the questionnaire independently, you may want to have them work in pairs. Have them take turns asking each other the questions. Each partner records the answers and calculates the personality type for the other.

Option: As a class, compare the results from the personality questionnaire with those from the color analysis. How do the two personality descriptions compare? Are they similar or different? Does one method work better than the other? Which one?

❻ Vocabulary Check Have students read the directions and then complete the activity independently or with a partner. Review the answers as a class.

> **Answers**
> 1. h 2. f 3. b 4. g 5. e 6. c 7. a 8. d

^{Link} *Workbook: Practice 2*

Talk About It

 Option: You may prefer to postpone this activity until after the grammar presentation if you feel students need extra help with understanding gerunds. You also might direct students to Workbook Practice 4.

Presentation

Note: The purpose of this activity is to develop fluency. Students should feel free to talk without fear of interruption for error correction. If you notice persistent errors, write them down for later reteaching or review.

❼ Have students read the instructions and the model conversation. Then have a pair of students read the conversation aloud for the class.

Have students work in pairs to complete the activity. You may want them to change partners once or twice and repeat the interview for additional practice. Make sure to allow enough time for students to complete the activity. Then ask them to report about the person or people they interviewed, either in small groups or as a class.

Option: Have students compile the results of the interviews on the board as lists of likes and dislikes. Then have them analyze the data to figure out which activities are the most popular and which are the least popular. You might also want to have them figure out whether gender or age plays a part in the most popular and the least popular activities.

Option: Have each student use the information from the interview to write a short paragraph about his or her partner's preferred free-time activities. Students might first need to gather additional information from their partners.

^{Link} *Workbook: Practice 3*

GRAMMAR

Gerunds

Preview

- To focus students' attention on gerunds, call on several students to name activities they enjoy doing and activities they don't enjoy doing. Elicit full sentences, and write a few of them on the board. (Example: I enjoy hiking.) Ask students what they notice about the form of the word following the verb. (It ends in **–ing**.) Elicit or explain to students that these words are gerunds, which function as nouns.

- You may want to review the spelling rules for adding –ing to verbs. Add **–ing** to the base form of the verb, except when the base form ends in **e** or with one vowel and one consonant. If it ends in **e**, drop the **e** before adding **–ing**; for example, **drive** becomes **driving**. If it ends with one vowel and one consonant, double the consonant before adding **–ing**; for example, **get** becomes **getting**.

Presentation

Have students read the explanation and the examples in the box. Point out that since gerunds are used as nouns, they can be subjects, objects of verbs, or objects of prepositions. Review the examples, making sure that students understand the terms **subject**, **object of verb**, and **object of preposition**. Point out that negatives can be used with gerunds, as in the second sentence.

6 **Vocabulary Check** The words and expressions on the left are from the previous questionnaire. Match them with the correct meanings on the right.

_____ **1.** to look forward to   **a.** acting according to one's beliefs

_____ **2.** to put off   **b.** to demand

_____ **3.** to insist on   **c.** dependable

_____ **4.** to avoid   **d.** wanting success

_____ **5.** outgoing   **e.** friendly; liking to talk to others

_____ **6.** reliable   **f.** to postpone

_____ **7.** idealistic   **g.** to stay away from

_____ **8.** ambitious   **h.** to be happy about something that is going to happen

Talk About It

7 Take turns interviewing a partner about his or her free-time activities.

Ask for information.

A: What do you enjoy doing in your free time?

Give information.

B: I enjoy listening to music and reading.

Ask for more information.

A: And what do you dislike doing?

Give more information.

B: I hate going to baseball games, but I go when my brother is playing.

GRAMMAR

Gerunds

A gerund is the –ing form of a verb, used as a noun. Gerunds can be subjects, objects of verbs, or objects of prepositions. They can also be in the negative.

> **A:** I enjoy **traveling** to exotic places. _(object of verb)_
>
> **B:** Not me. I hate **not having** a hot bath. _(negative gerund)_
>
> **A:** I look forward to **breaking** the routine. _(object of preposition)_
>
> **B:** Exotic **traveling** is only fun when I can watch it on TV. _(subject)_

1 Complete the conversation with the correct gerund form.

MOTHER: Henry, I've asked you ten times to cut the grass. Quit
(1. put off) _____ it _____ . Do it. Now!

HENRY: I don't feel like **(2. cut)** _____ it now, Mom. I'm
reading a really interesting book.

MOTHER: But the yard looks horrible! The neighbors are going to criticize us
for **(3. cut)** _____ the grass. You know how they complain
about **(4. see)** _____ messy yards.

HENRY: Oh, Mom. Can't we talk about something different?

MOTHER: No, Henry, you are not going to get out of **(5. do)** _____ this
anymore. I want that grass cut today, and that's that!

HENRY: OK, Mom, if you insist on **(6. have)** _____ your way, I'll do it,
but I don't feel like **(7. do)** _____ it now.

Verbs Followed by Infinitives/Gerunds

Some verbs are followed by infinitives, some by gerunds, and some by either form.

Verb + Infinitive		Verb + Gerund		Verb + Infinitive or Gerund		
ask	need	avoid	finish	begin	hate	start
choose	plan	consider	mind	can't stand	like	stop
decide	refuse	deny	miss	continue	love	remember
expect	want	enjoy	quit	dislike	prefer	

2 **Check Your Understanding** Complete the dialogue with the
gerund or infinitive form of the verb in parentheses.

A: Tell me about yourself and I'll guess your sign.

B: OK. I want **(1. travel)** _____ more and I really enjoy
(2. visit) _____ faraway places.

A: So you like **(3. travel)** _____ , but you prefer
(4. go) _____ to exotic places. Do people accuse you of
(5. be) _____ too adventurous?

B: Yes, but I can't stand **(6. be)** _____ inactive. People also
criticize me for **(7. remember, *neg.*)** _____ details.

A: You're like me. You need **(8. see)** _____ the bigger
picture. You must be an Aries.

3 Work with a partner. Find out your partner's sign. Then, read the
description for this sign in the horoscope on page 47. Ask questions
to see if your partner really has these personality traits.

Example:

A: So, you're a Scorpio. Do you really keep on working until a job is finished?

B: Yeah, I'm determined to finish everything I start.

A: Do you dislike talking about your feelings?

B: No, I don't mind discussing them with close friends.

❶ Have students read the instructions and then complete the exercise independently. Then have them compare answers with a partner.

Answers
1. putting ... off 2. cutting 3. not cutting
4. seeing 5. doing 6. having 7. doing

 Option: You might want students to identify the function of each gerund. (object of verb, negative gerund, object of preposition, or subject)

Link *Workbook: Practices 4, 5*

Verbs Followed by Infinitives/Gerunds

Preview

- Ask students how infinitives are formed. (with **to** + the base form of the verb) Elicit examples of sentences with infinitives.

- To focus students' attention on the relationship between infinitives and gerunds, write the following sentences with gerunds on the board:

  I like traveling.

  I also enjoy skiing.

  Ask whether the gerunds in these sentences could be replaced by infinitives. Elicit that an infinitive is possible only with the first sentence. (I like to travel.) Ask students to explain why. (The verb **like** takes infinitives or gerunds, but the verb **enjoy** takes only gerunds.)

- Introduce the term **astrological sign** if you didn't do so earlier.

Presentation

Have students read the explanation and the lists of verbs in the box. Review the explanation and the lists as a class.

☑ ❷ **Check Your Understanding** Remind students that some words can be followed by both the gerund or the infinitive form. (Refer them to the right side of box. Review words with students.) Then have students complete the exercise independently and check their answers in pairs.

Answers
1. to travel 2. visiting 3. to travel/traveling
4. to go/going 5. being 6. to be/being
7. not remembering 8. to see

Option: Have students write pairs of sentences—one using an infinitive and one using a gerund—for the verbs that can be followed by either infinitives or gerunds.

Option: Write the following conversation on the board or on an overhead transparency, or make a copy for each student. Have students underline each gerund and circle each infinitive. Have them label each gerund as a subject (*S*), object of a verb (*O*), or object of a preposition (*OP*).

A: What's your sign?

B: I'm not sure.

A: Wait! Let me guess! Do you like <u>staying</u> *(O)* at home?

B: Yes. In fact, I hardly ever want (to go) out. I just prefer <u>staying</u> *(O)* home. I like (to visit) friends, though.

A: Do your friends and family criticize you for <u>being</u> *(OP)* too moody?

B: Yes. They accuse me of <u>being</u> *(OP)* too emotional, but I don't think I am. I'm a very sensitive person, and I feel bad when they say that.

A: Do you hate <u>meeting</u> *(O)* new people and <u>talking</u> *(O)* in public?

B: Yes, I do. <u>Meeting</u> *(S)* new people is hard for me, and I always avoid <u>speaking</u> *(O)* in public. Basically, I'm a really shy person.

A: Gee, you're a perfect Cancer. You were born between June 21 and July 20, right?

B: No. In fact, I was born at the beginning of January.

❸ Read the directions and the example as a class. If necessary, say the names of the zodiac signs on page 47 so that students can hear the correct pronunciation. Then have the partners complete the activity. (*Answers will vary.*)

❹ Read the directions and the example as a class. Then have partners take turns asking and answering questions like those in the example. (*Accept any answer students can justify from the horoscope.*)

🜨 **Option:** Have students work in groups or as a class to discuss why so many people like to read their horoscopes in newspapers and magazines. Do these people really believe that astrologers can predict the future by studying the stars?

❺ Read the directions and the example with the class. Then have students write true sentences about themselves. (*Answers will vary.*)

🜨 **Option:** Display pictures of people from magazines. Have students work in pairs or small groups to describe the people, using **be afraid of**, **be good at**, **can't stand**, **doesn't mind**, **enjoy**, **insist on**, **look forward to**, **plan on**, and **put off**. Have them share their descriptions with the class.

Aquarius (January 21–February 18) Creative and idealistic; loves daydreaming about making a better world; can be selfish.

Pisces (February 19–March 21) Sensitive and gentle; enjoys meeting people and making new friends; can be superficial.

Aries (March 22–April 21) Active and adventurous; can't help getting excited about new projects; enjoys traveling.

Taurus (April 22–May 21) Generous and good at saving money; enjoys investing in the stock market; can be stubborn.

Gemini (May 22–June 21) Cultured and clever; prefers reading and talking; takes on many projects at once.

Cancer (June 22–July 21) Home-loving and conservative; dislikes traveling and tries to avoid making changes; sometimes too emotional.

Leo (July 22–August 21) Confident and organized; not afraid of making mistakes; often insists on being the leader.

Virgo (August 22–September 21) Organized and precise; can't stand having a messy house; always finishes doing what he or she starts.

Libra (September 22–October 21) Peace-loving and charming; always tries to avoid arguing with people; enjoys telling jokes.

Scorpio (October 22–November 21) Determined and intelligent; keeps on doing a job until it is finished; dislikes talking about feelings.

Sagittarius (November 22–December 21) Sincere and cheerful; loves talking to people and making them laugh; avoids making decisions.

Capricorn (December 22–January 20) Reliable and careful; insists on doing a good job; often avoids listening to other people's opinions.

4 The following statements are all incorrect. With a partner, ask and answer questions to find out what's wrong.

Example:

Aquarians dislike thinking about changing the world.
A: Do Aquarians dislike thinking about changing the world?
B: No, Aquarians love thinking about making the world better.

a. Cancers can't stand staying at home.
b. Capricorns seldom worry about doing a good job.
c. Geminis are criticized for not reading.
d. Leos insist on following a leader.
e. Libras enjoy arguing.
f. Pisces avoid making new friends.
g. Scorpios rarely insist on finishing a project.
h. Virgos don't mind having a messy house.

5 On a sheet of paper, write two sentences for each verb in the box. Express your true feelings.

Example:

I can't stand eating in tourist places on vacation.

afraid of	can't stand	love
avoid	don't mind	plan on
be criticized for	insist on	put off
be good at	look forward to	remember

6 With a partner, ask and answer questions using the cues in Exercise 5.

Example:

A: What are you looking forward to?

B: I'm looking forward to graduating this year. What about you?

A: I'm looking forward to seeing the Grand Canyon this summer.

 7 **Express Yourself** Write a paragraph describing your personality. List at least five traits. Then in groups of three, read your paragraph aloud. Ask each other questions.

LISTENING and SPEAKING

Listen: Our Many Faces

1 **Before You Listen** Draw faces in the circles. Then look at the chart of faces on page 49. What do you think the conversation will be about?

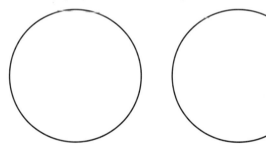

 Taking Notes When you listen and take notes, you focus on key words and ideas. To save time as you write, use words and phrases, not complete sentences. Also, be sure to develop a set of abbreviations and symbols that works for you.

Common Abbreviations	Common Symbols
w/ (with)	= (the same as)
w/o (without)	≠ (not the same, opposite)
approx. (approximately)	& (and)
inclu. (includes, including)	@ (at)
n.b. (note well, important)	✳ (important)
e.g. (example)	—> (result)
cf. (compare)	# (number, number of)
sum. (in summary)	? (confusing, questionable)

6 Read the directions and the example with the class. Then have partners take turns asking and answering questions using the cues in Exercise 5.

 Workbook: Practices 6, 7, 8, 9, 10

7 Express Yourself Read the directions with the class. Then divide students into groups that don't include partners from Exercise 6. Encourage students to use their sentences from Exercise 5.

LISTENING and SPEAKING

Listen: Our Many Faces

Presentation

1 Before You Listen Have students read the instructions and then draw the faces. Encourage them to draw quickly without careful thought. Then ask students what they think the conversation in Exercise 2 will be about.

➡ Taking Notes Have students read the strategy and the chart of abbreviations and symbols. Then ask them whether they already use abbreviations and symbols when they take notes. If so, what are some of the abbreviations and symbols they use? You might want to write some of them on the board. Emphasize that each person should develop his or her own system. Next, you might want to say a few sentences and ask students which words from the sentences are key words that should be included in notes. For example, you might say, *What is **personality**? Over the years scientists have developed different definitions of personality. For example, some scientists define personality as the way a person thinks, feels, and acts. (Possible responses:* personality, diff. defs. of personality, one: way a person thinks, feels, acts)

🎧 ❷ Have students read the instructions. Then focus their attention on the chart. Play the recording or read the audioscript aloud two or more times. Remind students to take notes using key words and phrases, not whole sentences. Let them listen again to check their answers.

Audioscript: The audioscript for Exercise 2 appears on page T145.

Answers

Answers will vary. **Happy:** normal, friendly, easygoing; enjoy being w/others; like telling stories or jokes; good sense of humor. **Ugly or Silly:** trouble developing personal relationships; feel threatened; to hide insecurity—act out roles; avoid risking true inner selves. **Angry:** trouble relating to others; don't trust others, open up, or admit being wrong; antisocial **Sad:** not antisocial; have deep feelings about people but often deny them; don't have strong self-images; try to be what others want them to be; need more confidence

---

❸ Have students read the directions and then complete the activity in pairs. You may want to ask some pairs to talk about their analysis of their drawings with the rest of the class. Ask students to tell what they think about this method of analyzing personality.

 Option: Have students write a short paragraph describing the personality of a close friend or family member. Next, have them ask that friend or family member to draw three faces. Then have them analyze the faces according to the information in the chart. Does their analysis fit the description in the paragraph? Have students discuss their results as a class.

📓 *Workbook: Practice 11*

Pronunciation

Preview

* Write the following conversation on the board.

  A: How did you get through the course?
  B: I asked for a lot of help.

Say the two lines of the conversation. Then say the second sentence twice, the first time fully pronouncing the **of**, the second time saying **lotta** for **a lot of**. Ask students to tell you the difference between the two ways you said the second sentence. Elicit that the first time you fully pronounced the **of** (/əv/) he second time you reduced it (/ə/).

* Have students practice the conversation, pronouncing **of** both ways.

Presentation

Have students read the explanation in the box independently. If necessary, review the meaning of **function words** (words such as prepositions, conjunctions, and articles that are used to connect other parts of speech, such as nouns, verbs, and adjectives).

🎧 ❹ Have students read the directions. Then play the recording or read the sentences aloud two or more times. Have students circle their answers. Then have them work in pairs to compare their answers. Let them listen again to check their answers.

Answers

A: /əv/; B: /əv/; A: /ə/; B: /əv/; A: /ə/

---

❺ Divide the class into pairs to practice reading the conversation. Then have several pairs read the conversation to the class. Have the other students listen to hear whether **of** is reduced.

 Workbook: Practice 12

Speak Out

Presentation

➡ **Discussing Feelings** Have students read the strategy and the expressions in the box. Can they think of other expressions that could be used? You might want to have students practice using these expressions by discussing situations that people might have strong feelings about. Examples include standing in a long line at a store, waiting for a friend who's often late, having a friend change plans at the

(Speak Out continues on page T50.)

2 Experts say that the way we draw faces shows different aspects of our personality. Listen to the conversation and complete the following chart by taking notes.

Faces	Personality Traits
Happy	
Ugly or Silly	
Angry	
Sad	

3 Work with a partner. Use the information in the chart to analyze each other's drawings and personalities. Does your partner agree with your analysis? Why or why not?

Pronunciation

Reducing of

Like other function words, the preposition **of** is usually unstressed in quick speech. When this happens, **of** /əv/ is sometimes reduced to /ə/.

 4 /əv/ or /ə/? Listen to the conversation and circle the pronunciation you hear.

A:	Have you ever thought **of** going to see a fortune-teller?	/əv/	/ə/
B:	I'm afraid **of** hearing what she'll say.	/əv/	/ə/
A:	You might hear a lot **of** interesting things.	/əv/	/ə/
B:	OK, I'll do it. So what's the price **of** advice?	/əv/	/ə/
A:	Don't worry. It won't cost a lot **of** money.	/əv/	/ə/

5 Practice reading the dialogue, focusing on reducing *of*.

Speak Out

STRATEGY **Discussing Feelings** When you talk about topics or events that are emotional, you can use certain expressions to discuss feelings.

Asking About Feelings	Expressing Feelings
Do you feel the same way?	I feel/don't feel the same way.
How do you feel about it?	That really irritates me.
Does that (bother) you?	Oh, I don't mind.

6 A pet peeve is something that irritates us. It's often a small thing. For example, one person may hate waiting for people. Another may dislike hearing whistling. List two or three of your pet peeves.

7 Work with a partner. Find out if your pet peeves bother him or her, too. Use the language for asking about and expressing feelings.

READING and WRITING

Read About It

1 Before You Read Read the title of the article and look at the drawings. What do you think the article is about?

STRATEGY **Using Graphics** Diagrams, drawings, graphs, and charts often accompany texts to help clarify meaning and illustrate important points. When you read, use graphics to help you understand the text more easily.

Your Personality in the Palm of Your Hand?

Throughout history, people have been fascinated by the mysteries of the human personality. In their efforts to find out how and why humans differ from each other, people have looked for answers in the
5 stars, in the analysis of handwriting, in the study of the shape of the head, and in the lines and shapes of the hand.

Anyone can look at a human hand and deduce some facts about the owner. For example, a hand
10 with blisters and calluses tells us its owner does physical labor. But some people have gone beyond that simple step to a much more exotic way of analyzing a person's character. Through the ages, these analysts have identified different lines and
15 shapes (called mounts) in the palm of the hand and have connected them to certain human personality traits.

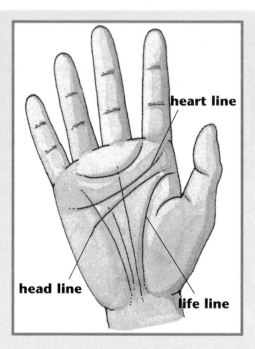

Experts in palm reading identify nine separate lines in the human palm. The length and clarity of these lines determine certain aspects of personality. Three of the most important lines
20 are the life line, the head line, and the heart line. A long life line shows that the owner will keep on living to a very old age. The head line is related to intelligence; a long, curved line shows that the owner is used to thinking imaginatively. The heart line shows love and affection. A short line indicates that the owner has problems expressing affection; in contrast, a long, strong line shows that the owner enjoys passionate relationships.

(Speak Out continued from page T49.)

last moment, and having several tests scheduled for the same day. Use expressions that ask about feelings, and have students respond with sentences expressing their feelings.

Note: The purpose of this activity is to develop fluency. Students should be energized to speak without fear of interruption for error correction. If you notice persistent errors, write them down for later reteaching or review.

❻ Have students read the explanation of a **pet peeve**. Then brainstorm with the class other pet peeves a person could have. Examples include people who don't turn off their radios when you're talking to them, people who talk on cell phones in restaurants, people who don't answer their e-mails, and people who change the TV channels continuously. Then have students list two or three of their own pet peeves.

❼ Have students read the instructions and then complete the activity. Encourage them to use the language for asking about and expressing feelings. Then ask individuals to describe their partner's pet peeves to a small group or the rest of the class.

Option: Do Exercise 7 as a polling activity rather than as pair work. Poll students about their pet peeves. Compile the results in a chart on the board. What is the most common pet peeve among the students?

Read About It

Presentation

❶ Before You Read Have students read the directions and answer the question. Then have them discuss as a class what they know about palm reading.

➡ **Using Graphics** Have students read the strategy. Ask them to give examples of types of books and other materials in which graphics are helpful. Also have them identify the different kinds of graphics that are used in these books. (diagrams in science books, maps in geography books, and so on) Then ask them how the two drawings on pages 50 and 51 might help them as they read the article. How would the article be more difficult if the drawings weren't included?

Have students read the article on pages 50 and 51 independently in class or for homework. If students read in class, you might want to set a time limit. Remind students to pay attention to the diagrams as they read.

Option: Have students read in pairs. One student reads while the other listens and looks at the diagrams. Have students switch roles.

❷ Have students read the directions and then complete the activity. When they are finished, have them compare their diagrams to the diagrams in the article.

Answers

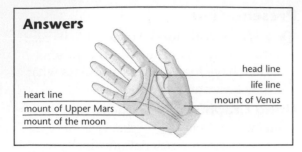

head line
life line
mount of Venus

heart line
mount of Upper Mars
mount of the moon

---

❸ Have students read the directions and then work independently to write the definitions. Remind them not to use their dictionaries. Then have students work in pairs to compare their answers.

Answers

Answers will vary. **a.** figure out **b.** work **c.** unusual **d.** having a round shape **e.** easily affected **f.** explaining the meaning of

---

Think About It

(*See page 52.*)

❹–❺ Have students read the directions independently and then discuss their responses as a class.

✸ **Option:** Have students write comprehension questions about the article and then exchange them in groups to get the answers.

✸ **Option:** Some students may be interested in finding out more about ways people have tried to analyze personality—through palm reading, graphology (the study of handwriting), phrenology (the study of the shape of the head), and so on. Have them research the subject and report their findings to the class. Be sure they discuss whether these methods are scientifically reliable.

✸ **Option:** Encourage students to talk about fortune-telling in their cultures. Is it common? Is it forbidden? Do many people believe in it? Do people in their cultures have other ways to analyze personalities? Have them describe them.

Write: A Personal Letter

(*See page 52.*)

Preview

Ask students whether they remember writing personal letters in which they described people they know. Encourage students to think of people they might describe in a personal letter. (a new boyfriend or girlfriend, a demanding teacher or boss, a mean neighbor, a funny coworker, or a new roommate)

Presentation

Have students read the explanation of a personal letter independently.

❻ Have students read the directions and then complete the activity. Have them work in pairs to compare their answers before checking them as a class.

25   In addition to identifying lines, readers also look at nine mounts, rounded parts of the palm, that indicate other character traits. These mounts can be flat, round, or very developed. Three of the important mounts are the mount of Venus, the mount of the
30 moon, and the mount of Upper Mars. A flat mount of Venus indicates poor health. If the mount of Venus is round, it shows that the owner works at having a healthy mind and body. It also indicates a love of being with and helping other people. The owner of a
35 round mount of the moon loves traveling and has a sensitive nature. A strongly developed mount of the moon can indicate creative thinking. A person with a flat mount of Upper Mars believes everything he or she hears; the owner trusts people. A very developed
40 mount of Upper Mars, however, indicates that the owner has difficulty in controlling anger and other strong emotions.

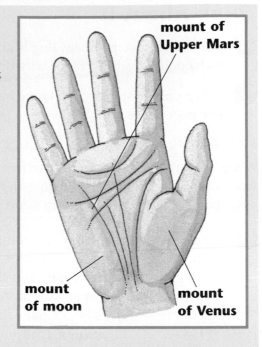

    By interpreting all the lines and mounts, experts in palm reading claim they can then describe a person's personality. It is the individual's decision whether or not to believe these readings.

2 Without looking back at the text, label the diagram. Use the words in the box.

> head line
> heart line
> life line
> mount of the moon
> mount of Upper Mars
> mount of Venus

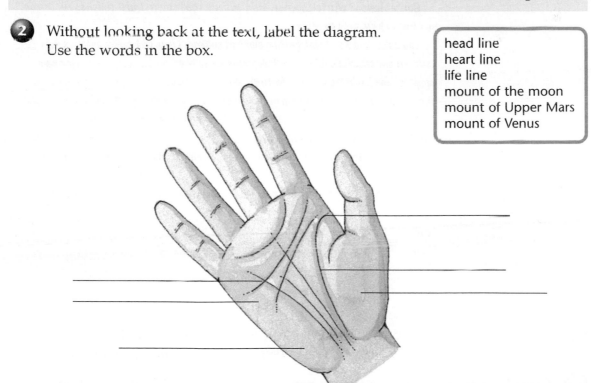

3 Review the article and write definitions of these words on a sheet of paper. Do not use a dictionary.

    a. to deduce (line 8)   **d.** rounded (line 26)
    b. labor (line 11)   **e.** sensitive (line 36)
    c. exotic (line 12)   **f.** interpreting (line 43)

Think About It

4 Do you believe palm reading is an accurate way to determine personality traits? Why or why not?

5 Have you or anyone you know had a palm reading? What was the experience like?

Write: A Personal Letter

When we write letters to friends or family, we are more casual and personal than when we write formal business letters. The greeting and closing, among other parts of the letter, are more informal.

6 Read this personal letter and compare it with the formal letters in Unit 1 (page 10) and Unit 3 (page 30). List the differences in the punctuation, in the greeting and the closing, and in the verb forms. Compare your answers with those of your classmates.

> January 2, 2000
>
> Dear Diana,
>
> Sorry I haven't written sooner, but I've been really busy. I just finished my exams, so I finally have time to write.
>
> You asked me how I was getting along at college. I love it! I really enjoyed my courses and teachers this term. I also have a really interesting roomate. Her name is Brigitte, and she's from Paris. At first, she had difficulty understanding English, so she had trouble keeping up with her courses. Now, after six months, she's doing just fine. Although sometimes she can't help speaking French, she insists on trying to speak English with me. I really like that. She's generous, intelligent, and lots of fun. I've invited her to stay at my parents' house for winter break, so you'll be able to meet her.
>
> I'm really looking forward to being back home. See you in a couple of weeks.
>
> Love,
> Linda

Write About It

7 Think of a person you'd like to describe to a friend. Brainstorm ideas about the person's personality. Then write a personal letter describing the person.

8 **Check Your Writing** Exchange papers with a partner. Use the questions below to offer feedback. Then revise your own paper as needed.

- Are the parts of the letter clearly marked?
- Is the writing appropriate for an informal letter?
- Is the description of the friend clear? Can you add other details?
- Are the verb forms correct?

Answers

Answers will vary. Possible responses:

The greetings: The business letters use titles followed by colons (Dear Sir or Madam: and Dear Ms. Datris:). The personal letter uses the first name followed by a comma (Dear Diana,).

The closings: The business letters use formal closings followed by the writer's full name (Sincerely, Diane M. Jackson; Yours sincerely, Freida Jackson). The personal letter uses an informal closing followed by the first name (Love, Linda).

Level of language and use of verb forms: The business letters use formal language (*I would very much like to talk with you about the position; I look forward to hearing from you soon*). They do not use contracted forms of verbs. The personal letter uses informal language (*You asked me how I was getting along at college. I love it!*). It uses the exclamation point to express excitement. It also uses contracted forms of verbs.

Write About It

❼ Have students think of an interesting person to describe to a friend. (Refer them to the people they named during the preview of the Write section.) Have them brainstorm ideas about the person's personality, plan a letter using their ideas, and then write a first draft of the letter.

☑ ❽ **Check Your Writing** After students have written their first drafts, have them work with partners to check the form, content, and style. Have partners give each other feedback before they write their final drafts.

 Workbook: Practice 13

Vocabulary Expansion: Compound adjectives
See page T144.

Answers

Answers may vary. Possible answers:

Positive: hard-working, well-respected, easygoing, outspoken, open-minded, well-educated, kindhearted, outgoing

Negative: ill-tempered, hardhearted, narrow-minded, absent-minded, tightfisted, two-faced, hardheaded

EVALUATION

See page TExi.

Unit 5 Achievement Test

Self-Check See **Check Your Knowledge**, page 40 of the Workbook.

Dictation Dictate the following sentences. For more information on dictation, see page TExv.

1. My sister enjoys traveling for business.
2. I prefer to travel for pleasure.
3. Last year my mother and I decided to visit Tokyo.
4. We loved visiting our relatives.
5. Next year we want to visit Shanghai.

Next, have students write five sentences about a place they would like to visit. Encourage them to use verbs that are followed by infinitives or gerunds. Refer them to the list of these verbs on page 46 in the Student Book.

Communication Skills

1. Lead a discussion about characters the students know from books, TV, the movies, or public life. Have them describe their personalities. Encourage students to use a range of words to describe the personalities.

2. Have students give their opinions about various activities such as traveling, paying taxes, speaking English, and doing errands. Pay attention to their use of gerunds and infinitives.

IF I HAD MY WAY

OBJECTIVES

- To talk about changes, dreams, and preferences
- To talk about unreal situations using the second conditional
- To contrast first and second conditionals
- To use the second conditional to ask for and give advice
- To listen in order to summarize
- To hear stressed syllables and rhythm in sentences
- To encourage and discourage
- To get meaning from context
- To write an analysis
- To understand and use the prefixes **under–**, **mis–**, and **over–**

GETTING STARTED

Warm Up

Preview

- Ask students wether they think most of the people they know are happy with themselves, that is, with their personality, appearance, and situation. Ask students to list three things they like about themselves and would not want to change. You may want students to share their lists in small groups.

- Write the words **impossible** and **improbable** on the board. Focus students' attention on the roots **possible** and **probable** and their meanings (that can happen, that is likely to happen). Then ask students what the prefix *im–* means (not). Next, ask students to give the meanings of both words (that will not happen, that will not likely happen). Finally, ask students to name changes that would be **possible** for someone to

make and changes that would be **impossible** to make. (*Examples:* possible: changing one's hairstyle; impossible: changing one's height, that is, without using shoes with platforms, etc.) Also ask them for examples of changes that are possible, but improbable. (*Example:* earning a million dollars a year)

Presentation

Have students read about the expression *if I had my way,* and ask several students to use it in a sentence.

❶ Have students read the instructions and work independently to write their lists. Then have them discuss their "wish lists" in pairs, small groups, or as a class. Make sure they tell whether their dreams are possible, improbable, or impossible. (If students do not want to reveal personal things they wrote, they should not be required to do so.)

❷ Have students read the instructions independently. Then have them work in small groups to complete the activity.

🎧 ❸ Have students read the instructions independently. Play the recording or read the audioscript aloud two or more times. Remind students that they do not have to understand every word in order to complete the activity. Let them listen again to check their answers.

Audioscript: The audioscript for Exercise 3 appears on page T155.

> **Answers**
> **a.** Mary **b.** Carlos **c.** Bruce

 Workbook: Practice 1

IF I HAD MY WAY

GETTING STARTED

Warm Up

"If I had my way" is an expression that means "if things could be the way I want them to be." People sometimes use this expression to talk about changes, dreams, and preferences. For example, a teacher might say, "If I had my way, vacation would start tomorrow."

1 Many of us dream about changing ourselves or our lives. Some people would like to have a different job or have different color eyes. Make a list of some things you might want to change about yourself. Then decide which changes are real possibilities for you and which are improbable or impossible.

2 Work in small groups. Compare your lists of things you might want to change about yourselves. Do you want the same things?

3 Listen to the conversations and decide who wants to change in some way. Circle the name.

   a. Mary   Chen   **b.** Carlos   Ellen   **c.** Bruce   Fatima

Figure It Out

A. *Doris is on vacation at the beach, chatting with a few of her friends.*

DORIS: Isn't this the life! I'm sure glad our vacation has started.

RAOUL: Yeah, but wouldn't it be great if vacation lasted all year long?

ALICE: Oh, I don't know. I think I'd get restless and bored.

RAOUL: No, you wouldn't, Alice. Just think of all the things you'd be able to do.

5 **ALICE:** Like what?

DORIS: Well, travel, for one thing. If you had all year, you'd be able to spend a month in twelve of the great cities of the world!

ALICE: Hey, you're right. I'd start with Paris and Istanbul. Then I'd go to Buenos Aires, Mexico City, Seoul, and ...

10 **RAOUL:** That sounds interesting, but if I had my way, I'd do something more exotic—like live in a small village in the Amazon or spend time observing wild gorillas in Africa.

ALICE: Hey, maybe vacations should last two years! I wouldn't be able to choose between the two.

15 **RAOUL:** Maybe vacations should last forever.

DORIS: If so, we'd need a vacation from our vacation.

B. *Doris is back at work after her vacation.*

FRANK: I think we should bring up our new advertising idea at tomorrow's meeting.

DORIS: You're right. If I were you, Frank, I'd raise
20 it right at the beginning.

DEREK: If we could get the support of the new president, the rest of the department would have to go along with our plan.

DORIS: Probably. But if you went to the president
25 directly, it would offend the vice-president. You know how oversensitive he is.

FRANK: Yes, but if he knew the president approved of our plan, I think he'd change his mind.

DEREK: Come on. Let's not be underhanded about
30 this. After all, we have the right formula. We know our sales would increase if we used ordinary people instead of professional models in our ads. Why can't he see that?

DORIS: I don't know. I think our sales have decreased because those
35 models look so fake. How can our customers believe them if they don't look authentic?

DEREK: I'm sure he'd go along with us if we could make him see that real people better reflect the way life really is.

FRANK: OK. You've inspired me. I'll propose the idea tomorrow.
40 Maybe we can convince him to try it on a temporary basis. Then if it works, we can make it a permanent policy.

Figure It Out

Presentation

Read Conversation A aloud as students listen. Students can listen with their books open or closed. Then have students read the conversation independently in class or for homework. Alternatively, have them read it in groups of three.

Have students answer the following questions, as a class or in groups. (*Answers will vary somewhat.*)

1. Why didn't Alice want the vacation to last all year? (She was afraid she'd get restless and bored.)

2. What kind of vacation does Doris suggest? (Doris suggests spending a month in twelve of the great cities of the world.)

3. What kind of vacation would Raoul prefer? (Raoul would prefer an exotic vacation in a far-off place.)

4. Why does Doris say they would need a vacation from their vacation? (A vacation that lasted forever would be tiring.)

Read Conversation B aloud as students listen. Students can listen with their books open or closed. Then have students read the conversation independently in class or for homework. Alternatively, have them read it in groups.

Have students answer the following questions, as a class or in groups.

1. Why are Frank, Doris, and Derek afraid to talk directly to the president about their plan? (They don't want to offend the vice-president.)

2. What is their new plan? (They want to use ordinary people in their ads instead of professional models.)

3. When will Frank propose the new plan? (tomorrow)

4. What will Frank try to convince the vice-president to do? (to try the plan on a temporary basis)

☑ ❹ **Vocabulary Check** Have students read the directions and complete the activity independently. Review the answers as a class.

Answers
1. e 2. g 3. c 4. f 5. b 6. a 7. d

❺ Have students read the directions and complete the activity independently. Then have them check their answers in pairs.

Answers
a. O b. S c. O d. S e. O

 Option: Have students find the following words in Conversation B on page 54 and use the context to figure out the meanings of the words. Have them write their definitions. Then have them work with partners to compare their definitions. You may also want them to write a sentence with each word.

to raise	formula	to inspire
to approve	to increase	to propose
to change one's mind	to decrease	basis

Link ***Workbook: Practice 2***

Talk About It

 Option: You may prefer to postpone this activity until after the grammar presentation (page 56) if you feel students need extra help with sentences that have hypothetical conditions and results.

Presentation

Note: The purpose of this activity is to develop fluency. Students should be encouraged to speak without fear of interruption for error correction. If you notice persistent errors, write them down for later reteaching or review.

❻ Have students read the instructions and the model conversation. Then have a pair of students read the conversation aloud for the class.

Have each student interview four other students and record their answers in the chart. Make sure to allow enough time for students to complete the activity. Then, either in groups or as a class, ask students to report about the people they interviewed.

 Option: Have students use the two questions to interview other students in their school. After students have recorded the answers, help them organize the information in two graphs on the board, one for each question. Then have them analyze the information. What were the most popular responses to each question? Finally, you might want to have students make posters listing the most original answers, the funniest answers, the most common answers, the most surprising answers, and so on.

Link ***Workbook: Practice 3***

☑ ④ **Vocabulary Check** Match the words with their meanings.

_____ **1.** to last (line 2)   **a.** dishonest; secretive

_____ **2.** restless (line 3)   **b.** easily bothered or irritated

_____ **3.** to bring up (line 17)   **c.** to mention; to talk about; to suggest

_____ **4.** to offend (line 25)   **d.** to show

_____ **5.** oversensitive (line 26)   **e.** to continue

_____ **6.** underhanded (line 29)   **f.** to upset; to make angry

_____ **7.** to reflect (line 38)   **g.** dissatisfied; nervous

⑤ Does each pair of words or expressions have the same (**S**) or opposite (**O**) meaning? Write **S** or **O**.

_____ **a.** Isn't this the life?/Life is not good.

_____ **b.** observing/watching.

_____ **c.** authentic/fake

_____ **d.** go along with/give support

_____ **e.** permanent/temporary

Talk About It

⑥ Interview four of your classmates to find out what they would do if they had the time and money. Write their answers in the chart.

Ask for hypothetical information.

A: What would you do if you had a lot of extra time?

Give information.

B: I wouldn't work. I'd study photography.

Ask for more information.

A: And what would you do if you had all the money you wanted?

Give more information.

B: I wouldn't waste any time. I'd travel around the world.

	Name	Time	Money
1.			
2.			
3.			
4.			

Talking About Unreal Situations: The Second Conditional

Conditional sentences usually consist of an *if* clause (condition) and a result clause, which can be in either order. First conditionals describe real or possible conditions and results.

Possible Condition	Possible Result
If our advertising plan **works**,	we **will make** it a permanent policy.
(If + *present tense*)	(will + *verb*)

We use the second conditional to talk about hypothetical or unreal conditions in the present or future. The result clause describes unreal consequences.

Hypothetical Condition	Hypothetical Result
If Alice **had** a year-long vacation,	she **would sail** around the world.
(If + *past tense*)	(would + *verb*)

1 **Check Your Understanding** Read the conditional statement. Then, check the statement that is true.

   a. If today were a holiday, I'd go to the beach.

      ____ Today is a holiday.   ____ Today is not a holiday.

   b. We'll buy a new car if we don't have any other expenses this year.

      ____ We hope to get a new car.   ____ We are sure we'll buy a new car.

   c. Bob would be considered for a promotion if he worked harder.

      ____ Bob will probably get a promotion.   ____ Bob doesn't work hard.

   d. If John has another offer, he won't take this job.

      ____ John might get another offer.   ____ John won't get another offer.

   e. Carmen would help if she weren't busy.

      ____ Carmen will probably help out.   ____ Carmen is busy.

2 On a separate sheet of paper, change the sentences from the first to the second conditional. Then compare your answers with a partner's.

Example:

If the supervisor has time, we will meet with him tomorrow.

If the supervisor had time, we would meet with him tomorrow.

   a. If our supervisors accept our plan, we will implement it immediately.

   b. If we implement our plan, sales will increase rapidly.

   c. If customers buy more products, the company's profits will rise.

   d. If the company shows more profits, the president will be grateful.

   e. If the president is grateful, he'll give us a year-long vacation and a raise.

GRAMMAR

Talking About Unreal Situations: The Second Conditional

Preview

- To review the first conditional, write the following possible conditions on the board and ask students to provide logical results.

  If you study hard, … (you will get into a good university).

  If you don't study hard, … (you will get a low grade).

  Ask students to identify for each sentence the condition clause, or **if** clause, and the result clause. For example, in the first sentence, the condition clause is "If you study hard," and the result clause is "you will get into a good university." Ask, *Can the positions of the condition clause and the result clause be reversed?* (yes) Ask students to reverse the clauses in the sentences. (*Example:* You'll get into a good university if you study hard.) Then focus students' attention on the meaning of these conditional sentences. Ask, *Do these sentences represent real possibilities?* (yes) Finally, have students practice using conditional sentences by asking them a few questions beginning, *What will happen if … ?* and having them answer them.

- To introduce the second conditional, mention an exotic, faraway place and ask students whether it is probable that they will live there soon. (no) Have students imagine what they would do in that exotic place if they actually lived there. Write the following sentences on the board.

  If I lived in (Bali), I would learn (Indonesian).

  If I lived there, I would also visit (the temples).

  Ask students to identify the condition clause and the result clause in each of

these sentences. Ask them how these conditionals differ from the others in form. Elicit that the verb in the condition clauses is in the past tense (**lived**) and the auxiliary verb in the result clause is **would** instead of **will**. Ask how these conditionals differ from the others in meaning. Elicit that they are about improbable or impossible situations. Finally, ask students to work in pairs to tell where they would visit if they could. Ask them to make sentences like the models. Have students share their sentences with the class.

Presentation

Have students read the explanations and example sentences silently in class or for homework. Then review the explanations with the class. Ask if the past tense form of the verb in the **if** clause indicates past time or refers to the present. (refers to the present) Ask students to think of additional examples using the second conditional. Point out that with the second conditional, the first- and third-person singular forms (**I**, **he, she, it**) use **were** rather than **was**.

Language Note: You may want to explain that in informal situations many speakers use **was**, instead of **were**, with **I, he, she**, and **it**.

Punctuation Note: You may want to focus students' attention on the comma used to separate clauses in the example sentences. Point out that the comma is always used when the **if** clause comes first. When the result clause is first, no comma is used.

☑ ❶ **Check Your Understanding** Have students read the directions and complete the activity independently. Then have them work in pairs to check their answers before reviewing them as a class.

Answers

a. Today is not a holiday. **b.** We hope to get a new car. **c.** Bob doesn't work hard. **d.** John might get another offer. **e.** Carmen is busy.

(*Exercise 2 discussion appears on page T57.*)

(*See Exercise 2 on page 56.*)

❷ After students read the instructions and the example, have them write the sentences independently and then compare their answers with a partner's. Then review the answers as a class.

Answers

a. If our supervisors accepted our plan, we would implement it immediately. **b.** If we implemented our plan, sales would increase rapidly. **c.** If customers bought more products, the company's profits would rise. **d.** If the company showed more profits, the president would be grateful. **e.** If the president were grateful, he would give us a year-long vacation and a raise.

❸ You may wish to elicit or present **yacht.** Have students complete the exercise independently. Then review the answers as a class.

Answers

Answers may vary. **1.** would … do **2.** won **3.** would stop **4.** wouldn't … get **5.** didn't have **6.** would buy **7.** would travel **8.** would … go **9.** would go **10.** Would … stop

Option: Tell students that you are thinking of someone in the class. They are to guess who the person is by asking, "If this person were a (boat), what kind of (boat) would (she) be?" Answer by saying, *If this person were a (boat), (she'd) be (an expensive yacht).* Students should ask about a kind of animal, bird, flower, car, house, tree, book, movie, building, perfume, shoes, jacket, and so on until someone guesses who the person is.

❹ Have students read the directions independently. Then review the sample conversations with the class before having the pairs develop their conversations. You may want to ask pairs to present their conversations to small groups or the rest of the class.

Answers

Conversations will vary. **a.** improbable **b.** probable **c.** probable **d.** improbable

Link *Workbook: Practices 4, 5, 6, 7*

3 Think of verbs that make sense in the conversation. Write the correct verb forms on the lines.

BOB: What (1.) _____ you _____ if you (2.) _____ $6 million?

TOM: That's easy. I (3.) _____ working immediately!

BOB: But (4. *neg.*) _____ you _____ bored?

TOM: Not at all. If I (5. *neg.*) _____ to work, I (6.) _____ a yacht, and I (7.) _____ to exotic places. I've always wanted to be a professional traveler.

BOB: That sounds fantastic. Where (8.) _____ you _____ first?

TOM: I (9.) _____ somewhere warm. That's for sure.

BOB: (10.) _____ you _____ playing the lottery?

TOM: Are you kidding? I'd buy it!

4 Read the situation. Is the result probable (real) or improbable (unreal)? With a partner, take turns asking and answering questions.

Examples:

- Sam isn't doing well in his job. His boss threatened to fire him.
  lose his job

A: Do you think Sam will lose his job? (*probable*)

B: Yes, he's had some big problems lately, but if he loses it, he'll just look for another one.

- Jill's doing very well in her job. In fact, her boss gave her a promotion.
  lose her job

A: Do you think Jill will lose her job? (*improbable*)

B: Of course not. Her boss loves her. But if she somehow lost her job, she'd get another one really fast.

a. Pam has wanted to visit New York City ever since she read about theaters on Broadway. She wants to go this year, but she has to pay her college tuition.   **go to New York this year**

b. The Wongs spend three hours a day driving to work in rush hour traffic. They'd like to live closer to work, so they're saving money to buy a new house.   **move closer to work**

c. Jason is having trouble with calculus. He missed a lot of classes at the beginning of the semester. Now he's trying to catch up, but he really doesn't understand it.   **fail the course**

d. Claudette has always wanted a red sports car, but she'll never earn enough money to buy one. This week she bought a lottery ticket. The chance of winning the lottery is 1 in 27,000,000.   **get a red sports car**

Asking for and Giving Advice

We also use the second conditional to ask for and to give advice.

> **If I were you, ...**
>
> **A:** My boss just gave me two months of paid vacation! What **would** you **do if** you **were** me?
>
> **B:** **If** I **were** you, I**'d rent** a house by the sea and **write** a screenplay.

 Were is used with all persons in unreal *if* clauses.

 5 **Express Yourself** Work with a partner. Read the situations. Take turns asking for and giving advice. Use the second conditional.

    a. You're twenty-one and you have a good job. Your boyfriend/ girlfriend wants to get married. You want to have children someday, but you're not sure you're ready to get married now.

    b. You work with a friend who is driving everyone crazy because she gossips all the time. She also gets offended when anyone criticizes her.

    c. The children in the apartment next to yours play music so loudly that you can't even hear your TV.

    d. Your eighteen-year-old son wants to move to another country, but you don't approve. You think it will be too dangerous for him.

    e. When you get home from shopping, you realize that the clerk has charged you too much money.

LISTENING and SPEAKING

Listen: Workplace Changes

 1 **Before You Listen** If you could have any kind of job you wanted, what would it be? Would you go to an office? Work at home? What would your workplace be like?

STRATEGY **Listening to Summarize** When you listen, it's a good idea to focus on the most important ideas and one or two of the most important details so that you can later summarize the main content of the conversation.

  2 The members of the Planning Committee at Ajax Corporation are discussing workplace changes they want to recommend. Listen and then complete the chart on page 59.

Asking for and Giving Advice

Preview

Ask students to pretend that a classmate has been having a problem with his car. Have students give advice to this classmate. Elicit the advice from the students. Then write it on the board.

Examples:

You should take your car to a mechanic.
You ought to have your car checked at
    the dealer's.
You should buy a new car.

Explain that another way of giving advice is to use the second conditional. Write the following advice on the board.

If I were you, I would buy a new car.

Presentation

Have students read the explanation and the examples independently in class or for homework. Then review the explanation and the examples with the class. Ask students to give examples of other situations in which the second conditional could be used to give advice. Have them also give the examples of advice for those situations. (*Example:* A situation in which a friend has a difficult roommate: If I were you, I would look for another roommate.) Remind students that in the second conditional **were** is used with all pronouns.

⑤ Express Yourself Have students read the directions independently. Then have them complete the activity with their partners. You may want to ask pairs to present their conversations to small groups or to the rest of the class. (*Answers will vary.*)

 Workbook: Practice 8

Listen: Workplace Changes

Presentation

❶ Before You Listen Have students read the questions independently. Then discuss their responses as a class. Have students note the different workplaces their classmates prefer.

➡ **Listening to Summarize** Have students read the strategy. Then ask them to give examples of situations in which people summarize what they've heard. (*Examples:* summarizing a lecture for a friend who wasn't in class, summarizing a movie, summarizing an important news story for someone who didn't hear it)

❷ Have students read the directions independently. Then focus their attention on the chart. Remind them to write down the main idea and one or two important details on each line of the chart. Then play the recording or read the conversation aloud two or more times. Have students write their responses.

Audioscript: The audioscript for Exercise 2 appears on page T155.

> **Answers**
> Answers will vary.
> **Idea 1:** flextime—employees work eight hours but can decide when to come and go
> **Idea 2:** home-based office hours—possible by connecting everyone's computer
> **Idea 3:** videophones—can be used for electronic conferences and meetings
> **Idea 4:** child-care facilities at the company for workers who have to stay late or live far away

T58

❸ Have partners compare their charts. Then review the answers as a class.

 Option: Ask students to talk about the ideas discussed by the committee. You might want to lead a discussion about the students' reactions to the ideas. Which of the ideas do they like best? Why? Which do they like the least? Why?

Link *Workbook: Practice 9*

Pronunciation

Presentation

Have students read the explanation independently in class or for homework.

🎧 **❹** Have students read the instructions independently. Then play the recording or read the sentences aloud two or more times. Be sure that everyone hears the stressed syllables and the rhythm. Next, have students work in pairs to say the sentences. Finally, ask several students to say the sentences to the class.

❺ Have students read the instructions and complete the activity independently or in pairs.

> **Answers**
> <u>What</u> would you <u>think</u> if I <u>sang</u> out of
>   <u>tune</u>?
> <u>Would</u> you <u>stand</u> up and <u>walk</u> out on <u>me</u>?
> <u>Lend</u> me your <u>ears</u> and I'll <u>sing</u> you a <u>tune</u>,
> <u>And</u> I'll <u>try</u> not to <u>sing</u> out of <u>key</u>.

 Workbook: Practice 10

Speak Out

Presentation

➡ **Encouraging and Discouraging** Have students read the strategy and the examples in the box on page 60. Focus attention on the language for encouraging and discouraging. Then write on the board, *The boss is in a really good mood, so I think I'll ask him today if we can have flextime.* Have students respond to the statement with the first expression for encouraging, **That's a wonderful idea**.

Next, write on the board, *The boss is in a really bad mood, but I think it's OK to discuss flextime with him today anyway.* Have students respond to this statement with the first expression for discouraging, **I'm not sure about that**. Have students think of additional situations and then ask them to make sentences for these situations with the other expressions for encouraging and discouraging, as appropriate.

Summary of Workplace Changes Discussed
Idea 1
Idea 2
Idea 3
Idea 4

3 Compare your summary with a partner's. Did you include main ideas and one or two important details?

Pronunciation

Rhythm

In English, we speak in thought groups. In each thought group, the stressed syllables, unstressed syllables, and pauses combine to create a special beat or rhythm. This beat is even and goes from stressed syllable to stressed syllable, no matter how many unstressed syllables fall between.

4 Listen to the sentences. Focus on how the stressed syllables carry the rhythm. With a partner, take turns saying the sentences.

	●		●		●
a. I		TAKE			TIME.
b. I	would	TAKE			TIME.
c. I	would	TAKE	a lot of		TIME.
d. I	wouldn't	TAKE	a lot of		TIME.
e. I	wouldn't	TAKE	a lot of your		TIME.

5 Read the excerpt from the Beatles' song, *A Little Help from My Friends*. Each thought group has four stressed syllables. Underline the stressed syllables.

What would you think if I sang out of tune?

Would you stand up and walk out on me?

Lend me your ears and I'll sing you a tune,

And I'll try not to sing out of key.

6 Listen to the song and check your answers. Then practice reading the lyrics with a partner.

Speak Out

STRATEGY **Encouraging and Discouraging** If you agree with someone's idea, it is common to offer encouragement or support. When you believe someone's idea is unwise or wrong, you can politely express discouragement.

Encouraging	Discouraging
That's a wonderful idea.	I'm not sure about that.
I completely support you on that.	I'd think about that again.
You've got a good point.	I don't think I can support you there.

 7 Work in groups of three. Each of you reads about a different situation, **A, B,** or **C.** Describe your situation to the group and try to agree on the best course of action. Use the language for encouraging and discouraging.

A. Lydia has tickets for a concert by her favorite band. She has just read in the paper that there are some fake tickets on the market. Lydia suspects that her tickets are fake because they were inexpensive. What would you do if you were Lydia?

B. Kevin is on the cleaning staff in a perfume factory. The company is famous for its secret perfume formula. Kevin thinks a manager may be a spy because he saw this person looking at other people's papers. What would you do if you were Kevin?

C. Paulina is working at her computer, and she accidentally discovers a way to make free long-distance phone calls with it. What would you do if you were Paulina?

READING and WRITING

Read About It

 Before You Read If you "had your way," how would you change the world?

 Getting Meaning from Context You can often figure out the meaning of unknown words from the context. Pay attention to other words and sentences, and to grammar and punctuation clues in the text that help clarify meaning.

Utopias: Nowhere Lands

Men and women throughout history have dreamed of a perfect world where people would live in peace and harmony. A vision of the best of all worlds came to be called utopia after Sir Thomas More came up with the term in 1516 to name his subjective vision of an ideal world. However, even before his time, philosophers, including Plato, had described perfect societies.
5 And since More's time, other dreamers have planned and even carried out their ideas for a better world.

Many of the world's great utopias were only theoretical, never to be carried out in reality. The creators, however, carefully planned every aspect of utopian life. They designed the physical appearance of their utopias, decided upon the ideal number of people to live in them,
10 and created systems for education, culture, politics, law, and economic life.

Note: The purpose of this activity is to develop fluency. Students should be encouraged to speak without fear of interruption for error correction. If you notice persistent errors, write them down for later reteaching or review.

❻ Have students read the instructions, break into groups, and complete the activity. Make sure students understand that they should talk about each situation and come to a consensus on the best course of action first. Have the groups compare their final decisions. (*Responses will vary.*)

 Workbook: Practice 11

READING and WRITING

Read About It

Preview

* Have students name some famous people who changed the course of history. (Possible answers include Christopher Columbus, Albert Einstein, Catherine the Great, Madame Curie, Abraham Lincoln, and Napoleon Bonaparte.) Have them explain how these people changed the world.

* Focus attention on the picture on page 61. What relationship do students think the picture might have to the reading? (If students don't have any ideas, have them read the first sentence of the text.)

Presentation

❶ **Before You Read** Have students read the directions independently. Then have them share their ideas in small groups or with the rest of the class. You might want to give them a few minutes to jot down their ideas first.

➡ **Getting Meaning from Context** Have students read the strategy. Make sure students understand the different kinds of context clues they can use.

Have students read the article independently in class or for homework. If they read it in class, you might want to set a time limit. Tell students to use context clues when they come across unfamiliar words. Ask them to think about the context clues they use in each case.

Option: Check comprehension by writing the following questions on the board or asking them orally. Have students work in pairs or in small groups to check their answers.

1. What is a utopia? (a vision of a perfect world where everyone lives in peace and harmony)

2. What did the planners of some utopias include in their plans? (physical appearance; number of people; systems for education, culture, politics, law, and economic life)

3. How did Sir Thomas More envision his utopia? (as an island divided into sections; groups of families chose elders to be in government; everyone worked six hours a day; people ate together in the town dining room; and criminals were made into slaves)

4. Who founded New Harmony, Indiana? What was New Harmony like? (Robert Owen; people were divided into groups in charge of farming, manufacturing, and education; families lived in their own homes but ate together in the town dining room; all children went to school; the town organized its own publications and cultural events)

5. What happened to New Harmony? Why? (It ended in 1828 because the people couldn't agree on the type of government to have.)

Option: Have students write questions of their own, based on the reading, and exchange them in groups. Have the groups share their questions and answers with the rest of the class.

❷ Have students read the directions and write the meanings of the words. Tell them not to be concerned with getting the definitions exactly right. Then have them check their dictionaries.

Answers
Answers will vary. **a.** a dream, thought, idea **b.** an idea or place of perfection (students will have personal ideas) **c.** personal **d.** to make happen, put into effect **e.** existing as an idea only **f.** to end, break up **g.** creators, people who established something **h.** the same

❸ Have students read the instructions and work in pairs to complete the activity. Remind them of the various clues mentioned in the strategy. What kinds of clues did students find most useful? How close do their definitions come to the actual definitions?

Think About It

Presentation

❹–❺ Have students read the directions independently. Then have them discuss their responses in pairs or in small groups. Have students write down their responses. Then ask individuals or groups to share their ideas with the class.

☸ **Option:** Divide the class into small groups. Have the groups plan their own utopias: Select a name and describe the physical setting (an island, top of a mountain), the number of inhabitants, the political structure (a king/queen, a president, a parliament, no government), the economic system (everything belonging to everybody, individual ownership), the structure for family and marriage (no marriage, children belonging to everyone), the system of punishment for crime (prison, alternatives to prison), and the system of education (formal schools, an alternative to schools, education for everyone, education for only some, practical subjects only).

Have the groups illustrate their utopias. Display the descriptions and illustrations. Discuss the similarities and differences.

T61

Write: An Analysis

(*See page 62.*)

Preview

• Have students work in pairs to consider whether they would move to a foreign country if they were offered a job there. Ask them to think about the advantages and disadvantages they would need to consider to make a decision. Have them make a list and share their lists with other pairs or small groups.

• Ask students to tell how they would organize their ideas in a paragraph that answers the question "Would you move to a foreign country if you were offered a job there?" Discuss students' ideas and the possible patterns of organization as a class. Compare responses with the model paragraph on page 62. (topic sentence, advantages, disadvantages, concluding sentences.)

Presentation

Have students read the explanation independently in class.

❻ Have students read the paragraph and complete the activity independently. Have them check their answers in pairs and then as a class.

Answers
1. TS 2. A 3. A 4. A 5. transition sentence 6. D 7. D 8. D 9. D 10. CS

❼ If necessary, review the meaning of logical connectors. (words whose main use is to show the relationships between ideas) Review the answers as a class.

Answers
Answers will vary. Numbers are student book sentence numbers. **3.** also = adds information **4.** Last (but not least) = signals the last point in the sequence **5.** On the other hand = shows contrast **7.** For example = begins an example **8.** In addition = adds information **9.** Finally = signals the last point in the sequence **10.** In conclusion = sums up; but = shows contrast

More, for example, described his utopia as a small island divided into many sections, each with its own town. Groups of families chose elders to be in the government. Together, the elders chose a prince to direct the government. Everyone had to work six hours a day and people ate together in the town dining room. The government never killed criminals—instead,

15 criminals were made into slaves.

Some people actually tried to create real utopias. One of them was New Harmony, Indiana. A wealthy factory owner, Robert Owen, started it in 1825. The people were divided into groups in charge of farming,

20 manufacturing, and education. There was one store, and every day workers got "work credits" to spend there. Families lived in their own homes, but everyone ate together in the town dining room. All children attended school, where they studied English,

25 math, science, philosophy, and farming. The town printed its own books and newspapers, and organized plays, concerts, and dances. However, there was disagreement over how to govern the community, and in 1828 the utopia dissolved.

New Harmony, Indiana

All founders of utopias have believed that humanity, if given the opportunity, would work

30 toward its own personal and social fulfillment. Their utopias have been very different in design, but all have had an identical goal: the creation of a society in which everyone works in peace for the common good.

2 Review the article. On a sheet of paper, write definitions of these words. Do not use a dictionary.

   a. vision (line 2)

   b. utopia (line 2)

   c. subjective (line 3)

   d. to carry out (line 5)

   e. theoretical (line 7)

   f. to dissolve (line 28)

   g. founders (line 29)

   h. identical (line 31)

3 Work with a partner. Compare the strategies you used to figure out meaning from context. Did you use the same strategies?

Think About It

4 Do you think a utopia can succeed? Why or why not?

5 What would your utopia be like? Name five features.

Write: An Analysis

When you write an analysis, you are evaluating an idea, a decision, or a course of action. To do this, it is useful to examine the advantages and disadvantages of the issue.

6 Read the paragraph. Label each sentence according to its function.
TS = Topic Sentence; **A** = Advantage; **D** = Disadvantage;
CS = Concluding Sentence. Sentence 5 has been labeled.

(**1**) If I were offered a job in another country, I would have to think carefully before accepting it. (**2**) One advantage would be that I could get to know a culture other than my own. (**3**) I would also be able to learn a new language in its natural context. (**4**) Last but not least, I am sure the entire experience would be fun and exciting. (**5**) On the other hand, I would have to give serious thought to such a move because there would also be disadvantages. (**6**) One disadvantage would be that I would have many things to learn in a short time. (**7**) For example, I would have to learn a new language immediately and get used to a new job. (**8**) In addition, it would be expensive to move and settle in. (**9**) Finally, I would probably miss my family and friends back home. (**10**) In conclusion, if I got the job, I think I would accept it to get the experience of living in a foreign country, but I think it would take time and patience to adapt and live there happily.

1. _____   6. _____
2. _____   7. _____
3. _____   8. _____
4. _____   9. _____
5. _transition sentence_ 10. _____

7 Work with a partner. Underline the logical connectors used in the paragraph above. Then identify the function of each one.

Example:

1. *If = a condition*

Write About It

8 Imagine you just got a job with a large company. They have given you the choice of working in one of their offices in a large city or in a small town. Write a paragraph in which you analyze the advantages and disadvantages to explain your choice. Use the paragraph in Exercise 6 as a model.

9 **Check Your Writing** Exchange papers with a partner. Use the questions below to give feedback. Offer any feedback for improving your partner's paragraph. When you get your paper back, revise as necessary.

> • Are the author's points well explained?
> • Are both advantages and disadvantages analyzed?
> • What transition words are used to signal relationships between ideas?

Write About It

❽ Have students read the directions independently. Then have them brainstorm first the disadvantages and advantages of working in a large city and then the disadvantages and advantages of working in a small town. Have them make a decision, based on their notes. Then have them write a paragraph in response to the question, using the paragraph in Exercise 6 as a model.

☑ **❾ Check Your Writing** Have students read the directions and then complete the activity. After partners have given each other feedback, have students revise their papers.

 Option: For additional experience, have students write a paragraph on one of the following topics. Students should make a decision and support it with an analysis.

1. You are given the opportunity to study abroad for one year. What are the advantages and disadvantages of studying abroad?

2. You are offered a job working after school every day and one day on the weekend. What are the advantages and disadvantages of accepting the job?

3. You are offered the choice of working at home or working in the office. What are the advantages and disadvantages of each possibility?

Link *Workbook: Practice 12*

Vocabulary Expansion: Prefixes *under–, mis–, over–* See page T145.

Answers
A. **1.** not enough, below normal
   2. wrongly, badly **3.** move excessive
B. **1.** overeat **2.** oversensitive **3.** underage
   4. misread **5.** undereducated **6.** overreact **7.** underpay **8.** misbehave
---

 Workbook: Practice 13

EVALUATION

See page TExi.

Unit 6 Achievement Test

Self-Check See **Check Your Knowledge,** page 48 of the Workbook.

Dictation Dictate the following sentences. Then have students write sentences about themselves by replacing the **if** clauses in sentences 2, 5, and 6 and the result clauses in sentences 1, 3, 4, and 7. For more information on dictation, see page TExv.

1. If vacations lasted all year, we would do something exotic like observe gorillas in Africa.
2. If I had more money, I would move to a foreign country.
3. If I have some free time this weekend, I'll go to the beach.
4. If I could make any change in our school, I would make the schedule more flexible.
5. If I study harder and make sure that I understand everything, I'll do well in this course.
6. If I were less selfish, I would have more friends.
7. If we lived in a utopia, everyone in our society would work in peace for the common good.

Communication Skills

1. Display a variety of pictures showing workplace and vacation situations. Have students describe each situation. Then lead a discussion about the pictures, trying to elicit the unit vocabulary. Which of these workplaces/vacations would students prefer?

2. Have students talk about what they would do in these situations.

What would you do …

… if you were in a bank and it was robbed?

… if you won the lottery?

… if you were a famous person?

… if you saw a UFO?

Review Units 4–6

Unit review exercises can be assigned for homework or done in class. You can use them in different ways.

- Give the review exercises as a quiz. Have students work alone and submit their answers to you.

- Give the review exercises as you would other exercises in the book. Students work alone and then compare answers with a partner.

- Have students work alone and then review answers as a class. Have selected students write their answers on the board. Then correct any errors as a class.

❶ Have students read the instructions independently and then complete the exercise. For general notes on the past perfect tense, refer students to Unit 4, page 35.

Answers
1. had delivered 2. had decorated 3. (had) set 4. had started 5. brought *or* had brought 6. had lit

❷ Have students read the instructions independently and then complete the exercise. For general notes on the past perfect tense, refer students to Unit 4, page 35; for general notes on the past perfect progressive, refer them to Unit 4, page 36.

Answers
1. had been working 2. had gotten 3. decided 4. Did … slip and fall 5. didn't think 6. finished 7. did … do 8. went 9. saw 10. had swollen

❸ Have students read the instructions independently and then complete the exercise. For general notes on gerunds, refer students to Unit 5, page 45; for general notes on verbs that take gerunds and verbs that take infinitives, refer students to Unit 5, page 46.

Answers
1. preferred doing/preferred to do 2. worry about making 3. decided to study 4. started preparing/started to prepare 5. began bringing/began to bring 6. enjoys being

1 Complete the passage with the correct form of the verb.

Frank was really excited about surprising his wife with a birthday party. He worked hard to get everything just right. By the time he baked the birthday cake, the florist **(1. deliver)** _____ the bouquet of roses. By 5:30 p.m. he **(2. decorate)** _____ the cake and **(3. set)** _____ the table with the best china. By the time he finished wrapping her birthday present, the guests **(4. start)** _____ to arrive. Some of them **(5. bring)** _____ presents, too. By 6:00 p.m., the food was ready and Frank **(6. light)** _____ the candles. Everything was ready, but there was a problem. Where was his wife?

2 Complete the conversation with the correct form of the verb. Use the simple past, past perfect, or past perfect progressive tense. Use the negative when necessary.

BETH: Hey, Fred, what happened to your arm?

FRED: It was so stupid. I **(1. work)** _____ in the garden for a while, and I **(2. get)** _____ really dirty. So I **(3. decide)** _____ to turn on the water and clean up.

BETH: **(4. slip and fall)** _____ you _____?

FRED: Yes, right there on the wet driveway. But I **(5. think)** _____ any more about it, you know. When I **(6. finish)** _____ dinner, my arm was hurting.

BETH: So what **(7. do)** _____ you _____?

FRED: Well, I **(8. go)** _____ to the hospital. I had to sit in the waiting room for hours! By the time the doctor finally **(9. see)** _____ me, my arm **(10. swell)** _____ to double its normal size!

3 Complete the passage with the correct form of the verbs in parentheses. Use the infinitive or gerund form for the second verb.

Juan **(1. prefer/do)** _____ things himself. For example, he used to **(2. worry about/make)** _____ mistakes on his tax forms. So he **(3. decide/study)** _____ at a tax preparation school. He did well, so he **(4. start/prepare)** _____ tax forms for his friends. Soon he had his own small business. His customers **(5. begin/bring)** _____ their friends to him, and his business grew. Juan quit his first job, and now he **(6. enjoy/be)** _____ his own boss.

4 Complete the sentences with the correct preposition.

   a. Jenny is interested _____ learning to play the saxophone.

   b. She's looking forward _____ studying jazz.

   c. She insists _____ waking her family up every morning with her saxophone.

   d. Jenny's family loves her, but they plan _____ continuing to use their alarm clocks to get up in the morning.

   e. They are worried _____ telling her to stop playing and hurting her feelings.

5 Complete the conversations with a logical verb and the correct form of the second conditional.

   1. A: My sister is angry because I borrowed her rollerblades.
       What _____ you _____ if you _____ me?

     B: I _____ to her, if I _____ you.

   2. A: If I _____ a raise, I _____ a new car.

     B: Not me. I _____ the extra money in a savings account.

   3. A: _____ you _____ better luck if you turned on the copier first?

     B: Yes, I suppose that _____ . Thanks!

   4. A: Why don't you come with us to the comedy club?

     B: I really shouldn't. If I _____ a final exam tomorrow morning, I _____ .

Vocabulary Review

Use the words in the box to complete the sentences.

ambitious	prodigy
bring up	theoretical
impress	drop out of
challenge	carry out

   1. Though most utopias were _____ , some were actually built.

   2. Amy is always trying to _____ everyone with her expensive clothes.

   3. Students who _____ school usually don't do well later.

   4. Make sure you _____ our suggestions at the meeting; we want them to hear our ideas.

   5. Mozart's accomplishments at such a young age mark him as a _____ .

   6. He's a very _____ man who will one day be company president, I'm sure.

   7. Learning a second language can be a big _____ .

❹ Have students read the instructions independently and then complete the exercise. For general notes on verb + preposition combinations, refer students to the explanation and exercises in the grammar section of Unit 5, pages 45–48.

Answers
a. in b. to c. on d. on e. about

❺ Have students read the instructions independently and then complete the exercise. For general notes on the second conditional, refer students to Unit 6, pages 56–58.

Answers
Answers will vary. **1.** A: What would you do if you were me? B: I would talk to her if I were you. **2.** A: If I got a raise, I would buy a new car. B: Not me. I would put the extra money in a savings account. **3.** A: Would/Wouldn't you have better luck if you turned on the copier first? B: Yes, I suppose that I would (have better luck). **4.** B: If I didn't have a final exam tomorrow morning, I would come/go.

Vocabulary Review

Have students read the instructions independently and then complete the exercise.

Answers
1. theoretical **2.** impress **3.** drop out of
4. bring up **5.** prodigy **6.** ambitious
7. challenge

What's So Funny?

OBJECTIVES

- To talk about humor
- To report what someone said
- To report what someone asked
- To listen for definitions of terms
- To use stress to check understanding
- To report someone else's ideas
- To recognize tone
- To write a definition paragraph
- To use **tell**, **say**, **speak**, and **talk**

GETTING STARTED

Warm Up

Preview

Have students work individually, in pairs or small groups, or as a class to make a word map for **funny**, brainstorming all the related words they can think of (laugh, joke, comic, comedy, smile, humorous, clown, etc.).

Presentation

❶ Have students read the unit title and then describe what people do when something is funny (smile, laugh, and so on). Have students read and answer the questions independently. Then discuss students' responses as a class.

Language Note: **What's so funny?** is commonly used as a phrase in two situations: (1) when someone is laughing and we don't understand the joke or the comical situation; (2) when we're annoyed that someone is laughing, for example, when we think they're laughing at us.

🌐 **Option:** If students had difficulty coming up with a list of things that make people laugh, you might write the following items on the board: *jokes; strange or unusual appearances; funny movies or TV shows; comic books; embarrassing situations, such as slipping on a banana peel; comedians; limericks; silly rhymes;* etc. Have students give an example of each and explain what makes it funny. You might also

ask them to give examples of famous comedians, comedies, cartoonists, and so on.

🎧 ❷ Have students read the directions as a class. Have them note the definition of **pun**. If students need extra help with the definition of a pun, ask, *What's black and white and read (/rɛd/) all over?* If no one can guess, give the answer (a newspaper). If necessary, write the question on the board. Have students explain the pun. (They had probably assumed that **read**, the past tense of **read** (/rid/), was **red**, the color, because it followed the names of two other colors. Ask if puns are common in their languages. Ask students to share some.

Play the recording or read the conversation aloud two or more times and have students write down their answers. Let them work in pairs to compare responses. Review the answers as a class.

Audioscript: The audioscript for Exercise 2 appears on page T156.

Answers
buy, purchase; by, past

 Workbook: Practice 1

🌐 **Option:** The cartoon on page 65 is by American cartoonist Gary Larson. Other popular American cartoonists include Matt Groening, the creator of *The Simpsons*; Jim Davis, the creator of *Garfield*, the cat; Gary Trudeau, the creator of *Doonesbury*; and Charles Schultz, the creator of *Peanuts*, featuring Charlie Brown and Snoopy. You may want to bring in one or more books by these artists for the class to read and enjoy.

🌐 **Option:** You may want to bring in cartoons from local sources or from other countries. Have students say which ones they find funny and why. If you've brought in cartoons from different cultures, ask students if they think humor is the same across cultures and if people from different cultures would understand and appreciate the various cartoons.

GETTING STARTED

Warm Up

1 A cartoon is usually intended to make people laugh. What do you think this cartoon is about? Do you think it's funny? Why or why not? Brainstorm a list of things that make people laugh. Share your list with the class.

2 Many jokes contain puns. A pun is a play on words that sound the same but have different meanings. Puns are funny because the meaning of a word is confused with that of another. Listen to the dialogue. Which word is being played on? Which word can it be confused with? Write the words and meanings on the lines.

Word 1: _____

Meaning 1: _____

Word 2: _____

Meaning 2: _____

Figure It Out

Linda Garcia is a reporter for the Jasper TV station. This morning she interviewed a famous comedian, Ed Davis, for the local news.

GARCIA: Welcome back, Mr. Davis. How does it feel to come back to your hometown now that you're a famous standup comic?

5 **DAVIS:** It feels the same way it did when I lived here. That's why I don't live here anymore. No, really, it's nice to be back.

GARCIA: I heard you're going to do a show at your old high school to raise money for the new high school fund.

10 **DAVIS:** That's right. It'll be this Friday evening at 8 o'clock at Jasper High.

GARCIA: You must have happy memories of your school days.

DAVIS: Yes, actually, my teachers are the ones who discovered my talent. They were always telling me what a clown I was. But at least my classmates thought my jokes were hilarious.

15 **GARCIA:** So you learned something here?

DAVIS: Yeah, and the first thing I learned was that other kids got bigger allowances than I did! No, seriously, I learned that success comes from hard work and confidence in yourself. But now I'd just like to invite everyone to the show! I think

20 it'll be a lot of fun, and so do my joke writers!

After the interview, this article appeared in the newspaper.

Ed Davis to Perform in Hometown

This weekend, Jasper's own comedian Ed Davis will star in a show at Jasper High to help raise money for the new building project. Davis will give an evening performance on Friday at 8:00 p.m.

Davis has good memories of his high school days. He said that his teachers were the ones who had discovered his talent because they had told him he was a clown. When asked if he had learned anything in school, Davis replied that he'd learned that other kids had gotten bigger allowances than he had. But seriously, he said that high school had taught him to observe people and to see humor in ordinary events. Finally, Davis attributed his success to his own hard work and self-confidence. He said he hoped that everyone in the town would come to the show. He said he'd be on his best behavior … as long as he could.

3 Vocabulary Check Match the words on the left with their meanings on the right.

_____ **1.** comic (line 4)
_____ **2.** to raise (line 9)
_____ **3.** memories (line 11)
_____ **4.** hilarious (line 14)
_____ **5.** allowances (line 17)
_____ **6.** to attribute (news article)

a. money given by parents to children
b. very funny
c. to give the cause of
d. person who tells funny stories
e. things you don't forget
f. to collect

Figure It Out

Preview

Ask students to brainstorm the ways newspaper reporters gather information about famous people. (by interviewing them, interviewing people who know them, following them and observing their actions, reading about them, etc.)

Presentation

Have students read the introductory paragraph independently. Then focus attention on the picture. Have them predict the questions the reporter might ask the famous comedian.

Read the conversation aloud two or more times. For this conversation, you will probably want the students to listen with their books closed to see if they "get" the humorous parts. If you read the conversation aloud, you might want to chuckle after each of the following parts: "That's why I don't live here anymore!" "They were always telling me what a clown I was!" and "... that other kids got bigger allowances than I did!" Then have students read the conversation independently, in class or for homework.

Option: Have students work in pairs or groups to underline the parts of the conversation they think are funny. Have them compare their answers as a class.

Option: Have pairs of students rehearse the conversation and perform it for the rest of the class.

Have students read the newspaper article independently in class or for homework. Have them look back at the interview to verify what the reporter wrote. Ask whether the reporter used the comedian's exact words in the article or if she reported them. You might want to draw students' attention to the differences between quoting someone and reporting what he or she said.

You might want to write the following questions on the board for students to answer. Encourage students to scan the conversation and article for any information they don't remember.

1. What is Mr. Davis's hometown? (Jasper)
2. Why is he visiting his hometown? (To do a show to raise money for his old high school)
3. What did his teachers think about him? (They thought he was a clown.)
4. What did his classmates think about him? (They though he was hilarious.)
5. What were some things he learned in school? (He learned that the other students got bigger allowances. He learned that success comes from hard work and confidence in oneself.)
6. What were some of the funny things he said in the interview? (*Answers may vary somewhat.* He doesn't live in his hometown anymore because it's the same now as when he had lived there. His teachers "discovered his talent" when he was the class clown. He learned that other kids got bigger allowances. His joke writers think the show will be a lot of fun.)

☑ ❸ **Vocabulary Check** Have students read the directions and complete the activity independently. Them have them compare their answers in pairs.

> **Answers**
> 1. d 2. f 3. e 4. b 5. a 6. c

 Workbook: Practice 2

Option: Bring in information about comedians and the types of comedy they do. Then have students choose a comedian to research. Have them report on their findings to the class. For example, for Bill Cosby, they might share the following information: He has done standup comedy; appeared in movies, TV series, and comedy shows; written books, etc. They might then discuss *Cosby*—what kind of humor it involves, whether they like it and find it funny, whether it's realistic, and how it compares with other TV comedies about family life.

Talk About It

Option: You may prefer to postpone this activity until after the grammar presentation (page 68) if you feel that your students need extra help in using reported speech.

Presentation

Note: The purpose of this activity is to develop fluency. The students should speak without fear of interruption for error correction. If you notice persistent errors, write them down for later reteaching or review.

4 Have students work in pairs to read the directions and then practice the conversation in the example. Ask one pair to read the conversation aloud to the rest of the class. Have the pairs complete the activity. You might want them to complete the activity as a class, calling on different pairs of students.

Before students begin the activity, check their understanding of the vocabulary. You might want to have each student scan his or her chart for unfamiliar words. Then have them consult their partners or their dictionaries for the meanings of these words.

Option: Ask students if they agree or disagree with the quotations. Have them explain why. Then have the class decide which quotations are the funniest, the truest, the most exaggerated, and so on.

Option: Have students look up sayings by other famous people and report them to the class. You might want to write the ones they feel are the best on a poster and put it on the wall.

Option: The following people are quoted in this unit. Have students use the Internet or the library to find out more about one of them. Have them find additional quotations and report them to the class. To find quotations, they might look in a book like *Bartlett's Familiar Quotations*.

Will Rogers, 1879–1935, U.S. actor and humorist

Jules Renard, 1864–1910, French writer

James M. Barrie, 1860–1937, Scottish novelist, short-story writer, and playwright

Albert Camus, 1913–1960, French novelist, short-story writer, playwright, and essayist

Charles Lamb, 1775–1834, English essayist and critic

Michel de Montaigne, 1533–1592, French essayist

Mark Twain (Samuel Clemens), 1835–1910, U.S. author and humorist

George Bernard Shaw, 1856–1950, Irish dramatist, critic, and novelist

Fred Allen, 1894–1956, U.S. comedian

Josh Billings (Henry Wheeler Shaw), 1818–1885, U.S. humorist

Thomas Hobbes, 1588–1679, English philosopher and author

Immanuel Kant, 1724–1804, German philosopher

Sigmund Freud, 1856–1939, Austrian neurologist; founder of psychoanalysis

 Workbook: Practice 3

Talk About It

4 Famous people in history have had interesting opinions on a variety of topics. Work with a partner. One looks at Chart A below and the other looks at Chart B on page 70. Take turns asking about and reporting on what these famous people said.

Example:

Will Rogers on people who talk about themselves: "I always like to hear a man talk about himself because then I never hear anything but good."

Will Rogers, American humorist, famous for poking fun at politicians

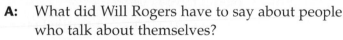
Ask what someone said.

A: What did Will Rogers have to say about people who talk about themselves?

Report what someone said.

B: He said that he always liked to hear a man talk about himself because then he never heard anything but good.

Chart A
Ask about these people's opinions:

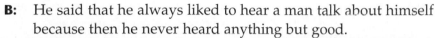

1. Jules Renard on solitude	**3.** Fran Lebowitz on life
2. James M. Barrie on age	**4.** Charles Lamb on work

Report on this information:

1. Montaigne on miracles: "I have never seen a greater miracle or monster than myself."

2. Mark Twain on education: "I have never let my schooling interfere with my education."

3. George Bernard Shaw on talking: "I believe in the discipline of silence and can talk for hours about it."

4. Fred Allen on remembering: "I always have trouble remembering three things: faces, names, and—I can't remember what the third thing is."

Mark Twain, American author

Fran Lebowitz, American author and comic

GRAMMAR

Reporting What Someone Said

When we report what someone said, we sometimes use the person's exact words, or direct speech. When we do not repeat the exact words, we use reported speech.

Direct Speech *(Baby-sitter and Child)*	Reported Speech *(Baby-sitter to Parent)*
Cindy said, "**I want** to go to the movies."	Cindy said (that) she wanted to go to the movies.
I told her, "**You went** to the movies **yesterday**."	I told her (that) she had gone to the movies the day before.
"**I haven't seen** *Funny Bones*," she complained.	She complained (that) she hadn't seen *Funny Bones*.
"**You'll see** it Friday," I explained to her.	I explained to her (that) she would see it this Friday.

1 In reported speech, we change the speaker's words in several ways. Look at the chart above. Find the words in bold print in direct speech. What do they become in reported speech?

Direct Speech   Reported Speech

a. I, want   _____*she*_____, _____

b. You, went, yesterday   _____, _____, _____

c. I, haven't seen   _____, _____

d. You, 'll see   _____, _____

When we report on a belief or general truth, we can either change the verb or not.

Samuel Butler once said, "Life is one long process of getting tired."

Samuel Butler once said that life is one long process of getting tired. (*His statement is still true today.*)

Some verbs of reporting require an object: *tell someone that* … With other reporting verbs, an object is optional: *explain (to someone) that* …

Cindy **told me** that she wanted to buy some comic books.

She **explained (to me)** that she had to report on early American comic strips.

2 Look at each of the verbs. Is an object required (**R**), or is it optional (**O**)? Circle **R** or **O**. Use the verb in a sentence to help you decide.

a. teach   R O   **c.** answer   R O   **e.** show   R O

b. report   R O   **d.** remind   R O   **f.** say   R O

GRAMMAR

Reporting What Someone Said

Preview

- Ask one student what he or she is going to do this evening. Report the statement to the class, using **said**, and write both the direct speech and the reported speech on the board. (*Example:* John said, "I'm going to watch TV this evening." John said that he was going to watch TV this evening.) Explain that the first sentence is an example of **direct speech** and the second is an example of **reported speech.** Ask students to tell you several differences between the two sentences. (The direct speech uses quotation marks; the reported speech uses **that; I** in direct speech becomes **he** in reported speech, and **am going to** becomes **was going to.**)

- Repeat the process, this time asking about something in the past to elicit different tenses. (*Example:* "What did you do after class yesterday?") Again, write both the examples of direct speech and reported speech on the board. (*Example:* Sandra said, "I did my homework after class yesterday." Sandra said that she had done her homework after class yesterday.) Ask students to identify the differences. (The direct speech uses quotation marks; the reported speech uses **that; I** in direct speech becomes **she** in reported speech; the past **did** becomes the past perfect **had done;** and **my** becomes **her.**)

- Ask questions similar to the two above, but this time write the answers as direct speech on the board and have students tell you what the corresponding reported speech is.

Presentation

Have students read the first part of the grammar explanation and the examples independently in class or for homework. Point out that **that** in reported speech can be included *or* omitted. Tell students to look carefully at the similarities and differences between the direct speech and reported speech in the box.

❶ Have students read the instructions and complete the exercise independently. Review the answers as a class. You might want to ask students what kinds of words change (pronouns, verbs, and time expressions) and how verb tenses change (present tense verbs change to past tense verbs, past tense and present perfect tense verbs change to past perfect tense verbs).

Answers
a. she, wanted b. she, had gone, the day before c. she, hadn't seen d. she, would see

To show that the verb doesn't have to change when reporting general truths or beliefs, write this quotation on the board: *Mark Twain said, "Everybody talks about the weather, but nobody does anything about it."* Point out that this statement was true when Mark Twain said it around a hundred years ago. Is it still true today? (Yes.) On the board write, *Mark Twain said that everybody talks about the weather but nobody does anything about it.* Point out that the verbs do not change in this situation.

Have students read the two other grammar explanations and the examples independently in class. Point out that the object referred to in the second explanation is the indirect object. You might want to have students make other sentences using **tell** (with an indirect object) and **explain** (*with* and *without* an indirect object).

❷ Have students read the instructions. Again, point out that the object referred to is an indirect object. Then have them complete the exercise independently or in pairs. Review the answers as a class.

Answers
a. R b. O c. O d. R e. O f. O

After reviewing the answers, point out that, in general, native English speakers prefer to use **report, answer,** and **say** without an *indirect object.*

❸ Have partners read the instructions and then write down their answers after discussing the sentences. Review the answers as a class.

Answers
Answers will vary somewhat.
a. He said that Anderson hurt the same nose that he had injured last year. **He was trying to say** that Anderson hurt his nose in the same way he had hurt it last year.
b. He said that McPherson was deliberately playing badly. **He was trying to say** that McPherson very much wanted to play well.
c. He said that X-rays showed that Yogi Berra's head had nothing in it. **He was trying to say** that the X-rays showed no injuries to Yogi Berra's head.

 Workbook: Practice 4

Reporting What Someone Asked

Preview

- To show the changes in reported questions, write these examples on the board.

  Jeff asked Gloria, "Will you help me?"
  Gloria asked Jeff, "What do you want me to do?"

  Jeff asked Gloria **if** she would help him.
  Gloria asked Jeff **what** he wanted her to do.

- Point out the use of **if** in the reporting of the yes/no question. Then have students work in pairs to compare the direct questions and the reported questions.

Presentation

Have students read the explanation and examples independently in class or for homework. Encourage them to look closely at each pair of direct question and reported question.

☑ **❹ Check Your Understanding** Have students read the directions independently and then complete the activity with a partner. After pairs have written and compared lists, discuss the differences as a class.

Answer
Direct questions use quotations and reported questions change tense (**can tell** to **could tell**, **is due** to **was due**) and pronouns (**you** to **she**, **your** to **her**). In addition, direct question word order changes in reported questions to statement word order, and yes/no reported questions add **if** or **whether**. Reported questions end with a period instead of a question mark.

❺ Have students read the directions independently. Then have them work independently or in pairs to complete the activity. Point out that **ask**, the main verb used to report questions, can be used with or without an object noun or pronoun. When students have finished, review the answers as a class.

Answers
Answers will vary somewhat; that is, proper nouns and pronouns can be used interchangeably, and various verbs can be used to introduce reported speech.
Eva said (that) she was really having trouble with English prepositions and verbs. Pete told her (that) he was great with grammar. Eva asked (him) if/whether he would help her. Pete asked (her) what she wanted to know. Eva asked (him) why a boy gets on a bus but a girl gets into a car. He said (that) it's because the boy doesn't have a driver's license. Eva asked (him) when he uses the present. Pete said (that) he uses the simple present for friends and the *perfect present* for his mother. (Point out to students that this answer is a pun.)

❻ Express Yourself Have students read the directions independently. Encourage them to use their imagination in thinking about the argument and writing the conversation. Tell them to include questions as well as statements. After students have reported their conversations to their partners, you might want to ask several pairs to report each other's conversations to the rest of the class.

(Exercise 6 Option appears on page T70.)

3 Sometimes people say things they don't mean to say. These "slips of the tongue" can be very funny. Read the sentences. Work with a partner. Discuss what you think these people said and what they intended to say.

   a. "Anderson has just injured his nose. It looks like the same nose he injured last year."
   He said …   He was trying to say …

   b. "McPherson is anxious to make a good showing. He wants to play in the worst way, and that's just what he's doing."
   He said …   He was trying to say …

   c. "Yogi Berra got hit in the head by a pitched ball. X rays of his head showed nothing."
   He said …   He was trying to say …

Reporting What Someone Asked

To introduce a reported yes/no question, we use *if* or *whether*. To introduce a reported information question, we use the question word. For both, we change the word order from question to statement form.

Direct Questions	Reported Questions
I asked Cindy, "Can you tell me about early cartoonists?"	I asked Cindy **if she could tell** me about early cartoonists.
"When is your report due?" I asked Cindy.	I asked Cindy **when her report was** due.

 4 **Check Your Understanding** Look at the chart above. How are direct and reported questions different? Work with a partner. On a sheet of paper, list as many differences as possible. Compare your list with another pair's.

5 On a sheet of paper, rewrite this conversation in reported speech.

   EVA: "I'm really having trouble with English prepositions and verbs."
   PETE: "I'm great with grammar."
   EVA: "Will you help me?"
   PETE: "What do you want to know?"
   EVA: "Why does a boy get on a bus, but a girl get into a car?"
   PETE: "It's because the boy doesn't have a driver's license!"
   EVA: "When do you use the present?"
   PETE: "I use the simple present for friends and the perfect present for my mother."

6 **Express Yourself** Imagine that you just had an argument with a good friend or your boss. Think of what your friend or boss accused you of and your responses. Write the dialogue. Then report the conversation to a partner.

Chart B
Ask about these people's opinions:

Ask about these people's opinions:

1. Montaigne on miracles   **3.** George Bernard Shaw on talking

2. Mark Twain on education   **4.** Fred Allen on remembering

Report on this information:

1. Jules Renard on solitude: "I enjoy solitude—even when I am alone."

2. James M. Barrie on age: "I am not young enough to know everything."

3. Fran Lebowitz on life: "Life is something to do when you can't get to sleep."

4. Charles Lamb on work: "I arrive very late at work in the morning, but I make up for it by leaving very early in the afternoon."

LISTENING and SPEAKING

Listen: Jokes

 Before You Listen Everyone likes to hear a good joke, but what is funny to one person may not be funny to another. Work with a partner and list topics that you think are funny.

 Listening for Definitions Speakers often define new or specialized terms with expressions such as *is called* and *is defined as*. They also define by example with words such as *for example, such as,* or *like*. Paying attention to these expressions helps you understand new words.

Jerry Seinfeld and cast

 Listen to the monologue and match the beginning of the sentence on the left with its ending on the right.

_____ **1.**	The point of a joke is	**a.** the beginning part that creates the situation.
_____ **2.**	The butt of a joke is	**b.** the necessary element that causes laughter.
_____ **3.**	The buildup is	**c.** the end of the joke that causes surprise.
_____ **4.**	The punch line is	**d.** the person or object the joke is about.

 Read the joke and answer the questions on page 71.

1. A doctor called his patient on the phone to give him the results of his tests.

2. "I have some bad news and some really bad news," said the doctor. "The bad news is that you have only twenty-four hours to live."

3. "Well," replied the patient, "if that's the bad news, what's the really bad news?"

4. "I've been trying to call you since yesterday," answered the doctor.

(Exercise 6 continued from page T69.)

 Option: Bring in or have the students bring in copies of magazines that feature articles about celebrities. (*Examples: People, Rolling Stone, Spy, Vanity Fair, Sports Illustrated.*) Have students work in pairs to find examples of the celebrities' words reported or quoted. Tell students to copy down the reported speech and the quotations. Then have them change the reported speech into quotations and the quotations into reported speech. If the celebrities are well known, you might want to have a pair of students say their words as reported speech without revealing their names, for example, "He/She said that …" Then have the other members of the class try to figure out who the celebrity is.

Workbook: Practices 5, 6, 7

LISTENING and SPEAKING

Listen: Jokes

Presentation

❶ **Before You Listen** Have students read the directions and then complete the activity. If students are having difficulty thinking of ideas, suggest some topics, for example, family members and tourists. You might also suggest that they start by thinking of jokes they know and like. Ask the partners to share their lists with the rest of the class. If students have listed such topics as fat people, race, or nationality, discuss why jokes on such topics could be offensive and hurtful.

➡ **Listening for Definitions** Have students read the strategy. Point out that definitions contain important background information for understanding main ideas.

❷ Have students read the directions. Then play the recording or read the audioscript aloud two or more times so that students can write their answers. Next, have students work in pairs to compare their answers. Review the answers as a class.

Audioscript: The audioscript for Exercise 2 appears on page T156.

> **Answers**
> **1.** b **2.** d **3.** a **4.** c

❸ Have students read the directions. Then have them work independently or in pairs to complete the activity.

> **Answers**
> **a.** 1 **b.** 4 **c.** the patient **d.** (*Answers will vary somewhat.*) Having only twenty-four hours to live is terrible, but this patient doesn't even have that—his twenty-four hours appear to be just about up.

Workbook: Practice 8

 Option: Have students write out their favorite jokes and analyze them in groups. Have them identify the four parts and decide why the jokes are successful.

Pronunciation

Preview

Write these sentences on the board.

"Is Bob coming tomorrow?"

"No, he's coming Friday."

Tell students that in this brief conversation two friends are discussing when a third friend, Bob, will come to visit them.

Have students guess which word in each sentence is the most heavily stressed. (tomorrow, Friday) To confirm the answers, say the sentences for the students, stressing *tomorrow* and *Friday*. Then have students repeat the sentences in pairs, using the appropriate stresses. Explain that these words are the most stressed because *when* Bob is coming to visit the two other friends is the most important information.

Presentation

Have students read the explanation and the examples independently in class or for homework. Then read the sentences aloud so that they can listen to the stresses. Make sure to stress the words in bold type.

❹ Have students read the directions and then work independently to complete the activity. Encourage them to think about how the conversations might sound and what information is the most important. You might divide the students into pairs to compare predictions.

🎧 ❺ Have students read the directions. Then play the recording or read the conversations in Exercise 4 aloud for students to check their predictions.

Answers

1. Who, dinner, Perry, That's, Barry 2. What time, party, What, me, I'm, I, invited 3. joke, didn't, like, everyone

---

❻ Have the partners practice the conversations. When they've finished, ask several pairs to read one or more of the conversations to the class, and have the other students listen to the stress patterns.

 Workbook: Practice 9

Speak Out

Preview

Ask students to give examples of situations in which people might want to report other people's ideas. Allow students to come up with a range of situations. Elicit that reporting other people's ideas is common in academic situations. History, literature, philosophy, psychology, and many other subjects involve discussing and writing about the ideas of many people.

Presentation

➡ **Reporting Someone Else's Ideas** Have students read the explanation and the examples of language for reporting other people's ideas. Explain that this strategy applies to writing as well as to speaking. You might want to inform students that if they don't signal that they are introducing someone else's idea, it can sound as though the idea is their own. Presenting someone else's idea as one's own is known as plagiarism and is an offense.

a. Which sentence is the buildup? _____

   b. Which sentence is the punch line? _____

   c. Who is the butt of the joke? _____

   d. What is the point of the joke? _____

Pronunciation

> **Using Stress to Check Understanding**
>
> We can use stress to emphasize a particular word. For example, when we don't understand something, we often stress that part of the sentence.
>
> **A:** **Where** did you say he was **going**?
>
> **B:** I said he was going to the **movies**.
>
> **A:** Oh, **I'm** sorry. **I** thought you said he was going to **Mary's**.

4 Read the conversations. Predict which word(s) should receive special stress. Underline each one.

   1. A: Who did you say was coming to dinner?

   　　B: I told you I invited Perry.

   　　A: That's funny. I heard you say Barry.

   2. A: What time are you going to the party?

   　　B: What party? No one asked me to go to a party!

   　　A: Oh, I'm sorry. I thought you were invited.

   3. A: Did you say you knew a good joke?

   　　B: No, I didn't. I don't like jokes.

   　　A: But everyone likes jokes.

5 Listen to the conversations. Were your predictions correct?

6 With a partner, practice reading the dialogues, focusing on stress patterns.

Speak Out

STRATEGY **Reporting Someone Else's Ideas** When you want to express in your own words what another person has said or written, you use certain expressions to signal that you are introducing someone else's ideas.

> In the words of (Thomas Hobbes), ...　　(Sigmund Freud) wrote/argued that ...
>
> (Immanuel Kant) said/stated that ...　　According to (Montaigne), ...

7 Work in groups of three. Each of you will read a different theory of humor and explain it to the group. Use the language for reporting someone else's ideas.

Sigmund Freud, Austrian psychologist

a. Thomas Hobbes's theory: The pleasure we feel at humor comes from our feeling of superiority over those we laugh at. Other people or groups seem inferior, and the joke teller and listener feel better than the others.

b. Immanuel Kant's theory: We see something as humorous because two ideas are connected that are not normally related. Things are out of their normal order and contrasted in an unexpected way.

c. Sigmund Freud's theory: We find humor in situations that bring us relief from conforming to society's expectations. We laugh because we can break social rules with no serious consequences, and as a result, we feel relief.

READING and WRITING

Read About It

 1 **Before You Read**

a. Every culture has legends, folktales, and fairy tales. List some fairy tales you know. Why do you think fairy tales remain popular generation after generation?

b. One well-known fairy tale is "Little Red Riding Hood." It is a story about a little girl, a basket of food, her grandmother, and a wolf. Can you tell this fairy tale?

 Recognizing Tone When you read, you understand more if you pay attention to tone—the attitude the writer adopts in the text. You can identify the writer's tone by the way he or she writes. A text can have a humorous tone, an ironic tone, an informative tone, or a persuasive tone, among others.

 2 Pay attention to the writer's tone as you read the story below.

The Little Girl and the Wolf

by James Thurber

One afternoon a big wolf waited in a dark forest for a little girl to come along carrying a basket of food to her grandmother. Finally, a little girl did come along and she was carrying a basket of food. "Are you carrying that basket to your grandmother?" asked the wolf. The little girl said yes, she was. So the wolf asked her where her grandmother lived and the little girl told him and he disappeared into the wood.

❼ Divide the class into groups of three to complete the activity. Have the groups read the directions. Then have some of the groups report their theories to the class. Does the class agree that the students have accurately reported their theories?

Option: As an alternative to the discussion method described in the Student Book, divide the class into three groups. Give each group a card or slip of paper on which you have written one of the three theories of humor. Have each group study and discuss its theory in preparation for explaining it.

After three or four minutes, have students form new groups of three, with one student from each of the previous groups. Have each student explain from memory the theory he or she studied. Encourage students to use the language for reporting ideas. Have each new group discuss all the theories as well as their own ideas.

Option: Have a class discussion on the three theories of humor. Do all the theories make sense to students? Which ones do they agree with? Why? Encourage students to use reported speech to introduce the ideas they want to comment on.

 Workbook: Practices 10, 11

Option: Bring in English-language newspapers and magazines with interviews; transcripts of speeches, debates, or discussions; editorials or letters to the editor; or articles discussing people's ideas. Have students read and report on a piece that is of interest to them. Make sure they use the language for reporting ideas and make the grammatical changes necessary for reported speech. You might want to encourage them to present their own ideas as well. Is it clear to the class which ideas are the students' and which are those of others?

READING and WRITING

Read About It

Preview

Ask, *In addition to jokes, what kinds of stories have people traditionally told?* (legends, folktales, fairy tales, myths, fables, etc.) If students have trouble answering, ask them what kinds of stories children usually listen to at bedtime or hear from their grandparents and parents?

Presentation

❶ Before You Read Have students read and discuss their responses to section **a** in pairs, in small groups, or as a class. Also, ask them to name their favorite fairy tales and explain why they like them.

Have students read and respond to section **b.** If no one can tell the story of "Little Red Riding Hood," tell students the story. If you know various versions of the story, tell the various versions and have students compare them and discuss similarities and differences.

➡ Recognizing Tone Have students read the strategy. Emphasize that tone is the writer's attitude toward his or her subject (topic). Make sure students understand each of the following tones: humorous, ironic, informative, persuasive. Explain the importance of this strategy. Ask, *What happens if we take seriously something that was intended to be ironic, or if we think something that was intended to persuade us was really intended to give us information?* You might want to bring in short texts that exemplify the tones mentioned.

❷ Focus attention on the cartoon on page 73. Have students describe it. What can they predict about the tone of the story by looking at the picture? Then have students read the story independently, in class, or for homework, keeping tone in mind.

Note: James Thurber, 1894–1961, was a well-known American humorist. As in this case, he illustrated his own stories.

Note: The Metro-Goldwyn lion is the lion that roars at the beginning of MGM movies.

T72

❸ Have students read the directions and answer the questions independently. Then have them compare their answers in pairs.

Answers

a. He was waiting for a little girl to come by with a basket of food for her grandmother. b. She was carrying a basket of food for her grandmother. c. He asked her if she was carrying the basket to her grandmother. d. She recognized him because he didn't look like her grandmother—even in her grandmother's nightcap and nightgown. e. She shot the wolf dead.

❹ Have students read the directions and then complete the activity independently. Then have them compare their answers in pairs.

Answers

a. basket b. woods c. nightgown and nightcap d. approached e. Metro-Goldwyn lion f. automatic

❺ Have students read the directions and then answer the questions in pairs, in small groups, or as a class.

Answers

humorous; second paragraph from "... for even ..." until the end of the moral.

❻ Have students read the directions independently and then complete the activity in pairs or small groups. Review the answers as a class.

Answers

Some answers may vary. Be sure students can explain their responses. a. informative b. humorous c. critical d. informative e. informative f. humorous

Think About It

(*See page 74.*)

❼–❽ Have students read the questions independently. Then have them answer them in pairs, in small groups, or as a class. If they discuss the questions in pairs or small groups, have individuals share their responses with the rest of the class. Make sure students discuss how this version differs from the traditional version of "Little Red Riding Hood." You may also want to introduce students to some well-known fables and their morals, for example, the fable "The Hare and the Tortoise" and its moral "Slow and steady wins the race."

✪ **Option:** Divide the class into pairs or groups. Distribute a copy of a fairy tale in English to each group. Have students write new versions of the fairy tale. They can write a modern comic version, as James Thurber did, or they can change the characters or the ending. Have the groups illustrate their versions with drawings or pictures cut out of magazines. Display the texts and pictures on posters around the classroom. Have students talk about how the stories they wrote are similar and how they are different. Have them vote on the best new story.

✪ **Option:** If you have students from different cultures, have each student bring in a fairy tale or folktale from his or her culture. If your students are all from the same culture, have each one research a fairy tale or folktale from a different culture to share with the class. Suggest that they use the Internet or the library, talk to someone from another country, telephone a consulate, and so on.

Once everyone has a story, have students record their stories. During several different class periods, play one or more of the stories for the class. The second or third time the students listen to a story, have them take notes. Then put them in small groups to retell the story, using their notes. Have each group write comprehension questions about the story to ask the other groups. After all the groups have asked their questions, collect the questions and use the best ones as a quiz for the whole class during the next class period.

When the little girl opened the door of her grandmother's house, she saw that there was somebody in bed with a nightcap and nightgown on. She had approached no nearer than twenty-five feet from the bed when she saw that it was not her grandmother, but the wolf, for even in a nightcap a wolf does not look any more like your grandmother than the Metro-Goldwyn lion looks like Calvin Coolidge. So the little girl took an automatic out of her basket and shot the wolf dead.

Moral: It is not so easy to fool little girls nowadays as it used to be.

Calvin Coolidge, U.S. president (1923–1929)

3 Answer the questions.

    a. What was the wolf waiting for?

    b. What was the little girl carrying?

    c. What did the wolf ask her?

    d. How did the little girl recognize the wolf in her grandmother's bed?

    e. What did the little girl do?

4 Use the context to find the words in the reading that match the following phrases. Do not use a dictionary.

    a. a container for carrying food

    b. a small forest

    c. clothes to sleep in

    d. came closer

    e. symbol of a movie company

    f. a gun or pistol

5 What tone does Thurber's story "The Little Girl and the Wolf" have—humorous, critical, or informative? Which of the writer's words or sentences helped you identify the tone?

6 Look at the book titles below and check the tone each book is likely to have. Mark an **✗** in the appropriate column.

Title	Humorous	Critical	Informative
a. *The Story of Superman*			
b. *Twenty Party Jokes*			
c. *Is Reading Comics Really Reading?*			
d. *Cartoons: A Reflection of Society*			
e. *Dorothy Parker: Humor That Hurts*			
f. *The Greatest Punch Lines*			

Think About It

7 Do you think James Thurber's version of "Little Red Riding Hood" is funny? Why or why not?

8 Do you agree with the moral of the story? Is the moral what makes the story funny? Why or why not?

Write: A Definition Paragraph

The topic sentence of a paragraph of definition usually includes the name of the item, the class to which it belongs, and identifying details that make the item different from others in its class. This sentence is followed by examples, descriptions, or comparisons that further develop and clarify the definition.

9 Look at the paragraph defining the word "fable." How does the writer develop the definition? Compare your ideas with a partner's.

A fable is a story that teaches a moral lesson using animal characters that talk and act like people. For example, in Aesop's fable of the fox and the grapes, a fox tries to reach some grapes to eat. When he is unsuccessful, he decides the grapes are sour. The lesson the story teaches is that we tend to belittle or think badly of what we can't have. Aesop is the best known writer of fables, but there are others such as La Fontaine, Joel C. Harris, and James Thurber. All of them use animals to describe human behavior and show us truths about ourselves that we might not accept in other ways.

Write About It

10 Choose one of the items in the box and write a one-paragraph definition. Be sure to include a clear topic sentence and support sentences that illustrate your definition. Use the model paragraph in Exercise 9 for help.

comedian	detective	prodigy
debate	joke	soap opera

11 **Check Your Writing** Work in groups of three. Exchange papers and give feedback using the following questions. Revise your own paper as needed.

- Does the topic sentence include the name of the item being defined, the class to which it belongs, and identifying details?
- Is the definition developed with examples, comparisons, or other details that clarify the term?

Write: A Definition Paragraph

Presentation

Have students read the explanation independently in class or for homework.

9 Have students read the paragraph independently and answer the question. Then have them compare their answers in pairs.

Answers

Answers will vary. A possible response is given.

The topic sentence says that a fable belongs to the class of stories; it is different from other stories in that it "teaches a moral lesson using animal characters that talk and act like people." The paragraph gives an example of a fable—Aesop's fable of the fox and the grapes—to illustrate the use of animal characters to teach a moral lesson. It then gives other examples of writers of fables. The last sentence explains why fables are written—they "show us truths about ourselves that we might not accept in other ways."

Write About It

Presentation

10 Have students choose an item to define. Before students write their definition paragraphs, encourage them to look again at the explanation and model paragraph in Exercise 9. To what class does their item belong? To what can it be compared, and what makes it different? How can it be described? What are some examples? What other details can they include?

☑ **11 Check Your Writing** Have students read the directions independently. Then have pairs of students exchange their first drafts and use the questions to check both the content and the organization. After they give each other feedback, using the questions in the box, have them write their final drafts.

 Workbook: Practice 12

Vocabulary Expansion: *Tell, say, speak, talk*
See page T146.

Answers
1. told 2. speak 3. talked 4. said 5. told

EVALUATION

See page TExi.

Unit 7 Achievement Test

Self-Check See **Check Your Knowledge,** page 56 of the Workbook.

Dictation Dictate the following joke about school to your students. For more information on dictation, see page TExv.

A little boy came home from school one day and told his mother he wasn't going back to school anymore. When his mother asked him why, he said that on Monday his teacher said that five and five make ten. On Tuesday, his teacher explained that seven and three make ten. On Wednesday, his teacher said that six and four make ten. The little boy told his mother that he wasn't going back to school until his teacher made up her mind.

Have students correct their dictation in small groups and then tell some jokes they know. If possible, their jokes should also be about school. Have each group decide on the funniest joke.

Communication Skills

1. Ask individuals to tell you what kinds of things they think are funny. Pay attention to the use of the vocabulary for comedy.

2. Ask students to tell you about a funny movie or TV show they saw recently. Encourage them to report on dialogue as well as action. Pay attention to their use of reported speech.

3. Have students tell a short story about something funny that happened to them at home, in school, or on the job. Pay attention to their use of tone.

SO THAT'S HOW ... !

OBJECTIVES

- To describe processes
- To use the passive voice in the present and past tenses
- To use the agent in the passive voice
- To identify the steps in a process
- To stress new information
- To express interest or indifference
- To use chronological order
- To write a process paragraph
- To understand and use the suffixes -er/-or, -ian, and -ist

GETTING STARTED

Warm Up

Preview

- Focus students' attention on the unit title. Elicit or explain when people might say it or similar expressions, such as *So that's how you do it! So that's it! So that's how it's done!* (when they find out how something is done)

- Write the word **mysteries** on the board. Ask students what meanings they know for the word. (They know, for example, the literary meaning from Unit 2.) Elicit or present the idea of mysteries as unsolved puzzles or unexplained processes. Ask students for examples, or mention mysteries such as the building of the pyramids and magic tricks.

Presentation

❶ Have students read the paragraph and write down some mysteries that they would like solved. Ask students to share their mysteries in small groups or as a class.

❷ Have students read the questions. Focus their attention on the labeled diagram of the toothpaste tube. Encourage students to say how they think the different-colored stripes are put into the tube.

❸ Have students read the instructions. Make sure everyone understands what to do. Play the recording or read the audioscript aloud two times. Have students work in pairs to compare their answers. Then have them listen again to check their work.

Audioscript: The audioscript for Exercise 3 appears on page T156.

> **Answers**
> a. 4 b. 2 c. 6 d. 1 e. 5 f. 3

 Option: Create a word map for the word **mystery**. Have students brainstorm words they associate with it. (See the Vocabulary Expansion Activity for Unit 1 on page T140.)

Workbook: Practice 1

Figure It Out

Preview

- Ask students whether they have ever been to the circus. What did they like best about it? Elicit or present **magician**. Ask students whether they have ever seen a magician at the circus or on TV. Encourage students to describe some of the tricks that they have seen magicians perform.

- Use the pictures on page 76 to elicit or present **compartment**, **hole**, **saw**, **exposed**, and **split**.

Presentation

Read the announcer's speech aloud as students listen. Tell them not to look at page 76 yet. Then ask students whether any of them have an idea of how magicians do this trick. Have students read the speech again silently.

SO THAT'S HOW ... !

GETTING STARTED

Warm Up

1 Magicians perform mysterious tricks. They saw people in half, pour liquids out of empty containers, and pull rabbits out of empty hats. Many ordinary things in life are mysteries, too. For example, how is the lead put into a pencil? What are some other mysteries you would like to know about?

2 Have you ever seen striped toothpaste? How do you think the different-colored stripes are put into the tube?

3 Listen to the explanation. Number the steps in the process from first (1) to last (6).

    a. The tube is squeezed and pressure is applied to the white paste.

    b. The small tube is filled with colored paste.

    c. As the white paste comes out of the tube, the colored paste is forced onto it through the slots.

    d. A small slotted tube is placed in the opening of a larger tube.

    e. Pressure is applied on the colored paste by the white paste.

    f. The long part of the tube is filled with white paste.

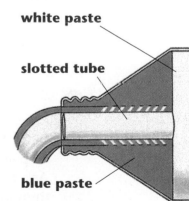

white paste

slotted tube

blue paste

Figure It Out

ANNOUNCER: And now, ladies and gentlemen, the great magician will attempt to saw a woman in half! Watch closely as she gets into the empty box. She leaves her head, hands, and feet exposed.

Now the magician is cutting through the box. Look closely as the halves of the box are moved apart. The woman is split in two, but she's still smiling! Look! A member of the audience is invited to shake her hand. Now the halves of the box are being moved together again. The magician is opening the box. The woman's getting out. And she's fine!

4 Now find out how the trick was done.

   a. A box is carried on stage and the magician shows the audience that it is empty. Meanwhile, a woman is hidden under the table, ready to crawl through the false bottom.

   b. The woman on stage is then invited into the box. Instead of occupying the entire box, she gets into the front compartment. The second compartment is occupied by the woman who was hiding under the table.

   c. The woman in the front sticks her head and hands through holes in the box. The second woman's feet are exposed through the holes of the back compartment.

   d. The box is sawed into two pieces by the magician. The two halves of the box are pulled apart and the audience is led to believe that the woman is split into two.

   e. Finally, the box is moved together again and is opened so the woman can get out. The woman isn't harmed.

5 **Vocabulary Check** Match the words and meanings.

_____	**1.** tricks	**a.**	to put on; to place on
_____	**2.** tube	**b.**	to push together
_____	**3.** to squeeze	**c.**	narrow openings
_____	**4.** pressure	**d.**	actions that seem impossible
_____	**5.** to apply	**e.**	section; part
_____	**6.** slots	**f.**	to move on hands and feet
_____	**7.** to expose	**g.**	a tool that cuts
_____	**8.** saw	**h.**	to show; to let be seen
_____	**9.** to crawl	**i.**	a long, thin hollow object
_____	**10.** compartment	**j.**	force

Talk About It

6 Two organizers of next month's international magicians convention are meeting to see if everything is getting done on time. Work with a partner. One of you looks at Organizer A's list on page 77, and the other looks at Organizer B's list on page 84. Ask and answer questions about the convention. Check the things that are done and fill in the times.

❹ Have students find out how the trick was done by reading the steps listed and looking at the corresponding pictures.

Option: Have students work in groups of five to retell and act out the magic trick. Have one student pretend to be the magician, another pretend to be the person to be sawed in half, and a third student pretend to be the person who is hidden. Instruct the other two students to say the steps in the trick to the first three, who should then act out what they hear.

☑ **❺ Vocabulary Check** Have students read the directions and complete the activity independently or with a partner. Review the answers as a class.

> **Answers**
> 1. d 2. i 3. b 4. j 5. a 6. c 7. h 8. g 9. f
> 10. e

Option: Have students report on magicians they have seen in person or on TV or magicians who are well known in their country. Have them find a picture, if possible, and write a short biographical paragraph about a magician. Encourage them to describe one of the tricks the magician is famous for.

 Workbook: Practice 2

Talk About It

Option: You may prefer to postpone this activity until after the grammar presentation (page 77) if you feel students need extra help with using the passive voice.

Presentation

Note: The purpose of this activity is to develop fluency. Students should talk without fear of interruption for error correction. If you notice persistent errors, write them down for later reteaching or review.

❻ Have students read the instructions and the model conversation silently. Then have a pair of students read the conversation aloud to the class. Have students work in pairs, and have each pair decide who will be Organizer A and who will be Organizer B. Focus students' attention on the example answer to Organizer A's question in Organizer A's chart. Explain that after Organizer B answers the first question, he or she asks the next question. Make sure students understand the words in the charts. Have students complete the activity. Review the completed charts as a class.

Option: Ask one or more pairs to perform their conversations for the class.

 Workbook: Practice 3

GRAMMAR

Describing a Process: The Passive Voice

Preview

- To introduce the idea of **processes**, have students brainstorm the steps involved in the process of planting seeds. (making holes in the ground, putting the seeds into the holes, covering the seeds with dirt, watering the area) Then elicit other processes. (baking a cake, assembling a new bicycle, and so on)

- Select one of the processes students mentioned, and elicit the steps of the process. Have students give the steps in full sentences using the impersonal **you** (for example, "First, you combine the flour, sugar, and salt"). Write the steps on the board.

- Point out to students that the **you** in these sentences is not important—it just means "anyone." Elicit that the focus of the sentences is on the steps in the process—that is, the actions—rather than on the person who is doing them.

- Tell students that there is a way to get rid of the **you** and to focus on the actions: using the passive voice instead of the active voice. Rewrite some or all of the sentences on the board as passives. (For example, "First, the flour, sugar, and salt are combined.")

- Ask students how the active and passive voice pairs on the board are different. (In the passive voice sentence, **the flour, sugar,** and **salt** is the subject and so comes before the verb instead of after it; the verb is **are combined** instead of **combine**.)

- Ask students to look at an active and passive pair of sentences and tell you in which sentence the subject does the action. (the active sentence—for example, someone does the action of combining the flour, sugar, and salt) Ask them in which sentence the subject receives the action, rather than doing it. (the passive sentence—for example, the flour, sugar, and salt become combined)

Presentation

Have students read the explanation and example sentences silently in class or for homework. Before students read the example sentences, you might want to ask them how they think a pencil is made. After they have read the examples, ask them to compare the active and passive texts, noticing the difference in the word order and in the verb forms. Ask, *How do you know whether to use **is** or **are** in a passive sentence?* (Use **is** if the subject of the passive sentence is singular and **are** if it is plural.)

Language Note: You might want to point out to students that **they** in the active sentences, like **you** in the active sentences in the preview, is an impersonal form, used to mean "people, someone/anyone."

Ask about an item.

A: Is the convention hotel reserved?

Answer and tell about time.

B: Yes, it is. It was reserved a year ago.

Ask about another item.

B: Has the equipment for tricks been ordered?

Answer and tell about time.

A: No, it hasn't, but it will be ordered tomorrow.

Organizer A

	List of Jobs	Done	When
1.	reserve a convention hotel	✓	*a year ago*
2.	order equipment for tricks	___	tomorrow
3.	pay for convention hotel space	___	_____
4.	send letters to performers	___	two months ago
5.	register members	___	_____
6.	print the programs	___	one month ago
7.	arrange shuttle transportation	___	_____

GRAMMAR

Describing a Process: The Passive Voice

When we explain a process, or how to do something, the actions are more important than the person or thing doing the actions. To emphasize the actions, we use the passive voice (*be* + past participle) instead of the active voice.

Active Voice (focus on agent)	**Passive Voice** (focus on action)
How they **make** pencils	How pencils **are made**
First, they **cut** the wood into slats.	First, the wood **is cut** into slats.
Then, they **cut** grooves in the slats.	Then, grooves **are cut** in the slats.
Next, they **place** strips of lead into the grooves, and they **fit** other slats over the ones with the lead.	Next, strips of lead **are placed** into the grooves, and other slats **are fitted** over the ones with lead.
They **glue** the slats together into boxes.	The slats **are glued** together into boxes.
Then they **cut** the boxes into strips, and they **shape** the strips into pencils.	Then the boxes **are cut** into strips, and the strips **are shaped** into pencils.

1 Here are the final steps in making a pencil. Change the sentences from the active to the passive voice.

    a. They paint the pencils. _____

    b. Then they add erasers. _____

    c. Finally, they sharpen the pencils. _____

2 Complete the passage with the passive voice. Use the simple present.

    Green olives **(1. pick)** _____ in the fall. They
(2. split) _____ with wooden hammers. Then they
(3. put) _____ into a barrel of water. After three or
four days, the water **(4. remove)** _____ and fresh water
(5. add) _____. This process **(6. repeat)** _____
four times. Next, the olives **(7. leave)** _____ in a spicy
liquid for three or four weeks until they are ready to be eaten.

The Passive Voice: Past Tense

The passive voice can also be used to talk about past actions (*was/were* +
past participle).

> The process for making pencils **was invented** by William Monroe in 1812.
>
> Before that, feather pens **were** commonly **used**.

3 **Check Your Understanding** Complete the passage about the
development of writing with the correct form of the active or passive
voice. Use the negative when necessary.

    In the earliest forms of writing, alphabets **(1. use)** _____.
Instead, people **(2. communicate)** _____ through pictures
of objects and people. However, the pictures **(3. be)** _____
unable to express abstract ideas such as "love" or "belief." As a result,
symbols **(4. invent)** _____ to represent sounds, syllables, and
later entire words. In many languages today, symbols such as &, %, $,
+, and = **(5. see)** _____ in everyday writing.

    The Chinese writing system **(6. develop)** _____ in around
1500 B.C., and even today symbols for both words and syllables
(7. use) _____. The writing system in the West mainly
(8. use) _____ an alphabet to represent sounds.
In early alphabets, symbols **(9. represent)** _____ only
consonant sounds. Later, those alphabets **(10. follow)** _____
by others with symbols for vowel sounds as well.

4 What kind of writing system does your language use? If it uses an
alphabet, are there any letters different from those in the English
alphabet? Does it have any special marks? With a partner, discuss
the differences between the writing system of your language and
that of English.

**Ancient Chinese
writing on bone**

❶ Have students read the directions and write the sentences independently. Then review the answers as a class.

Answers
a. The pencils are painted. **b.** Then erasers are added. **c.** Finally, the pencils are sharpened.

🌐 **Option:** Have students tell how pencils are sharpened with a knife or razor and how they are sharpened with a pencil sharpener. Encourage them to use the passive voice in their descriptions.

❷ After students read the instructions, have them complete the sentences independently and then compare their answers with a partner's. Then review the answers as a class.

Answers
1. are picked **2.** are split **3.** are put
4. is removed **5.** is added **6.** is repeated
7. are left

🌐 **Option:** Show drawings of another process that is fairly simple to explain. Display the drawings and provide students with the steps written in the active voice. Have students write the steps in the passive voice on a sheet of paper.

The Passive Voice: Past Tense

Presentation

Have students read the explanation independently. Ask them to look at the example sentences. Point out that the passive voice can also be used to talk about past actions by using the past form of *be* (was/were) and the past participle.

☑ ❸ **Check Your Understanding** Have students read the instructions. Then have them complete the activity in pairs. Review the answers as a class.

Answers
1. weren't used **2.** communicated **3.** were
4. were invented **5.** are seen **6.** was developed **7.** are used **8.** uses **9.** represented
10. were followed

❹ Have students read the questions and instructions and, if possible, work with partners who speak the same language. (*Answers will vary.*)

🌐 **Option:** Have pairs of students who speak the same language make a list of differences between the English alphabet and the alphabet of their native language. For example, the Spanish alphabet does not have the letter **k**, and it uses **ch** as a separate letter. Then lead a class discussion about the various differences.

 Workbook: Practices 4, 5, 6

Using an Agent

Preview

Write the following sentences on the board.

The beautiful chocolate cake at the party last night was made by the new baker.

That cake was eaten in no time. When I went to get a piece, it was all gone.

Ask students to tell who did the action in the first sentence. (the new baker) Tell students that we call the person or thing doing the action in the sentence the **agent**. Ask, *What word comes before the agent in a passive sentence?* (by) Then ask, *Who did the action in the second sentence?* (We don't really know from the sentence—presumably some of the people at the party.) Tell them that some passive sentences in English specify who the agents are but that many do not.

Presentation

Have students read the grammar explanation and example sentences silently in class or for homework. Make sure that students understand why the agent is needed in the last sentence but not in the others. (The agent in the last sentence is known and important.)

❺ Have the pairs read the instructions and example and then take turns asking and answering the questions.

Answers

a. Who produced the first successful automobile? The first successful automobile was produced by Gottlieb Daimler and Karl Benz in 1887 in Germany. **b.** Who sent the first telephone message? The first telephone message was sent by Alexander Graham Bell in 1876 in North America. **c.** Who made the first electric light? The first electric light was made by Thomas Edison (United States) and Joseph Swan (Britain) in 1878–1879. **d.** Who invented the first battery? The first battery was invented by Alessandro Volta and Luigi Galvani in 1786 in Italy.

---

❻ **Express Yourself** Have students read the instructions and work on writing their trivia questions independently. Tell students that, if possible, their trivia questions should be about inventions, discoveries, and similar facts. When they have finished writing their questions, have them complete the activity with their partners. Encourage students to try to answer their partner's questions. *(Answers will vary.)* When they have finished, you may want to ask students to tell the class a fact they learned from their partner.

Option: Write these situations on the board.

1. Describe to someone how to plant a tree.

2. Tell a friend your weekend activities.

3. Teach a person to change a tire.

4. Explain to someone how to get a driver's license.

5. Ask a circus performer about the people in the circus.

6. Tell a friend how to cook your favorite dish.

Have students work with partners and figure out in which situations they could use the passive. (1, 3, 4, 6) Then ask the partners to choose one of those situations and develop a dialogue about it. You may want to have pairs of students share their conversations with the class.

Option: Have students do research in books or on the Internet to find out how a magic trick is done—for example, how a rabbit is pulled out of an empty hat. Have them write the steps of the process using the passive voice as appropriate. Then have them tell the class how the trick is done.

 Workbook: Practice 7

Using an Agent

In passive sentences, the doer of the action, the agent, is often left out because it is not necessary. When the agent is mentioned to complete the meaning of the sentence, it is introduced by the preposition *by*.

Using the Agent in the Passive Voice

Olives **are picked** in the fall

(Unimportant agent—we don't need to know who picks them.)

Olive trees **were** first **cultivated** in the Mediterranean regions.

(Unknown agent—we don't know who first cultivated them.)

Olives **are eaten** in all Mediterranean countries.

(Understood agent—we know that people eat them.)

Olives **were introduced** in California **by Father Junipero Serra**.

(The agent completes the meaning of the sentence.)

---

5 Work with a partner. Use the cues to ask and answer questions.

Example:

perform/first heart transplant

Dr. Christian Barnard/South Africa/1967

A: Who performed the first heart transplant?

B: The first heart transplant was performed by Dr. Christian Barnard in South Africa in 1967.

a. produce/first successful automobile
   Gottlieb Daimlier and Karl Benz/1887/Germany

b. send/first telephone message
   Alexander Graham Bell/1876/North America

c. make/first electric light
   Thomas Edison (United States) and Joseph Swan (Britain)/1878–1879

d. invent/first battery
   Alessandro Volta and Luigi Galvani/1786/Italy

6 **Express Yourself** Use an encyclopedia, the Internet, or another information source to write five trivia questions of your own. Ask a partner your questions. If he or she doesn't know the answer, be prepared to give it.

Example:

A: What was discovered by Marie Curie in 1911?

B: Radium was discovered by Marie Curie in 1911.

A: When were talking movies developed?

B: I think talking movies were developed around 1930.

Listen: Diamonds and Pearls

1 **Before You Listen**

    a. Almost everyone enjoys giving and receiving presents. What kinds of presents do you usually give friends or family?

    b. One traditional present is jewelry. How many kinds of jewelry can you name?

STRATEGY → **Identifying Steps in a Process** When listening to find out how something works or how something is done, it is important to focus on the order of steps in the process. Pay attention to words and expressions that signal the order. These include time clauses and expressions such as *first, next, then, the next step, after, the last part,* and *finally.*

2 Listen to find out how pearls are made. Complete the sentences.

    a. A pearl _____ inside an oyster.

    b. A grain of sand _____ inside the animal's shell.

    c. The animal _____ by the foreign object.

    d. A special substance _____ by the oyster.

    e. The object _____ by this substance.

    f. After many coverings, a pearl _____.

    g. The process takes approximately _____ years.

3 Listen to find out how diamonds are formed. Then put the steps of the process in order from 1 to 7.

    _____ **a.** The diamonds are mined or discovered.

    _____ **b.** Each diamond is studied before making a cutting plan.

    _____ **c.** Carbon is changed into cubic crystals by enormous heat and pressure.

    _____ **d.** Facets are formed by polishing the diamond's surface.

    _____ **e.** When all 58 facets are polished, the diamond is ready to be set.

    _____ **f.** The material carrying the diamonds is forced up to the earth's surface.

    _____ **g.** The material is cut following the marks made in india ink.

LISTENING and SPEAKING

Listen: Diamonds and Pearls

Presentation

❶ Before You Listen Ask several students when their birthdays are and what presents they got for their last birthday. (If birthday presents are not the custom, ask about some occasion when presents are given.) Then have students read the questions independently. Discuss their responses as a class. You may want to make a list on the board of the kinds of jewelry they name.

➡ **Identifying Steps in a Process** Have students read the strategy. Point out that this is similar to listening for the order of events in a narrative and that many of the time expressions used are the same. You might want to have students look again at the description of the process of making a pencil on pages 77–78 in the grammar section. How would this description seem different if the time expressions weren't used? (It would be harder to read and understand.)

🎧 **❷** Play the recording or read the audioscript aloud twice. Let the students compare their answers and listen again if necessary.

Audioscript: The audioscript for Exercise 2 appears on page T156.

> **Answers**
> Answers may vary slightly. **a.** is formed
> **b.** is caught **c.** is irritated **d.** is made
> **e.** is covered **f.** is formed **g.** seven

🎧 **❸** Have students read the instructions and make sure that they understand what to do. Remind them that they don't have to understand every word to understand the order of the steps in a process. You may want to have students read the steps silently before they listen. Then play the recording or read the audioscript aloud two or more times. Let students compare their answers and listen again if necessary.

Audioscript: The audioscript for Exercise 3 appears on page T156.

> **Answers**
> **a.** 3 **b.** 4 **c.** 1 **d.** 6 **e.** 7 **f.** 2 **g.** 5 (The correct order of the steps: 1. Carbon is changed into cubic crystals by enormous heat and pressure. 2. The material carrying the diamonds is forced up to the earth's surface. 3. The diamonds are mined or discovered. 4. Each diamond is studied before making a cutting plan. 5. The material is cut following the marks made in india ink. 6. Facets are formed by polishing the diamond's surface. 7. When all 58 facets are polished, the diamond is ready to be set.)

Option: Have students investigate how natural pearls are found in the sea by divers or how cultured pearls are made and harvested. Have them report their findings to the class.

Option: Have students do research to find out how other jewels are formed in their natural state. Or have them find out how pieces of jewelry are made. Have them report their findings to the class.

 Workbook: Practice 8

Option: Have students talk about traditional presents in their culture(s). Have them first identify and describe the occasions when presents are traditionally given. Then have them list and describe the presents that are appropriate for each occasion.

Option: Have students work in groups to design machines that perform a process or function. The machines could be practical or whimsical—for example, a machine that does homework, a machine that peels bananas, a machine that walks the family dog, and so on. Have students draw their machines on poster paper and explain how they work to the class. As a follow-up, have students write paragraphs explaining how their machines are operated and display them with the posters on the wall.

Pronunciation

Presentation

Have students read the information in the box. Say the example sentences for students and discuss the examples as a class. Do they understand why the boldfaced words in the sentences are important? Can the students hear that these words are stressed when you say the sentences? Have students look at how the stress differences in the answers relate to the different information that the questions are asking for.

④ Have students work in pairs to read the dialogue and circle the words. Emphasize that there is no single way to stress these sentences, but encourage them to think about what information is new and/or important. (*For answers, see Exercise 5.*)

Language Note: You may want to explain to students that **to have a long face** is an expression meaning "to look unhappy."

⑤ Play the recording or read the audioscript aloud, so that students can check their answers in Exercise 4. Ask students if their answers matched what they heard.

Audioscript: The audioscript for Exercise 5 appears on page T157.

> **Answers**
> A: I have a great joke.
> B: I hate jokes.
> A: This one's good.
> B: Do I have to listen to it?
> A: Yes, but you don't have to laugh.
> B: Go ahead.
> A: Well, this horse walks into a coffee shop…
> B: And the waiter says, "Why do you have such a long face?"
> A: How did you know?
> B: Well, all you had to do was look.

⑥ Have students practice the dialogue in pairs. After they have read it once, have partners switch roles and read it again. You may want to have some pairs present the dialogue to the class, focusing as before on stress.

Workbook: Practice 9

T81

Speak Out

Presentation

➡ **Expressing Interest or Indifference**
Have students read the strategy and the examples in the box. Ask, *What does indifference mean?* (lack of interest) Point out to students that in using expressions that show indifference, they must be careful to avoid offending others. Expressions showing indifference should usually be used only with friends or, for example, when someone is asking about whether one is interested in something.

Have students practice some of the language in the box by mentioning some possible topics for a conversation and having students express interest or indifference. (*Example: Should we talk about some recent movies?* "That sounds a little boring." *How about the chemical content of paint—should we talk about that?* "I'm not really interested in …")

Note: The purpose of this activity is to develop fluency. Students should be free to talk without fear of interruption for error correction. If you notice persistent errors, write them down for later reteaching or review.

⑦ Have students read the instructions silently. Then have a pair of students read the example conversation aloud to the class. Have students write their lists individually, including as many topics as they can think of, and then work in groups to complete the activity. (*Responses will vary.*) You might want to have each group decide on three topics that interest everyone in the group and then present their topics to the class. Have the rest of the class show interest or indifference. Are there topics that more than one group thought of? Which topics do students find especially interesting?

 Workbook: Practice 10

Pronunciation

 Read the dialogue. In each thought group, circle the word(s) that present new or important information.

> **A:** I have a great joke.
> **B:** I hate jokes.
> **A:** This one's good.
> **B:** Do I have to listen to it?
> **A:** Yes, but you don't have to laugh.
> **B:** Go ahead.
> **A:** Well, this horse walks into a coffee shop ...
> **B:** And the waiter says, "Why do you have such a long face?"
> **A:** How did you know?
> **B:** Well, all you had to do was look.

 Listen to the dialogue and check your answers. Did you get the joke?

With a partner, practice reading the dialogue, focusing on stress and intonation.

Speak Out

 Expressing Interest or Indifference In conversation or discussion, you can use expressions to show interest in or indifference to what is being said.

Showing Interest	Showing Indifference
I'm really interested in ...	I'm not really interested in ...
We'd like to learn more about ...	... doesn't really interest us.
I've always wanted to know why ...	I don't really care about ...
That sounds interesting.	That sounds a little boring/dull.

 Brainstorm a list of things you would like to learn about (for example, how special effects are created in movies or why women tend to live longer than men). Then work in groups of three. Share the items on your lists and take turns politely expressing interest or indifference.

Example:

A: You know, I've always wanted to find out how people swallow swords and swallow fire without getting hurt.

B: Really? I don't care about magic tricks, but I am interested in how trainers teach animals to act and do stunts in movies. I find that fascinating!

C: Not me. I'm more interested in things like dreams and what they mean.

READING and WRITING

Read About It

1 Before You Read

a. One of the world's most famous magicians was Harry Houdini. What do you know about him?

b. Houdini was known for his incredible escapes. Scan the reading to find the answers to these questions.

   1. What was one of Houdini's most famous tricks called?

   2. What was constructed for Houdini to get into?

   3. What was the tugboat used for?

 **Using Chronology to Understand Process** In reading about a process, you will understand more if you notice words that describe the time and sequence of the steps involved. Not every step is introduced with a time word, however, so it is also important to notice the order in which sentences without time words follow each other.

Houdini: Master of Escape

The magician Harry Houdini (1874–1926) was especially well-known for his spectacular and dangerous escapes. Not content to escape from a simple pair of handcuffs or a box, Houdini developed tricks which involved very real elements
5 of danger and fear.

One of Houdini's most fantastic tricks was called the "Challenge to Death." Each time he carried out this trick, Houdini and his audience met on a pier on a river or canal. First, in full view of the audience, a large wooden box or
10 crate was constructed. A small hole was cut in the bottom of the crate so it would sink. Members of the audience were invited to inspect the crate to make sure there was no false wall or bottom and to make sure the hole was too small for Houdini to crawl out of.

Harry Houdini, escape artist

READING and WRITING

Read About It

Preview

- Return to the topic of magic tricks and magicians by leading a short discussion about them. Ask questions such as *What other kinds of tricks do magicians do besides sawing a person in half? Can it be dangerous to be a magician?*

- Focus attention on the photo of Houdini. Encourage students to talk about what kind of person they think he was.

- Present pictures of different types of **construction** to introduce **carpentry**.

Presentation

❶ Before You Read Ask students the question in **a**. Then have them work independently to find the answers to the questions in **b**. You may want to elicit from students what the reading strategy of scanning consists of before they begin to scan. (looking at a text quickly to find specific bits of information)

Answers

1. "Challenge to Death" **2.** a large wooden crate **3.** to take the crate out from the shore and to bring it back

---

➡ Using Chronology to Understand Process Have students read the strategy. Students have already seen how time expressions can help them understand processes. The point here is that they can't always rely on time expressions. Authors avoid overusing time expressions, as too many sentences with time expressions would be awkward. Since steps are nearly always given in the order in which they occur, when students don't see time expressions, they can rely on sentence order.

Have students read the article independently in class or for homework. Encourage them to read without using dictionaries. If students read in class, you may want to set a time limit.

Option: To check comprehension, write the following questions on the board or ask them orally. If you have students write their answers, have them work in pairs or small groups to check their answers. *(Answers will vary somewhat.)*

1. Who was Harry Houdini? (a famous magician who was known for his spectacular and dangerous escapes)

2. Where was Houdini's audience whenever he performed the "Challenge to Death" trick? (on a pier on a river or canal)

3. What was done to the crate that made it sink? (A small hole was cut in the bottom of it.)

4. What did Houdini and his assistants do to show the audience that he shouldn't have been able to escape? (They handcuffed Houdini and put him inside the crate, hammered the crate shut with strong nails, and tied a thick rope around it.)

5. What happened that made the audience amazed? (Houdini was sitting on top of the crate when it was pulled out of the water, even though the crate was undamaged and was still tied with the rope.)

❷ Have students scan the article independently to find the words that belong in each of the two categories. Then have them compare lists in pairs.

Answers

Answers will vary.
Tools and Carpentry: wooden, box, crate, constructed, hole, cut, wall, bottom, hammered, nails, rope, tied **Ships and Sailing:** pier, river, canal, shore, tugboat, water

❸ After students read the instructions, refer to the article as they complete the exercise. Tell them to write down the time words that show the chronology. Check answers and time words as a class.

Answers

3 (Next), 2 (Then), 1 (First), 7, 6 (Finally), 4 (At this point), 5 (Then)

🜂 **Option:** Some of the words found in this unit can be used as different parts of speech, for example, He used a **saw** [noun] to **saw** [verb] the woman in half. Have students find other words in the article and the rest of the unit that belong to more than one part of speech. (Answers include escape, trick, cut, sink, hammer, nail, pressure.) Then have students use the words in sentences, with one sentence for each part of speech. *(Answers will vary.)*

Think About It

❹ – ❺ Have students read the questions independently. Then have them discuss their responses in pairs, in small groups, or as a class. Ask individuals or groups to share their ideas with the class.

🜂 **Option:** Have students work in pairs or small groups to write more discussion questions. Then have them give their questions to another pair or group to discuss.

Note: Students will find out how Houdini escaped when they do Workbook Practice 11. If students do not have workbooks, you may want to provide them with the explanation: Before the performance, a pair of nail cutters was hidden on Houdini's body. Once he was inside the crate, Houdini used a secret spring to open the handcuffs. Next, he used

the nail cutters to take several nails out of the top of the crate, and he moved the top aside. Then he crawled out and put the top back in place. He sat on top of the crate as it was pulled out of the water. Then, out of sight of the audience and before the boat got back to shore, Houdini's assistant removed the broken nails and secretly hammered in new nails. As a result, the audience inspected an undamaged crate.

Biographical Note: Harry Houdini was probably born in Budapest, Hungary, although his family came to the United States when he was very young. His original name was Erik Weisz; he took the stage name Houdini from the French magician Jean-Eugène Robert-Houdin. He performed in circuses at an early age, but in 1900 he began to be known internationally for his unusually dangerous escapes. "Challenge to Death" was a typical Houdini trick. In 1926, Houdini died as a result of a stomach injury.

🜂 **Option:** Have students find out more information about Houdini and, if possible, how his other tricks were done. Have them report their findings to the class.

🜂 **Option:** Have students work in small groups to brainstorm words they associate with tools and carpentry (for example, hammer, nails, wrench, drill, screwdriver, screw). Then have them compare lists as a class.

 Workbook: Practice 11

Write: A Process Paragraph
Preview

Elicit the definition of a process. (actions that are carried out step by step) Then have students brainstorm situations in which they would need to write a description of a process. (a lab report, an explanation of how to use a machine, a list of procedures for completing a project) Ask students where they have read about processes. (in textbooks, in instructions for operating a machine or constructing something, and so on)

Presentation

Have students read the explanation independently in class.

15   Then Houdini was handcuffed and closed up inside the crate. Next, the crate was hammered shut with strong nails, and a thick rope was tied around it. At this point, the members of the audience were asked to examine the nails and the rope. Then the crate, with Houdini inside, was taken out a short distance from shore on a tugboat. Finally, the crate was lowered into the water.

        As time passed, the audience anxiously waited for Houdini to appear. Suddenly, the crate
20   was pulled out of the water with Houdini sitting on top, waving to his fans on shore. As the crate was brought back to the pier, the audience could see that it was still undamaged and tied with the rope, exactly as it was when it had been lowered into the water. Everyone was amazed.

 Scan the article for words related to the categories and write them in the correct column.

Tools and Carpentry	Ships and Sailing

 Number the steps in Houdini's "Challenge to Death" in chronological order. Be ready to name the time words in the article that show chronology.

_____ A rope was tied around the crate.

_____ Houdini was handcuffed and nailed inside the crate.

_____ A large wooden crate was constructed.

_____ The crate was pulled out of the water with Houdini on top.

_____ The crate was lowered into the water.

        The audience was asked to examine the rope and the nails.

_____ The crate was taken away from the shore.

Think About It

 How do you think Houdini escaped? Share your ideas with the class.

5 Some magicians and circus performers such as high-wire artists regularly risk their lives to entertain the public. Do you think this is right? Why or why not?

Write: A Process Paragraph

A process paragraph is a step-by-step description of how something is done or how something happens. The topic sentence of a process paragraph often states the end result of the process. Then the steps in the process are described in chronological order.

6 Which items do you think should be included in a description of a process? Check the boxes.

☐ Give an explanation of your feelings. ____

☐ State the end result. ____

☐ Explain the results of a step, if necessary. ____

☐ Identify the process you are describing. ____

☐ Compare this process to another. ____

☐ Tell each of the steps. ____

☐ Define unfamiliar or new terms. ____

7 Number the steps in logical order for a process paragraph. Write the number on the line.

Write About It

8 Write a paragraph describing a process you know well. Use paragraphs 2 and 3 of the reading on Houdini as a model. Save your rough draft as a model for Workbook Practice, Unit 6.

 9 **Check Your Writing** Work in small groups. Read each of your group member's papers. Write comments or suggestions on the back of each paper. When you get your own paper back, use your group members' comments and the questions below to revise your paragraph.

- Does the topic sentence identify the process being described?
- Does the writer define any unfamiliar terms?
- Is each step presented in the correct order?
- Are time words used to signal the order of the steps? Are they used correctly?

Organizer B

List of Jobs	Done	When
1. reserve a convention hotel	✓	a year ago
2. order equipment for tricks	____	_____
3. pay for convention hotel space	____	three months ago
4. send letters to performers	____	_____
5. register members	____	in two weeks
6. print the programs	____	_____
7. arrange shuttle transportation	____	four months ago

❻ Have students complete the exercise independently. Have them compare their answers in pairs and then review them as a class.

Answers

State the end result; Explain the results of a step, if necessary; Identify the process you are describing; Tell each of the steps; Define unfamiliar or new terms.

❼ Have students work in pairs to complete the activity. Check answers as a class.

Answers

1. Identify the process you are describing.
2. State the end result. 3. Tell each of the steps. 4. Explain the results of a step, if necessary./Define unfamiliar or new terms. (Both of these take place as needed.)

Write About It

Presentation

❽ Have students read the instructions independently. Then have students work in pairs to brainstorm possible processes, and decide on the one they want to write about. Have them write their first drafts independently. Remind them to include a topic sentence and to use time expressions when appropriate. Students should save their rough drafts as a model for Workbook Practice 12.

☑ **❾ Check Your Writing** Have students exchange papers in small groups, and make sure that each group member gives feedback. Tell students that it is especially important to act on comments that two or more readers have made. Have them write their final drafts.

 Workbook: Practice 12

Vocabulary Expansion: Suffixes –er/–or, –ian, –ist See page T147.

Answers

A. 1. musician 2. psychologist 3. builder 4. politician 5. driver 6. comedian 7. technician 8. instructor 9. debtor 10. biologist
B. *Answers will vary.*

EVALUATION

See page TExi.

Unit 8 Achievement Test

Self-Check See **Check Your Knowledge** on page 64 of the Workbook.

Dictation Dictate the following process to your students. For more information on dictation, see page TExv.

To wash dishes properly, several steps must be followed. First, any food on the plates is put into the garbage. Then the kitchen sink is filled with hot water and dishwashing liquid. Glasses are washed first, followed by plates and dishes. After the plates are washed, all the silverware is cleaned. Finally, all the pots and pans are washed. Then the sink is emptied of the dishwater, and it is cleaned.

Then have the students write how another common household chore is done (for example, making a bed or dusting). You might also want to have the students brainstorm a list of household chores and then rank them according to their preferences, using the number 1 for the chore they each mind doing the least.

Communication Skills

1. Display pictures of different kinds of containers (barrel, compartment, crate, tube), tools (hammer, nail, rope, saw), and substances (lead, liquid, paste). You may want to show real objects instead of pictures. Mix up the items so that they are not together in their categories. Then have students classify the objects. Tell them to name other items that go in each category. Have them also tell how at least one object from each category is used. Watch for the correct use of vocabulary and the passive.

2. Have students choose a process they are familiar with (changing a roll of film or preparing some kind of food), and describe the steps using the passive voice. As an alternative to this activity, you might want to show students a series of pictures that illustrate a process and have them describe the steps in the passive.

HOME SWEET HOME

OBJECTIVES

- To talk about houses and home repairs
- To use the structures **have someone do**, **get someone to do**, and **make someone do**
- To use passive **have something done** and **get something done**
- To express purpose
- To listen to confirm predictions
- To hear and pronounce /i/ versus /ɪ/
- To ask for clarification and clarifying details
- To understand spatial organization
- To write a descriptive paragraph
- To understand and use **make** versus **do**

GETTING STARTED

Warm Up

Preview

- Write **Home Sweet Home** on the board. Elicit or present the difference between **house** and **home**. (**House** refers to just the physical structure, the building; **home** means the house or other place where you live.) Explain that **Home Sweet Home** is a common expression in North America. Ask students what they think it means and if there are similar expressions or sayings in their cultures. Encourage them to talk about what they think makes a house a home.

- Review **carpentry** (see Exercise 2 on page 83 in the Student Book) and present **plumbing**, and other terminology for doing repairs around the house. Ask students what kind of book they should consult to find out how to fix a sink (a book on plumbing), build some shelves (a book on carpentry), or repair a light switch (a book on electrical work).

- **Option:** Have students work in pairs. Have them look at the **floor plans** on page 85 and find the similarities and differences between them. Encourage them to talk about the various rooms, their size and shape, and where they are located in each plan.

- **Option:** Display pictures of different types of homes—apartments, mansions, castles, farmhouses, cottages, houseboats, caves, tents, igloos, and so on. Then have students discuss why they think people choose to live in one type of home over another.

Presentation

❶ Have students read the questions silently and write notes for their answers. When they finish, have them work with partners to find out what their partners know how to do, and what they want to learn to do and why. Then have students talk about their partners in groups or as a class. Make sure they say why their partners wants to learn particular skills.

🎧 ❷ Have students listen to the conversation. Which house is Jenny interested in buying? (floor plan 1) Play the recording or read the audioscript aloud. Remind students that they do not have to understand every word in order to complete the activity.

Audioscript: The audioscript for Exercise 2 appears on page T157.

 *Workbook: Practice 1*

Figure It Out

Preview

- Ask students whether they would prefer to live in the city or the country. Have them work independently, in pairs, or in small groups to list the advantages and disadvantages of each. Have them share their ideas with the rest of the class.

- Elicit or present **remodeling, water pipe, roof, plumber, install/installation, sprinkler system, to replace,** and **to replant.**

(Figure It Out continues on page T86.)

T85

1.   2.

GETTING STARTED

Warm Up

1 Do you like to work around the house? What kinds of things do you know how to do—carpentry? electrical work? gardening? painting? plumbing? What would you like to learn to do? Why?

2 Jenny is interested in buying one of the houses above. Listen to the conversation. Circle the number of the correct floor plan.

Figure It Out

Tom and Liz Santucci have recently bought an abandoned farmhouse that they plan to fix up. They're looking at the house now and talking about the kinds of repairs that will need to be done to get their house in shape.

      LIZ: So how are we going to get all this remodeling done, Tom?

     TOM: Well, I can do the electrical installation myself, but I'll need someone to help me out. Can your brother give me a hand?

     LIZ: I'm sure he wouldn't mind lending a hand. But who will we
5   have replace all the water pipes?

     TOM: Well, my cousin's a plumber. I'll get her to do the job. She owes me a favor and she's efficient.

     LIZ: Great! You know our first priority, though, is the roof. I'm sure it'll have to be repaired. We don't want leaks this winter.

10   **TOM:** You're right. I'll have some estimates done next week. Then we'll be able to choose the least expensive.

Liz: And I want to have the whole house repainted. We'll make the kids help out. I can get my sister's kids to join in, too.

Tom: As for the outside, the back yard is a disaster. Can I get you to
15 replant the garden?

Liz: That's the fun part. If you get the sprinkler system installed, I'll make the kids help me plant flowers and vegetables.

Tom: You know, Liz, this house is going to look like new!

Liz: Don't forget the swimming pool. You promised the kids.

20 **Tom:** Well, unless we get a loan from the bank, we won't be able to afford it this year. Let's make it the first thing we have done next year. Until then, I'll get the hose, you turn on the water!

 3 **Vocabulary Check** Match the words and their meanings.

____ **1.** abandoned (introduction)	**a.** someone who repairs water pipes
____ **2.** remodeling (line 1)	**b.** to help me
____ **3.** to give me a hand (line 3)	**c.** calculation of approximate cost
____ **4.** plumber (line 6)	**d.** money borrowed
____ **5.** estimate (line 10)	**e.** left alone; unlived in
____ **6.** loan (line 20)	**f.** changing to make new or different

Talk About It

4 The Wu family wants to convert an old Victorian house into a restaurant. Two family members are discussing what work still needs to be done. With a partner, ask and answer questions using the cues.

Example: paint/tables and chairs

Ask about work.

A: What else needs to be done?

Describe work.

B: The tables and chairs need to be painted.

Offer solution.

A: I'll get someone to paint them.

Respond and describe immediate action.

B: OK. I'll have them delivered to the shop.

---

a. clean/ovens
b. install/new refrigerators
c. put up/new sign
d. order/tablecloths
e. clean up/parking lot
f. repair/cash register
g. connect/gas
h. print/new menus
i. build/deck

(Figure It Out continued from page T85.)

- Introduce **abandoned**. Discuss why things, people, animals, etc. get abandoned.

- Ask students if they needed something to be done, would they look for someone who was **efficient**? Why?

Option: Display a picture of an old house to elicit or present some of the words.

Presentation

Read the conversation on pages 85 and 86 aloud as students listen with their books open or closed. Then have students read the conversation silently in class or for homework.

Language Note: In American English, **yard** refers to the land around a house and **garden** to the part of the yard used for growing flowers and vegetables. (In British English, garden is often used the way **yard** is in American English.) After the initial presentation of the conversation, have students answer the following questions, as a class or in groups, to check comprehension.

1. Does Tom understand electricity? (yes)
2. Who else knows about electricity? (Liz's brother)
3. Is the plumbing in good condition? (no)
4. How will they decide who to ask to put on the new roof? (They'll have an estimate done and will then choose a company that's least expensive.)
5. What is Liz going to ask her sister's children to do for her? (help paint)
6. Will Liz and Tom have a swimming pool put in this year? (only if they can get a loan from the bank; otherwise, they'll have it done next year)

☑ ❸ **Vocabulary Check** Have students read the directions and then complete the activity independently or with a partner. Review the answers as a class.

Answers
1. e 2. f 3. b 4. a 5. c 6. d

Option: Ask individuals to retell parts of the conversation from memory. You may want to choose new narrators after every few sentences. Give cues when needed.

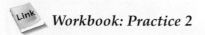 *Workbook: Practice 2*

Talk About It

Option: You may prefer to postpone this activity until after the grammar presentation (page 87) if you feel students need extra help with the structures.

Presentation

Note: The purpose of this activity is to develop fluency. Students should feel free to talk without fear of interruption for error correction. If you notice persistent errors, write them down for later reteaching or review.

❹ Have students read the instructions and the model conversation. Then have a pair of students read the conversation aloud for the class. Students can then work in pairs to continue the conversation using the cues. Encourage them to use language similar to that in the example. Then have pairs of students present their conversations to the class.

Option: To extend the activity, write the following cues on the board. Ask students to think of others and add them to the list.

print/new menus   paint/dining room
connect/the gas   deliver/food
put/an advertisement for the restaurant/in the newspaper

Option: Ask one or more pairs to perform their conversations for the class. Have the rest of the class listen and request clarification if necessary.

Option: Ask students to imagine the work that would need to be done if they opened a gym, staged a rock concert, put on a play, built a school, and so on. Have them work in pairs or small groups to list the things that they would need to have done. Then have them make up dialogues using the items on their lists as cues. Encourage them to use structures similar to those in the example in Exercise 4.

 Workbook: Practice 3

GRAMMAR

Getting Things Done

Preview

- Have students work in pairs or small groups to brainstorm personal services that other people usually do for them—for example, cut their hair and deliver their newspaper. Then ask them to think of jobs around the house that they usually have other people do—for example, fix the plumbing. List all their ideas on the board. Then ask students to match professions or people to the items in the list—for example, cut hair: hairdresser or barber.

- Write the following sentences on the board.

  You don't usually cut your hair yourself. You have the hairdresser cut your hair.

  Have students work in pairs to make similar sentences about the services and people listed on the board. Ask individuals to share their sentences with the class.

- Next to the sentence *You have the hairdresser cut your hair*, write: *You'll have the hairdresser cut your hair, You'll get the hairdresser to cut your hair, You'll make the hairdresser cut your hair*. Elicit the differences in forms and meanings between the sentences.

Presentation

Have students read the grammar explanation and examples in the box. Go over the example sentences to make sure that students see the form and meaning differences among these three related structures. (**get** takes **to** + verb; **make** has the sense of "to force someone to do something")

☑ ❶ **Check Your Understanding** Have students read the instructions and complete the exercise independently. Then have them compare answers with a partner. Review the answers as a class.

> **Answers**
> 1. had 2. had 3. get 4. make (or have)
> 5. get

Have students read the explanation for the structures in the passive voice. Read aloud the examples in the language box. Elicit other examples from students, and write them on the board.

🜨 **Option:** If students need help with the difference between the active and passive versions of these structures, you may want to write the following chart on the board. Elicit which expressions focus on the action (the passives) and which focus on the person doing the job (the actives). Elicit the difference in the form of the verb. (the passives use past participles) Finally, elicit which verb we use **to** with. (**get** in the active voice)

Active			
get	someone	to do	something
have		do	
Passive			
get	something	done	(by someone)
have			

❷ Have students read the instructions and complete the exercise independently. Then have them compare answers with a partner. Review answers as a class.

> **Answers**
> 1. reinstalled 2. done 3. paid 4. hung
> 5. put up 6. repaired

Getting Things Done

Sometimes we cannot or do not want to do a task ourselves. In these cases, we can *have someone do* the task, we can *get someone to do* it, or we can even *make someone do* it.

> I'll **have** the plumber **fix** the sink. (= *ask or hire him*)
>
> Then I'll **get** my father **to install** the lights. (= *persuade him to*)
>
> And I can **make** my sister **help**. (= *force her to*)

☑ **1** **Check Your Understanding** Read the conversation and fill in the blanks with the correct form of *have*, *get*, or *make*.

A: You're never going to believe what happened today!

B: I know. You **(1.)** _____ the carpenters install your new kitchen cabinets.

A: That's right. And I **(2.)** _____ my sister arrange all my dishes inside. Then, a half hour later, I heard a huge crash! The cabinets came crashing down!

B: You're kidding me! You're going to **(3.)** _____ the carpenters to come back and install them again, aren't you?

A: You bet! And I'm going to **(4.)** _____ them pay for the dishes, too!

B: Yeah, and **(5.)** _____ them to deliver the dishes, too.

When we want to stress the action being done, we use the passive voice. We *have something done* or we *get something done*.

> We **had** our roof **repaired**.   (*have* + noun + past participle)
>
> Then we **got** the house **repainted**.   (*get* + noun + past participle)

2 Complete the conversation with the correct form of the verb.

B: Have you had your kitchen cabinets **(1. reinstall)** _____ yet?

A: I tried to, but I couldn't get it **(2. do)** _____ by the same company. They said it wasn't their responsibility. I'm really upset.

B: Can you get the repairs **(3. pay)** _____ by the insurance company?

A: They blamed it on the walls and refused to pay.

B: How are you going to get the cabinets **(4. hang)** _____? Are you going to do it yourself?

A: Are you kidding? I'd probably hang them upside down.

B: Why don't you have them **(5. put up)** _____ by your brother?

A: Good idea. I got my ceiling **(6. repair)** _____ by him once.

3 Complete the passage with the correct form of the verb.

In 1967, Daniel K. Ludwig, one of the richest men in the world, was worried that the world would run out of food and paper, so he started an incredible project to solve the problem. He had his lawyers **(1. buy)** _____ 4 million acres of Amazonian jungle along the River Jari. Next, he had the jungle **(2. clear)** _____. Then he made his construction workers **(3. put in)** _____ 2,600 miles of road and 45 miles of railroad track. After that, he had an entire Japanese paper mill **(4. ship)** _____ to the site. To supply wood for the paper mill, he had 250,000 trees **(5. plant)** _____. He even had trees **(6. bring in)** _____ from Indonesia. He got farmers **(7. grow)** _____ rice and ranchers **(8. raise)** _____ cattle. He had houses **(9. build)** _____ for his workers. Unfortunately, though, insects ate the crops, the trees from Indonesia wouldn't grow, and many workers got tropical diseases. Ludwig had several experts **(10. fire)** _____, but the project continued to fail. Finally, after fifteen years, Ludwig gave up and went back to the United States. He had lost $1 billion.

Clearing the jungle for the Jari project

Working in the rice fields for the Jari project

4 With a partner, ask and answer questions with *have, get,* and *make.* Use the list of occupations in the box and the cues below.

electrician	repair person
gardener	roofer
technician	mechanic
painter	carpenter

Example:

You have a leaky faucet.

A: What would you do if you had a leaky faucet?

B: I'd get a plumber to fix it. What would you do?

A: I'd make my wife fix it.

a. Your car won't start.
b. Your house needs painting.
c. Your computer broke.
d. Your oven is leaking gas.
e. You want some new kitchen cabinets.

f. You need to install a burglar alarm.
g. Your yard is a mess.
h. Your garage roof is leaking.
i. Your window broke.
j. Your car battery died.

❸ Have students complete the exercise independently or with a partner. Then review their answers as a class.

Answers
1. buy 2. cleared 3. put in 4. shipped
5. planted 6. brought in 7. to grow
8. to raise 9. built 10. fired

❹ Have students read the instructions and the example silently. You may want to present **technician** (someone with a particular skill to fix a specific thing) and review the other key vocabulary. Then have a pair of students read the example aloud. Have students work in pairs to ask and answer the questions. *(Answers will vary but should be logical and follow the pattern in the example.)*

 Option: For each item, have a pair of students perform their conversation for the class.

Link *Workbook: Practices 4, 5, 6*

Option: Write the following statement and questions on the board or make a copy for each student. Have students work in pairs or small groups to answer the questions.

We would all like to have certain things done for us to improve the quality of our lives. What things would you like to have done to your home? What would you like to have done at your school or workplace? What would you like to have done in your city? What would you like to have done to your car or to the bus or subway you usually take?

Expressing Purpose

Preview

Tell students that people have many reasons for doing the things they do. Tell them that when we ask about reasons, we ask **why** questions.

Presentation

Have students read the grammar explanation and the example conversation in the box independently.

Write this question on the board: *Why did the Elliotts take out a loan?* Have students brainstorm some answers. Write one of the students' answers on the board in the following ways:

They took out a loan in order to redecorate their house.

They took out a loan so that they could redecorate their house.

Go over the explanation and examples as a class. Make sure students understand that the words in parentheses—**in order** and **that**—are optional and can be omitted. Use the examples to make sure that students understand that (**in order**) **to** and **so** (**that**) have the same meaning and understand how they differ in form (**in order to** is followed by the verb in its base form; **so that** is followed by a clause—that is, by a subject and a verb). Point out that the clause following **so** (**that**) generally includes a modal like **would** or **could**. To reinforce these points, ask students what the first example sentence would be if it had **so** (**that**) and what the second example sentence would be with (**in order**) **to**. (She took out a loan so that she could remodel her house. She remodeled it in order to have a second bedroom.)

Ask students to give additional examples of questions with **why** and answers that express purpose.

❺ Have students read the directions and complete the sentences independently. Encourage them to use their imaginations. Have students go over their answers in pairs or in a small group. When students have finished, have some students share their answers with the class. (*Answers will vary.*)

 ❻ **Express Yourself** Read the question aloud to the class. Before students start working in pairs, have them brainstorm some ideas independently. Encourage them to use their imaginations. If they could make any kind of improvements they wanted, what would they do? What changes would make the place where they live ideal? Then have students work with their partners. Remind them to use some structures for getting things done and for expressing purpose. When they have finished, ask several students to report their partners' ideas to the class.

Workbook: Practice 7

LISTENING and SPEAKING

Listen: A Special House

Presentation

❶ **Before You Listen** Read the questions aloud to the class. Lead a short class discussion about ghosts and spirits. Encourage students to express their opinions and the reasons for them.

Expressing Purpose

We use (*in order*) *to* + verb or *so* (*that*) + clause to tell the purpose behind actions.

> **A:** Why did Liz take out a loan?
>
> **B:** She took out a loan **(in order) to remodel** her house.
>
> **A:** Why did she remodel her house?
>
> **B:** She remodeled it **so (that) she would have** a second bathroom.

5 Mr. and Mrs. Sanchez have just made the following home improvements. What do you think was the purpose of each? Complete the sentences with *in order to* or *so that*.

a. They had a fireplace built _____

b. They had a skylight put in _____

c. They had one of the bedrooms made into an office _____

d. They had a second phone line installed _____

e. They had a new garage door installed _____

f. They had the driveway enlarged _____

g. They had an alarm system installed _____

h. Idea of your own: _____

 6 **Express Yourself**

What kinds of improvements have you made or would you like to make to your room, house, or apartment? Share your ideas with a partner.

LISTENING and SPEAKING

Listen: A Special House

 Before You Listen Some people believe in the existence of ghosts or spirits. Do you? Do you think that some people can communicate with spirits? Why or why not?

Listening to Confirm Predictions You can sometimes predict what a conversation will be about. Then, when you listen, you focus on information that tells you whether your predictions are accurate or not. You confirm your predictions.

Stairway to ceiling, Winchester house

 2 You are going to hear a talk about a special house. Read the statements and write **T** (true) or **F** (false). Then listen to confirm your predictions.

_____ **a.** I'm going to hear about a house haunted by ghosts and spirits.

_____ **b.** I'm going to find out how a movie set was constructed for a recent horror movie.

_____ **c.** I'm going to find out about an unusual house and why it was built.

 3 Listen again and complete the chart.

1. Year of purchase of farmhouse:	
2. Original number of rooms:	
3. Location of farmhouse:	
4. Reason why work was begun:	
5. Number of carpenters who worked:	
6. Number of years work continued:	
7. Number of rooms at present:	
8. Unusual features:	

Pronunciation

/i/ versus /ɪ/

The vowel sounds **/i/** as in **leave** and **/ɪ/** as in **live** are very common in English. These sounds are similar, but **/i/** is held longer than **/ɪ/**. Each sound has a number of different spellings.

4 Predict the pronunciation of each word and write it in the correct column.

leave	these	rid	reasons	he's	list	slip	sit	heat	fit
live	this	read	risen	his	least	sleep	seat	hit	feet

/i/	/ɪ/
leave	_live_

→ **Listening to Confirm Predictions**

Have students read the strategy. Explain that with listening, as with reading, making predictions about what will come next can help them better understand the main ideas.

🎧 ❷ Tell students to apply the strategy to the talk they will hear. Focus their attention on the photograph of one of the stairways in the Winchester house. Ask, *What is unusual about this stairway?* Then have students make their predictions independently. *(Answers will vary.)* Play the recording or read the audioscript aloud. After students have listened, ask them whether their predictions were accurate or not.

Audioscript: The audioscript for Exercises 2 and 3 appears on page T157.

🎧 ❸ Have students look over the chart. Then have them listen again one or more times and fill in the chart. Have them work in pairs to compare answers. Let them listen once more to check their answers. Then ask what they think of Mrs. Winchester and her house.

> **Answers**
> 1. 1884 2. 8 3. the Santa Clara Valley in California 4. Mrs. Winchester believed that spirits told her to change the design of the house 5. 22 6. 38 7. 160 8. Answer may include doors that opened into the air, stairs that went to the ceiling, stairs that went around in circles, six kitchens, forty bedrooms, forty seven fireplaces, 467 doors, 10,000 windows.

🌐 **Option:** Ask students why they think Mrs. Winchester followed the spirits' building instructions. (suggest that Mrs. Winchester believed that as long as she kept building on the house and communicating with the spirits, she wouldn't die.)

🌐 **Option:** Have students work in pairs to act out a conversation between Mrs. Winchester and a spirit. One student plays Mrs. Winchester and the other plays a spirit. Have student playing the spirit give various instructions as he/she imagines they were given to Mrs. Winchester.

Have student playing Mrs. Winchester respond to each instruction by making comments and asking questions about how the changes are to be made. The "spirit" should answer these questions.

🌐 **Option:** Ask individuals to retell parts of the story in their own words using the information in the chart.

🌐 **Option:** Have students share any stories they have heard about spirits communicating with people. Alternatively, have them research such stories, by asking other people or by using the library or Internet.

 Workbook: Practice 8

Pronunciation

Preview

- Write this sentence on the board:

  How long ago did Sam **(leave/live)** _____?

  Say the sentence with either **leave** or **live** and ask students to decide which one you said. You might want to have the students raise their left hands for **leave** and their right hands for **live**.

- Explain that the vowel (/i/) in **leave** is longer than the vowel (/ɪ/) in **live**. Ask students to repeat these pairs of words: **leave—live, sheep—ship, feel—fill, eat—it**. Then write some of the pairs of words on the board. You might want to call attention to the fact that many times one vowel letter represents the shorter sound and two vowel letters the longer sound, although there are exceptions (for example, **me, he, she**).

Presentation

Read the explanation aloud to the class.

❹ Have students fill in the columns with their predictions independently.

> **Answers**
> /i/ **leave:** these, read, reason, he's, least, sleep, seat, heat, feet
> /ɪ/ **live:** this, rid, risen, his, list, slip, sit, hit, fit

🎧 **❺** Play the recording or read the audio-script aloud. Have students check their answers in Exercise 4. Let them listen again, if necessary. As a follow-up, read the words aloud in each column, pausing for students to repeat.

Audioscript: The audioscript for Exercise 5 is found on page T157.

❻ Have students read the instructions. Elicit ideas about the meaning of the saying. Have students mark their answers to items **a–d** independently. Then ask them again what the saying means. Next, have students work in pairs to compare their answers and to think of exceptions to the rules. Have them share their lists with the class. Compile a list on the board.

> **Answers**
> **a.** /i/ **b.** /i/ **c.** /e/ **d.** /aɪ/ **e.** Answers will vary. Possibilities include meant, aisle, piece, priest.

❼ Have students read the directions and make sure that they understand what to do. (Student A should read the sentences on page 91 while Student B circles the correct words in the chart on page 94, and Student B should read the sentences on page 94 while Student A circles the correct words on the chart on page 91.) After students have completed the activity in pairs, review the answers as a class.

☻ **Option:** You may wish to point out that **list** (page 94, item 5) has a different meaning here (tilt to one side).

> **Answers**
> A listens and circles **1.** sleep **2.** feel **3.** this **4.** hit **5.** list
> B listens and circles **1.** ship **2.** leave **3.** he's **4.** meal **5.** bit

 Workbook: Practice 9

Speak Out

Presentation

➡ **Asking for Clarification and Clarifying**
Have students read the strategy. Focus their attention on the box containing the language for asking for clarification and clarifying. Model and elicit the expressions in the box. For example, describe a process and include clarifying details. Then describe a process and have students ask for clarification.

Note: The purpose of this activity is to develop fluency. Students should be free to talk without fear of interruption for error correction. If you notice persistent errors, write them down for later reteaching or review.

❽ Have students read the instructions and the list of household tasks. Have a pair of students read the example conversation on page 92 aloud for the class. Then have students get into groups of three or four and complete the activity. Circulate and help with vocabulary as needed. Remind students to use the language for asking for clarification and clarifying details.

☻ **Option:** Have students demonstrate for the class something they know how to do, such as how to fix a bike or wash windows. Or have them bring in something they built, such as a key rack or a birdhouse, and explain how they built it. Remind students to clarify details as they explain the process. Encourage the class to ask for clarification when appropriate.

 Workbook: Practice 10

5 Now listen and repeat each pair of words. Did you write each word in the correct column?

6 When talking about English sounds and spellings, people say, "When two vowels go walking, the first one does the talking." What do you think this means? Read the examples and circle the answers. (See page 131 for IPA symbols.)

   a. The vowels **ee** in *sleep, sheep,* and *feet* are pronounced /i/ /ɪ/
   b. The vowels **ea** in *leave, eat,* and *least* are pronounced /i/ /ɪ/
   c. The vowels **ai** in *paid, rain,* and *main* are pronounced /e/ /aɪ/
   d. The vowels **ie** in *pie, lies,* and *died* are pronounced /e/ /aɪ/
   e. Can you think of exceptions to these rules? List them.

7 Work with a partner. First, A reads the sentences below and B circles the words on page 94. Then B reads the sentences on page 94 and A circles the words here.

A reads:	A listens and circles:	
1. Hal got on a really big ship.	**1.** sleep	slip
2. I don't know when they'll leave.	**2.** feel	fill
3. He's sailing to the islands.	**3.** these	this
4. Soon he'll get served his meal.	**4.** heat	hit
5. Hal only wants a little bit.	**5.** least	list

Speak Out

Asking for Clarification and Clarifying In conversation, when certain points or statements are not clear, it's important to ask the speaker for clarification. Also, you should make sure your statements and explanations are clear to others by clarifying what you mean.

Asking for Clarification	Clarifying
So first you … ?	What I mean is …
Could you explain how to … ?	Let me explain again …
Can you go over that again?	Let me put it another way. You …

8 Work in groups of three or four. Explain to your group how to do one of the tasks in the box. You can also use your own ideas.

change a lightbulb	put up wallpaper	fix a broken window
fix a leaky faucet	set up a computer	repair a brick wall
hang some pictures	build bookshelves	plant a tree

Example:

A: It's easy to change a fuse. First, you kill the power to the circuit panel, unscrew the fuse, or pull it out if it's a cartridge type, and replace it with the same type. Then you turn the power back on, and you're done.

B: So first you do something to the circuit panel? Could you go over that part again?

A: Sure. What I mean is you have to turn off the electricity first.

READING and WRITING

Read About It

1 **Before You Read** Did you have a favorite toy when you were a child? What special meaning did it have for you? Do you remember how you got it? Do you still have it? Tell the class about it.

 STRATEGY **Understanding Spatial Organization** When describing a place, writers often use spatial organization. You will understand better if you notice whether the details are organized from general to specific or specific to general, from outside to inside or inside to outside, or from front to back or back to front.

Play Palace

England is well-known for its impressive architecture, but few people realize that one of its most beautiful examples is only 92 inches (2.3 meters) high. Queen Mary's dollhouse, designed
5 by the British architect Sir Edwin Lutyens in 1920, is an exquisite working reproduction of a royal home of the period, realistic and functional in every perfect detail.

Sir Lutyens employed more than 150
10 craftsmen to ensure the authenticity of his design. He had a lawn of green velvet laid out and a beautiful miniature garden put in to the east, where flowers traditionally catch the morning sun.

Detail of the day nursery in Queen Mary's dollhouse

To guard the palace, Lutyens had figures of sentries at attention placed around the grounds. He
15 even had a garage built to hold several toy limousines and a mechanic's workshop constructed, complete with miniature tools. The house itself has three floors. The exterior walls of the house are made of wood, carved and painted to resemble stone. Lutyens had a mechanism installed that raises and lowers the walls electrically so the interior rooms can be reached. He had workmen put real marble and parquet floors in the rooms, along with windows that slide open
20 and doors that lock. He had plumbers create a system for hot and cold running water, which runs from silver faucets.

READING and WRITING

Read About It

Preview

Ask students to name some common toys. You might want to bring in pictures of some toys for students to name or to match to names you write on the board.

Presentation

❶ Before You Read Read the questions aloud to the class and have individuals respond. For larger classes, have students share their stories in groups.

Option: Have students each write their favorite toy on a slip of paper. Collect the papers, then read them aloud. Ask the class to guess which toy is the favorite of which class member.

➡ **Understanding Spatial Organization** Have students read the strategy silently. Tell them to practice using this strategy as they read the passage.

Option: While students are reading the strategy, draw on the board a pyramid or other simple object that has a top, bottom, inside, and outside. Then use the object to illustrate the different types of text organization. Show students that writers can approach a description from many different angles. Begin by showing that they can start from the bottom (point to the bottom of the object) and move up to the top (point to the top). Then use the object to illustrate other spatial organizations: top to bottom, outside to inside, inside to outside, general to specific, and specific to general.

Focus students' attention on the pictures. Have them describe the pictures, and have them predict what relation the pictures have to the article.

Have students read the article independently in class or for homework. Encourage them to read without dictionaries. If students read in class, you may want to set a time limit.

Option: To check comprehension, write the following questions on the board or ask them orally. You might want to have students check their answers in pairs or small groups. (*Answers will vary somewhat.*)

1. Describe the dollhouse in one sentence. (It is a perfect, functional miniature reproduction of a royal home.)

2. What did Sir Edwin Lutyens have made for the outside of the palace? (a lawn and garden, sentries to guard the palace, a garage, and a workshop)

3. Describe the outside of the palace. (It has wooden walls carved and painted to look like stone.)

4. What are some of the objects inside? (velvet and lace curtains, gold and china objects, miniature books, drawings and paintings, a stocked wine cellar, and so on)

5. What were some of the materials used to make the dollhouse? (silver, marble, velvet, lace, wood)

6. Where is the dollhouse now? (It's on display in Windsor Castle.)

You might want to have students make up three more questions about the dollhouse to ask each other.

❷ Have students work independently to read the directions and figure out the meaning of the words. Then have them work with partners to check their answers. If necessary, allow partners to check a dictionary to settle any differences.

> **Answers**
> Answers will vary somewhat. **a.** copy **b.** skilled workers **c.** truth, reality, genuineness **d.** very small, tiny **e.** guards, soldiers **f.** land around a building **g.** look like, be similar to **h.** to make an exact copy **i.** books **j.** to show or exhibit

Option: You may want to give students these additional words to figure out from context. Have them write synonyms or short definitions. *(Answers will vary.)*

1. functional (line 7) (capable of being used)

2. exterior (line 16) (outside)

3. interior (line 18) (inside)

4. stocked (line 30) (filled)

5. exhibited (line 37) (shown)

❸ Have students complete the exercise independently, compare their answers in small groups, and justify their choices.

> **Answer**
> **c.** outside to inside

Option: You may want to write the following discussion questions on the board or make a copy for each student. Have students talk over their ideas in pairs, in small groups, or as a class. Ask individuals to share their ideas with the class.

1. Some people believe that it is not a good idea to give dolls and dollhouses only to girls to play with. They think boys need to express their feelings by playing with these toys, too. Do you agree with this idea? Why or why not?

2. Clearly, Queen Mary's dollhouse required a large amount of money and a lot of effort to build. Do you think this is a good way for money to be spent? Why or why not? Does it make a difference whether the object is kept private or exhibited in public?

Option: Have students go to the library and research other famous miniatures—for example, model ships, cars, airplanes, or trains. Have them report their findings to the class. After students have completed the Write About It activities on page 94, you may want to have them write a description of a miniature they researched.

Option: Have students do one of the following: write a paragraph describing a favorite childhood toy; bring a toy to class and tell about it; write a paragraph comparing toys from the past to toys found in stores today. (you may wish to have students do the writing options after Write About It on page T94.)

Write: A Descriptive Paragraph

Preview

- Ask students how they would describe the classroom. Where would they start their description, and how would they organize it spatially? Ask also which details they think would be important to describe. What feeling about the classroom would these details give listeners? Is this feeling accurate?

- Ask students if they have ever written a physical description of a person, place, or thing in a letter to someone. Have them talk about the description and how they organized it. You may want to have students work in pairs to brainstorm situations in which they would need to write descriptions.

Presentation

Have students read the explanation independently. Ask students what controlling idea—that is, attitude or feeling—seemed to be expressed by the description of Queen Mary's dollhouse. (admiration or appreciation of the perfection, realism, elegance, and so on) Have them give examples of details that contribute to this attitude or feeling about the dollhouse. Point out that the description does not contain any details that contradict the controlling idea.

In addition, Sir Lutyens had seamstresses make elegant curtains of velvet and lace, carpenters
25 duplicate Chippendale and Queen Anne furniture, and interior decorators find objects of gold and china, as well as more than 700 drawings and paintings. Lutyens found bookbinders and had them create more than 200 tiny leather-bound volumes for the library. He even had the wine
30 cellar stocked with miniature bottles, each one filled with a few drops of the best wines!

Because of Luyten's concern for detail, Queen Mary's dollhouse is a perfect duplicate in miniature of the finest royal home. So that everyone could
35 appreciate the art and craftsmanship that went into the building of this beautiful play palace, the dollhouse was exhibited in public in 1924, and has remained on display in Windsor Castle ever since.

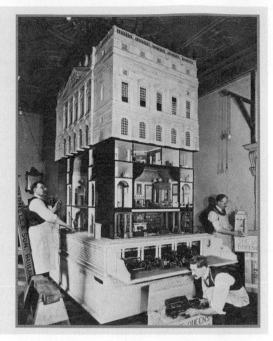

2 Use the context to figure out the meaning of the words below. Write synonyms or short definitions on the lines.

   a. reproduction (line 6) _____

   b. craftsmen (line 10) _____

   c. authenticity (line 10) _____

   d. miniature (line 12) _____

   e. sentries (line 14) _____

   f. grounds (line 14) _____

   g. to resemble (line 17) _____

   h. to duplicate (line 24) _____

   i. volumes (line 29) _____

   j. to display (line 38) _____

3 How is the description of the Play Palace organized in the article? Circle the letters.

   a. top to bottom   **d.** inside to outside

   b. bottom to top   **e.** specific to general

   c. outside to inside   **f.** general to specific

Write: A Descriptive Paragraph

When you write a description of a place, you create a vivid picture in words for the reader. In addition to organizing your ideas logically, by space or by importance, you should give the description a controlling idea. Think of this idea as your attitude or feeling about the place. This idea will keep the paragraph focused and allow you to include specific details.

4 Read the paragraph describing a room and answer the questions.

It is clear from just looking at my sister's room that she is a musician. As you open the door, a set of musical chimes makes a melody. To the right of the door is a large bookcase filled with books on composers, sheet music, and her collection of compact discs and tapes. On the right wall is a long shelf with all of her awards, certificates, and prizes from different musical competitions. Under that shelf is her old upright piano. Next to the piano are her guitar case, her violin case, and her flute case. On the night table next to her bed are a radio alarm clock and a little bust of Beethoven. The posters above her bed show all of her favorite musicians and composers. On the other side of her bed is a comfortable chair, where she spends hours listening to music from her stereo system, which is very large and takes up most of the left wall. Even her desk, to the left of the door, is covered with books on music, her own compositions, and autographed pictures of musicians she has seen at concerts. It is safe to say, after seeing her room, that my sister lives for music.

    a. How is the paragraph organized?

    b. What is the controlling idea of the paragraph? Circle it.

    c. Underline all the details that relate to the controlling idea.

    d. What is the purpose of the concluding sentence?

Write About It

5 Brainstorm a list of places that have been important in your life (for example, your bedroom, the family kitchen, a treehouse, the basement, the schoolyard, an office, a hospital room, a park, a beach, etc.). Choose one of these places to describe in a paragraph.

6 Brainstorm specific details that will help create a picture in words for your readers. Decide how you will organize the details in a logical way. What is your general attitude or feeling about the place? Write a topic sentence that presents this controlling idea. Then write the paragraph.

 7 **Check Your Writing** Exchange paragraphs with a partner. What place has your partner described? Use the questions below to give feedback to your partner. When you get your paper back, revise as necessary.

> • What is the controlling idea of the description?
> • Is this idea supported with enough details?
> • How is the description organized? Is it clear and logical?

B reads:	B listens and circles:	
1. The captain had to sleep a bit.	**1.** sheep	ship
2. Now how does he feel?	**2.** leave	live
3. He likes this a lot better.	**3.** he's	his
4. Oh my, did they hit a rock?	**4.** meal	mill
5. Help, the ship's starting to list!	**5.** beat	bit

4 Have students read the paragraph and answer the questions independently. Then have them check answers in pairs or as a class.

Answers

a. spatially, around the room from right to left **b.** The controlling idea is the first sentence: "It is clear from looking at my sister's room that she is a musician." **c.** The many nouns related to music should be underlined, as should their modifiers. **d.** to reinforce the controlling idea

Write About It

Presentation

5 Have students brainstorm the places independently. Encourage them to think of as many places as they can and to list them all. Then have students think carefully before choosing the one place they would like to describe. Can they remember the place in detail? Do they have an attitude or feeling about the place?

6 Again, encourage students to think of as many details as possible when brainstorming and then to think carefully about which details they should actually use in their description. Remind them that these details should fit with their controlling idea. After they have written a topic sentence with their controlling idea, they may want to make a sort of outline by listing the details they think they will use in a logical order. Have them complete their first drafts.

☑ **7** **Check Your Writing** Have pairs of students exchange their first drafts and use the questions to check both the information and the organization. Have them give each other feedback before they write their final draft.

🜨 **Option:** Have students describe their "dream house." Tell them to brainstorm details that are a part of the house and its grounds and to list them. Then have them write a paragraph following the instructions for Exercise 6. Have individuals read their descriptions to the class.

 Workbook: Practice 11

Vocabulary Expansion: *Make versus do*
See page T148.

Answers

1. make 2. made 3. do 4. make 5. made
6. did 7. made 8. made 9. did 10. made
11. making 12. made 13. do 14.. made

 Workbook: Practice 12

EVALUATION

See page TExi.

Unit 9 Achievement Test

Self-Check See **Check Your Knowledge,** page 72 of the Workbook.

Dictation Dictate the following paragraph. When students have finished, have them rewrite the paragraph so that it tells about how they would like to remodel their home. For more information on dictation, see page TExv.

Maybe at some time in the future, I will be able to have my apartment remodeled. If this happens, I'll make many changes. I'll have a carpenter build a deck on my fourth-floor apartment so that I'll finally be able to sit outside. I'll have each room painted a different color of the rainbow. I'll get an electrician to install strings of tiny bright lights on all the ceilings. And I'll have the entire apartment soundproofed so that I won't have to worry about neighbors and noise.

Communication Skills

1. Show students a picture of an old, run-down house. Tell students to imagine that they are repairing the old house. Ask them to say what they think will need to be done. Listen for the names of workers, household items, and construction terminology.

2. Ask students to talk about errands or things that need to be done in their own lives. Pay attention to the structures they use to talk about getting things done and to express purpose.

Review Units 7–9

Unit review exercises can be assigned as homework or done in class. You can use them in several ways:

- Give the review exercises as a quiz. Have students work alone and submit their answers to you.

- Give the review exercises as you would other exercises in the book. Have students work alone and then compare answers with a partner.

- Have students work alone and then review answers as a class. Have selected students write their answers on the board. Then correct any errors as a class.

❶ Have students read the instructions independently and then complete the exercise. For general notes on reported speech, refer students to Unit 7, pages 68–69.

> **Answers**
>
> Answers will vary somewhat; for example, verbs used to report speech will vary.
>
> Namiko said (that) she needed some help.
>
> Hiroshi asked (her) what the matter was.
>
> Namiko said (that) she was having a party on Friday and (that) she wanted it to be perfect.
>
> Hiroshi asked (her) whether/if she had bought enough to eat and drink.
>
> Namiko said (that) she had plenty and (that) she had been cooking all week but (that) she was worried about the music.
>
> Hiroshi said (that) she could borrow his CD collection. He said that it was/is huge.
>
> Namiko told Hiroshi (that) he was the greatest. She also told him (that) now the party would be a hit.

❷ Have students read the instructions independently and then complete the exercise. For general notes on the passive voice, refer students to Unit 8, pages 77–79.

> **Answers**
>
> 1. died 2. was preserved 3. was covered 4. was found 5. (was) taken 6. is being kept/is kept 7. has been collected/is being collected/is collected 8. (has been) stored/(is being) stored/(is) stored

❸ Have students read the instructions independently and then complete the exercise. For general notes on the passive voice and agents with the passive, refer students to Unit 8, pages 77–79.

> **Answers**
>
> a. The winning goal was kicked in the last seconds of the game by Fernandez. b. Useful information is found on the Internet. c. In the United States, cereal is often eaten for breakfast. d. The papers were graded by Professor Kohn. e. The invitations will be printed tomorrow.

1 Write the conversation in reported speech.

NAMIKO: "I need some help."

_____

HIROSHI: "What's the matter?"

_____

NAMIKO: "I'm having a party on Friday and I want it to be perfect."

_____

HIROSHI: "Did you buy enough to eat and drink?"

_____

NAMIKO: "I have plenty, and I've been cooking all week, but I'm worried about the music."

_____

HIROSHI: "You can borrow my CD collection. It's huge."

_____

NAMIKO: "You're the greatest. Now the party will be a hit."

_____

2 Complete the passage with the correct form of the verb. Use the passive voice when appropriate.

Over 5,000 years ago, a hunter (**1. die**) _____ in the mountains on the border of Italy and Austria. His body (**2. preserve**) _____ because it (**3. cover**) _____ by snow and ice for thousands of years. In 1991, he (**4. find**) _____ and (**5. take**) _____ to the University of Innsbruck, where scientists are learning a lot about him. Now his body (**6. keep**) _____ in a special environment there, along with his clothes, tools, and hunting weapons. Information about him (**7. collect**) _____ and (**8. store**) _____ in a database at the university.

3 Change the sentences from active to passive voice. Use the agent only when necessary.

a. Fernandez kicked the winning goal in the last seconds of the game.

_____

b. Many people find useful information on the Internet.

_____

c. In the United States, people often eat cereal for breakfast.

_____

d. Professor Kohn graded the papers.

_____

e. The company will print the invitations tomorrow.

_____

4 Complete the conversation with the correct form of the verb.

DAN: Congratulations on your promotion, Kim.

KIM: Thanks, Dan. The best part is my new office! The first thing I did was have the painters (**1. come in**) _____ and (**2. paint**) _____ the walls and ceiling.

DAN: Did you have your office (**3. redecorate**) _____, too?

KIM: Yes. I had new shelves (**4. install**) _____ and an extra-large desk (**5. build**) _____ for me. And I got new carpet (**6. put in**) _____ as well. Now I am having my daughter (**7. shop**) _____ for a couple of nice paintings for the walls.

DAN: It will look great when you're done. Have your daughter (**8. get**) _____ some plants for a finishing touch.

5 Give the purpose of each action. Use *(in order) to* + verb or *so (that)* + clause.

a. Why did Greg stay up all night?

_____

b. Why did you walk to work today? Where's your car?

_____

c. Why did Cathy call you last night?

_____

e. Why did your brother borrow your tools?

_____

Vocabulary Review

Use the words in the box to complete the sentences.

estimate	remodel	hilarious	jokes	miniature
plumber	pressure	process	saw	theories

1. We should _____ our kitchen. We really need more space.
2. Toothpaste comes out of the tube when _____ is applied.
3. The play we saw last night was _____; we laughed till we cried!
4. Several philosophers have developed _____ of humor.
5. I can't cut wood with this old thing; I need a new _____.
6. Let's get an _____ to see how much it would cost to fix the roof.
7. My aunt collects _____ teapots, cups, and saucers. She has hundreds!
8. He's not good at telling _____, but he does have a great sense of humor.
9. The _____ by which olives are prepared is fascinating.
10. The leaky faucet is driving me crazy. Call a _____ to fix it!

❹ Have students read the instructions independently and then complete the exercise. For general notes on structures used to talk about getting things done, refer students to Unit 9, page 87.

> **Answers**
> 1. come in 2. paint 3. redecorated
> 4. installed 5. built 6. put in 7. shop
> 8. get

❺ Have students read the instructions independently and then complete the exercise. For general notes on structures used to express purpose, refer students to Unit 9, page 89.

> **Answers**
> Answers will vary. Possible answers: **a.** Greg stayed up all night (in order) to study for his English test/so (that) he could study for his English test. **b.** I walked to work today (in order) to get some fresh air/so (that) I could get some fresh air. My car was at home. **c.** Cathy called me last night (in order) to invite me to her party on Friday/so (that) she could invite me to her party on Friday. **d.** My brother borrowed my tools (in order) to build a bookcase/so (that) he could build a bookcase.

Vocabulary Review

Have students read the instructions independently and then complete the exercise.

> **Answers**
> 1. remodel 2. pressure 3. hilarious
> 4. theories 5. saw 6. estimate 7. miniature
> 8. jokes 9. process 10. plumber

MYSTERIES OF SCIENCE

OBJECTIVES

- To talk about scientific mysteries
- To speculate about the past
- To use **may have, might have, could have, must have** + past participle
- To express past ability or missed opportunity
- To draw logical conclusions about the past
- To distinguish between fact and opinion
- To pronounce the reduced forms of **have** in past modals
- To use formal language in writing
- To determine the meanings of phrasal verbs from context

GETTING STARTED

Warm Up

Preview

- Write the unit title, **Mysteries of Science**, on the board. Explain that scientists are always trying to solve mysteries. Elicit or mention the kinds of mysteries scientists have solved or are working on solving. (*Examples:* finding cures for illnesses such as AIDS and learning about other planets)

- Elicit or present the words **conclusive**, **creature**, **dinosaur**, **lake**, **monster**, and **sophisticated**. For example, ask students how a lake is different from the ocean or the sea. (It's smaller, has fresh water, and is surrounded by land.) Ask students to tell about what they know about dinosaurs. Then explain that scientists have used sophisticated, or advanced, methods to study dinosaurs and that they have some conclusive findings about when the dinosaurs existed.

Language Note: **Loch** is a Scottish word that means "lake." The pronunciation of **loch** is /lɑk/.

Presentation

❶ Have students read the information and think about the questions. Then have them work in pairs or small groups and to think of mysteries that scientists have not yet been able to explain. Have the pairs or groups share their ideas with the rest of the class.

🎧 ❷ Have students read the instructions. Play the recording or read the audioscript aloud two or more times and have students write their answers. (You may want to mention that 750 feet is approximately 230 meters.) Review the answers as a class.

Audioscript: The audioscript for Exercise 2 appears on page T157.

> **Answers**
> 1. 750 2. Scotland 3. monster 4. dinosaur
> 5. lake 6. 1,500 7. 1980s 8. photographs

🌀 **Option:** Have students work in groups of three to act the parts of a radio interviewer and two people who have seen the Loch Ness monster. Have the interviewer ask questions and have the witnesses describe their experiences.

🌀 **Option:** Tell students to imagine that someone saw a strange kind of monster in their own town and to write short newspaper articles about the incident. Encourage them to illustrate their articles with drawings of the monster. You might want to post the articles on the classroom walls.

🌀 **Option:** Review meanings of suffixes *–ist*, *–er/–or* (one who practices, does, or believes in; one whose profession is) before students are assigned Workbook Practice 1.

 Workbook: Practice 1

GETTING STARTED

Warm Up

1 Many scientists spend their lives trying to solve mysteries, such as how migrating birds find their way over long distances or how the pyramids in Egypt were built. Can you think of any mysteries scientists have not been able to explain? Share your ideas with the class.

2 Listen and write the correct words on the lines.

Loch Ness is a huge body of water,
(1.) _____ feet deep, located in
(2.) _____. Many people think that a kind
of **(3.)** _____ or **(4.)** _____ lives
in this **(5.)** _____. It was first seen over
(6.) _____ years ago, and there have been
many sightings since then. An attempt to find the creature through the use of sophisticated scientific instruments took place in the **(7.)** _____, but no conclusive evidence was found. There are, however, **(8.)** _____ which seem to show a large, living being swimming in the lake.

The creature "Nessie" at Loch Ness

Figure It Out

The students in Miss Catucci's history class have just heard a classmate's report on Loch Ness. Now, after class, they are talking about another mystery.

Nazca, Peru

SALLY: Kenji's report on Loch Ness was great. What a mystery!

CHRIS: I've always wanted to go to Nazca in Peru to see those mysterious drawings
5 on the ground. Some of them are over forty miles long!

SALLY: Were they carved in the ground?

CHRIS: Yeah, they're amazing. There are animals, plants, human heads, and
10 complex geometric figures. And some of the drawings show things that the ancient civilizations couldn't have known about, like African lions.

ANDY: Do you think the Incas might have
15 carved them?

CHRIS: Well, the local Indians say they were made even before the Incas lived there.

ANDY: What were they for?

CHRIS: Nobody knows exactly. Astronomers think they must have been
20 part of a huge star chart.

SALLY: But some anthropologists think primitive people might have drawn them for sacred or religious purposes.

CHRIS: There's even a really strange theory involving UFOs …

SALLY: Oh yeah. Some people say that the long lines and marks may have
25 served as a landing field for flying saucers! And who knows? It could be true!

CHRIS: Well, if you look carefully, there is one drawing that looks a lot like an astronaut in a space helmet … It's amazing.

3 Vocabulary Check Match the words on the left with their meanings. The first three are from Exercise 2 on page 97.

_____ **1.** creature
_____ **2.** sophisticated
_____ **3.** conclusive
_____ **4.** to carve (line 7)
_____ **5.** primitive (line 21)
_____ **6.** flying saucer (line 25)
_____ **7.** helmet (line 28)

a. cut into
b. of long ago
c. protective head covering
d. unidentified round object seen in the sky
e. very complex and advanced
f. a living animal or person
g. convincing; final

Figure It Out

Preview

- Elicit or present **geometric**, **carved**, **primitive**, **sacred**, **religious**, **UFO**, **flying saucer**, and **space helmet**. Use pictures, drawings on the board, and/or synonyms as appropriate. For example, for UFO and flying saucer, show the picture on page 99 and tell students that it can be called a UFO, for unidentified flying object, or it can be called a flying saucer, because it looks like a plate. Ask students to tell what they have seen or read about sightings of UFOs.

- Ask students if they have ever seen **artifacts** (objects made by human work, such as a primitive tool) or read about any early civilizations, such as the Incas or the Aztecs. If any students have some knowledge about an early civilization, have them share their knowledge with the class.

Presentation

Focus students' attention on the photograph, which shows ancient drawings on the ground at Nazca, in Peru. Ask students to describe what they see in it. Then ask them to predict what the conversation will be about.

Read the conversation aloud as students listen. Students can listen with their books open or closed. Then have them read the conversation independently in class or for homework.

Have students answer the following questions about the conversation, as a class or in groups, to check comprehension.

1. Who gave a report on Loch Ness? (Kenji)
2. Where would Chris like to go? Why? (to Nazca in Peru, to see the mysterious drawings there)
3. What do the drawings show? (animals including African lions, plants, human heads, geometric figures)
4. Who carved the drawings into the ground? (maybe primitive people who lived there before the Incas)
5. What was the purpose of the drawings? (No one knows for sure—some astronomers think they were part of a star chart; some anthropologists think they were drawn for religious purposes; some people say flying saucers landed there.)

☑ ❸ **Vocabulary Check** Have students read the directions and complete the activity independently. Review the answers as a class.

> **Answers**
> 1. f 2. e 3. g 4. a 5. b 6. d 7. c

 Workbook: Practice 2

Talk About It

Option: You may prefer to postpone this activity until after the grammar presentation (page 99) if you feel that your students need extra help with past modal auxiliaries.

Presentation

Note: The purpose of this activity is to develop fluency. Students should be free to talk without fear of interruption for error correction. If you notice persistent errors, write them down for later reteaching or review.

❹ Have students read the instructions and model conversation. Then have a pair of students read the conversation aloud for the class. Have students work in pairs to complete the activity. Then ask pairs of students to perform their conversations for the class.

Option: Have students continue the activity using the following cues. Be sure they use **who** for persons and **what** for things.

1. Kevin/his brother
2. ambulance/police car
3. recording/live performance
4. the victim's sister/her cousin
5. real gun/toy gun

 Workbook: Practice 3

GRAMMAR

Speculating About the Past

Preview

- Elicit or present the meaning of **speculating**. (thinking/guessing based on facts) To introduce the idea of speculating about the past, have students work in pairs or small groups. Ask them if they know for certain why there are no longer dinosaurs. (Even scholars do not know for certain.) Ask students to brainstorm some possible reasons. (*Examples:* There wasn't enough food for them; a meteorite killed them.) Have them report their reasons, and write them on the board.

- Remind students that when we speculate about the present, we use the modal aux

iliaries **may**, **might**, and **could**. (*Example:* It may rain today.) Then explain that **may**, **might**, and **could** are also used to speculate about the past. Write a sentence on the board that makes a speculation about the past. (*Example:* Scientists don't know for sure, but dinosaurs might have disappeared because there was not enough food for them.)

- Ask students what follows the modal in the sentence you wrote. (**have** + past participle) Then have students make similar sentences based on the speculations they had made. Write their sentences on the board.

- Write the sentence on the board:

    Jane could have left early.

    Elicit the negative and interrogative forms of **could have left** in the sentence. (Jane couldn't have left early. Could Jane have left early?) Then write on the board:

    Peter might/may have gone to the store.

    Elicit the negative forms of **might have** and **may have** in the sentence. (Peter might not/may not have gone to the store.) Explain that this means that it is possible that Peter did not go to the store. Tell students that **could not have** + past participle is not used in this sense. (The uses of **couldn't have** are explained on pages 100 and 101.)

Presentation

Have students read the grammar explanation and examples independently in class or for homework.

❶ Have students read the instructions and the paragraph independently. Help with any unfamiliar vocabulary. Have students complete the exercise independently. Then have them compare answers in pairs. Review answers as a class.

Answers
1. might/may/could have existed
2. might/may/could have disappeared
3. might/may/could have survived
4. might/may/could have come
5. might/may/could have been
6. might not/may not have represented
7. might/may/could have drawn

Talk About It

 You and a friend are trying to figure out what you have just seen and heard. You have different interpretations. With a partner, ask and answer questions using the cues.

Example: weather balloon/UFO

Ask for information.
A: What do you think it was?

Speculate about the past.
B: I don't know. I think it might have been a weather balloon.

Give firm belief.
A: I think it was probably a UFO.

Admit possibility.
B: Well, I guess it could have been either one.

a. star/meteorite
b. dog/wolf
c. plane/giant bird
d. ship/sea monster

e. tomato sauce/blood
f. doorbell/phone
g. shadow/ghost
h. trick/magic

GRAMMAR

Speculating About the Past

When we speculate or guess about things in the past that we are unsure of, we use *may have, might have,* or *could have* + past participle.

> Here are two theories on what killed the dinosaurs 140 million years ago:
>
> A meteorite **may have hit** the earth and **caused** their death
>
> The dinosaurs **might not have survived** because of the climactic changes that the Earth experienced.

 Read the mystery and the theories. Write the correct form of the verb on the line. Use *might, may,* or *could.* Use the negative when necessary.

In 1929, the Piri Re'is map was discovered in the imperial archives in Istanbul. Piri Re'is, an admiral in the Turkish navy, had a map of the Atlantic Ocean made in 1513. His map had accurate drawings of Africa and South America and the still undiscovered Antarctica. There were several speculations about this map:

a. A civilization sophisticated enough to make these maps
(**1. exist**) _____ before the 1500's. The civilization
(**2. disappear**) _____, but a few of their
maps (**3. survive**) _____.

    b. The maps (**4. come**) _____ from intelligent visitors from outer space.

    c. The map (**5. be**) _____ a fake.

    d. The part of the map below South America (**6. represent**) _____ Antarctica at all. A mapmaker (**7. draw**) _____ an imaginary part to the map, as was often the custom.

2 Read each situation and make a speculation for B's response.

  1. A: I really don't know what happened to this computer.

    B: _____

    A: Yes, possibly. Spilling tea on the keyboard would damage it.

  2. A: Who could have been trying to communicate with us?

    B: _____

    A: Stop it! You're scaring me! She's been dead for years!

  3. A: Wow! The Garcias have just remodeled their house and now a trip to Tunisia? I didn't know they were so well-off.

    B: _____

    A: Or maybe they inherited it from a long-lost cousin.

  4. A: How did Marta get to work this morning?

    B: _____

    A: Oh, that's right. Her car's still in the garage.

  5. A: What a strange robbery. The thieves knew exactly where the money was.

    B: _____

    A: Gee, I didn't think of him, but why would he?

  6. A: Where do you think Sam's been? I hope he's OK.

    B: _____

    A: That's possible. He's been talking a lot about needing to get away.

Expressing Past Ability or Missed Opportunity

We use *could have* + past participle to talk about our ability to do something in the past or to talk about opportunities that we had but didn't take advantage of.

A: Did you see the dinosaur exhibit at the Natural History Museum last week?

B: No, but I **could have seen** it. I was in the neighborhood. (*missed opportunity*)

A: So why didn't you?

B: I **couldn't have gone to** the exhibit and also to the movies. (*past ability*)

---

3 Think of three missed opportunities in your life and write them on a piece of paper. Then, with a partner, take turns interviewing each other.

Example:

A: Tell me about some of your missed opportunities.

B: In college, I could have studied in Madrid for a semester.

A: So what did you do instead?

B: I stayed in California and studied Spanish there.

❷ Have students read the instructions and make sure that everyone understands what to do. Have students work in pairs to complete the dialogues. Then have pairs read the completed dialogues to the class.

Answers

Answers will vary. Possible answers:
1. Someone might/may/could have spilled tea on it. **2.** The previous owner of the house might/may/could have been trying to communicate with us. **3.** They might/may/could have won the money in a lottery. **4.** She might/may/could have taken the bus. **5.** (Dan) might/may/could have told them where it was. **6.** He might/may/could have gone on a vacation.

 Workbook: Practice 4

Expressing Past Ability or Missed Opportunity

Preview

• Remind students that **could** is used to express past ability. (*Example:* When I was young, I could speak Spanish fluently.) Explain that **could have** + past participle is used to express a past ability that was possible but didn't become actual. That is, it expresses the idea of "would have been able to." (*Example:* When I was young, I could have spoken

English fluently, but I didn't have any English-speaking friends to talk to.) Use this sentence to point out the closely related sense of missed opportunity.

• Give students a problem someone had in the past and have them brainstorm ways that the person would have been able to solve the problem. For example, tell students, *A friend of mine was locked out of her house last night and spent the whole night in her car. How could she have gotten into her house?* Elicit sentences with **could have** + past participle. (*Example:* She could have called the police.) Write the sentences on the board.

Presentation

Have students read the grammar explanation and examples independently in class or for homework.

Pronunciation Note: Tell students that **could have** is often pronounced /ˈkudəv/ or /ˈkudə/.

❸ Have students read the instructions and the example independently. Then have a pair of students read the example interview aloud for the class. After students have written down their missed opportunities independently, have them carry out the interviews in pairs. Encourage them to ask follow-up questions, as in the example. Have some pairs present their interviews to the class.

 Workbook: Practice 5

Drawing Logical Conclusions About the Past

Preview

- To introduce the idea of drawing logical conclusions, give students a piece of information. For example, say, *John wasn't feeling well last weekend, and yesterday he wasn't in class.* Have students brainstorm several possibilities as to why John wasn't in class. Then ask them to choose the most logical one. (that John was sick) On the board, write:

  We're not absolutely certain, but given the information we have, John must have been sick.

  Then say that to draw logical conclusions about the past, we use **must have** + past participle.

- Repeat the procedure to show students how to make negative statements expressing near certainty about the past—that is, statements we make when we're almost certain something was impossible. For example, say, *John didn't know there would be a test and he didn't do any studying for it. How do you think he did on the test?* After students have answered, write on the board:

  We're not absolutely certain, but given the information we have, John couldn't have done well.

  Point out that this sentence uses **couldn't have** + past participle.

Presentation

Have students read the grammar explanation and examples independently in class or for homework. You might point out that the forms **must not have** and **couldn't have**, as in the examples, are more common than **mustn't have** and **could not have**.

4 Read the instructions and example aloud to the class. Then have pairs of students take turns asking and answering questions based on the cues. Encourage them to use the sentence contexts to figure out any unfamiliar words.

Answers

Answers will vary somewhat. **a.** They must have had cookies and milk for a snack. **b.** Someone must have taken a shower. **c.** The jeans and shirt must have fit one of the thieves. **d.** They must have listened to the latest CD of the Broken Bones Band, and they must have left recently. **e.** They must have taken Mrs. Santelli's jewelry. **f.** They must have gone out the garage door and closed it, or they must have walked by it.

Option: Have students use the information in Exercise 4 to write a newspaper article about the break-in at the Santellis' house. You may want to have them write a follow-up article that describes the capture of the thieves and makes speculations about their motives. Encourage students to use their imaginations.

☑ **5 Check Your Understanding** Have students complete the activity independently in class or for homework and then compare answers in pairs.

Answers

Answers may vary. We would be likely to use these modals in all these situations except in explaining how to do something or in applying for a scholarship.

---

6 Express Yourself Have students work in pairs to choose an appropriate situation for using modals in talking about the past. After they have written their dialogues, have them practice reading them to another pair. Then ask pairs to perform their dialogues for the class.

Option: Have students write sentences about the past using **might have, may have, could have**, and **must have** and these time expressions:

1. in ancient times   4. prior to this
2. several years ago   5. yesterday
3. at that time

 Workbook: Practices 6, 7

(*Exercise 6 Options continue on page T102.*)

Drawing Logical Conclusions About the Past

When we have enough information to draw a logical conclusion about events or situations in the past, we use *must have* + past participle.

> Jack invited over 100 guests to his party. It **must have cost** a fortune.
> The guests left right after dinner. They **must not have had** a good time.

When we are almost certain that something was impossible, we use *couldn't have* + past participle.

> Pablo **couldn't have been** at the party last night. He was at work all night.

 4 Last night there was a break-in at the Santelli's. Detectives are inspecting the evidence for clues. Work with a partner. Read the evidence and make logical conclusions about what happened.

Example: A window was broken.

A: Why do you think they broke the window?
B: They must have crawled into the house through the window.

   a. Traces of cookies and milk were found on the kitchen counter.
   b. There was a wet towel in the shower.
   c. A pair of jeans and a white shirt were missing from Mr. Santelli's room.
   d. The Broken Bones Band's latest CD was still playing in the living room.
   e. All of Mrs. Santelli's jewelry was missing.
   f. The garage door was closed, but a ring was found on the ground outside the door.

 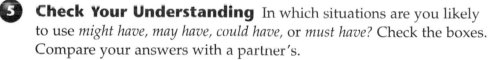 **5** **Check Your Understanding** In which situations are you likely to use *might have, may have, could have,* or *must have?* Check the boxes. Compare your answers with a partner's.

   ☐ You missed the end of a movie and you're guessing how it ended.
   ☐ You're wondering why a fellow student was absent the other day.
   ☐ You're explaining to a friend how to use a cellular phone.
   ☐ You are talking about life in dinosaur times.
   ☐ You are applying for a scholarship for a free English course.

 6 **Express Yourself** Work with a partner. Imagine yourselves in one of the situations above. Then write a dialogue and read it to another group.

Listen: Tropical Rain Forests

1 **Before You Listen** An ecosystem consists of all the animals and plants in a particular area and the interdependency between them. What do you know about the rain forest ecosystem? Discuss with a partner.

STRATEGY **Recognizing Facts and Opinions** When listening, it is important to know whether you are hearing facts or opinions. Certain expressions help signal each.

Facts	Opinions
The fact is that …	In my opinion …
Research shows that …	As I see it …
Experts in the field agree that …	Most people think …

2 Listen to a panel discussion about the world's tropical rain forests. Then decide if the following statements were presented as fact or opinion. Write **F** (fact) or **O** (opinion) on the line.

_____ **a.** Rain forests are mysterious and beautiful.

_____ **b.** Rain forests are vital sources of oxygen.

_____ **c.** It's impossible to imagine the size of Amazonia.

_____ **d.** Rain forests consist of five layers that coexist in a delicate balance.

_____ **e.** It's a tragedy that sections of the rain forest have been cut down.

_____ **f.** Young organizations are ineffective in defending the rain forests.

3 Listen to the discussion again and complete the chart.

1. Locations of major rain forests _____

_____

2. Area of Amazonia in square miles _____

3. Number of species in one square mile of Amazonia _____

4. Number of layers in a rain forest _____

Pronunciation

Reducing *Have* with Past Modals

When followed by a word beginning with a consonant, ***have*** /hæv/ in past modals is usually reduced to /əv/, or in fast talk, to /ə/. When followed by a vowel sound, /əv/ is not reduced to /ə/.

A: The 100 giant statues on Easter Island are still a mystery.

B: Who **could have** carved them?   /kʊd hæv/→/kʊdəv/ or /kʊdə/

(Exercise 6 Options continued from page T101.)

⊕ **Option:** Have students speculate and draw conclusions about these situations using the modals in parentheses. Have them use each modal in a separate sentence.

1. The doctor called. Sarah's just been taken to the hospital. (might have, must have)
2. Carol's just bought a new house and a new car! (could have, must have)
3. I don't know why I didn't do well on that test. I studied for it. (couldn't have, must not have)
4. How did Tom get so sunburned? (must have, could have)

⊕ **Option:** Bring in or have students bring in pictures of tools and machines of types that are no longer used. (A library should be a good source of pictures.) Have students work in pairs and take turns guessing what the machines were used for. Encourage students to use the language for speculating about the past and for drawing logical conclusions.

LISTENING and SPEAKING

Listen: Tropical Rain Forests

Presentation

❶ **Before You Listen** Have students read the explanation of *ecosystem* and the question. Then have them discuss in pairs what they know about rain forest ecosystems. Have pairs share their knowledge with the class.

➡ **Recognizing Facts and Opinions** Have students read the strategy. Present or elicit a few sentences with some of the expressions given and/or similar expressions. To do this, use topics presented earlier in the unit. (*Example:* Experts agree that dinosaurs became extinct about 140 million years ago. *or* In my opinion, we'll never really understand why dinosaurs became extinct.)

🎧 ❷ Have students read the instructions. Then play the recording or read the audioscript aloud. If necessary, play the recording or read the audioscript again so that students can check their answers. Review answers as a class.

Audioscript: The audioscript for Exercises 2 and 3 appears on page T158.

> **Answers**
> **a.** O **b.** F **c.** O **d.** F **e.** O **f.** O

🎧 ❸ Have students read the chart. Then play the recording or read the audioscript aloud. After students have filled in the chart, have them work in pairs to compare answers. If necessary, let them listen again to check their answers.

> **Answers**
> **1.** Western Africa, southeast Asia, South America **2.** 2.5 million square miles **3.** 117 **4.** five

 Workbook: Practice 8

Pronunciation

Preview

- Write the following conversation on the board.

  A: Where could Jack be?

  B: I don't know. He must have left early.

  Read the conversation to students, pronouncing **must have** as /məstəv/. Ask them how you pronounced **must have**. If necessary, read the conversation again so students can answer your question. Write the second sentence in the conversation three more times, replacing **must have** with **might have**, **may have**, and **could have**. Ask students how **might have**, **may have**, and **could have** might be pronounced. Call on students to say the sentences.

- Tell students that /məstəv/ can be reduced to /məstə/. Read the sentence on the board with **must have** (He must have left early.) pronouncing **must have** as /məstə/. Have students pronounce **must have** and then **might have**, **may have**, and **could have** in this way. Then have them say the sentences with these reduced forms.

Presentation

Have students read the explanation and example. Say **could have** in the three pronunciations, and have students repeat. Then have students practice saying the sentence in the example with the three different pronunciations of **could have**.

🎧 ❹ Have students read the instructions. Play the recording or read the audioscript aloud two or more times. If necessary, let students listen again to check their answers. Then have them repeat each sentence after they hear it.

Answers
a. /meəv/ **b.** /maɪtə/ **c.** /kudəv/ **d.** /məstəv/

🎧 ❺ Have students read the instructions. Play the recording or read the audioscript aloud. If necessary, let students listen again to check their answers. Then have them repeat each sentence after they hear it.

Answers
a, c, c, b, c

❻ Have students practice the dialogue in pairs. Then call on some pairs to perform it for the class.

 Workbook: Practice 9

Speak Out

Preview

Write **Speculating about the past** on the board. Then tell students, *My brother always writes to me once a week, but he hasn't written to me for the last three weeks.* Have students make speculations about this situation, eliciting sentences such as "He could have forgotten." and "He might have broken his arm." Write some of the sentences on the board.

Presentation

➡ **Speculating About the Past** Have students read the strategy and the expressions in the box. Point out that they have already used **might have**, **may have**, and **could have**

to speculate about the past. Point out also that **It might/may/could have been** are equivalent in meaning to **Maybe it was** or **It's possible that it was**.

Note: The purpose of this activity is to develop fluency. Students should be free to talk without fear of interruption for error correction. If you notice persistent errors, write them down for later reteaching or review.

❼ Have students read the instructions and the example. Then assign each student a text—**A**, **B**, or **C**—to read independently. Have all the students who were assigned to read a text sit together in a group. Tell them to help each other remember the information in the text. Give them a four- or five-minute time limit to learn the information.

☯ **Option:** Have students form groups of three in which each person reads a different text. Have them close their books and tell each other the information. After each person tells about his or her text, the group should talk about possible explanations. Encourage students to use the expressions for speculating about the past.

Pronunciation Note: In text **B** on page 104, the place name *Lascaux* is pronounced /la'sko/.

Geographical Note: Easter Island, also called Rapa Nui or Isla de Pascua, belongs to Chile and is located in the Pacific Ocean 3,200 kilometers (2,000 miles) west of Chile's coast. It covers an area of 130 square kilometers (50 square miles).

☯ **Option:** You might want to give students these questions for additional practice in making speculations about the texts.

1. Who built Stonehenge?
2. How and why was Stonehenge built?
3. Who painted the sophisticated paintings in the caves at Lascaux?
4. Why were so many of the statues on Easter Island left unfinished?

(*Exercise 7 Options continue on page T104.*)

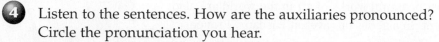

4 Listen to the sentences. How are the auxiliaries pronounced? Circle the pronunciation you hear.

a. Some think ancient South Americans **may have** carved the statues.   /meəv/   /meə/

b. Others think the Polynesians **might have** built them.   /maɪtəv/   /maɪtə/

c. Scholars say the statues **could have** actually been images of chiefs.   /kʊdəv/   /kʊdə/

d. Experts conclude they **must have** all been made from volcanic rock.   /məstəv/   /məstə/

5 Predict the pronunciation of *have*. Then listen and confirm.

		a	b	c
A:	How could they have forgotten?	/hæv/	/əv/	/ə/
B:	They might have been really busy.	/hæv/	/əv/	/ə/
A:	They must have confused the day.	/hæv/	/əv/	/ə/
B:	Could they have actually gotten lost?	/hæv/	/əv/	/ə/
A:	Yes, but they could have called anyway.	/hæv/	/əv/	/ə/

6 Work with a partner. Read the dialogue in Exercise 5 aloud. Reduce *have* and link it to the previous word.

Speak Out

 Speculating About the Past When you are not sure of something that happened in the past, you use certain expressions to indicate your uncertainty.

... might/could have (been) ...	Maybe it was ...	I wonder if ...
(It) may/might have (been) ...	Isn't it possible that ...	Perhaps ...

7 Work in groups of three. Each of you should read a different text independently. Then close your books. Take turns reporting on what you read. Then discuss possible explanations.

Example:

A: So, why do you think the people of Rapa Nui carved those statues?

B: Well, it may have been for religious reasons.

C: Or possibly it was to frighten away invaders coming to the island.

A. Nobody knows exactly who built the Stonehenge monument on the Salisbury Plain in England, but we do know that it is very ancient. Parts of the stone circle were probably begun around 2200 B.C. Later generations added to the construction over a period of nine centuries. There are different theories as to why Stonehenge was built. Some people think it was a castle, others an observatory from which to watch the stars, and still others a calendar in stone. Equally unclear is how Stonehenge was built. The stones are truly enormous and heavy, yet they were transported from places far away.

Stonehenge

Unit 10

103

B. Some of the most beautiful works of art in the world are also some of the most ancient. In a series of caves at Lascaux, France, sophisticated paintings of animals were painted by a primitive people between 15,000 and 20,000 years ago. Many important questions remain unanswered. How did an ancient people achieve such works of beauty? How did they know how to prepare the paints they used? How did they have an idea of perspective (making flat drawings appear to have depth) when this technique was not rediscovered in art until the fifteenth century? Why did they paint their pictures high up on hidden walls in secret caves where no one could easily see them? Why did they paint them at all?

Cave painting at Lascaux

C. In 1772, a Dutch navigator discovered more than 250 huge statues on an island only thirty-five miles around. This island, called Rapa Nui or Easter Island, is located in the Pacific Ocean, far away from any other land, and it is covered with huge stone statues representing a lost race of people. The 100 or so statues that are finished are extremely heavy, and yet they are carved so carefully that they have perfect balance. There are also more than 150 unfinished statues, and the abandoned tools of the builders lie around them on the ground. Who do the statues represent? Who carved them? Why did they carve them? No one knows for sure.

Easter Island

READING and WRITING

Read About It

1 **Before You Read**

    a. Look at drawing **a**. Is the hat taller than it is wide? Use your ruler to measure it. Was your guess correct?
Look at drawing **b**. Are the lines the same length? Use your ruler to check. Were you right?

    b. Work with a partner. Figure out how the optical illusions trick the eye. Tell the class your theories.

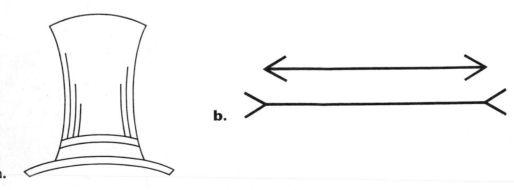

(Exercise 7 Options continued from page T103.)

 Option: Before the Speak Out activity, tell students that you are going to give them a quiz afterward and that the quiz may include dates and other details. (The purpose of the quiz is to encourage each person to provide accurate and complete information to the others in the group.) When students have completed the activity, have them take the quiz.

Possible questions:

1. Where is Stonehenge? (Salisbury Plain, England)

2. When was the stone circle begun? (around 2200 B.C.)

3. Where did the stones come from? (from places far away)

4. Where are the famous cave paintings in France? (Lascaux)

5. When were they painted? (between 15,000 and 20,000 years ago)

6. Were the paintings easy to see? (No, they were high up on hidden walls in secret caves.)

7. How many statues are on Easter Island? (more than 250)

8. What are they made of? (stone)

9. Is Easter Island near other land? (No, it is very far away from other land.)

Link *Workbook: Practice 10*

Read About It

Presentation

❶ **Before You Read** Have students read the instructions and answer the questions in **a** independently. To measure the top hat, they should measure the height from the tallest point and they should measure the width of the brim. To measure the lines, they should only measure the straight lines, not the arrowheads. (The height and the width of the hat are the same; the two lines are the same length.)

Explain that the drawings are **optical illusions**. Elicit the meaning of optical illusions. (Optical illusions are things that are not the way they appear to be.) Have students complete **b**. Encourage individuals to share their theories with the class.

Note: You might want to explain to students that optical illusions play on the way we usually see things. For the picture of the top hat, we tend to perceive a real top hat as being tall; we usually do not consider the width of the brim. The two parallel lines with the shorter angled lines are called an angle illusion. The angles change our perception of the length of the parallel lines.

➡ **Distinguishing Between Fact and Opinion** Have students read the strategy. Briefly review the expressions for facts and opinions on page 102. Explain that using this strategy will help in understanding the text.

Have students look at the title of the article and the picture and predict what the article will be about. Then have them read the article independently in class or for homework. Encourage them to read without dictionaries. If students read in class, you may want to set a time limit.

🌀 **Option:** To check students' comprehension, write the following questions on the board or ask them orally. If you have students write their answers, have them work in pairs or small groups to check their answers. (*Answers may vary.*)

1. What are some examples of the laws of nature? (that a compass points north and water flows down a hill)

2. What happens to tourists driving on the Croy Brae hill? (When they think they are going down the hill, their cars slow down and they are really going up, and the opposite is true of the other side of the hill.)

3. What are some of the strange things that happen in the Oregon Vortex? (balls roll uphill, smoke makes spirals; compasses don't work, but people automatically lean north; and a person approaching an observer seems to get shorter)

4. What are some of the theories about why the natural laws are different for some places on earth? (the effects are optical illusions; there are local variations in the earth's magnetic field; the places affect our balance and perceptions)

❷ Have students complete the exercise independently and then share their answers in small groups or as a class.

Answers
Answers for the **facts** will vary. The three **opinions** are found in the last two paragraphs of the article; words that help distinguish them from facts include **feel**, **think**, **must be**, and **believe**.

Think About It

❸ – ❹ Have students answer the questions in pairs or groups and then share their answers with the class.

🌀 **Option:** Have students look in the library or on the Internet for other examples of strange natural phenomena and then report their findings to the class.

Distinguishing Between Fact and Opinion When you read, you
will understand better if you notice the difference between information
presented as fact and as opinion.

Tricks of Nature

Most people expect the laws of nature to be obeyed. That
is, they expect a compass to point to the north and water to
flow down a hill. But these natural laws that we take for
granted do not hold in some places on the planet. In places
5 such as Croy Brae, Scotland, and Sardine Creek, Oregon,
U.S.A., the laws of nature that we normally experience are
not in effect.

When tourists driving their cars in Scotland come to the hill
called Croy Brae, they think they are dreaming. The road
10 appears to go downward, and yet, when drivers slow their cars
to go down the hill, their cars stop. The road that looks as if it is
going down really goes up! People experience the same sensation
on the other side of the hill, too. When drivers accelerate their cars
in an attempt to go up the hill, they go down! If a car is left on the hill
15 without its brakes on, it will move up the hill rather than down as well.

People also feel confused in a place called the Oregon Vortex in the United States. In a
circular spot 165 feet (49.5 meters) in diameter, the laws of nature change. In the vortex, balls
roll uphill and smoke makes spirals. A heavy iron ball suspended from the ceiling hangs at an
angle. Compasses don't work in the circle, but people standing in it automatically lean toward
20 magnetic north! A person moving away from an observer there seems to get taller instead of
shorter, and a person coming toward the observer seems to get shorter.

No one has yet been able to explain why the normal laws of nature do not hold in these
places around the world. Some scientists and observers feel that the effects are really optical
illusions. Others think that there must be local variations in the earth's magnetic field that
25 cause changes in normal behavior.

Still others believe that these places somehow affect our sense of balance and change our
perceptions of how things are. But whatever the theories, the facts show that natural laws are
different for some places on Earth.

2 Underline three examples of facts in the text. Circle three examples
of opinions. What words or context helped you distinguish among
them? Share your ideas with the class.

Think About It

3 What do you think causes the strange effects in the places described
in the text?

4 Do you know of any other places in the world where the laws of
nature seem different? Tell the class what you know.

Write: Using Formal Language

The language that we use in academic writing and in business letters is more formal than that used in speaking and in personal letters. Formal written language often includes more complex sentence structures, more sophisticated vocabulary, and full forms instead of contractions.

 Read the following pairs of sentences and check which you think is more appropriate for formal writing.

- a. ☐ I apologize for not writing sooner, but I have been out of town.
  ☐ I'm sorry I haven't written sooner, but I've been busy.
- b. ☐ Bill went on an archaeological dig, and he found a fossil.
  ☐ While digging at an archaeological site, Bill found a fossil.
- c. ☐ Maybe the dinosaurs died because the climate changed.
  ☐ The dinosaurs might not have survived climatic changes.

6 Read the passage. Underline the word or words that you think are more suitable for formal writing. Answers may vary.

Mummies have long held an almost magical fascination. People around the world have been curious about Egypt's elaborate ritual of death and by the (**1. extreme/great**) care devoted to (**2. preserving/keeping**) bodies (**3. forever/for eternity**).

A "mummy" is a remarkably preserved body, a corpse that has (**4. withstood/fought**) decay and putrefaction. The process can be intentional or accidental. In either case, the corpse's (**5. falling apart/dissolution**) has been (**6. arrested/stopped**), and the effects of time slowed. The final result is a human form which, with its (**7. things/belongings**), ornaments, and clothing, becomes the physical representation of another time.

Write About It

7 You work for UPR, Inc. (**U**nusual **P**henomena **R**esearch, Incorporated). As chief researcher, you need to write a formal letter responding to Mr. S. Genova about a series of strange lights he saw moving at high speed across the sky. In your letter, you want to thank him for his report and tell him that your researchers investigated the phenomenon and concluded that the lights were not UFOs (unidentified flying objects). Tell him what the lights might have been. In closing, invite him to submit another report any time he sees unusual phenomena. Be sure to include all the parts of a formal letter and to use formal language.

  Check Your Writing Exchange papers with a partner. Use the questions below to give feedback to your partner. When you get your paper back, revise as necessary.

- Does the letter have all the parts of a formal letter?
- Is the language appropriate for a formal letter?
- Is the content accurate?
- Are verb forms used correctly?

Write: Using Formal Language

Presentation

Have students read the explanation. You might want to have them look back over the unit to find examples of formal language, with complex sentence structures and sophisticated vocabulary, and share their examples with the class.

❺ Have students read the instructions and complete the exercise independently. Then have them discuss in pairs, in small groups, or as a class which words and structures led them to choose as they did.

Answers

a. I apologize for not writing sooner, but I have been out of town. **b.** While digging at an archaeological site, Bill found a fossil. **c.** The dinosaurs might not have survived climatic changes.

❻ Have students complete the exercise individually and discuss their answers in pairs or small groups or as a class.

Answers

Answers may vary. **1.** extreme **2.** preserving **3.** for eternity **4.** withstood **5.** dissolution **6.** arrested **7.** belongings

Write About It

Presentation

❼ Go over the instructions with the class. Make sure that students understand all the vocabulary. Before students write their letters, have them refer to the business letter on page 30. Then have them write their first drafts using appropriate form and language.

☑ **❽** **Check Your Writing** Have students exchange first drafts with partners and use the questions to check the format, language, and information. Have them give each other feedback before they write the final draft.

 Workbook: Practice 11

Vocabulary Expansion: Determining phrasal verb meaning from context See page T149.

Answers
a. 5 b. 6 c. 4 d. 2 e. 7 f. 1 g. 3

EVALUATION

See page TExi.

Unit 10 Achievement Test

Self-Check See Check Your Knowledge, page 80 of the Workbook.

Dictation Dictate the following paragraph. Then have students rewrite the paragraph in informal language (that is, as if they were talking to someone). For more information on dictation, see page TExv.

In addition to studying optical illusions, scientists study illusions that involve other senses. For instance, the sound of a clock is a steady, unaccented sound, with each beat being identical. Yet instead of hearing tick tick tick tick, we hear tick tock tick tock, because our brain automatically organizes and interprets sounds as meaningful patterns.

Communication Skills

1. To elicit some target vocabulary, show students pictures of some ancient ruins, drawings, or cave paintings. Ask them to describe the pictures and make speculations about life in an ancient civilization. Encourage students to speculate about the people, their religion, whether they were primitive or sophisticated for their time, what kinds of animals lived there, and so on. As they speak, listen for the correct use of vocabulary and structures.

2. Have students talk about a mysterious happening or unexplained mystery, such as the Loch Ness monster, the Egyptian pyramids, the disappearance of the dinosaurs, or UFO photographs. Tell students to make speculations about it. Listen for the correct use of the past modals.

SADDER BUT WISER

OBJECTIVES

- To talk about learning from experience
- To ask for and give advice about the past
- To speculate about past actions and their consequences
- To use past modals to express advice, criticism, and regret
- To use the third conditional to speculate about the past
- To listen in order to make inferences
- To reduce **have** in negative past modals
- To describe the opposite of past reality
- To personalize for greater appreciation of fiction
- To write a persuasive paragraph
- To understand idioms with **run**

GETTING STARTED

Warm Up

Preview

- Ask students if they understand the expression **sadder but wiser**. Elicit experiences from students that they think have made them **sadder but wiser**. (*Note:* If students don't feel comfortable talking about something personal, let them tell about someone else's experience or make up a story that illustrates the expressions.)

- Ask students, *What do people often give to help someone who has a problem?* (advice) Then ask students to give examples of three common problems and write them on the board. Elicit some logical solutions to these problems. Encourage students to use the language they know for giving advice (page 58), and introduce **should**, **ought to**, and **had better** and the first and second conditionals (page 56).

Presentation

❶ Have students read the explanation and question independently. Review as a class the experiences the students shared in the previous section. Were these experiences examples of **sadder but wiser**? Have some students tell the class their partner's story.

❷ Have students read the instructions. Play the recording or read the audio-script aloud two or more times. Let students listen again to check their answers, if necessary.

Audioscript: The audioscript for Exercises 2 and 3 appears on page T158.

> **Answers**
> 1. Yes 2. No 3. Yes

❸ Have students read the instructions and listen to the conversations again. Then have them share their ideas in groups or as a class. Make sure they give the reasons for their opinions.

 Workbook: Practice 1

Option: Write the following expressions on the board and have students categorize them. Which ones do we say to accept advice? Which ones do we say to reject advice?

a. That's a good idea. (accept)
b. I suppose it's the best thing to do. (accept)
c. I don't think that's the best course of action. (reject)
d. Oh, I don't know. (reject)
e. I think you're right. (accept)
f. I don't think I could do that. (reject)
g. What a great solution! (accept)
h. I don't see how that would work. (reject)

Figure It Out

Preview

- Use the picture on the top of page 108 to elicit or present **brake**, **flat tire**, **spare (tire)**, **headlight**, and **windshield**. Ask whether anyone has ever changed a flat tire. Where is the spare kept in the car?

(Preview continues on page T108.)

GETTING STARTED

Warm Up

1 Sometimes people don't take good advice. If things later turn out badly, they might look back and regret their actions, but also learn from them. We say they are "sadder, but wiser." Have you had an experience that made you sadder, but wiser? Share your story with a partner.

2 Three people are asking for advice. Listen to the conversations. Circle *Yes* if the person agrees to the advice and *No* if the person doesn't.

    a. Alice   Yes   No

    b. Carlos   Yes   No

    c. Michiko   Yes   No

3 Listen to the conversations again. Do you agree with the advice given? Why or why not? Share your ideas with the class.

Figure It Out

4 Read the conversations and decide who is the sadder but wiser person in each.

A.   **HANK:**   Great! Just great! Now what do we do? Here we are in the middle of nowhere with a flat tire and no spare! We'll never get to the beach.

5

10

15

TONY: Yeah, but there's nothing we can do about it now.

HANK: This is all your fault! Everybody warned you about this car, Tony! You should have listened to us when we told you not to buy this old wreck! Look at it! The windshield's cracked; one headlight doesn't work …

TONY: I couldn't afford anything better. This car was a real bargain!

HANK: If you had saved up more money, or if you had looked a little harder, you could have bought something more dependable.

TONY: Yeah, my sister told me the same thing, but if I had followed her advice, I would have bought a motorcycle instead.

HANK: And we wouldn't be stuck out here now!

B. **PATIENT:** I know I should have stuck to a better diet and gotten more exercise, but I didn't have the time. Now I have this terrible stomachache!

20 **DOCTOR:** If you had followed my advice, you wouldn't have gotten so sick. Now we'll have to admit you to the hospital for tests and possibly for treatment.

PATIENT: Oh no, I can't believe it. I can't miss more work.

DOCTOR: If you had acknowledged you had an ulcer, you wouldn't have

25 aggravated your condition. If you had stopped smoking, relaxed, and watched your diet, your ulcer wouldn't have gotten so bad.

PATIENT: But, Doctor, aren't ulcers caused by stress? If I had quit smoking, I would have been even more of a nervous wreck than I am now!

DOCTOR: Well, you can't go on like this. You have to get off the fast track and slow

30 down.

PATIENT: I suppose if I'm stuck in the hospital, I'll have no choice!

C. **REPORTER:** So, Ferrer, would the score have been any different if you had played the last five minutes

35 of this game?

FERRER: I'd like to think so! But I couldn't go on. My knee was killing me. When I sprained it last week, the doctor told me to stop playing, but I didn't take his advice. I decided to play tonight anyway. I just

40 didn't want to let the team down.

REPORTER: Maybe you should have taken your doctor's advice more seriously.

FERRER: I guess so. The coach shouldn't have let me play. Now I'll probably need surgery and be on the

45 bench for the rest of the season.

(Preview continued from page T107.)

Has anyone ever had an accident or problem involving one of these items?

- Talk about students' experiences at the doctor's office or the hospital to elicit or present **stomachache, to admit (to a hospital), condition, sore, to sprain, surgery, to treat, treatment,** and **ulcer.**

- Talk about a basketball team or another sports team students are familiar with to elicit or present **captain, coach, on the bench, point, score, season,** and **team.** Who are the coach and the captain of the team? Who sits on the bench a lot? What was the score of the last game? Who scored the most points?

- Focus attention on the pictures on page 108. Ask students to predict what the conversations will be about.

Presentation

④ Read the instructions and the conversations on pages 107–108 aloud as students listen. Students can listen with their books open or closed. Then have students read the conversations silently in class or for homework. After the initial presentation of the conversations, have students answer the following questions, as a class or in groups, to check comprehension.

Conversation A

1. Who bought a used car? Why? (Tony. He couldn't afford anything more expensive.)
2. Where were Hank and Tony going when the car broke down? (to the beach)
3. What's wrong with the car? (It has a flat tire and no spare, a cracked windshield, and a headlight that doesn't work.)
4. What would Tony have bought if he hadn't bought the car? (a motorcycle)

Conversation B

5. What had the doctor previously advised? (a healthy diet, exercise, and no smoking)
6. What is wrong with the patient? (She has an ulcer.)
7. Who is stressed out? (the patient)
8. How is the patient going to stop smoking? (She'll be stuck in a hospital and won't be allowed to smoke.)

Conversation C

9. Did Ferrer finish playing the game? Why or why not? (No. His knee hurt too much.)
10. Did Ferrer think the coach did the right thing? (No. He said the coach shouldn't have let him play.)
11. What did the doctor advise? (not to play in the game)
12. Who won the game? (the other team)

Have students discuss the conversations in groups or as a class and decide on the "sadder but wiser" people.

Answers

A: Tony B: Patient C: Ferrer

Option: Have students work in pairs to read the conversations aloud. Then have them close their books. Ask individuals to retell each conversation from memory. You may want to write some key words on the board to help them remember the conversations.

Option: Have students work in pairs. One student is a volunteer who works on an advice hot line, and the other is a person who phones the hot line for help with a problem. (An advice hot line is a telephone number people can call if they need advice.) Have them make up problems and advice and act out several phone calls. Have pairs perform their conversations for the class.

☑ **❺ Vocabulary Check** Have students read the directions and complete the matching exercise. Review the answers as a class.

> **Answers**
> 1. h 2. d 3. g 4. f 5. c 6. a 7. b 8. e

 Option: Have students work in pairs or small groups to look back at the conversations and figure out the meanings of **bargain, cracked, stuck, to stick to, to go on,** and **to let (someone) down** from the context. Have them share their ideas with the class. Ask students how the meanings of **stuck** and **to stick to** are different. (**Stuck** is an adjective meaning "can't move"; **to stick to** is a verb meaning "to continue.")

Link *Workbook: Practice 2*

Talk About It

 Option: You may prefer to postpone this activity until after the grammar presentation (pages 109–110) if you feel students need extra help with past modals and the third conditional.

Presentation

Note: The purpose of this activity is to develop fluency. Students should be free to talk without interruption for error correction. If you notice persistent errors, write them down for later reteaching or review.

❻ Have students read the instructions and the model conversation independently. Then have a pair of students read the model conversation aloud for the class. Help with any unfamiliar vocabulary in the items. Have students complete the activity in pairs. Encourage them to use language like that in the example dialogue. Then ask pairs to perform their conversations for the class.

Link *Workbook: Practice 3*

GRAMMAR

Using Past Modals: Advice, Criticism, and Regret

Preview

- Elicit types of problems a person could have. (financial, health, educational, family, professional, and so on) Have students work in pairs or small groups to think of a problem in the present. (Example: a neighbor who plays music too loudly) Have a pair state their problem to the class and ask for advice. Have the other students give them advice. Make sure the students use **should have** or **ought to have**. Write one of the conversations on the board.

- Restate the students' problem situation as a past problem. Say, for example, *Last night I couldn't sleep because of my neighbor's loud music.* Elicit the time period when the restated problem took place. (in the past) Using the advice from the original situation, write a conversation with past modals on the board, for example:

  A: What should I have done?

  B: You should have asked your neighbor to turn down the music.

- Elicit the form used to give advice about the past. (**should have** + past participle) You might want to point out the similarity to the forms introduced in Unit 10 for speculating about the past (the modals **may have, could have,** or **might have** + past participle).

- Have students work in pairs to form the negative and interrogative of **should have**. Then tell them to put **ought to** in the past. (**ought to have** + past participle) Explain that negatives are formed with **should have**, *not* with **ought to have**. Mention that questions with **ought to have** usually include **do you think**.

Presentation

Have students read the grammar explanation independently in class or for homework. Review the grammar explanation and example conversation with the class.

(*Presentation continues on page T110.*)

5 **Vocabulary Check** Match the words with their meanings.

——— **1.** wreck (line 7)   **a.** state; illness
——— **2.** dependable (line 13)   **b.** points made in a game
——— **3.** to admit (line 21)   **c.** to make worse
——— **4.** ulcer (line 24)   **d.** reliable; that can be counted on
——— **5.** to aggravate (line 25)   **e.** person who instructs a team
——— **6.** condition (line 25)   **f.** stomach problem caused by stress
——— **7.** score (line 33)   **g.** to enter into
——— **8.** coach (line 43)   **h.** broken-down vehicle; person who is
                                         in bad shape physically or mentally

Talk About It

 6 You and your neighbor have lots of problems. With a partner, take
turns stating the problems and giving advice.

Example: electric bill/cut off electricity

State past problem.

A: I forgot to pay my electric bill, and they cut off my electricity.

Give advice about the past.

B: That's terrible! You should have paid your bill when you got it.

Agree but give excuse.

A: You're right. I know I should have, but I forgot.

Criticize about the past.

B: If you had paid it on time, they wouldn't have shut off your lights.

---

a. medicine/condition worse   **e.** red light/got ticket
b. so much fried food/got stomachache **f.** stressed out/developed ulcer
c. hole in roof/damaged carpet   **g.** broken glass/got flat tire
d. gas/ran out on highway   **h.** cheap computer/broke down

GRAMMAR

Using Past Modals: Advice, Criticism, and Regret

To ask for and give advice about the past, to criticize past actions, and to
express regret, we can use *should have* or *ought to have* + past participle.

TONY:	OK, I made a mistake. So what **should I have done**?
MIKE:	First of all, you **shouldn't have bought** an older-model computer.
TONY:	Well, what do you think I **ought to have bought**?
MIKE:	You **should have gotten** something faster with more memory, and you **ought to have asked** someone like me for advice.

1 Complete the conversations with B's response. Use *should* or *ought to*.

1. A: We're lost. I don't remember how to get to Jane's house.

    B: _____

    A: I know, but I was sure I would remember.

2. A: I woke up late and missed my ten o'clock appointment.

    B: _____

    A: I know, but I went to bed so late that I forgot.

3. A: My feet are killing me. I can't walk another step.

    B: _____

    A: I know, but I didn't think we would walk so far.

4. A: My new pants don't fit. They're way too baggy.

    B: _____

    A: I know, but I didn't have time to.

Speculating About the Past: The Third Conditional

We use the third conditional (*if* + past perfect, *would/could have* + past participle) to speculate about hypothetical or unreal conditions in the past. We also use it to soften our criticism of past actions.

> **A:** **If** Mia **had practiced** harder, she **could have won** the piano competition.
>
> **B:** Yeah, I guess **if** she **hadn't been** so confident, she **would have spent** more time playing the piano and less time at the mall.

2 Look at the examples above and answer the questions.

    a. Did Mia win the piano competition?

    b. What did she spend her time doing? Why?

3 Read about the ecological mistake. Write the correct form of the verb on the line. Use the negative when necessary.

In 1960, ecologists introduced the Nile perch into Lake Victoria to provide the people with more food; however, the Nile perch ate most of the 300 other species of fish in the lake.

    a. If the ecologists **(1. know)** _____ what the perch would do, they **(2. put)** _____ them into the lake.

    b. If the perch **(3. eat)** _____ the other fish, the local population **(4. have)** _____ a greater food supply.

Unfortunately, the Nile perch also ate the fish that helped control schistosomiasis, a deadly disease. As a result, the disease spread rapidly throughout the lake region.

    c. Schistosomiasis **(5. spread)** _____ around the lake if there **(6. be)** _____ Nile perch in the water.

(Presentation continued from page T109.)

Ask students to state one or two problems in the past. Then have individuals ask for and give advice for these problems using **should have** and **ought to have**.

Language Note: Should have is more commonly used than **ought to have**, which is somewhat more formal.

Pronunciation Note: Should have is commonly pronounced "should've" (/ˈšudəv/) or "shoulda" (/ˈšudə/). For possible pronunciations of **shouldn't have**, see Pronunciation on page 113.

❶ Have students complete the conversations independently. Then have them check their answers in pairs. Review answers as a class.

> **Answers**
> Answers will vary somewhat. **1.** You should have asked her for directions. **2.** You should have set your alarm clock. **3.** You should have worn more comfortable shoes. **4.** You should have tried them on in the store.

 Workbook: Practices 4, 5, 6, 7

Speculating About the Past: The Third Conditional

Preview

- Tell students that Pete got a very low grade on his last test because he didn't study. Then write the following sentence on the board:

  If Pete had studied, he probably would have gotten an A.

  Ask, *Did Pete study?* (no) Ask, *Did he get an A?* (no) Tell students that when we talk about a condition and a result that are imaginary or contrary to the facts, we use the third conditional.

- Elicit the form of the third conditional. [**If** + past perfect (= **had** + past participle), **would have** + past participle]

- Ask students to compare the form of the second conditional (**If** + past tense, **would** + verb) with that of the third conditional. Write an example of the second conditional on the board.

If Pete studied, he **would** pass the course.

Write the same sentence using the third conditional on the board.

If Pete **would have** studied, he **could have** passed the test.

Then elicit a comparison of the time reference of the two conditionals. (the second conditional: present and future; the third conditional: past)

Presentation

Have students read the grammar explanation and examples independently in class or for homework. Review the grammar explanation and examples with the class. Elicit additional examples using the third conditional.

❷ Have students answer the questions and discuss the answers as a class.

> **Answers**
> **a.** no **b.** She spent her time at the mall because she was confident she would win.

❸ Have students read the instructions and look over the reading passage and sentences about it. Point out that in some places either **would** or **could** can be used. Have students complete the exercise independently. Then have them work in pairs to compare their answers. Review answers as a class.

> **Answers**
> **a.** 1. had known 2. wouldn't have put
> **b.** 3. hadn't eaten 4. could/would have had
> **c.** 5. wouldn't/couldn't have spread
> 6. hadn't been **d.** 7. hadn't grown
> 8. would/could have caught **e.** 9. had been
> 10. would/could have had **f.** 11. hadn't been
> 12. could/ would have dried
> **g.** 13. could/would have smoked 14. had had

❹ Have students read the instructions and
a. Ask, *Did Martin stick to his exercise program?* (yes) Then ask, *Did Martin gain a lot of weight?* (no) Then say, *This is what really happened: Martin stuck to his exercise program, and he didn't gain a lot of weight.* Have students work in pairs to complete the activity by asking and answering similar questions about each sentence.

Answers

Answers may vary somewhat. **a.** Martin stuck to his exercise program, and he didn't gain a lot of weight. **b.** Khalid didn't take my advice, and he bought the cell phone. **c.** Lin didn't practice hard enough, and she didn't win the competition. **d.** Angela didn't tell the truth, and she wasn't so happy. **e.** The building didn't have a fire alarm, and one or more people were hurt.

❺ Have students read the directions and the example independently. Then have a pair of students read the example aloud for the class. Have students work in pairs to complete the activity. You may want to ask some pairs to perform their conversations for the class. *(Responses will vary but should follow the pattern in the example.)*

The Nile perch was an enormous fish sometimes weighing over 200 pounds. As a result, the small fisherman couldn't catch it.

d. If the Nile perch **(7. grow)** _____ to such sizes, the fishermen **(8. catch)** _____ them without any problems.

e. If the fisherman **(9. be)** _____ able to catch the Nile perch, they **(10. have)** _____ much more food to eat.

Finally, the Nile perch were too oily to be dried in the sun, so people had to smoke them. However, firewood was very limited.

f. If the fish **(11. be)** _____ so oily, the people **(12. dry)** _____ them in the sun to preserve them.

g. The people **(13. smoke)** _____ the fish if they **(14. have)** _____ more wood.

4 Read the sentences. Then tell what really happened.

a. If Martin hadn't stuck to his exercise program, he would have gained a lot of weight.

b. If Khalid had taken my advice, he wouldn't have bought that cell phone.

c. If Lin had practiced harder, she would have won the competition.

d. Angela would have been happier if she had told the truth.

e. No one would have been hurt if the building had had a fire alarm.

5 With a partner, take turns reading the situations, criticizing and agreeing.

Example:

A: Sidney made a big mistake with the accounts at work but didn't tell his boss. When his boss found out about it, she fired him.

B: He should've told her about it immediately.

A: I agree. If he had told her, she wouldn't have fired him.

a. Even though Jeff didn't feel well, he insisted on going out. He got caught in the rain, and now his condition is worse. He has a terrible headache and a sore throat.

b. The step on the Wintermute family's front porch was broken, but they didn't get it fixed. When the mail carrier came, he fell and sprained his ankle.

c. Carl took cash with him on his trip to Bali instead of taking traveler's checks. He lost the cash.

d. Lisa didn't have her driver's license but drove her brother to the airport anyway. The police pulled her over and took her to the police station.

6 **Check Your Understanding** Check the situations in which you are likely to use *should have, ought to have, could have,* or *would have.* Compare your answers with a partner's.

☐ You bought a used car last week and now it doesn't work.

☐ You just changed apartments and need to have a phone installed.

☐ You need some advice on how to apply for a driver's license.

☐ You got a flat tire last week and never got it fixed. Now you have another flat tire and no other spare.

☐ Although your landlady didn't allow pets, you moved your cats in anyway. Now she wants you to get rid of them or move.

7 **Express Yourself** With a partner, think of another situation you would use past modals in. Imagine yourselves in the situation and write a dialogue.

LISTENING and SPEAKING

Listen: Job Performance

1 **Before You Listen** Some people manage their time well and have a lot of energy for their work. How well do you manage your time? How efficient are you in your work?

STRATEGY **Making Inferences** When information is not directly stated by a speaker, you can use the knowledge you have about the situation as well as other information that is explicitly stated to make inferences or guesses about the situation.

2 The Personnel Director at Stone College had appointments with several students today. Listen to the conversations and read the inferences. Is there enough information in the conversations to make each inference? Write **Y** (yes) or **N** (no).

1. ____ **a.** Jane and Enrique have worked together for a long time.
   ____ **b.** Enrique is an economics major.
   ____ **c.** Jane and Enrique care about punctuality and responsibility.
   ____ **d.** Jane owes money for the courses she is taking.

2. ____ **a.** Tim doesn't respect the professor he works for.
   ____ **b.** Tim is unconcerned when people can't find him in the office.
   ____ **c.** Tim has a problem with dizziness.
   ____ **d.** The Personnel Director judges students on their work performance and rewards them accordingly.

☑ ❻ **Check Your Understanding** Have students read the instructions and check their answers independently. Then have them compare answers with a partner.

> **Answers**
> We would be likely to use these forms in all the situations except the second and third.

 ❼ **Express Yourself** Have students work in pairs to read the instructions and think of an appropriate situation. Then have them write a dialogue—including past modals and the third conditional—for the situation they have chosen. Have pairs perform their dialogues for the class.

📖 *Workbook: Practices 8, 9*

LISTENING and SPEAKING

Listen: Job Performance

Presentation

❶ **Before You Listen** Have students respond to the questions in pairs, small groups, or as a class. Then have students discuss attitudes toward work and the qualities of a good employee. What attitudes and qualities do employers want their employees to have?

➡ **Making Inferences** Have students read the strategy independently. Point out that this strategy is very important for listening (and for reading), as in any conversation (or text) a lot of meaning is conveyed without being directly stated. You might want to give students an example of making inferences. (If you hear someone say, "I'm going to stay up all night studying and will finish studying on my way to school," you can infer that he's a student, that he has a test tomorrow, that he's not yet fully prepared for the test, and that he probably doesn't drive to school.)

🎧 ❷ Play the recording or read the audioscript aloud two or more times. Give students enough time to write their answers. Let them listen again to check their answers. Then have students discuss their answers in small groups or as a class. Have them explain how they were able to make the inferences.

Audioscript: The audioscript for Exercise 2 appears on page T159.

> **Answers**
> Answers may vary somewhat. **1. a.** N **b.** N **c.** Y **d.** Y **2. a.** Y **b.** Y **c.** N **d.** Y

📖 *Workbook: Practice 10*

Pronunciation

Preview

- On the board, write the following conversation.

  A: Did Jack stay till the end of the party?

  B: Yeah. He should have gone home earlier, but he was having such a good time.

  Ask students how **should have** is pronounced when reduced. (/šudəv/ or /šudə/) Then write: If he had gone home, he would have gotten my phone call.

  Ask them how **would have** is pronounced when reduced. (/wudəv/ or /wudə/) Have students practice saying the sentences quickly with the reduced forms.

- Elicit some consequences of Jack not going home. (*Example:* If Jack hadn't stayed out so long, he wouldn't have missed the phone call.) Then elicit what he should and should not have done (*Example:* He shouldn't have stayed so long.) Encourage students to use the negative forms **shouldn't have** and **wouldn't have** and to pronounce them /šudnəv/ and /wudnəv/.

Presentation

Have students read the explanation independently. Then read the example sentences aloud. Have students repeat the sentences aloud.

Pronunciation Note: When spoken at a normal speed, **shouldn't have** and **wouldn't have** are pronounced /šudnəv/ and /wudnəv/. When they are pronounced quickly, usually in informal speech, they are pronounced /šudnə/ and /wudnə/. If pronounced very quickly, /d/ often becomes a part of /n/ and is not pronounced: /šunə/ and /wunə/.

❸ Play the recording or read the audioscript aloud two or more times and have students fill in their answers. Then have them compare answers with a partner. Let them listen again to check their answers.

Audioscript: The audioscript for Exercise 3 appears on page T160.

Answers
1. shouldn't have 2. wouldn't have
3. shouldn't have 4. should have 5. should have 6. would have

❹ Have students read the instructions. Then have them practice the conversation in pairs. You might want to have some pairs read the conversation to the class and have other students listen for use of reductions.

 Workbook: Practice 11

Speak Out

Presentation

➡ **Describing the Opposite of Past Reality** Have students read the strategy and the language in the box. You might want to set up a situation to elicit or present the language. For example, say, *I was in a hurry yesterday. I couldn't find a parking place, so I parked in a no-parking zone. My sister was with me and she advised me not to park there. While I was in a shop, the police towed my car away.* Encourage students to use the third conditional to say what you should and shouldn't have done to avoid having your car towed away.

Note: The purpose of this activity is to develop fluency. Students should be free to speak without fear of interruption for error correction. If you notice persistent errors, write them down for later reteaching or review.

❺ Have students read the instructions and example independently. Give them some time to think about the person and advice they want to tell about. Have two students read the example aloud to the class. Then have students carry out the activity in pairs. Remind them to use some of the language in the box. Ask individuals to retell one of their partner's experiences to the class.

Option: Have students write paragraphs about the influential people in their lives and the advice those people gave.

(*Exercise 5 Options continue on page T114.*)

T113

Pronunciation

3 Listen to the dialogue. Write in the missing words.

A: You **(1.)** _____ run that red light!

B: I had to. Otherwise, the guy behind me **(2.)** _____ been able to stop in time.

A: Yes, but you **(3.)** _____ had to stop so suddenly. You **(4.)** _____ seen that guy behind you, and you **(5.)** _____ just slowed down.

B: I suppose you're right. If the police had seen me, I'm sure they **(6.)** _____ given me a ticket.

4 With a partner, take turns reading the two roles in the conversation above. Try to use the reductions whenever possible.

Speak Out

STRATEGY ➤ **Describing the Opposite of Past Reality** Use the third conditional to describe the opposite of what actually happened.

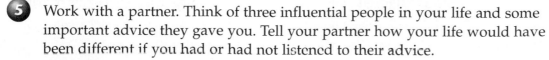

If I hadn't done that, I ...	If you had listened to her, you ...
(That) wouldn't have happened If ...	I would never have ... if he hadn't ...

5 Work with a partner. Think of three influential people in your life and some important advice they gave you. Tell your partner how your life would have been different if you had or had not listened to their advice.

Example:

A: My older sister gave me some of the best advice I've ever gotten. She was so practical. If I hadn't taken her advice, I'd never have been hired for the job I have now.

B: My uncle is the one who most influenced my decisions. I would never have gone to college if he hadn't convinced me to believe I could do it.

Read About It

 Before You Read Much of the reading we do is to get information. But we also read for pleasure. What are some of the stories, articles, poems, or books you have recently read for fun? Compare your list with a classmate's.

 Personalizing Part of the pleasure of reading fiction is allowing yourself to feel as certain characters do and to get caught up in an emotional response. As you read the story, you become part of it, and you relate the story to your own situation and feelings.

See Ya!
by Diane Pinkley

[1] "See ya," my daughter said, as I went to the boarding line with her brother and sister. We were going to the United States to live. Back to my mother's house. My daughter was staying, just legally old enough to do so without my permission. I remember barely seeing her last quick wave through the dim plane window.

[2] "See ya." My own mother had hated that expression. "What do you see?" she would ask, whenever I used it. "Do you really see me?"

[3] Now two of my children and I were living in my mother's house. The silent house that had always had flowers in vases on small shiny tables. The house that she had devoted so many careful hours of cleaning and polishing to. I remember the housedress with the ruffle at the neck that she liked to do her cleaning in. I remember surprising her as she gazed out on a sunny afternoon through half-polished glass, rag in hand. "See ya," I would say, as I ran out to a low-slung car full of wild friends. "See ya," I would yell, as we roared away. "Don't wait up!"

[4] "I can't anymore," she'd say. "Who could keep up with someone as wild as you?"

[5] It didn't seem to surprise her that I went off to live in Europe. "I knew it. Bohemians, poets, and artists in foreign slums," she said. "I just knew it. I saw it coming. What kind of life is that?"

[6] It didn't seem to surprise her when I telephoned to say I was staying for good. I had gotten married. "I'm glad for you," she said. Her voice sounded far away.

[7] If only I could hear it now.

[8] She was surprised when I phoned to say I was coming with her three grandchildren for a visit. "They're old enough to travel now," I said. "They should see you."

[9] We five spent eight days together in this very house, full of shining mirrors reflecting the afternoon sun. "I'm not so young, you know," she said. "I have no energy. It must be the kids making me tired." She'd taken to staying in her bedroom, resting in bed, having only toast and tea.

(Exercise 5 continued from page T113.)

Option: Have students write letters to an advice columnist describing a problem they had in the past. Tell them that they can either use a real problem or make one up. Have them exchange their letters with partners. Then have them act as advice columnists for their partners and write responses using past modals and the third conditional. Post the letters and responses on a wall in the classroom for everyone to read.

READING and WRITING

Read About It

Presentation

❶ Before You Read Have students read the paragraph and write their lists independently. Have them compare their lists in pairs. Then write some of the titles on the board. Are there some titles that are very popular in the class? Are they mysteries? romance? other fiction? comic books?

➡ **Personalizing** Have students read the strategy independently. Then elicit some emotional responses a writer can try to bring out. (anger, sadness, fear, and so on)

Have students look at the title of the story. Ask, *When do we use the expression "See ya"?* (informal leave-taking) Ask, *Based on the title, what do you think the story might be about?* After students answer, have them read the first two paragraphs. Then ask again what they think the story might be about.

Have students read the story independently in class or as homework. Encourage them to read without dictionaries. If they read the story in class, you may want to set a time limit. Ask students to tell their reactions to the story. Can they relate to the situation? In what way?

❷ Have students work independently, in pairs, or in small groups to answer the questions. Then have them share their answers with the rest of the class. Make sure they support their opinions with lines from the reading.

Answers

Answers will vary somewhat. **a.** The mother felt that her daughter (the narrator) wasn't very close to her—that her daughter was out-of-reach and that she didn't have any influence over her. **b.** While her mother was alive, the narrator thought her mother didn't understand her, couldn't deal with her, and wasn't really interested in her. After her mother's death, the narrator realized her mother really had been sick when she last visited her, and she regretted her impatient behavior and really missed and appreciated her mother. **c.** The narrator's daughter was mentioned to suggest that the narrator is developing the same kind of relationship with her daughter that she had with her mother. Predictions about their relationship will vary. **d.** Answers will vary.

❸ Have students work independently to read the instructions and complete the exercise. Then have them compare answers with a partner or as a class.

Answers

a. See ya **b.** barely **c.** vases **d.** rag **e.** slums **f.** deal with

❹ Have students work with partners to read the instructions and to find the different meanings. Then discuss the meanings as a class.

Answers

There are six different meanings: **1.** goodbye, so long (paragraph 1) **2.** see with eyes (paragraph 1) **3.** perceive, know (paragraph 2) **4.** predict (paragraph 5) **5.** get to know, meet (paragraph 8) **6.** understand the truth and not be fooled (paragraph 10, *see through*)

Think About It

❺–❻ Have students talk over their opinions in pairs, in small groups, or as a class. If students are comfortable talking about their families, ask individuals to compare relationships in their families to those in the story. They can also talk about relationships in other families they know. Remind students to use past modals when they explain the advice they would have given.

Option: In addition to the questions in Exercises 5 and 6, have students think about and respond to these questions: Which character in the story is sadder but wiser? Why is she sad? What did she learn?

Option: Over a period of time, have students read and think about other short stories. You may want to ask students to go to the library and choose interesting short stories to bring back to the class. Then make copies of the best stories for all the students to read and analyze. Remind students that many short stories can be found in anthologies.

Write: A Persuasive Paragraph

Preview

Present or elicit a couple of situations where we want to persuade someone to adopt our point of view about something. (*Example:* You feel that one kind of computer is most efficient, but your boss is about to order another type of computer for the office. You might try to convince your boss of your point of view.) Then have students work in pairs and brainstorm situations in which they might need to use persuasion in writing. Have the pairs report their ideas to the class.

Presentation

Have students read the introductory information independently. Then explain that the sentence with the point of view is the topic sentence of the paragraph. Ask them why they think the writer's point of view is stated in the first sentence of the paragraph. (In order to persuade the reader of your ideas, it's best to make your ideas clear right away.) Point out that each reason is developed with supporting information. Have students discuss why outlines might be especially useful for persuasive writing.

[10] "Mother," I said. "Don't think you are fooling me for a minute. Don't think I can't see through you. I know what you're doing. You're hiding. You just can't deal with me. Not now, not ever."

[11] "Oh honey," she said. Her voice sounded far away.

[12] If only I could hear it now.

[13] I learned of my mother's death a year later. "See ya," I had said upon leaving for Europe, impatient with her days in bed, angry at her hiding from me. "See ya."

[14] If only I could.

2 Answer the questions.
  a. What were the mother's feelings about the narrator of the story? How do you know?
  b. What were the narrator's feelings about the mother while the mother was alive? After the mother was dead? How do you know?
  c. Why is the narrator's own daughter mentioned in the story? What do you think will happen to their relationship?
  d. What was your own emotional response to the story?

3 Find the words in the paragraphs that have similar meanings to these words and expressions. Work without a dictionary.

Paragraph 1
  a. Bye
  b. hardly

Paragraph 3
  c. decorative containers
  d. cleaning cloth

Paragraph 5
  e. poor, dirty housing

Paragraph 10
  f. understand and accept someone's actions

4 How many ways does the writer use the verb *see?* Discuss the different meanings with a partner.

Think About It

5 Are the relationships in the story similar to or different from the relationships in your own family? How are they alike or different?

6 What should the people in the story have done differently? What advice would you have given each person?

Write: A Persuasive Paragraph

We sometimes write to persuade people to agree with a particular opinion. When we write a persuasive paragraph, we start by stating our point of view. We then give reasons why our readers should agree. Making an outline of main points is helpful in organizing and developing reasons.

7 The city of Arnold decided to close Fifth Avenue to traffic. Read the outline of one writer's opinion and the writer's completed paragraph below.

I.	(Point of View)	City should have closed Fifth Avenue earlier.
II.	(Reason)	Closed street attracts more shoppers.
	A. (Support)	People enjoy benches, flowers, fountains.
	B. (Support)	Business increased 25 percent since street closed.
III.	(Reason)	Money is being invested in area.
	A. (Support)	New businesses opened.
	B. (Support)	Old businesses were remodeled.
IV.	(Reason)	Parking is no problem.
	A. (Support)	Business doubled in parking lot on Fourth Avenue.
	B. (Support)	New lot was opened on Sixth Avenue.
V.	(Conclusion)	City should have acted last year.

The city of Arnold should have closed Fifth Avenue to traffic one year ago. First and most important, the changes have attracted shoppers to the downtown area. This is because the city planner designed the street with the shopper in mind. For example, they put in benches to sit on, flowers to look at, and fountains to enjoy. Shop owners state that business has increased by 25 percent since the street was closed to traffic. Secondly, the changes have attracted investment in the downtown area. Several new businesses have opened, and the older stores have been remodeled. Finally, some critics warned that closing Fifth Avenue would lead to parking problems, but this simply has not happened. Business at the city parking lot on Fourth Avenue has doubled, and a new lot has opened on Sixth Avenue. The success of this project proves that the city should have blocked traffic from Fifth Avenue a year ago when first proposed by shop owners.

Write About It

8 You don't agree with the writer. Which of these arguments would you use to persuade people that closing the street was a mistake?

a. Traffic has increased on other downtown streets.
b. People don't like walking from the parking lot.
c. Prices have gone up because of the remodeling.
d. The benches and flowers cost a lot of money.
e. Children might get used to playing in the street.

9 Make an outline and write a paragraph to persuade people to agree with you.

  10 **Check Your Writing** Exchange papers with a partner. Use the questions below to give feedback to your partner. When you get your own paper back, revise as necessary.

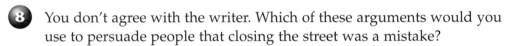

- Does the writer state his or her point of view in the first sentence?
- Does the writer give enough reasons to support his or her opinion?
- Are these reasons supported with details?

7 Have students read the outline and the writer's paragraph on page 116 independently. Then have students work in groups or as a class to discuss how the writer developed the ideas in the outline into a paragraph. Also have them discuss how the paragraph was organized.

Write About It

Presentation

8 Have students read the arguments independently and choose the arguments they think are most persuasive. Then have them work in pairs, in small groups, or as a class to compare their choices and to brainstorm other possible arguments against closing the street.

9 Have students write an outline for their argument using the outline in Exercise 7 as a model. As in that outline, each reason should be supported. Then have students write their first draft. Remind them to include a topic sentence, a concluding sentence, and transitions between the reasons.

☑ **10 Check Your Writing** Have students exchange papers with partners and use the questions to check content and format. Have them give each other feedback. Have them write their final drafts.

 Workbook: Practice 12

Vocabulary Expansion: Determining meaning from context—Idioms with *run* See page T150.

Answers
a. 5 b. 6 c. 3 d. 2 e. 7 f. 4 g. 1

EVALUATION

See page TExi.

Unit 11, Achievement Test

Self-Check See **Check Your Knowledge**, page 88 of the Workbook.

Dictation Dictate the following story. Then have students use the story as a model for their own contrary-to-fact story, where a minor event has major consequences as a result of a chain of circumstances. For more information on dictation, see page TExv.

Paul is the captain of our basketball team. Last night, the cafeteria served smoked perch. If the cafeteria had served pizza, Paul would have eaten it. But he didn't eat the perch, so at about midnight he was hungry. If he had listened to my advice, he would have eaten a banana. If he had eaten a banana, he would have been fine. Instead, he ate a gallon of ice cream. He woke up with a terrible stomachache and couldn't get out of bed. If he had played in the game today, he would have scored a lot of points and we would have won. The coach said that we should have played better. But I know that the problem was that smoked perch.

Communication Skills

1. Display pictures of a doctor's office, a basketball game or another team sport, and/or a car accident. Have students describe the pictures. Encourage them to use the unit vocabulary. Listen for the correct use of the vocabulary.

2. Have students talk about something they did in the past that did not turn out well. Have them tell what other course of action they could have taken and how things would have been different. Listen for the correct use of past modals and of the third conditional.

WISHFUL THINKING

OBJECTIVES

- To talk about the environment and other world issues
- To make wishes about the past, present, and future
- To use constructions with **wish**
- To listen to identify speakers' roles
- To place stress on consecutive content words
- To evaluate and justify ideas
- To outline texts
- To write a persuasive letter
- To recognize and understand related word forms

GETTING STARTED

Warm Up

Preview

Write **wishful thinking** on the board. Ask students what this phrase might mean. Elicit or explain that **wishful thinking** is believing that something you want to be true really is true—for example, on finishing a test you hadn't studied for, you might think that it wasn't so hard after all and that you got an A (only to find out later that you'd gotten a C). Ask students whether they ever do any wishful thinking.

Presentation

❶ Have students read the explanation and question independently. You might want to give an example about yourself to start the discussion. Have students share their answers in pairs. Then have individuals describe one of their partner's wishes to the class.

🎧 ❷ Play the recording or read the audioscript aloud so students can mark their answers. Have students work in pairs to compare their answers and then listen again to check them, if necessary.

Audioscript: The audioscript for Exercise 2 appears on page T160.

T117

> **Answers**
> 1. color of eyes 2. dancing 3. shyness

✿ **Option:** Write the following questions on the board or make copies for students. Play the recording or read the audioscript again for them to write their answers.

Conversation 1
1. What class do students have together? (biology)
2. Is the new boy friendly or unfriendly? (friendly)

Conversation 2
3. When is the party? (Friday)
4. Who does the boy want to impress? (Dorothy)

Conversation 3
5. Who is Lucy talking to? (Mr. Allen)
6. What is Mr. Allen's advice? (to participate more in class)

❸ Have students read the explanation and question independently. Then have them respond to the question in groups or as a class.

 Workbook: Practice 1

Figure It Out

Preview

- Initiate a discussion of the environment to elicit or present the meanings of **disposal**, **toxic waste**, **chemicals**, **extinct**, **conserve**, and **regulation(s)**. Use photographs, drawings on the board, and/or synonyms as appropriate. Encourage students to say what they think they could do to help conserve **resources** (a reserve or source of supply, support, or assistance).

- Ask students to name other world issues besides the environment. (war, weapons control, disaster relief, poverty and hunger, and so on) What issues do students feel are the most pressing?

(*Figure It Out continues on page T118.*)

GETTING STARTED

Warm Up

1 Most people would like some things about their lives to be different from the way they really are. Some short people would like to be taller; some single people would like to be married. What things in your life would you like to be different? Describe your wishes to a partner.

2 Listen to the conversations. What do the speakers wish were different? Circle the answer.

Conversation 1:	height	color of eyes	weight
Conversation 2:	dancing	studying	skiing
Conversation 3:	humor	intelligence	shyness

3 In the United States, people make wishes on special occasions. They make a wish when they blow out birthday candles or when they see a shooting star. When do people make wishes in your culture?

Figure It Out

A reporter is asking people what important changes they would like to see in the world for the third millennium.

A.   **REPORTER:**   And what is your wish for the future, young man?

   ALFRED: I want people to realize that we are slowly killing the planet. I wish people would stop polluting the air we breathe and the water we drink.

Unit 12

5	REPORTER:	Can you be more specific?
	ALFRED:	Yeah. Companies all over the world have emptied dangerous chemicals into our rivers and oceans. I wish there were mandatory, planetary regulations about the disposal of toxic waste.
10	CARL:	But wait. Industry has voluntarily spent millions of dollars to cut down on pollution and solve the toxic waste problem.
	ALFRED:	All I know is that before we had so much new technology, people seemed to respect nature more. I wish people cared as much about saving the environment as they do about creating new machines.
15	ROXANNE:	I agree. Take the rain forests, for example. If they're destroyed, we'll lose important sources of oxygen, and hundreds of species of plants and animals will become extinct. What a shame!
	ALFRED:	Let's hope that humans are not one of those species!

B.

REPORTER: And how about you, Miss? What are your hopes and wishes for the new millennium?

JUSTINE: I agree with Alfred. We should protect the environment and conserve our natural resources, and the most important resource on our planet is people.

REPORTER: What exactly do you mean by that?

JUSTINE: Well, millions of people have died in senseless wars. I wish people would stop fighting. I wish people truly believed in peace.

REPORTER: That's an idealistic view. Ever since weapons were invented, people have used them to fight in wars.

JUSTINE: I know, but I wish they had never been invented. If governments didn't spend so much money on weapons, they could use that money to explore ways of benefiting people.

ALFRED: Hey, I wish I could vote for you for president! You sound like you would reform the world!

☑ ④ Vocabulary Check Match the words on the left with their definitions on the right.

_____	**1.** to breathe (line 4)	**a.**	poisonous
_____	**2.** mandatory (line 7)	**b.**	willingly
_____	**3.** disposal (line 8)	**c.**	to control the use of; to save
_____	**4.** toxic (line 8)	**d.**	to help; to be good for
_____	**5.** voluntarily (line 9)	**e.**	to take air in and out of the body
_____	**6.** source (line 15)	**f.**	required by order or law
_____	**7.** extinct (line 16)	**g.**	to change to make better
_____	**8.** to conserve (line 23)	**h.**	no longer existing
_____	**9.** to benefit (line 35)	**i.**	removal; getting rid of
_____	**10.** to reform (line 37)	**j.**	place from which something comes

(Figure It Out continued from page T117.)

Presentation

Read the conversations on pages 117 and 118 aloud as students listen. Students can listen with their books open or closed. Then have students read the conversations independently in class or for homework.

After the initial presentation of the conversations, check comprehension by having students answer the following questions.

1. What does Alfred wish? (He wishes that people would stop polluting the air and water.)

2. What specific example of an environmental problem does Alfred mention? (A lot of companies have emptied dangerous chemicals into our rivers and oceans.)

3. Who agrees with Alfred? (Roxanne)

4. Who disagrees with Alfred? (Carl)

5. What is Justine concerned about? (She's concerned about war and weapons control.)

6. Which speakers are idealists? (Alfred and Justine)

In addition, you might want to have students discuss the following questions as a class or in groups.

1. Do you agree with Alfred or with Carl? Explain your answer.

2. Do you agree with Justine? Why or why not?

Option: If there are strong differences of opinion in the class, you may wish to organize an informal debate about one or more of the issues.

Option: Have groups of five students work together to act out the parts of the reporter, Alfred, Carl, Roxanne, and Justine. Have them practice the conversations and then perform them from memory for the class.

Option: Discuss the statement "What a shame!" (line 16). Have students share, with a partner or the class, situations where another student would respond with "What a shame!"

☑ ❹ **Vocabulary Check** Have students complete the exercise independently in class or for homework. Ask individuals to share their answers with the class.

> **Answers**
> 1. e 2. f 3. i 4. a 5. b 6. j 7. h 8. c 9. d
> 10. g

Option: Write **benefit, care, control, reform,** and **respect** on the board and point out that these words can be used as nouns or verbs. Have students work with partners to make up pairs of sentences using each word as a noun and as a verb.

Write **empty** on the board. What two parts of speech can this word be? (verb and adjective) Have students find **empty** in Conversation A. (line 6) What does **empty** mean in this context? (to pour out)

 Workbook: Practice 2

Talk About It

Option: You may prefer to postpone this activity until after the grammar presentation on pages 119–120 if you feel students need extra help with structures with **wish**.

Presentation

Note: The purpose of this activity is to develop fluency. Students should be free to speak without fear of interruption for error correction. If you notice persistent errors, write them down for later reteaching or review.

❺ Have students read the instructions and the example conversation independently. Then have a pair of students read the example conversation aloud. Have students complete the activity in pairs, switching roles after they have done half. Encourage students to use language similar to that in the example. Have pairs perform their conversations for the class.

Option: Have students suggest additional categories. (height, talent) Then have them continue the activity using these categories.

Option: Have students work in pairs or groups to survey other students, family members, etc. about their three main wishes for the world. Have them record their findings and report them to the class. Make a chart showing the results of the survey. What did people seem to be most unhappy with? Were wishes similar or different for different age groups? for men and women? for older and younger people?

GRAMMAR

Wishing for Changes to the Present

Preview

- To introduce wishing about the present, have students work in pairs or small groups to brainstorm three things about

their city they would like to change. (*Example:* "We have too much traffic on Main Street. I'd like Main Street to be closed to traffic.") When they have finished, list some of their ideas on the board. Explain that when we express a desire for something to be different from the way it is now, we are wishing about the present.

- Write sentences with **wish** paraphrasing one of the ideas on the board. For example, for *I'd like Main Street to be closed to traffic,* write:

  I wish Main Street <u>were</u> closed to traffic.

  I wish cars <u>weren't</u> allowed to use Main Street.

  I wish drivers <u>couldn't drive</u> on Main Street.

  I wish we <u>didn't have</u> any traffic on Main Street.

- Have students work in pairs to make similar sentences about the other ideas listed on the board. Have them report some of their sentences to the class.

- Write a few of the students' sentences on the board. Then elicit the form used for wishing for changes in the present. (**wish** + past tense)

Presentation

Have students read the grammar explanation and examples independently in class or for homework.

☑ ❶ **Check Your Understanding** Have students read the instructions and complete the exercise individually. Discuss the answers as a class. Remind students that the use of the past tense to talk about the present and the use of **were** for all persons are the same as with the second conditional.

Answers
a. past b. were c. could *or* were able to

Talk About It

 5 You are surveying people about changes they would like in their lives. With a partner, ask and answer questions. Use the cues and your imagination.

Example: age

Ask about a wish.

A: What do you wish were different in your life?

Tell about a wish.

B: I'm seventy-four now. I wish I were a lot younger.

Ask for an explanation.

A: And why is that?

Give an explanation.

B: If I were younger, I'd go to the Amazon to help save the rain forests.

An example of deforestation

a. job	**d.** languages	**g.** appearance
b. travel	**e.** money	**h.** health
c. friends	**f.** education	**i.** idea of your own

GRAMMAR

Wishing for Changes to the Present

We wish for things that are different from reality. We use present wishes to express regret or complaint about the current situation. Wishes take conditional verb forms since the wish is for something not real or possible.

Present Reality	Wish for Present Change
The air **is** polluted.	I **wish** the air **weren't** polluted.
We **can't drink** the water in our lakes.	I **wish** we **could drink** the water.
Anti-pollution laws **aren't strict enough**.	I **wish** the anti-pollution laws **were** stricter.
Justine **can't reform** the world.	She **wishes** she **were able to reform** the world.

  1 **Check Your Understanding** Circle the answer or answers.

a. To wish for changes in the present, the verb in the clause after *wish* changes to: present   past   past perfect

b. To wish for changes in the present, the verb *be* with all persons changes to: *is   are   were*

c. To wish for changes in the present, the modal *can* changes to: *could   were able to*

2 Complete the passage with the correct form of the verb. Use a negative form when necessary.

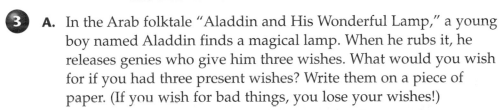

DAUGHTER: Being a teenager is boring! I wish I
(1. be) _____ older.

MOTHER: It's not always great being older. I wish I
(2. have) _____ to worry about you kids
all the time.

DAUGHTER: Well, I wish I (3. need) _____ to go to
school. And I wish I (4. have) _____
enough money to travel around the world. In fact,
I wish I (5. can) _____ leave this town and
never come back.

MOTHER: Yeah, and I wish I (6. have) _____ a million
dollars so I could buy a yacht and go with you.

DAUGHTER: Oh, don't you wish we (7. can) _____ live
like that? It would be a dream come true!

3 **A.** In the Arab folktale "Aladdin and His Wonderful Lamp," a young
boy named Aladdin finds a magical lamp. When he rubs it, he
releases genies who give him three wishes. What would you wish
for if you had three present wishes? Write them on a piece of
paper. (If you wish for bad things, you lose your wishes!)

B. With a partner, ask and answer questions about your wishes.

Wishing for Changes to the Past

We make wishes about the past to express regret or complain about something in the
past. Since the wish is for something unreal, we use conditional verb forms.

Past Reality	Wish for Change to the Past
I **studied** French in the United States.	I **wish** I **had studied** it in France.
I **couldn't speak** French when I went to France.	I wish I **had been able to speak** French.
My sister **couldn't go** to France with me.	I wish she **could have gone** with me.

4 Karl is a very successful businessman now, but when he was younger,
he led a wild life. Now he has several regrets about those years.
Work with a partner. Take turns being Karl and telling about
your regrets.

Example: dropped out of college/didn't study

A: If you could change anything about your life, what would
it be?

B: I wish I hadn't dropped out of college.

A: Well, why did you drop out?

B: I had no time to study. I wish that I had studied harder.

❷ Have students read the directions and write their answers independently. Then have a pair of students read the conversation aloud and have the rest of the class compare their answers.

Answers
1. were 2. didn't have 3. didn't need
4. had 5. could 6. had 7. could

 Workbook: Practice 4

❸ Have students read the question and write their wishes independently. Then have them work in pairs to find out about each other's wishes. *(Answers will vary.)* Have students share their partners' wishes with the class. You might want to take a poll to find out the three most popular wishes.

Wishing for Changes to the Past

Preview

• To introduce wishing about the past, have students brainstorm past actions that had bad consequences. *(Example: "I drove my father's car without his permission, and I had an accident.")* Write a few of their ideas on the board. Explain that when we want something in the past to be different from the way it was, we are wishing about the past.

• Write sentences with **wish** about one of the ideas. For example, for *"I drove my father's car without his permission, and I had an accident,"* write:

I wish I <u>had been</u> more careful.

I wish I <u>had known</u> how to drive better.

I wish I <u>hadn't taken</u> my father's car.

• Have students work in pairs to make similar sentences about some of their other ideas listed on the board. Have them report the sentences to the class.

• Write a few of the students' sentences on the board. Then elicit the form for wishing in the past. (**wish** + past perfect tense)

Presentation

Have students read the grammar explanation and examples independently in class or for homework. Point out that in their use of the past perfect or **could have** + past participle, these sentences are similar to third conditionals.

❹ Have students read the instructions and example independently. Then have a pair of students read the example conversation aloud for the class. Have students work in pairs to complete the activity. Remind them to take turns starting the conversations. After students have completed the activity, have pairs perform the conversations for the class.

Answers
Sample conversations.
a. I wish I hadn't wrecked my brand new car. *Well, how did you wreck it?* I ran a stop sign. I wish I hadn't run the stop sign.
b. I wish I hadn't lost my first job. *Well, why did you lose it?* I didn't take it very seriously. I wish I had taken it more seriously.
c. I wish I had invested my money. *Well, why didn't you invest it?* I spent it on nothing. I wish I hadn't spent it on nothing.
d. I wish I hadn't gotten divorced. *Well, why did you get divorced?* I wasn't flexible enough. I wish I had been more flexible.
e. I wish I hadn't sold my old records. *Well, why did you sell them?* I needed some money. I wish I hadn't needed the money.
f. I wish I hadn't lost track of old friends. *Well, why did you lose track of them?* I moved away. I wish I hadn't moved away.

🜨 **Option:** You may wish to have students write out the conversations as homework.

🜨 **Option:** Have students work in pairs to write more cues like those in Exercise 4. Then have them give their cues to another pair to use to continue the activity.

5 Have students read the instructions and example conversation independently. Then have a pair of students read the example conversation aloud for the class. Have students work in pairs to complete the activity. Explain that student A starts each conversation by reading the cue aloud, and that students should take turns starting the conversations. After students have completed the activity, have pairs perform the conversations for the class.

Answers

Answers will vary somewhat, but answers like these are probable for student B: **a.** I wish I had applied earlier. **b.** I wish I had brought it in sooner. **c.** I wish I had bought it on sale. **d.** I wish I had gotten it fixed. **e.** I wish I hadn't failed it. **f.** I wish I had bought gas before we left.

 Workbook: Practice 3

6 Have students read the instructions and example conversation independently. Give them some time to think about the items in the list. Have students work in pairs to complete the activity. *(Answers will vary.)* Have students perform some of their conversations for the class. You may want to discuss some of the items as a class. Do any students have similar regrets?

Option: Have students write paragraphs about things they wish they had done differently. Have them give reasons for their wishes.

Option: Have students ask family members about things they wish they had done differently in their lives. Have them record their findings and organize their findings into a chart. Have students indicate in the charts whether the family members they interviewed were male or female, old or young, and so on. Then have individuals share their charts with the class. Finally, have students analyze the information in the charts to see if they can make any generalizations about the wishes of males vs. females, the old vs. the young, and so on.

 Workbook: Practice 5

a. wrecked my brand new car/ran a stop sign
b. lost my first job/took it more seriously
c. invested my money/spent it on nothing
d. got divorced/was more flexible
e. sold my old records/needed some money
f. lost track of old friends/moved away

5 Work with a partner. Take turns using the cues to start a conversation and wishing about the past.

Example:

A: Where have you been? The concert is almost over!
B: I know. I wish I had left home earlier. The traffic was awful!
A: Well, I could have told you it would be bad.

a. I'm sorry, we can't accept your application. The deadline was yesterday.
b. Sorry, but your guarantee was only for three months. You'll have to pay for the repairs now. The guarantee has expired.
c. You paid how much? I just saw the same computer on sale for considerably less.
d. I told you to get the roof fixed before it rained!
e. How could you have failed the math test? It was so easy!
f. I can't drive much farther. We're almost out of gas.

6 Looking over your life, you probably see things that you wish you had done differently. With a partner, take turns asking and answering questions about the things in the list.

Example: family

A: What do you wish you had done differently with regard to your family?
B: I wish I had spent more time with my grandparents.
A: I know what you mean. I wish I had, too.

a. school
b. home life
c. work
d. vacation
e. relationships
f. idea of your own

Wishing for Changes to the Future

To wish for future changes, we use *would* or *could*. We often use future wishes to criticize, complain, or suggest.

Present Reality	Wish for Change to the Future
My boss **isn't going to give** me any time off.	I **wish** he **would give** me time off.
I **can't take** a vacation next year.	I **wish** I **could take** a vacation next year.

7 We all like to think that things will get better in the world. Look at the world issues in the box and think of your wishes for the future. Write five of your wishes on a sheet of paper.

> **World Issues**
>
> deforestation   nuclear weapons   handgun control
> water pollution   global warming   drug abuse
> extinction of animals equal rights for minorities   population growth
> idea of your own

8 **Express Yourself** With a partner, express your most heartfelt wish for future change. Try to persuade your partner to agree with you.

LISTENING and SPEAKING

Listen: Share a Wish

1 **Before You Listen** Who do you usually share your wishes with? Explain. What kinds of things do you usually wish for?

STRATEGY **Recognizing Speakers' Roles** In listening, it is important to be able to identify a speaker's position, job, or function in a particular situation. Recognizing the role of each speaker helps you understand more fully why and how each one of the speakers communicates.

2 Listen to the five conversations. What relationship do the speakers in each conversation have? Write the number of the conversation on the line.

_____ **a.** mother/daughter   _____ **e.** teacher/student
_____ **b.** lawyer/client   _____ **f.** neighbor/neighbor
_____ **c.** coach/player   _____ **g.** boss/assistant
_____ **d.** friend/friend   _____ **h.** doctor/patient

Wishing for Changes to the Future

Preview

- To introduce wishing about the future, have students brainstorm things about their city they would like to see changed within the next ten years. (*Example:* I want less pollution.) Write a few of their ideas on the board. Explain that when we want something to be different in the future, we are wishing about the future.

- Write sentences with **wish** about one of the ideas; for example, for "*I want less pollution*," write:

  I wish we <u>could reduce</u> the amount of pollution.

  I wish the government <u>would do</u> something about pollution.

  I wish industries <u>would find</u> cleaner ways of making their products.

  I wish people <u>wouldn't throw</u> litter on the ground.

- Have students work in pairs to make similar sentences about their own ideas. Then have them share their sentences with the class.

- Write a few of the students' sentences on the board. Then elicit the forms for wishing in the future. (**wish** + **would** or **could** + base form of verb)

Presentation

Have students read the grammar explanation and examples independently in class or for homework.

❼ Have students read the instructions and the list of world issues independently. Give help with any unfamiliar vocabulary. Then have students write down their five wishes independently. (*Answers will vary.*)

❽ **Express Yourself** Ask students to decide which wish is most important to them. Then have students work with partners. Do their partners agree that the change they are wishing for is important? If not, can they persuade their partners to agree? After the pairs have completed the activity, discuss the wishes as a class.

Option: Bring in posters with slogans for change on them, or write the following slogans on the board:

Save the Whales
Only You Can Prevent Forest Fires
Smokers Die Younger
Save the Children
Save the Planet
No More War
Don't Be a Litterbug

Have students read the slogans and tell what the groups who wrote the slogans would like to see changed in the future. Have students make a sentence with **wish** for each slogan, as either a written or an oral exercise.

Option: Have students discuss how they would like to improve their school's environment. Possibilities include cleaning up the classrooms, halls, or schoolyard; painting the rooms; planting trees in the schoolyard; putting plants in classrooms; putting up a poster in the library requesting students to be quiet. Then have students work in pairs or in small groups to write sentences about their wishes for school improvement.

LISTENING and SPEAKING

Listen: Share a Wish

Presentation

❶ **Before You Listen** Have students read and respond to the questions in pairs, in small groups, or as a class.

➡ **Recognizing Speakers' Roles** Have students read the strategy independently. You might want to point out that this is something we usually do without thinking and ask students whether they can remember any examples of when they understood a situation, in real life or in a movie, by understanding the relationship between the speakers.

❷ Have students read the instructions, the question, and possible answers independently. Then play the recording or read the audioscript aloud two or more times. Have students compare their

(*Exercise 2 continues on page T123.*)

(Exercise 2 continued from page T122.)

answers with a partner. Let them listen again if necessary.

Audioscript: The audioscript for Exercise 2 appears on page T160.

> **Answers**
> a. 4 b. 1 d. 2 f. 5 g. 3

 Option: Have students write short dialogues for the remaining sets of relationships: coach/player, teacher/student, doctor/patient. Remind them to use at least one **wish** sentence. Have students perform their dialogues for the class.

Link *Workbook: Practice 6*

Pronunciation

Preview

• Write these phrases on the board:
  a new car
  a black suit
  a tall building
  a nice person

  Ask students to predict, for each of the phrases, which syllables are stressed.

• Say the phrases aloud and have students check their ideas. (Make sure you put more stress on the noun than on the adjective.) Explain that, as content words, nouns and adjectives receive stress, whereas **a**, an article, doesn't.

Presentation

Have students read the explanation and the examples independently in class or for homework. Then read the examples aloud, stressing the syllables in boldface type, and

have students repeat them. Review the examples to make sure that students can hear the differences in stress and that they understand the rules that account for the differences (for example, **White House**, as a name, acts as a single noun, rather than as an adjective + noun, like **white house**).

❸ Have students work in pairs to read the instructions and complete the activity in two steps.

> **Answers**
> The following combinations should be underlined. Syllables in boldface type have the strongest stress. **A:** main **road**; **B:** long **walk**; **A:** **water**falls; **B:** Golden State **Highway**, tall **trees**, green **grass**, blue **birds**, beautiful blue **sky**, aspen **trees**; **A:** fresh **fruit**, tall **trees**, green **grass**, nice **view**

 ❹ Play the recording or read the audioscript aloud and have students check their answers. Have students discuss the answers with their partner and then as a class.

❺ Have students practice the dialogue in pairs. Then have some pairs read it aloud to the class.

Link *Workbook: Practice 7*

Speak Out

Presentation

➡ **Evaluating and Justifying** Have students read the strategy and the expressions in the box. Ask students to name situations where they might use these strategies. Present or elicit the expressions by discussing a relevant school or class issue with students.

Pronunciation

Saying Content Words Together

When two content words come together, one word is slightly more stressed than the other. When an adjective and noun come together, the stress is usually on the noun, but it can also be placed on the adjective to convey special meaning.

         ●   ●   ●   ●

Jo lives in a white **house**.   The president lives in the **White** House.
(any house that is white)   (a specific house)

When two nouns come together, the first one is usually more stressed.

            ●   ●   ●

Clean up the toxic **waste** problem.

3 Work with a partner. Read each sentence and underline all the *adjective + noun* and *noun + noun* combinations. Predict which syllable should carry the strongest stress and put a large dot (●) over it.

A: I wish we had taken the main road.

B: But I thought you wanted to take a long walk.

A: I did. If only we'd get to the waterfalls already.

B: On Golden State Highway, you wouldn't have been able to see tall trees, green grass, or blue birds. And look at that beautiful blue sky, and those colorful aspen trees.

A: Well, I'm tired and hungry. I wish we had brought fresh fruit or chips or something. You can't eat tall trees, green grass, or a nice view.

4 Listen and confirm your predictions. Discuss the ones you got wrong. Try to figure out why.

5 Take turns reading the dialogue to each other, focusing on stress.

Speak Out

STRATEGY

Evaluating and Justifying Sometimes you need to examine an idea or action by looking at its strengths and weaknesses. After evaluating, you justify your acceptance or rejection of the idea by explaining the reasons behind your decision.

Evaluating	Justifying
Let's look at the pros and cons.	I think that ... because of three main reasons.
It's important to keep in mind that ...	The main reason for choosing ... is ...
All things considered, I think that ...	We would benefit by this action because ...

6 Are you a wishful thinker? Do you think it's better to be a wishful thinker or an entirely practical person? Share your ideas with a partner.

7 Do some wishful thinking now. On a sheet of paper, write a wish about each category below. Try to be specific.

space exploration	world economy	world politics
weather control	useful inventions	languages
medical discoveries	world environment	wars

8 Work in small groups. Imagine that three of the wishes that the members of your group made could come true. Evaluate the wishes and choose the three best ones. Then justify your choices to the class.

Example:

A: I wish humans could establish a long-term colony on Mars. Just think how our scientific knowledge would expand!

B: Well, that's one advantage, but keep in mind that the money for a project like that could probably be better spent on Earth.

C: I agree. We would benefit more by focusing on problems here and now, such as feeding the hungry or protecting the environment.

READING and WRITING

Read About It

1 **Before You Read** Many organizations have been formed to help improve the world. Work with a partner. List as many of these organizations as you can and tell what they do.

STRATEGY **Outlining a Text** When you read, you understand better when you notice the main ideas and supporting details of a text. Outlining these main ideas and details helps you see the organizational structure the writer used and understand the text better.

UNICEF: Working for a Better World

The United Nations International Children's Emergency Fund (UNICEF) was created by the United Nations in 1946 to provide food, clothing, blankets, and medicine to children who
5   needed help after World War II. While providing this immediate assistance, UNICEF officials realized that there was a need for long-range programs to benefit children all over the world. To this end, the organization changed its focus as well as its name. Today it is known as the United Nations Children's Fund.

Note: The purpose of this activity is to develop fluency. Students should talk without fear of interruption for error correction. If you notice persistent errors, write them down for later reteaching or review.

❻ Have students read the questions and think about them independently. Then have them share their ideas with their partner. If desired, discuss the questions as a class.

❼ Have students read the instructions and the categories independently. Clarify vocabulary as necessary. Then have students write their sentences independently.

❽ Have students read the instructions and example dialogue independently. Then have them look again at the language for evaluating and justifying on page 123 and at its use in the example in Exercise 8. Have three students read the example dialogue aloud for the class. You might want to have them extend the dialogue in the example. Then have students work in groups to complete the exercise. Have each group evaluate the wishes its members made in Exercise 7 and choose the best three wishes. Remind students to use the language for evaluating and justifying, both in discussing their wishes and in explaining their choices to the class.

Option: Have each group make a poster to illustrate the wish it chose as the best one. They could show, for example, a collage of doves for "We wish there were peace on earth," photos of clean and dirty water for "We wish people would stop polluting our rivers," and so on. Have students sign their posters and display them for the class.

Option: Have students work in groups to create public service messages for television. Their messages can be about the environment or any other issues that interest them. Have each group present its message to the class. Encourage students to use the structures and expressions they've been practicing in this unit in presenting their messages.

Read About It

Presentation

❶ Before You Read Have students work in pairs to read the instructions and to write their lists. Then have them share lists as a class. (The students can list Greenpeace, the United Nations, Amnesty International, the World Bank, the World Health Organization, and other such organizations.)

➡ **Outlining a Text** Have students read the strategy. Suggest that they read a text through once and then outline it as they read it a second time. You might want to review outline format, discussing how roman numerals are used with main ideas, capital letters with details supporting the main ideas, and Arabic numerals with details that support the supporting details.

Have students read the article independently in class or for homework. If students read in class, you may want to set a time limit. Check comprehension by having students answer the following questions. (*Answers may vary somewhat.*)

1. Who founded UNICEF? (the United Nations)

2. What is the main purpose of UNICEF? (to help children all over the world through health and education programs)

3. Who does UNICEF help educate? (nurses, teachers, child welfare specialists, parents)

4. How does UNICEF get its money? (through voluntary contributions mostly from governments and through various fund-raising activities)

❷ Have students read the instructions and complete the exercise independently. Review answers as a class.

Answers
1. d 2. a 3. e 4. c 5. b 6. f

✦ **Option:** Write these words from the article on the board.

aid	establish	provide
contribute	goals	purpose
create	help	sponsor
equipment	objectives	supplies

Have students work in pairs or groups to group the words with similar meanings. Encourage them to refer to the article if they need to figure out the meanings of any of the words. (Word groups: aid, contribute, help, provide, sponsor; equipment, supplies; goals, objectives, purpose; create, establish)

❸ Have students read the instructions and complete the exercise independently. Then have them check their answers in pairs or groups.

Answers
Outlines will vary somewhat.
  I. Origin of UNICEF
    A. year of founding 1946
    B. original purpose to provide food and supplies to children needing help after World War II
  II. Present-Day Goals of UNICEF
    A. Developmental/Humanitarian
      1. supplies disease-control programs, health centers, schools
      2. supports projects that help reduce infant mortality rates
      3. provides emergency relief following disasters, wars, or epidemics
    B. Educational
      1. provides funds for training nurses, teachers, and child welfare specialists
      2. sponsors classes in nutrition, child care, parenting, and basic education

  III. Sources of Support for UNICEF
    A. Voluntary contributions
    B. Other Funds
      1. Sale of greeting cards
      2. Television benefits hosted by famous personalities
      3. Other types of fund-raising activities supported by private citizens

✦ **Option:** Have students write out a summary of the article in class or for homework. Encourage them to base their summary on the outline they completed.

Think About It

(*See page 126.*)

Presentation

❹ – ❺ Have students read the questions independently. Then have them carry out the discussion in pairs, in small groups, or as a class. If they haven't contributed to an organization, would they like to? Why or why not? What kind of organization would they contribute to? What can they do as individuals to make the world a better place.

Write: A Persuasive Letter

(*See page 126.*)

Preview

Have students work in pairs or small groups to list the parts of a formal letter. (return address, date, inside address, greeting, body, closing, signature) See the writing sections in Units 1 and 3 and discuss what should be included in a persuasive paragraph. (a statement of your point of view and reasons for your opinions) (See the writing section in Unit 11.)

Presentation

Have students read the explanation independently in class or as homework.

T125

In order to aid children the world over, UNICEF today combines humanitarian and developmental goals by helping over 100 countries plan and expand services in the areas of health and education. For example, in the field of health care, UNICEF provides supplies and equipment for disease-control programs, health centers, and school food plans. It also supports projects that help reduce infant mortality rates, such as immunization programs and food supplement projects. In addition, UNICEF still provides emergency relief following disasters, wars, or epidemics. In the field of education, UNICEF provides funds for training nurses, teachers, and child welfare specialists. It also sponsors classes in nutrition, child care, and parenting, as well as in basic education.

UNICEF, with a multimillion dollar budget, provides its many services thanks to voluntary contributions, most of which come from governments. Other funds are acquired through the sale of greeting cards, television benefits hosted by famous personalities, and other types of fund-raising activities supported by private citizens. UNICEF succeeds because concerned people around the world, rather than just wish that the world were a better place, contribute their effort, money, and time to make it better for our children and our future.

2 Use the context to match the words on the left with their meanings on the right.

_____ **1.** long-range (line 7)   **a.** to make larger
_____ **2.** to expand (line 12)   **b.** science of eating properly
_____ **3.** mortality (line 16)   **c.** support; assistance
_____ **4.** relief (line 18)   **d.** not immediate
_____ **5.** nutrition (line 21)   **e.** death
_____ **6.** contribution (line 23)   **f.** donation; gift

3 Use information from the reading to complete the outline.

I. Origin of UNICEF
   A. year of founding _____
   B. original purpose _____
II. Present-day Goals of UNICEF
   A. Developmental/Humanitarian
      1. supplies disease-control programs, health centers, schools
      2. supports _____
      3. _____
   B. Educational
      1. _____
      2. _____
III. _____
      1. voluntary contributions
      2. _____
      3. _____
      4. _____

Think About It

 Have you ever contributed money or volunteered your services to an organization like UNICEF? Explain.

 Whose responsibility is it to make the world a better place? What can you as an individual do?

Write: A Persuasive Letter

We sometimes write formal letters to persuade people to agree with our point of view about an issue, idea, or action. As in a persuasive paragraph, we first state our point of view and then give reasons for our opinions, including examples and the quoted opinions of authorities, if possible. This kind of letter may end with a call to action, such as voting a particular way, joining an organization, or removing a product from stores. All the parts of a formal letter are included in a persuasive letter.

Write About It

 A large international company is planning to donate $5 million to the arts. The chairperson of the donation committee has asked for letters from citizens about worthy recipients. Work with a partner. Choose a worthy recipient from your city or country (an art museum, orchestra, children's theater, etc.). Make an outline of the reasons why you think that recipient should get the money. Then write a persuasive letter to the chairperson. The address is:

Chairperson, International Arts Committee
MegaCorp
5769 West Parson Avenue
New York, New York 10022

  Check Your Writing Exchange letters with a partner. Use the questions below to give feedback to your partner. When you get your own paper back, revise as necessary.

- Does the letter include all the parts of a formal letter?
- Is the point of view well supported?
- Does the letter end with a call for action?
- Is the letter persuasive?
- Is the letter grammatically correct?

Write About It

Presentation

6 Have students read the instructions independently. Then have them work in pairs to complete the activity.

☑ **7 Check Your Writing** Have students work in pairs to exchange their first drafts and to use the questions to check both the information and format. Have them give each other feedback before they write the final draft.

Option: Divide the class in half. Give each half of the class the letters written by students in the other half. Explain that each half of the class is the International Arts Committee at MegaCorp and must read the letters to decide who will get the money. Have each group choose a chairperson. Then have them read their letters, evaluate them, and decide who should win the money. Each chairperson should then announce the recipient and summarize the reasons why the recipient was chosen.

 Workbook: Practice 8

Vocabulary Expansion: Word forms See page T151.

Answers
Some categories may have more than one answer. Possible completed chart:

Verb	Noun	Adjective	Adverb
1. appreciate	appreciation, appreciativeness	appreciative	appreciatively
2. compete	competition, competitiveness	**competitive**	competitively
3. conclude	conclusion, conclusiveness	conclusive	**conclusively**
4. **criticize**	criticism, critic, critique, criticalness	critical	critically
5. develop	development, developer	**developmental**	developmentally
6. idealize	ideal, idealist, idealism	idealistic	**idealistically**
7. purpose	**purpose**	purposeful, purposeless	purposefully purposelessly
8. **respect**	respect, respectability, respectfulness	respectable, respectful	respectfully
9. use	**use**	usable, useful, useless, used	usefully, uselessly
10. volunteer	volunteer	**voluntary**	voluntarily

EVALUATION

See page TExi.

Unit 12 Achievement Test

Self-Check See Check Your Knowledge, page 94 of the Workbook.

Dictation Dictate the following summary of the reading. As you dictate, tell students where to leave blank spaces for the missing information. Then have students use information from the reading to complete the sentences. For more information on dictation, see page TExv.

UNICEF was created by _____ in _____ to provide food, clothing, blankets, and _____ to children who needed help after _____. Today UNICEF helps countries provide services in the areas of health and _____. As before, it provides emergency help after disasters, wars, or _____. In addition, it sponsors _____ in nutrition and child care. UNICEF meets its multi-million-dollar _____ through contributions, which are mainly from _____, and through _____ activities, such as the sale of _____.

Communication Skills

1. Give students a number of pictures that show environmental problems and/or solutions. Have them talk about the pictures in pairs or small groups. As they talk, pay attention to their use of the unit vocabulary.

2. Have students talk about things they wish for themselves and for the world. Pay attention to their use of the structures with **wish**.

Answers for Dictation
The United Nations 1946; Medicine; World War II; education; epidemics; classes; budget; governments; fund-raising; greeting cards

REVIEW UNITS 10–12

Unit review exercises can be assigned for homework or done in class. You can use them in several ways.

- Give the review exercises as a quiz. Have students work alone and submit their answers to you.

- Give the review exercises as you would other exercises in the book. Students work alone and then compare answers with a partner.

- Have students work alone and then review answers as a class. Have selected students write their answers on the board. Then correct any errors as a class.

1 Have students read the instructions independently and then complete the exercise. For general notes on modals used to speculate about the past, express past ability, and draw logical conclusions about the past, refer students to Unit 10, pages 99–101; for general notes on past modals used to criticize, refer them to Unit 11, page 109.

Answers
1. might have been/could have been
2. might have knocked over/could have knocked over 3. shouldn't have told
4. couldn't have made

2 Have students read the instructions independently and then complete the exercise. For general notes on modals used to speculate about the past, refer students to Unit 10, page 99.

Answers
Answers will vary. 1. He/She might have been sick. 2. There may have been a robbery. 3. It could have been a flying saucer. 4. The letter might have been from her boyfriend. 5. The person could have had the wrong fax number.

3 Have students read the instructions independently and then complete the exercise. For general notes on past modals used to express advice, criticism, and regret, refer students to Unit 11, page 109.

Answers
Answers may vary somewhat. 1. should have dressed. 2. should have arrived
3. should have remembered 4. should have allowed 5. should have described
6. shouldn't have done

1 Complete the conversation with the correct form of the verb. Use *might, could, must,* or *should.* Use the negative when necessary. More than one answer may be possible.

Tom: Kay! Did you hear that noise? What do you think it was?

Kay: I don't know, Tom. It **(1. be)** _____ the neighbor's cat.

Tom: That didn't sound like a cat to me.

Kay: The cat **(2. knock over)** _____ the garbage can again.

Tom: No, it sounded more like someone forcing a door open or something.

Kay: You **(3. tell)** _____ me that. You're scaring me!

Tom: Listen!

Kay: I did hear it that time. You're right. A cat or dog **(4. make)** _____ that sound. Should we call the police?

2 Write sentences speculating about the past.

1. Today was the final exam, but the teacher never showed up.

   _____

2. Police surrounded your neighbor's house.

   _____

3. An object with a bright, flashing light moved across the sky.

   _____

4. Carol opened a letter and began to jump up and down in excitement.

   _____

5. You got eight faxes from someone you never heard of.

   _____

3 Complete the passage with the correct form of a verb from the list. Use *should* or *shouldn't.*

allow	do
arrive	dress
describe	remember
perform	expect

Roger went to an important job interview, but he didn't get the job. There are several things he did wrong. For example, he had on old jeans and a torn T-shirt. He **(1.)** _____ more appropriately. His appointment was for 10:00 a.m., but he showed up at 10:18. He **(2.)** _____ on time. He didn't have a copy of his résumé with him. He **(3.)** _____ to take a copy of his résumé. Every time the interviewer spoke, Roger interrupted. He **(4.)** _____ her to finish her sentences before speaking. When the interviewer asked questions about his work experience, he complained about his former bosses. He **(5.)** _____ his experience, not his feelings. Finally, he asked the interviewer for a date. He certainly **(6.)** _____ that!

4 Complete the sentences with the correct form of the verb.

a. It is so hot in here! I wish the landlord (turn off) _____ the heat!

b. These drinks aren't cold. I wish we (have) _____ some ice.

c. Steve wishes he (sing) _____ opera, but he has a terrible voice!

d. Ann's motorcycle is old. She wishes she (buy) _____ a new one.

e. I never took a foreign language course in school. I sure wish I (study) _____ a foreign language back then.

f. Alice couldn't come to the meeting, but she phoned to say she wishes she (attend) _____.

g. My sister went to the Broken Bones concert. I wish I (go) _____, too.

h. Wilma didn't do well on the test. Now she wishes she (pay) _____ more attention in class.

i. Sam says he isn't going to play sports this year at school, but I sure wish he (try out) _____ for the basketball team.

Vocabulary Review

Use the words in the box to complete the sentences.

benefit	funds
budget	extinct
conclusive	deal with
mandatory	sophisticated
stick to	wreck
weapon	cut down on

1. Our department got a bigger _____ for next year. Now we'll have enough money to finish the project!

2. Now the photocopier has broken down again, as if I don't already have enough problems to _____ in this office!

3. Our understanding of human genetics has become _____.

4. Even though I'm taking flu medicine, I feel terrible. I'm still a _____!

5. It's important to protect endangered species. Otherwise, they will become _____.

6. Listen, John. It's in our _____ to compromise on this issue. Your refusal is holding up progress.

7. I saw you eating chocolate! Why won't you _____ your diet?

8. In most people's minds, there is still no _____ evidence to prove the existence of UFOs.

9. The professor asked for additional _____ in order to finish the study.

10. Attendance is _____. If you don't come to class, you will receive an "F."

❹ Have students read the instructions independently and then complete the exercise. For general notes on structures used to express wishes about the present, refer students to Unit 12, page 119; for general notes on structures used to express wishes about the past, refer them to Unit 12, page 120; for general notes on structures used to express wishes about the future, refer them to Unit 12, page 122.

Answers
a. would turn off b. had c. could sing
d. could buy e. had studied/could have studied f. could have attended g. had gone/could have gone h. had paid
i. would try out

Vocabulary Review

Have students read the instructions independently and then complete the exercise.

Answers
1. budget 2. deal with 3. sophisticated
4. wreck 5. extinct 6. benefit 7. stick to
8. conclusive 9. funds 10. mandatory

Base Form	Simple Past	Past Participle
be: am, is, are	was, were	been
become	became	become
begin	began	begun
bend	bent	bent
bite	bit	bitten
blow	blew	blown
break	broke	broken
bring	brought	brought
build	built	built
buy	bought	bought
catch	caught	caught
choose	chose	chosen
come	came	come
cost	cost	cost
cut	cut	cut
do	did	done
draw	drew	drawn
drink	drank	drunk
drive	drove	driven
eat	ate	eaten
fall	fell	fallen
feel	felt	felt
fight	fought	fought
find	found	found
fit	fit	fit
fly	flew	flown
forget	forgot	forgotten
freeze	froze	frozen
get	got	gotten
give	gave	given
go	went	gone
grow	grew	grown
have, has	had	had
hear	heard	heard
hide	hid	hidden
hit	hit	hit
hold	held	held
hurt	hurt	hurt
keep	kept	kept
know	knew	known
leave	left	left

IRREGULAR VERBS

Base Form	Simple Past	Past Participle
lend	lent	lent
lie	lay	lain
lie	lied	lied
light	lit	lit
lose	lost	lost
make	made	made
mean	meant	meant
meet	met	met
pay	paid	paid
put	put	put
quit	quit	quit
read	read	read
ride	rode	ridden
ring	rang	rung
rise	rose	risen
run	ran	run
say	said	said
see	saw	seen
sell	sold	sold
send	sent	sent
set	set	set
sing	sang	sung
sit	sat	sat
sleep	slept	slept
speak	spoke	spoken
speed	sped	sped
spend	spent	spent
stand	stood	stood
steal	stole	stolen
strike	struck	struck
swim	swam	swum
take	took	taken
tell	told	told
think	thought	thought
throw	threw	thrown
understand	understood	understood
wake	woke	woken
wear	wore	worn
win	won	won
write	wrote	written

THE INTERNATIONAL PHONETIC ALPHABET

IPA SYMBOLS

Consonants

/b/	**b**a**b**y, clu**b**	/s/	**s**alt, medi**c**ine, bu**s**
/d/	**d**own, to**d**ay, sa**d**	/š/	**s**ugar, spe**ci**al, fi**sh**
/f/	**f**un, pre**f**er, lau**gh**	/t/	**t**ea, ma**t**erial, da**t**e
/g/	**g**ood, be**g**in, do**g**	/θ/	**th**ing, heal**th**y, ba**th**
/h/	**h**ome, be**h**ind	/ð/	**th**is, mo**th**er, ba**th**e
/k/	**k**ey, cho**c**olate, bla**ck**	/v/	**v**ery, tra**v**el, o**f**
/l/	**l**ate, po**l**ice, mai**l**	/w/	**w**ay, any**o**ne
/m/	**m**ay, wo**m**an, swi**m**	/y/	**y**es, on**i**on
/n/	**n**o, opi**n**ion	/z/	**z**oo, cou**s**in, alway**s**
/ŋ/	a**n**gry, lo**ng**	/ž/	mea**s**ure, gara**g**e
/p/	**p**aper, ma**p**	/č/	**ch**eck, pi**c**ture, wa**tch**
/r/	**r**ain, pa**r**ent, doo**r**	/ǰ/	**j**ob, refri**g**erator, oran**g**e

Vowels

/ɑ/	**o**n, h**o**t, f**a**ther	/o/	**o**pen, cl**o**se, sh**ow**
/æ/	**a**nd, c**a**sh	/u/	b**oo**t, d**o**, thr**ough**
/ɛ/	**e**gg, s**ay**s, l**ea**ther	/ʌ/	**o**f, y**ou**ng, s**u**n
/ɪ/	**i**n, b**i**g	/ʊ/	p**u**t, c**oo**k, w**ou**ld
/ɔ/	**o**ff, d**augh**ter, dr**aw**	/ə/	**a**bout, pen**c**il, lem**o**n
/e/	**A**pril, tr**ai**n, s**ay**	/ɚ/	mo**th**er, Satur**d**ay, doct**or**
/i/	**e**ven, sp**ea**k, tr**ee**	/ɝ/	**ear**th, b**ur**n, h**er**

Diphthongs

/aɪ/	**i**ce, st**y**le, l**ie**	/ɔɪ/	**oi**l, n**oi**se, b**oy**
/aʊ/	**ou**t, d**ow**n, h**ow**		

THE ENGLISH ALPHABET

Here is the pronunciation of the letters of the English alphabet, written in International Phonetic Alphabet symbols.

a	/e/	n	/ɛn/
b	/bi/	o	/o/
c	/si/	p	/pi/
d	/di/	q	/kyu/
e	/i/	r	/ɑr/
f	/ɛf/	s	/ɛs/
g	/ǰi/	t	/ti/
h	/eč/	u	/yu/
i	/aɪ/	v	/vi/
j	/ǰe/	w	/'dʌbəlˌyu/
k	/ke/	x	/ɛks/
l	/ɛl/	y	/waɪ/
m	/ɛm/	z	/zi/

UNIT VOCABULARY

STARTING OUT

Nouns
course
diagram
policy
rectangle
square
triangle

Verbs
to get the facts
to influence

UNIT 1

Nouns
acceptance letter
achievement
awareness
basics
characteristic
letter of inquiry
letter of
   recommendation
principal
resource
strategy
tuition

Verbs
to accomplish
to associate
to get across
to get along with
to get better
to hire

to join
to make progress
to memorize
to obtain
to participate
to reduce
to request
to require
to subscribe to
to take advantage of

Adjectives
artificial
consistent
natural

Adverbs
already
still
yet

Expression
on your own

UNIT 2

Nouns
account
accountant
assistant
blood
cash
certainty
evidence
fiancé, fiancée
housekeeper
killer
lawyer
motive
mystery
robbery
safe
silverware
subway
sum
suspect
victim
widow

Verbs
to brag
to check
   (something) out
to come up with
to commit
to disturb
to fire
to force
to kill
to lock

Adjectives
familiar (with)
furious
illegal
valuable

UNIT 3

Nouns
acquaintance
citizen
client
colleague
landlord
manager
opening
order
overtime
patient
permission
personnel
   department
persuasion
power
request
role
rush hour
tenant

Verbs
to allow
to appreciate
to contribute
to convince
to encourage
to expect
to frustrate
to let
to order
to permit
to remind
to share
to warn

Adjectives
flexible
frustrating
inflexible
strict

Expressions
depending on
in ages
sense of humor

UNIT 4

Nouns
ability
champion
chess
field
goal
level
math
philosopher
prodigy
symphony

tournament
violin

Verbs
to admire
to challenge
to compose
to concentrate
to correspond
to drop out
to earn
to get a raise

to make (one's) mark
to measure
to publish
to range
to recognize
to replace
to solo

Adjectives
average
exceptional

foreign
gifted
remarkable
superior
talented

Adverbs
exceptionally
rapidly

UNIT 5

Nouns
aspect
cause
compliment
prestige
stock market
trait

Verbs
to analyze
to avoid
to catch up

to criticize
to daydream
to deny
to feel like
to have (one's) own way
to impress
to insist on
to invest
to look forward to
to mind
to put off

Adjectives
ambitious
charming
cheerful
clever
competitive
conservative
controversial
cultured
determined
easygoing
generous

gentle
idealistic
lonesome
optimistic
organized
outgoing
precise
reliable
sensitive
sincere

UNIT 6

Nouns
formula
founder
promotion
utopia
vision
yacht

Verbs
to approve of
to bring up

to carry out
to decrease
to dissolve
to eliminate
to get rid of
to go along with
to inspire
to last
to observe
to offend

to propose
to raise
to reflect
to threaten

Adjectives
authentic
exotic
fake
ideal
identical

oversensitive
permanent
restless
romantic
subjective
temporary
theoretical
underhanded
wild

UNIT 7

Nouns	humor	theory	to raise (money)
allowance	joke	volume	to reply
clown	media	X ray	to star
comedian	memory		to suggest
comic	miracle	**Verbs**	
discipline	pun	to attribute	**Adjectives**
generation	solitude	to inform	hilarious
guarantee	talent	to injure	humorous
		to interfere	

UNIT 8

Nouns	liquid	saw	to pass
barrel	magician	stripe	to pick
compartment	nail	trick	to remove
crate	oyster	tube	to split
diamond	paste		to squeeze
hammer	pearl	**Verbs**	
handcuffs	pressure	to crawl	**Expression**
hole	process	to cultivate	in full view
lead	rope	to expose	

UNIT 9

Nouns	interior decorator	technician	to leak
bookshelf	loan	wallpaper	to mind
brick	mechanic		to remodel
bricklayer	metalworker	**Verbs**	to repair
cabinet	pipe	to arrange	to replace
carpenter	plumber	to connect	to replant
carpentry	priority	to convert	to resemble
electrician	repairs	to decorate	
estimate	reproduction	to deliver	**Adjectives**
faucet	roof	to duplicate	abandoned
fence	roofer	to give (someone) a hand	electrical
fireplace	shape	to install	
installation	system		

UNIT 10

Nouns
anthropologist
archaeologist
astronomer
attempt
biologist
botanist
civilization
creature
dinosaur
ecosystem
flying saucer
geographer
geologist
ground
helmet
lake
meteorite
monument
oceanographer
purpose
religion
species
volcano
zoologist

Verbs
to balance
to carve
to erupt
to locate
to migrate
to transport

Adjectives
ancient
complex
conclusive
geometric
local
primitive
sacred
sophisticated

UNIT 11

Nouns
ache
bargain
brake
captain
coach
condition
fault
headlight
point
score
season
sore
spare
surgery
team
tire
treatment
turn signal
ulcer
windshield
wreck

Verbs
to acknowledge
to admit (to a
  hospital)
to aggravate
to be stuck
to go on
to let (someone)
  down
to pull over
to run (a red light)
to run out of
to run over
to sprain
to stick to
to think
  through
to treat

Adjectives
cracked
dependable
flat
stuck

UNIT 12

Nouns
benefit
capital punishment
chemical
contribution
control
disposal
exploration
extinction
industry
millennium
nutrition
organization
peace
regulation
relief
source
species
speed limit
toxic waste
weapon

Verbs
to benefit
to breathe
to conserve
to empty
to expand
to pollute
to reform
to respect

Adjectives
extinct
long-range
mandatory
senseless
useless
voluntary

Adverb
voluntarily

INDEX

Numbers indicate units.

CONTENTS

SCOPE AND SEQUENCE

Unit	Theme	Topics	Functions	Grammar	Listening and Speaking	Reading and Writing	Pronunciation	Vocabulary Expansion
1	Making Progress	Language learning, learning strategies, learning styles	• To analyze learning strategies • To talk about progress in learning • To summarize	Present perfect tense; *Already, yet, still*	**Listening:** Sound Off ➡ Listening for distinctions **Speaking:** A universal language ➡ Summarizing	**Reading:** The Human Brain ➡ Identifying main ideas **Writing:** A letter of inquiry	Consonant clusters with *–ed* endings	Using word maps
2	Whodunit?	Robbery, mystery	• To speculate • To predict • To make deductions • To express certainty and uncertainty	Degrees of certainty; Modal auxiliaries	**Listening:** What's on TV? ➡ Listening for details **Speaking:** What's Your Future? ➡ Expressing certainty and uncertainty	**Reading:** The Meeting ➡ Confirming predictions **Writing:** A narrative	Stress on two-syllable words	Descriptive adjectives
3	Because I Told You To!	Authority, societal roles	• To talk about orders, requests, permissions, persuasion, and advice • To use formal and informal language • To use language appropriate to one's roles	Orders, requests, permission, persuasion, advice; *Make, have, let*	**Listening:** It's in the Tone ➡ Listening for tone **Speaking:** Asking for permission ➡ Using formal and informal language	**Reading:** Roles in Human Society ➡ Recognizing definitions and examples **Writing:** A letter of application	Contrastive stress	Using a dictionary
4	Child's Play	Child prodigies, intelligence, I.Q. Test	• To talk about things that happened earlier in the past • To ask for confirmation and to confirm details • To ask for and indicate understanding	Past perfect tense; Past perfect progressive tense	**Listening:** A Child Prodigy ➡ Identifying causes and results **Speaking:** Solving a problem ➡ Confirming understanding	**Reading:** Mozart: Child Prodigy ➡ Understanding paragraph structure **Writing:** Coherence	Using intonation to ask a yes/no question	More about using a dictionary
5	The Real You	Ways of understanding personalities	• To talk about likes, dislikes, and preferences • To talk about personality traits • To discuss feelings	Gerunds; Verbs followed by infinitives, gerunds	**Listening:** Our Many Faces ➡ Taking notes **Speaking:** Pet peeves ➡ Discussing feelings	**Reading:** Your Personality in the Palm of Your Hand? ➡ Using graphics **Writing:** A personal letter	Reducing *of*	Compound adjectives
6	If I Had My Way	Druthers, fantasies, preferences	• To talk about preferences • To talk about hypothetical situations and actions • To ask for and give advice • To encourage and discourage	Talking about unreal situations: The second conditional; Asking for and giving advice	**Listening:** Workplace Changes ➡ Listening to summarize **Speaking:** What would you do? ➡ Encouraging and discouraging	**Reading:** Utopias: Nowhere Lands ➡ Getting meaning from context **Writing:** An analysis	Rhythm	Prefixes *under–, mis–,* and *over–*

T138

Unit	Theme	Topics	Functions	Grammar	Listening and Speaking	Reading and Writing	Pronunciation	Vocabulary Expansion
7	What's So Funny?	Humor, jokes, puns, cartoons, sense of humor, theories of humor	• To report what someone said • To report what someone asked • To recognize tone	Reporting what someone said; Reporting what someone asked	**Listening:** Jokes ➡ Listening for definitions **Speaking:** What is humor? ➡ Reporting someone else's ideas	**Reading:** The Little Girl and the Wolf ➡ Recognizing tone **Writing:** A definition paragraph	Using stress to check understanding	*Tell, say, speak,* and *talk*
8	So That's How … !	Mysterious process	• To describe process • To use chronological order • To express interest and indifference	Describing a process: The passive voice; The passive voice: Past tense using an agent	**Listening:** Diamonds and Pearls ➡ Identifying steps in a process **Speaking:** That's interesting … ➡ Expressing interest or indifference	**Reading:** Houdini: Master of Escape ➡ Using chronology to understand process **Writing:** A process paragraph	Stressing new information	Suffixes *–er/–or, –ian,* and *–ist*
9	Home Sweet Home	Home repair and improvement	• To talk about things that need to be done • To express purpose • To ask for clarification and to clarify	Getting things done; Expressing purpose	**Listening:** A Special House ➡ Listening to confirm predictions **Speaking:** How to … ➡ Asking for clarification and clarifying	**Reading:** Play Palace ➡ Understanding spatial organization **Writing:** A descriptive paragraph	/i/ versus /ɪ/	*Make* versus *do*
10	Mysteries of Science	Scientific puzzles and mysteries	• To speculate and draw conclusions about the past • To express possibility or ability in the past • To use formal language	Speculating about the past; Expressing past ability or missed opportunity; Drawing logical conclusions about the past	**Listening:** Tropical Rain Forests ➡ Recognizing facts and opinions **Speaking:** Explaining mysteries ➡ Speculating about the past	**Reading:** Tricks of Nature ➡ Distinguishing between fact and opinion **Writing:** Using formal language	Reducing *have* with past modals	Distinguishing phrasal verb meaning from context
11	Sadder but Wiser	Lack of foresight in our lives, consequences of unwise decisions	• To ask for and give advice about the past • To speculate about past actions and the consequences of these actions • To describe the opposite of past reality	Using past modals: Advice, criticism, and regret; Speculating about the past: The third conditional	**Listening:** Job Performance ➡ Making inferences **Speaking:** Influential people ➡ Describing the opposite of past reality	**Reading:** See Ya! ➡ Personalizing **Writing:** A persuasive paragraph	Reducing *have* with negative past modals	Idioms with *run*
12	Wishful Thinking	Making the world a better place, personal improvement	• To make wishes about the past, present, and future • To evaluate and justify	Wishing for changes to the present; Wishing for changes to the past; Wishing for changes to the future	**Listening:** Share a Wish ➡ Recognizing speakers' roles **Speaking:** A wish ➡ Evaluating and justifying	**Reading:** UNICEF: Working for a Better World ➡ Outlining a text **Writing:** A persuasive letter	Saying content words together	Related word forms

Unit 1

Making Progress

Using word maps

One way you can learn vocabulary is to use word maps. It is easier to remember new words if you group them according to meanings and associations they have for you. For example, to make a word map for the word **resources**, first write the word and draw a box around it. Next, think of a word that you associate with **resources**. Write the word, draw a circle around it, and connect it to the box around **resources**. Then do the same thing with other related words.

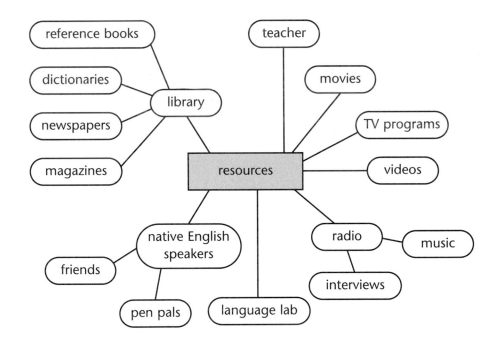

Expand the word map below. Then choose four more words from the vocabulary list for Unit 1 and make a word map for each one. Compare your maps with those of a partner.

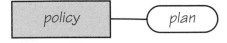

Unit 2

Whodunit?

Descriptive adjectives

A. The following words are descriptive adjectives.

Fill in the chart with words from the list that describe people. Some words can go in more than one category.

tall	well-built	chubby	brown	scrawny
dark	blond	thin	small	big
medium height	curly	red	short	scar
double chin	middle-aged	straight	green	heavy-set
black	gray	large	bald	old
young	long	overweight	little	blue

1. Age	
2. Height	
3. Weight/body type	
4. Hair	
5. Facial characteristics	

B. *Can you think of any other descriptive adjectives? Add them to the chart in Part A.*

Name _____ Date _____

Because I Told You To!

Using a dictionary

A. *Dictionaries give more information than just the meanings of words. Look at this portion of a dictionary page. Which of these things can you find? Circle the letters.*

a. parts of speech (noun, verb, etc.)

b. examples of words used in sentences

c. etymologies (histories of words)

d. a pronunciation guide

e. pictures

f. pronunciations of words

B. *Use your dictionary to find the information to answer the following questions. Write the answers on a sheet of paper.*

					retired	retrospection

a hat	i it	oi oil	ch child	⎧ a in about
ā age	ī ice	ou out	ng long	⎪ e in taken
ä far	o hot	u cup	sh she	ə = ⎨ i in pencil
e let	ō open	ù put	th thin	⎪ o in lemon
ē equal	ô order	ü rule	¥H then	⎩ u in circus
ėr term			zh measure	< = derived from

re trib u tive (ri trib′yə tiv), *adj.* paying back; bringing or inflicting punishment in return for wrongdoing. —**re trib′-u tive ly,** *adv.*

re trib u to ry (ri trib′yə tôr′ē, ri trib′yə tôr′ē), *adj.* retributive.

re triev al (ri trē′vəl), *n.* 1 act of retrieving; recovery. 2 possibility of recovery.

re trieve (ri trēv′), *v.,* **-trieved, -triev ing.** —*v.t.* 1 get again; recover: *retrieve a lost pocketbook.* See **recover** for synonym study. 2 bring back to a former or better condition; restore: *retrieve one's fortunes.* 3 make good; make amends for: *retrieve a mistake.* 4 find and bring to a person: *A dog can be trained to retrieve game.* —*v.i.* find and bring back killed or wounded game. —*n.* act of retrieving; recovery. [< Old French *retruev-,* a form of *retrouver* find again < *re-* again + *trouver* to find] —**re triev′a ble,** *adj.*

re triev er (ri trē′vər), *n.* 1 dog trained to find killed or wounded game and bring it to a hunter. 2 person or thing that retrieves.

retro-, *prefix.* backward; back; behind, as in *retrocede.* [< Latin < *retro* back]

re tro ac tive (ret′rō ak′tiv), *adj.* acting back; having an effect on what is past. A retroactive law applies to events that occurred before the law was passed. —**ret′ro ac′tive ly,** *adv.* —**ret′ro ac tiv′i ty,** *n.*

retriever (def. 1)—2 ft. (61 cm.) high at the shoulder

1. At the top of every dictionary page there are two **guide words**. The one on the left is the first word on the page. The one on the right is the last word on the page. Each word that is listed is called an **entry**. A word may have more than one entry. Find the entry or entries for **permit**. What are the guide words on the page? Does permit have more than one entry. Why?

2. These are abbreviations for parts of speech: **n., v., adv., pron., prep**. What does each one mean? What parts of speech can **permit** be used as?

3. How many definitions does your dictionary give for the noun **permit**? For the verb **permit**? Where is the stress on the noun? On the verb?

4. Look up the following words in your dictionary. For each, write the guide words you found on the page, the number of syllables in the word, the syllable that has the stress, the part of speech the word belongs to, and the number of definitions it has. If a word has more than one entry, write the pronunciation, the part of speech, and the number of definitions for each entry.

    a. boss   **c.** allow   **e.** patient

    b. role   **d.** work   **f.** refuse

Unit 4

Child's Play

More about using a dictionary

In Unit 3, you used a dictionary to get information on the parts of speech, number of syllables, and stress patterns of words. Dictionaries also contain information on pronunciation, spelling, and etymology (word history).

A. Dictionaries use symbols to represent sounds. Key words are used to show which sounds the symbols represent. The symbols and key words are given in a chart that is at the front or back of the dictionary and in some dictionaries on every page.

Find the pronunciation symbols and key words in your dictionary. Write the symbols and key words for the underlined sounds in these words.

	Symbol	Key Words		Symbol	Key Words
1. genius			**4.** opera		
2. best			**5.** sing		
3. that			**6.** chess		

B. Dictionaries show the accepted way to spell words. Some words have more than one accepted spelling.

Write the spellings your dictionary gives for each of the following words.

1. dialog _____   **4.** alright _____

2. theater _____   **5.** program _____

3. gray _____   **6.** traveled _____

C. Many dictionaries provide the **etymology** of each word. That is, they show what language a word began in and how it developed into its current form.

*Check whether your dictionary includes etymologies. If it does, look up the word **accomplish** and write its etymology.*

_____

_____

_____

Unit 5

The Real You?

Compound adjectives

You can usually figure out the meaning of compound adjectives by analyzing the words that make them up. Many compound adjectives include a present participle or a past participle.

Compound adjectives can be used to describe personalities.

A. *Categorize the following words as positive or negative personality characteristics. Use your dictionary if necessary.*

hard-working	ill-tempered	hardhearted	absent-minded	two-faced
well-respected	outspoken	well-educated	kindhearted	outgoing
easygoing	open-minded	narrow-minded	tightfisted	hardheaded

Positive Personality Traits	Negative Personality Traits

B. *Do you know any other compound adjectives that describe personalities? Add them to the chart in Part A.*

Unit 6

If I Had My Way

Prefixes under–, mis–, over–

A prefix is placed at the beginning of a word and changes the meaning of the word in some way. Three common prefixes are *under–*, *mis–*, and *over–*.

> The boy has been sick so long that he's now **underweight**.
>
> I'm thinking of changing jobs because my boss has **misunderstood** everything I've tried to do on our project.
>
> We don't go to that restaurant anymore because the waiter **overcharged** us for our meals twice.

A. *Circle the correct answers.*

1. *Under–* probably means: before   not enough   below normal

2. *Mis–* probably means: wrongly   badly behind   after

3. *Over–* probably means: all   every   more excessive

B. *Use the prefixes to make new words. Write them in the correct columns. Then find your new words in your dictionary. What words weren't in the dictionary?*

	under–	mis–	over–
1. to use incorrectly		misuse	
2. to eat too much			
3. extremely sensitive			
4. not of full age			
5. to read wrongly			
6. poorly educated			
7. to react excessively			
8. to pay too little			
9. to behave incorrectly			

Unit 7

What's So Funny

Tell, say, speak, talk

The words **tell** and **say** are very similar in meaning but are used differently. **Tell** is used with a noun or a pronoun that indicates the person something is told to, but **say** is often used without mentioning (the name of) a person to whom something is said.

> **Luis:** Carol **said** she had a great joke. Do you and Sofia want to hear it?
>
> **Sara:** I want to hear it, but I don't know about Sofia. Yesterday she **told me** that she didn't like most jokes.

The words **speak** and **talk** are similar in meaning but are often used differently. We usually use **speak** in formal situations and in referring to the ability to converse in a language. We use **talk** in informal situations and in referring to a conversation between people.

> **Kenji:** Hey Paul! When can we **talk** about your trip to Italy? I guess you can **speak** Italian now, right?
>
> **Paul:** Yeah, I can **speak** it OK.
>
> **Maria:** Excuse me, Paul, the boss would like to **speak** to you.
>
> **Paul:** Sure, I'll be there right away.

*Complete the sentences with a correct form of **tell**, **say**, **speak**, or **talk**.*

Last week, my boss asked me if I would give a presentation on humor and the media. I **(1.)** _____ her that I got really nervous when I had to **(2.)** _____ in front of large groups of people. Then a friend at work **(3.)** _____ to me about my decision. He **(4.)** _____ that I knew the most about the topic. When I saw my boss again, I **(5.)** _____ her that I would be happy to do the presentation.

Unit 8

So That's How ... !

Suffixes –er/–or, –ian, –ist

The suffixes –er/–or, –ian, and –ist all indicate "the one who does."

> The play was ruined by the **actor** who forgot his lines.
> The smiling woman was sawed in half by the **magician**.
> The trapeze artist was the best **performer** in the circus.

A. *Fill in the chart with words ending in –er/–or, –ian, or –ist. Then check your answer in the dictionary.*

Definition	Word
1. one who plays music	
2. one who knows psychology	
3. one who builds	
4. one who works in politics	
5. one who drives	
6. one who performs comedy	
7. one who knows a technical area	
8. one who instructs	
9. one who has debts or owes money	
10. one who knows biology	

B. *Do you know anyone who "does something"? What does he or she do? Complete the chart with words that use the suffixes –er, –or, –ian, or –ist.*

Definition	Word
1.	
2.	
3.	
4.	

Unit 9

Home Sweet Home

Make versus *do*

Make and **do** can be confusing. In general, **make** carries the idea of "construct, produce, or prepare." **Do** carries the idea of "perform or carry out an activity."

> Alice **is making** a dress to wear to the wedding.
> Tom **made** a delicious dessert for the dinner party.
> My brother **does** his homework right after school.
> Kevin **did** all the shopping and cleaning today.

Certain words and expressions are associated with each verb.

Add any expressions you can think of to the chart. Then complete the sentences with the correct form of **make** *or* **do**.

Make			Do		
money	an appointment	noise	housework	an exercise	a puzzle
an effort	a mistake		homework	an errand	
a decision	the bed		a favor	the dishes	

My day began late. So I had to **(1.)** _____ an effort to get out of bed. I **(2.)** _____ a quick cup of coffee and left the house. I didn't have time to **(3.)** _____ the dishes or **(4.)** _____ my bed.

On my lunch hour, I **(5.)** _____ a dentist appointment and **(6.)** _____ some other errands. My boss was angry with me. because I was out of the office a long time and I had **(7.)** _____ a mistake on an important report. I was upset the rest of the afternoon. But I **(8.)** _____ an important decision—to look for another job!

When I got home, I **(9.)** _____ my exercises, **(10.)** _____ my dinner, and went to bed. I couldn't sleep because my neighbor was **(11.)** _____ a lot of noise, so I **(12.)** _____ another decision—to look for another apartment!

I was finally beginning to fall asleep when the phone rang. It was my boyfriend. He wanted me to **(13.)** _____ him a big favor, but I said I couldn't. Then I **(14.)** _____ my last decision—to look for another boyfriend!

Unit 10

Mysteries of Science

Determining phrasal verb meaning from context

Phrasal verbs are sometimes called two- and three-word verbs. The meaning of these verbs is often different from the meaning of the verb alone.

A. *Use the context to match each italicized expression with its meaning.*

Have you ever wanted to **(1.)** *look for* buried treasure? **(2.)** *Pick up* a shovel and **(3.)** *set off for* Oak Island in Mahone Bay, Nova Scotia. People have known that someone buried treasure there in 1795, but no one has been able to **(4.)** *figure out* a way to **(5.)** *get* it *out of* the ground. The gold is protected by a series of wooden barriers and tunnels. Many people tried to find the gold, but so far they have all had to **(6.)** *give up*. But one day someone will figure out how to **(7.)** *get to* the buried treasure. Why shouldn't it be you?

_____	**a.** remove from	_____	**e.** reach, arrive at
_____	**b.** stop trying	_____	**f.** search for
_____	**c.** invent, discover	_____	**g.** travel to
_____	**d.** get, grab		

B. *Here are some more phrasal verbs. Can you figure out their meanings? How are the meanings of these phrasal verbs different from the meanings of the verbs alone?*

look up	turn down	get on
run into	stick with	call off

C. *Write some phrasal verbs. Then work with a partner to compare your lists. Were any of the words the same? Do you know the meaning of all the words on your lists? Use your dictionary to clarify a meaning, if necessary.*

Unit 11

Sadder but Wiser

Determining meaning from context— Idioms with *run*

The word **run** is a part of many idiomatic expressions.

Use the context to match each italicized word or expression with its meaning.

My day didn't start out well. Usually, I **(1.)** *run in* the park in the morning, but this morning I couldn't because I was feeling too **(2.)** *run down*. You see, I had a bad cold. I got out of bed to take some cold medicine, but the bottle was empty. I had **(3.)** *run out of* medicine, so I had to drive to the drugstore. On my way there, I **(4.)** *ran over* a kid's bicycle left in the street, but no one saw me. I wasn't lucky on the way home either. I **(5.)** *ran a red light* and a policeman saw me. He **(6.)** *ran my name through* a computer and found out I hadn't paid any of my traffic tickets, so he brought me here. Let me tell you, I was surprised to **(7.)** *run into* my very own lawyer, here in jail! And I was going to call *him* to ask for advice!

_____ **a.** did not stop for   _____ **e.** see unexpectedly

_____ **b.** put information in   _____ **f.** hit and broke

_____ **c.** did not have any more   _____ **g.** go by moving legs fast

_____ **d.** very tired

Unit 12

Wishful Thinking

Related word forms

When you know the meaning of one form of a word, you can expand
your vocabulary by recognizing related forms. Look at these words related
to **benefit**.

Verb	Noun	Adjective	Adverb
benefit	benefit	beneficial	beneficially
	benefactor	beneficent	beneficently
	beneficence		
	beneficiary		

*Complete the chart with as many forms of each word as you can without using
your dictionary. Then check your dictionary for additional forms and add them
to the chart.*

Verb	Noun	Adjective	Adverb
1. appreciate			
2.		competitive	
3.			conclusively
4. criticize			
5.		developmental	
6.			idealistically
7.	purpose		
8. respect			
9.	use		
10.		voluntary	

Student Book Audioscript

UNIT 1: Making Progress

Page 1, Exercise 2

Announcer: Conversation A

Mrs. Lopez: Alice, I want to tell you how pleased I am with your piano playing. Congratulations! You've really improved a lot in the last few months!

Alice: Why, thank you, Mrs. Lopez. I've been practicing for more than three hours a day. You've really been a good teacher, too.

Mrs. Lopez: Thank you, Alice. But your hard work has helped. I think you're more than ready for the concert now.

Alice: I hope so. It's been hard work, but I've enjoyed it.

Announcer: Conversation B

Boy: Hey, Mom, I got a 95 on my history test and a 91 in math.

Mom: Really? Good for you! I'm really proud of how much better you're doing this year.

Boy: Yeah, and to think that just last year I was getting 70's in most of my classes!

Announcer: Conversation C

Mr. Leary: Judy, you're going to have to learn to park the car better if you want to get your driver's license. I'm trying to be patient with you.

Judy: I know, Dad, but when I drive with you, I get all-nervous.

Mr. Leary: Well, don't worry. We'll go out again tomorrow. Now let's drive home.

Page 6, Exercise 2

Announcer: Hello, everybody, and welcome to another edition of *Sound Off*. Our guest today is Mr. Charles Rowe, an expert on learning styles. Mr. Rowe, why are learning styles important?

Rowe: Learning styles are important because we all have them! We learn in different ways, and if we are aware of the common learning styles, we can do a better job of teaching or learning.

Announcer: How many common learning styles are there?

Rowe: Experts in the field have developed many names for different learning styles, but the four most commonly recognized are visual, tactile, auditory, and kinesthetic.

Announcer: Visual, tactile, auditory, and kinesthetic. How are they different from one another?

Rowe: Well, let's look at visual learners first. On the most basic level, visual learners learn through their eyes. This means that they understand directions much better if someone shows them what to do, rather than if someone tells them. To remember things, they "see" or visually reproduce things in their minds, for example, a map on a page. Visual learners notice all the details of their surroundings. In class, for example, they enjoy looking at books, posters, and pictures.

Announcer: That seems logical. What about tactile learners? Do they learn by touching?

Rowe: Why, yes, they do! They learn and remember better when they can touch an object or manipulate something. Tactile learners are usually very good with machines and physical procedures. In class, tactile learners often have to have something in their hands while they listen or read—a pencil or an eraser, for instance.

Announcer: That's very interesting. Are tactile learners pretty common?

Rowe: That's a good question. There seem to be fewer tactile learners than visual and auditory learners, but many experts now think that there are many more tactile and kinesthetic learners than they had previously thought.

Announcer: You said that auditory learners are more common than tactile learners. What are the characteristics of auditory learners?

Rowe: Just as visual learners use their eyes, auditory learners use their ears. They learn better by hearing than by seeing. They understand directions after the first or second repetition, and they can usually repeat a joke or story after hearing it only once. This is because they use rhythm and sound to help them remember things. They know, for example, the words to all the popular songs on the radio. In class they can more easily memorize than students with other learning styles.

Announcer: We've now heard about visual, tactile, and auditory learners. How are kinesthetic learners different from the others?

Rowe: Kinesthetic learners learn through movement. They often draw or fold pieces of paper or move their pens and pencils around on their desks as they study or listen. They're good with machines, and they like to take things apart and put them back together. They need to carry out directions physically to understand them, and they use movement and rhythmic routines to help them remember.

Announcer: Very interesting, Mr. Rowe. Well, I guess I'm an auditory learner because I can pick up the words to songs really easily. How about you listeners? I'm sure Mr. Rowe has given us all something to keep in mind as we try to learn new things. Thank you very much, Mr. Rowe, for being our guest on today's edition of *Sound Off*.

Rowe: You're welcome.

UNIT 2: Whodunit?

Page 11, Exercise 3

Woman: You're late! I thought you might not come. Do you have your tools?

Man: Yeah, I got 'em. Where's the safe?

Woman: Shhh. I have the key to the back door. There. It's open. Follow me.

Man: Where are you? It's so dark in here that I can't see a thing.

Woman: Be quiet! Someone might hear you! Come on. We have to go through the kitchen and into the dining room.

Man: This way?

Woman: No, that's the laundry room. Come this way. To the left.

Man: Now what?

Woman: Come on. We have to go into the hall and turn left again.

Man: Is the safe in the living room?

Woman: No, it's not. The living room's the other way. Now will you please be quiet! Just follow me to the end of the hall. Then we'll turn right into the study.

Man: OK, lady. You're the boss.

Woman: Here. It's through this doorway. The safe is under that picture on the wall by the bathroom. Can you get it open?

Man: I sure can. That's what you're paying me for …

Page 16, Exercise 2

Narrator: And at midnight, viewers are in luck! On Channel 5 at 12 o'clock, another thrilling episode of *Midnight Mystery Theater*. Tonight's episode is titled "The Victim," and it features those two great stars, Peter Carleton and Joan Young. Peter Carleton is a doctor who decides that he doesn't love his wife anymore. Joan Young plays his wife. When she mysteriously becomes ill, she begins to suspect that her husband and his beautiful assistant are planning a very final goodbye. Can she find evidence of the crime before it's too late? Find out tonight at midnight.

Page 17, Exercise 4

A: Are you making any progress on the Federa case?

B: Well, we didn't progress much at first, but we know a lot now.

A: Who do you suspect stole the jewelry?

B: Our main suspect is Ruby Diamond.

A: Hey, didn't the police convict her for stealing jewelry a few years ago?

B: Yeah. She was a convict at Folsom Prison for six years.

A: How do you know that? Did you see her police record?

B: No, the police didn't record it in their files. We noticed it while we were investigating the Federa case.

A: Is it true the thief left a present for the Federa family when she took the jewels?

B: Yes, it is. She left a box of chocolates on the pillow. It's really an interesting case. I'll present all the evidence in court tomorrow.

UNIT 3: Because I Told You To!

Page 21, Exercise 2

Narrator: Conversation 1

Doctor: Are you nervous all the time?

Margaret: Yes, and I'm really tired.

Doctor: How long have you been feeling this way?

Margaret: Well, ever since I got my promotion.

Doctor: You should take a couple of days off and get some rest. And be sure to eat healthy food and get regular exercise.

Narrator: Conversation 2

Police Officer: Do you know that you drove right through that red light?

Margaret: Oh, I didn't even see it! I was thinking about my job.

Police Officer: Can I see your driver's license, please?

Margaret: Of course. Here you go.

Police Officer: You'd better think more about driving. I'm going to have to give you a ticket, Ma'am.

Narrator: Conversation 3

Margaret: I'm really frustrated! I'll never get all this work done this afternoon!

Secretary: Would you like me to stay late and help you?

Margaret: I'd really appreciate that. Tomorrow you can come in later if you want.

Secretary: No problem. I didn't have anything planned for this evening anyway.

Margaret: Oh, Mark, what would I ever do without you?

Narrator: Conversation 4

Margaret: I love my job, but it's really hard to work and take care of my family.

Father: Well, your mother and I did it when you and your brother were children.

Margaret: Yes, but in those days, Grandma lived with you.

Father: Oh dear, you're not inviting us to live with you, are you?

Page 26, Exercises 2 and 3

Announcer: Conversation a

Father: (*angry*) I told you a hundred times not to do that! I can't believe you refuse to listen to me!

Son: I'm sorry, Dad.

Father: Go to your room right now and don't come out until I say so.

Announcer: Conversation b

Sarah: (*persuasive*) Oh, come on, Gloria. We'll have so much fun. My parents are letting me go, and I want you to come, too.

Gloria: I don't know if my mother will let me go.

Sarah: Well, let's ask her together.

Announcer: Conversation c

Mother: (*worried*) Oh, John, what if something happened to him? I begged him to come home by ten o'clock because of the rain and the storm. Oh, I'm so upset!

Father: Mary, it's all right. He's a good driver. Just relax and trust him. He'll be home soon.

Announcer: Conversation d

Alex: (*angry*) Look, Mark, she made me go with her! I wanted to play cards with you and the rest of the guys.

Mark: Just calm down, will you?

Alex: Okay, just forget it.

Announcer: Conversation e

Woman: (*uncertain*) Well … , I don't know … I might go, but I'm not sure … I might go if he decides to go …

Friend: Well, I advise you to go. It would be the best thing for everyone.

Announcer: Conversation f

Husband: (*persuasive*) Honey, you promised me! You told me to go ahead and get the tickets and I did! Now, come on, you know you want to …

Wife: I guess you're right. I'll get my coat.

Pages 26, 27, Exercises 4 and 5

A: Are you sure you want Jeff to do the dishes?

B: Yes, I want him to do them this time. Paula did them last time.

A: Then, what do you want her to do?

B: I want her to watch the baby.

A: You know … I think you're nicer to her than to him.

B: I am not. I'm nice to them both. They both have to learn to help around the house.

UNIT 4: Child's Play

Page 33, Exercise 2

Narrator: Good morning, class. Today we are going to learn about the Stanford–Binet Test. The Stanford–Binet Test is used to measure intelligence. Since 1916, clinical psychologists, psychiatrists, and educational counselors have used this test to measure areas such as judgment, attention, reasoning, knowledge of vocabulary, spatial relationships, and other qualities of intelligence. The results of the Stanford–Binet Test are expressed in numbers. These numbers represent different intelligence quotients. In the Stanford–Binet system, the number 100 indicates normal or average intelligence. Higher numbers indicate higher intelligence, and lower numbers indicate lower intelligence. For example, "superior" intelligence is classified as falling within the range of 120 to 139. A person who has an I.Q. of 150 or above is classified as "very superior." A person with retardation has an I.Q. of below 70.

Page 38, Exercise 2

Doctor: Well, Mrs. Roberts, we've finished our tests and our examination of your son.

Mrs. Roberts: Oh, Doctor. I'm so worried. He was doing so well in school and in his special studies due to his high I.Q. But now I think he's losing his intelligence little by little!

Doctor: Don't worry. That's not the case at all. Dan is as intelligent as he ever was. He's a child prodigy with an I.Q. of 165.

Mrs. Roberts: But what's wrong then? He doesn't want to read or watch TV or use his computer. And because he isn't interested in school anymore, he isn't passing any of his subjects! In fact, he says he wants to drop out!

Doctor: Now, Mrs. Roberts, try to understand. He is feeling a lot of pressure from you and his teachers. Since you expect him to excel in everything, he's reacting to this pressure by giving up. Shutting down, if you will. Am I making myself clear?

Mrs. Roberts: Yes, I understand. But if I accept his present behavior, then it will just get worse! We only want what's best for him, after all. We want him to excel in everything because he can do it if he wants to!

Doctor: I'm sure you …

Mrs. Roberts: Why, Doctor, by the time Dan was three, he had already learned to read—by himself! And he had learned to use his father's computer by the time he was five!

Doctor: Yes, I know that. But you have to remember that he's still a child, so he needs to play with other kids. He needs to have time to himself, time to dream or do nothing. And most of all, he needs to know that you love him even if he isn't perfect.

Mrs. Roberts: Of course we love him! And it's because we love him that we want him to do his best and have the best possible future!

Doctor: I know what you mean. But right now, Dan doesn't want to be different from any of the other children he knows. Since he wants to be like other kids in the neighborhood, he doesn't want anyone to know that he's a prodigy. In fact, that is why he's stopped working and studying for now.

Mrs. Roberts: Do you mean it's a temporary condition?

Doctor: More than likely. Most child prodigies go through several stages during childhood. Just be sure to let him be like the other kids once in a while.

Mrs. Roberts: I see. Well, doctor, I'm feeling much better as a result of our conversation. Thank you.

Page 38, Exercises 4 and 5

A: You mean you don't recognize Steveland Morris's music?

B: Steveland Morris?

A: That's Stevie Wonder's real name.

B: No kiddin'. He's won several Grammy awards?

A: Yeah, and he was one of Motown's child prodigies. By the age of thirteen, he'd already had his first Motown hit.

B: He was only thirteen?

A: Yeah, and he was blind, too.

B: Blind? Wow, that's incredible.

UNIT 5: The Real You?

Page 43, Exercise 2

Lecturer: Today, class, we're going to continue our discussion of different ways to analyze our personalities. We will look at the relationship between colors and personality. First, let's take a look at the three primary colors: red, yellow, and blue.

According to studies carried out in North America, people who prefer the color red usually have strong personalities. They like expressing their opinions. They insist on saying whatever they think and feel, even if it is sometimes negative. They're confident people who enjoy meeting others and being in social situations.

In contrast to the "reds," people who choose blue are generally quiet and gentle. They don't like showing strong emotions. "Blues" feel that they should control what they say and do. They like spending time by themselves, and they like analyzing themselves.

Another group includes people who prefer yellow. They are normally cheerful, friendly people who prefer looking at the positive side of things. They don't like thinking about problems or serious subjects very much. Often "yellows" prefer hiding strong emotions, like fear or anger.

The analysis of colors is just another system that people have created to understand personalities. We will discuss other ways to analyze personality traits in our next class.

Page 49, Exercise 2

Interviewer: So, Doctor, if I understand you correctly, you're saying that when people draw faces, they are actually saying how sociable they are.

Doctor: Yes, or how unsociable! For example, when people draw angry faces, it usually means that they have trouble relating to other people. They avoid trusting people, and they resist opening themselves up to others. They seldom admit being in the wrong. People often consider them to be antisocial.

Interviewer: Aren't they similar to people who consistently draw sad faces? I mean, aren't they both antisocial?

Doctor: Well, there are some similarities, but people who draw sad faces aren't antisocial. They often deny having deep feelings about people, but they do have them. In fact, they want to have relationships with others. They just don't have strong self-images. They try to be what others want them to be. Believing in themselves and being more confident would help them to adjust.

Interviewer: Don't most of us just draw normal faces?

Doctor: Well, if you mean happy faces, yes. Most people draw happy faces. This means that most of us are normal, friendly, easygoing people who enjoy being with others. People in this category like going out and having an active social life. They often like telling funny stories or jokes. They have a good sense of humor.

Interviewer: Like people who draw clown faces or silly faces, right?

Doctor: Actually, no. People who draw silly or ugly faces are really showing their difficulties in developing personal relationships. They often feel threatened by other people and they hide their feelings of insecurity by acting out roles. They avoid risking their true inner selves by covering them up.

Interviewer: What about people who are just bad artists?

Doctor: Well, it seems that no matter how bad the drawing, it still reflects aspects of the artist's personality.

Interviewer: How fascinating! I'm sure our listeners would be interested in other ways to analyze their personalities. I hope you'll come back and talk with us on another show.

Page 49, Exercise 4

A: Have you ever thought of going to see a fortune-teller?

B: I'm afraid of hearing what she'd say.

A: You might hear a lot of interesting things.

B: OK, I'll do it. So what's the price of advice?

A: Don't worry. It won't cost a lot of money.

UNIT 6: If I Had My Way

Page 53, Exercise 3

Narrator: Conversation a

Chen: Hi, Mary. Is that a new dress?

Mary: Oh hello, Chen. Yes, it is. It was a birthday present.

Chen: Well, you look very pretty.

Mary: Thanks, but it's not really my style. If I were taller, the dress would look a lot better.

Narrator: Conversation b

Ellen: Carlos, could you come here a minute?

Carlos: Sure, Ellen.

Ellen: I have to key in this report for the boss, but I can't read your handwriting.

Carlos: Sorry. I know my handwriting is terrible. If I had the time, I'd take a word processing course. Then you wouldn't have to do it for me.

Narrator: Conversation c

Fatima: Bruce, would you mind not smoking here? The smoke really bothers me.

Bruce: Sure, Fatima, I'm sorry. You know, I have been trying to quit smoking, but the pressure at work just gets to me.

Fatima: I know. You can do it if you want to, though. Maybe you could chew gum.

Page 58, Exercise 2

Bob: Thanks for your input on that, Bill. Our next item on the agenda is our report on changes in the workplace. I suggest we begin by brainstorming any and all of the things we would like to see happen. Then, later, we can focus on which ideas to keep and which ideas to discard.

Ann: Good idea, Bob. I'd like to begin by suggesting the idea of flextime.

Bob: Could you elaborate on that, please?

Ann: Of course. More and more businesses today are allowing their employees to decide for themselves when they start work and when they leave work. As long as they work a typical eight-hour day, they are free to come and go when they please. Their hours are flexible.

Bill: And you think that would work here, Ann?

Ann: Sure, Bill. We don't manufacture products, so we don't have a factory assembly line. We're a service company that is all office-based. It would be easy to implement flextime for all of the employees.

Bill: Well, that's something to think about.

Pat: Here's another idea. How about home-based office hours? Many of us, I'm sure, would like to work on our computers at home.

Ann: Pat, that's a wonderful idea!

Bill: How would that work, exactly?

Pat: With the technology we have today, Bill, it would be easy to connect all of our computers with the office and each other. It would be cost-effective, too.

Bob: So, if we did this, it would mean we could stay at home and do our work and communicate with each other through our computers.

Ann: You could even be in your pajamas all day!

Pat: Very funny. But true!

Bill: But what about staff meetings? Conferences with clients?

Bob: I suppose we could come into the office one or two days a week to meet with people.

Pat: Well, we could, but these days, everything can be done electronically. How about this idea? If we had a videophone system, we could have conferences and meetings with clients without having to be in the same place. We'd see each other on video.

Bob: Got it. OK, any other suggestions?

Bill: I have an idea I'd really like to see become a reality.

Ann: What's that, Bill?

Bill: Well, as you know, I'm the new father of a beautiful baby boy, and I would like to see child-care facilities here at the company. Many businesses today provide some sort of child care for workers who have to stay late or live far away. The study I read said that productivity on the part of parents who had company child care increased by almost 12 percent.

Pat: Really? Well, that's certainly an idea to consider. Any more suggestions?

UNIT 7: What's So Funny?

Page 65, Exercise 2

Sue: Oh, hi, Pat!

Pat: Hi, there, Sue. What are you up to?

Sue: Well, there are some great sales going on at the mall, so I thought I'd go shopping. Why don't you come with me? It's always more fun to shop with someone.

Pat: Well, I'd love to go shopping, but it's near the end of the month, and I don't have any money left!

Sue: That's too bad, Pat. It would have been fun.

Pat: You go ahead and have fun anyway. But you know, the hardest part about being broke is watching the rest of the world go buy!

Page 70, Exercise 2

Narrator: Why do we laugh at jokes? What is it in a joke that causes laughter? One of the reasons we laugh at jokes is that the structure or the design of a joke prepares us to think in a certain way. Almost all jokes follow a similar structure, and all the parts of a joke have specific functions. For example, the beginning part of a joke is called the buildup. The buildup gets us ready to listen to the joke. It tells the situation, and it creates expectations or tension. The end of the joke is called the punch line. The punch line provides the surprise or the relief from tension created by the buildup. Often, jokes and stories have a butt. The butt is the object, person, or group of people that the joke talks about. The butt is made fun of or made to seem ridiculous. We laugh at the butt of the joke. Not all jokes have butts, but all jokes do have a point. The point is the important, essential, or primary element that causes the laughter. The point is achieved through surprise, embarrassment, exaggeration, or lack of logic. All these elements together form the structure of a joke.

Page 71, Exercises 4 and 5

Narrator: Conversation 1

Man: Who did you say was coming to dinner?

Woman: I told you I invited Perry.

Man: That's funny. I heard you say Barry.

Narrator: Conversation 2

Woman: What time are you going to the party?

Man: What party? No one asked me to go to a party!

Woman: Oh, I'm sorry. I thought you were invited.

Narrator: Conversation 3

Man: Did you say you knew a good joke?

Woman: No, I didn't. I don't like jokes.

Man: But everyone likes jokes.

UNIT 8: So That's How ... !

Page 75, Exercise 3

Announcer: To get that toothpaste with the colored stripes onto your toothbrush requires several steps. In the factory, when the toothpaste tube is ready to be filled, a small hollow tube with slots in its sides is placed in the opening of the larger tube. The small tube is then filled with blue toothpaste. Next, the large tube is filled with white toothpaste. When you squeeze the toothpaste tube, pressure is applied on the white paste. The white paste then applies pressure on the blue paste. As the paste comes out of the tube, the blue paste comes out of the slots and forms stripes on the white paste.

Page 80, Exercise 2

Chris: That's a pretty ring you have on, Judy.

Judy: Thanks, Chris. It was a present for my birthday. It's a real pearl.

Chris: How can you tell?

Judy: Well, it's hard to tell just by looking, but real pearls are usually a little irregular. They're not perfectly round like the false ones.

Chris: So how do they make pearls?

Judy: Nobody makes them. Real pearls come from oysters—you know, those things your mother makes soup with.

Chris: You're kidding!

Judy: No, really. A pearl is formed inside an oyster.

Chris: How?

Judy: Well, it happens when a grain of sand or a little piece of rock is caught inside the oyster's shell. If the oyster can't get it out, it begins to irritate the oyster.

Chris: Then what happens?

Judy: A special substance is made by the oyster to protect itself. The sand or rock is covered by the substance so it doesn't irritate the oyster anymore.

Chris: And that's it?

Judy: More or less. The oyster keeps on covering the sand or rock with more layers of substance, and after about seven years, a pearl is formed.

Chris: That's really interesting.

Page 80, Exercise 3

Narrator: Diamonds as we know them are formed twice: once deep under the surface of the earth, and a second time in the hands of an expert diamond cutter. How do diamonds make their way from under the earth to shine on velvet-covered trays in jewelry stores?

First of all, for diamonds to be formed in the earth, the mineral carbon must be positioned deep underground in layers of molten rock, or magma, far below the earth's surface. At this depth, the carbon is then acted upon by enormous heat and pressure, which cause it to form cubic crystals.

Next, pressure and movement from deep underground force the material carrying the diamonds upwards and outwards. This material, often the bluish rock called kimberlite, is shaped into funnel-like pipes as it's forced to the surface layers of the earth.

Once near or on the earth's surface, the diamonds may be mined from rock or simply discovered in rivers or alluvial deposits. After they've been cleaned, sorted, and weighed, the diamonds are ready to be evaluated by the diamond cutters.

In the process of diamond cutting, experts first study each diamond very carefully to make a plan for the cutting of the stone. The paths for cutting the diamond are traced onto the rough diamond with India ink, after which the stone is cut by cleaving or sawing.

After the cutting, facets are formed by polishing the diamond's surface with oil and diamond dust. Finally, when all fifty-eight facets of a brilliant-cut diamond shine with fire and brilliance, it's ready to be set as a piece of beautiful jewelry.

Page 81, Exercises 4 and 5

A: I have a great joke.
B: I hate jokes.
A: This one's good.
B: Do I have to listen to it?
A: Yes, but you don't have to laugh.
B: Go ahead.
A: Well, this horse walks into a coffee shop . . .
B: And the waiter says, "Why do you have such a long face?"
A: How did you know?
B: Well, all you had to do was look.

UNIT 9: Home Sweet Home

Page 85, Exercise 2

Jenny: Hello.
Alice: Hi, Jenny.
Jenny: Oh, hi, Alice. How are you?
Alice: Just fine, thanks. I tried to call you a couple of times yesterday, but you weren't home.
Jenny: I know. I was out looking at houses again.
Alice: I thought you were going to buy the one on Jefferson Street. Why are you still looking?
Jenny: Oh, I wasn't really happy with that one. If I bought it, I'd have to have a lot of work done on it, and that's expensive. But now I've found a house I'm really interested in buying.
Alice: Oh, yeah? What's it like?
Jenny: It's a red brick house with two bedrooms. It's just the right size. It has a living room, one bathroom, and a small kitchen.
Alice: Will you have to eat in the kitchen?
Jenny: No, there's a small dining room, too.

Alice: It sounds great. Is there a garage?
Jenny: No, but there is a driveway. I can get a garage built later on, if I want to.
Alice: Great. I'm glad you found what you want. Is it very far away?
Jenny: Not really. It'll take me about twenty minutes more to get to work, that's all.
Alice: Well, I hope it works out for you. Now, what I'm really calling about is my dinner party on Saturday. Do you think you could give me a hand?
Jenny: Of course. I'll be glad to. I'm great with a microwave!

Page 90, Exercises 2 and 3

Announcer: In 1884, Mrs. Sarah Winchester bought an eight-room farmhouse in the Santa Clara Valley in California. There, for thirty-eight years, she had twenty-two carpenters and many other workmen alternately build and tear down one of the strangest houses ever constructed.

Mrs. Winchester believed that she could communicate with spirits, and she had a special room set up where she would receive instructions. In their conversations each evening, the spirits had Mrs. Winchester write down their plans for the building to be done the next day. Then the next morning, Sarah would get her chief carpenter to carry out the new design.

Some of the spirits' ideas were unusual, to say the least. They had Mrs. Winchester install doors that opened into the air instead of into rooms. They had some stairs built that went up to a ceiling, and they had other stairs made that went around in circles.

In the thirty-eight years that Mrs. Winchester had work done on the house, 750 rooms were built. But Sarah had many of them torn down and replaced when the spirits told her to do so. Today, though smaller, the Winchester house remains an architectural wonder that covers 6 acres. It presently contains 160 rooms, 3 elevators, and 40 stairways. Still in existence are the 6 kitchens, 40 bedrooms, and the original 47 fireplaces. The 467 doors and 10,000 windows that Sarah had put in are still in place as well. Today, only tourists look out of those windows or go up and down those stairs, except, perhaps, the spirits that had Mrs. Winchester build her house.

Page 91, Exercise 5

leave, live	list, least
these, this	slip, sleep
rid, read	sit, seat
reason, risen	heat, hit
he's, his	fit, feet

UNIT 10: Mysteries of Science

Page 97, Exercise 2

Announcer: Loch Ness is a huge body of water, seven hundred and fifty feet deep, located in Scotland. Many people think that a kind of monster or dinosaur lives in this lake. It was first seen over fifteen hundred years ago, and there have been many sightings since then. An attempt to find the creature through the use of sophisticated scientific instruments took place in the 1980s, but no conclusive evidence was found. There are, however, photographs which seem to show a large, living being swimming in the lake.

Page 102, Exercises 2 and 3

Bob: Today our panel is going to discuss the world's rain forests. Most of us think rain forests are mysterious and beautiful, but the fact is that they are much more than that—they are vital sources of the oxygen we all need to breathe to survive.

Ann: That's right, Bob, and these oxygen factories are located on different parts of the globe. For example, major rain forests are found in western Africa and in southeast Asia, and research shows that the most famous and the largest rain forest is Amazonia, located in South America. It is larger than all of western Europe together and covers about $2\frac{1}{2}$ million square miles. Can you believe it? To me, it's impossible to imagine a forest that large!

Greg: Same here, but regardless of their size, Ann, all rain forests have many of the same characteristics. Scientists tell us that in their natural state, rain forests consist of five different layers. These five layers coexist in a very delicate balance.

Pat: That's right. Isn't it amazing that forests have adapted to this system? Just think about it. Starting with the bottom layer, the dark floor of the rain forests, we find ferns and herbs that grow in a layer of decaying vegetation. Then, above them, in the second layer, there are very young trees, palms, and plants that can exist with very little sunlight.

Bob: Yeah, Pat, and then, growing above them is a third or middle layer of trees. They have wide tops and grow up to 40 feet high or so. These trees are often covered with orchids and even cacti. Above them is still another layer, a higher fourth layer of trees that grow to be 60 to 80 feet tall.

Greg: Yeah, and those trees grow very close together, so they get a lot of the available sunlight. And the last layer, the very top layer of trees, grows even higher, to 135 feet or more into the sky. In my opinion, that has to be a really impressive sight.

Ann: I agree. It's almost as impressive as the incredible range of life found in the rain forests. For instance, we now know that the rain forests contain literally thousands of unusual and exotic species of plants and animals that have never even been seen in the rest of the world! Pat has some statistics on that, right?

Pat: That's right. In fact, in only one square mile of Amazonia, botanists have found 117 different species of trees, lianas, vines, and other plants. And zoologists have found equal numbers of exotic birds, frogs, and butterflies.

Greg: And biologists estimate that many thousands of other species exist that still have not been discovered. Isn't that incredible? I'd love to discover a new plant or animal species.

Bob: Well, Greg, it's not so great when you realize that they may never be discovered. What's terrible about it is that human beings are disturbing the delicate ecosystem of the rain forest. The balance that exists now is very fragile, and humans are upsetting that balance.

Pat: In fact, scientists sat that many other life forms may never be identified because large sections of the rain forests have been cut down.

Ann: In my opinion, it's a real tragedy. And more sections of the rain forests disappear each year. Just think what we might have learned about all the species that lived in those miles of rain forest!

Greg: Well, fortunately, many organizations and even governments are now working to make people aware of this destruction.

Bob: As I see it, they're still young organizations and so they're not very effective. I don't think they have the experience or money that they need to make a big impact.

Greg: What difference does it make if some organizations are new? They're all working hard to protect the rain forest. After all, it takes time to get their message to the public. The world is slowly becoming aware of how serious this problem is.

Pat: Let's hope so. People have to understand the importance of the rain forests to our life on Earth. It will be great when that day finally arrives.

UNIT 11: Sadder but Wiser

Page 107, Exercises 2 and 3

Narrator: Conversation a

Lucy: Hi, Alice. How're you doing?

Alice: Awful!

Lucy: What's wrong?

Alice: I don't know what to do. Smoking isn't allowed in our office, but every time the boss is away from the office, Bob lights up a cigarette! I've asked him not to smoke a hundred times, but he does it anyway. He must have smoked two packs already today! I'm really tired of it. What do you think I should do?

Lucy: Well, Alice, I think you should tell your boss. He might get angry with Bob, but so what? You've asked Bob not to smoke, but he keeps on doing it. If the boss fires him, it's his own fault.

Alice: I think you're right. I'll talk to the boss tomorrow. This is horrible! Why can't Bob just follow the rules like everyone else?

Narrator: Conversation b

Tim: You look frustrated, Carlos. What's the matter?

Carlos: It's my family again. They just don't understand that I'm nineteen, and I want to be independent.

Tim: Did you have another argument?

Carlos: Yeah. My parents just don't think I'm independent enough to live alone. They think I never stick to anything for very long and that I won't be able to hold onto my job. And they don't think I'll be able to support myself with my job either.

Tim: Well, why don't you move in with your older brother? Then when you save up some more money, you can look for your own apartment.

Carlos: Are you kidding? My older brother just got married! Now is not the time to ask. I guess I'll just be stuck at home forever!

Narrator: Conversation c

Teresa: Michiko! How are you? I haven't seen you for a while. Are you still the captain of the basketball team?

Michiko: I'm OK, I guess. And yes, I'm still captain, but I think I might have to quit the team.

Teresa: But why? You're the best player we've ever had!

Michiko: It's just that I don't have a lot of time to practice. I have a job now. And practice takes at least four hours a week. I just don't think I can go on working and playing as well as going to school.

Teresa: Of course you can! You can't let the rest of the team down. If time is your problem, why don't you talk to your coach and see if you can work out some kind of solution?

Michiko: I suppose I could do that.

Teresa: Of course. In fact, you ought to ask the coach to schedule the practices on the nights you don't work. Then you could keep your job and play on the team, too.

Michiko: That's a great idea! I'll talk to the coach and see what she says. Great seeing you again, Teresa.

Page 112, Exercise 2

Narrator: Conversation 1

Personnel Director: Come in, Jane. You too, Enrique. I called you both in to talk about the special project you're doing for the Economics Department. Professor Phillips is very pleased with your work.

Jane: Thank you.

Enrique: And thank Professor Phillips, too, when you see her.

Personnel Director: She was particularly pleased at how cooperative you have been. She told me that you helped each other out when there were problems, and that you didn't even mind sharing the same desk.

Enrique: That's right. Jane knows a lot about the database program we had to use, and she gave me lots of good advice. If she hadn't showed me how to run that program, it would have taken me twice the time to do my part of the work.

Jane: And Enrique helped me with some of the economics terminology and with all the statistics. That was really helpful for a sociology major like myself!

Personnel Director: She also said that both of you managed your time very well. You came on time and stayed focused on your work while you were in the office. You met all of your deadlines, too.

Enrique: Well, once or twice we really had to push ourselves to meet them, but the extra hours were worth it. We got it done.

Personnel Director: Well, I'm very happy to tell you that Professor Phillips wants you to work with her for the rest of the school year. And because you both did so well, I'm going to change your job classification status so that you earn $2.50 more per hour on the next project. Congratulations.

Jane: That's wonderful! The extra money will help pay my tuition. Thanks.

Enrique: Thank you. We really appreciate what you've done.

Narrator: Conversation 2

Personnel Director: Tim? Please come in. Are you OK?

Tim: Yeah, I guess. So how come I had to come in today?

Personnel Director: Well, Tim, I thought it would be a good idea if I gave you some feedback on the work you've been doing for Professor Swan.

Tim: Oh, man. What now?

Personnel Director: What do you mean, "what now"? Has something happened that I don't know about?

Tim: Well, kind of. I mean, that guy …

Personnel Director: You mean Professor Swan.

Tim: Yeah. Professor Swan is really obsessed with every little detail, you know? He practically had a heart attack this morning just because I filed some of the data from the book he's doing in the wrong place. I mean, *I* knew where it was. All he had to do was ask.

Personnel Director: I see. Well, it seems that you aren't actually *in* the office much of the time so that he can ask you about things.

Tim: Yeah, well. You know, it's really dark and stuffy in that office. And there's hardly any room to work.

Personnel Director: Tim, I was referring to the fact that you are almost always late. And you often leave early, according to other people in the department.

Tim: Oh, once in a while. It's not like it's the end of the world. What do they expect for $6.00 an hour?

Personnel Director: I see. Could I ask you about what happened on Tuesday of last week? I'd like to hear it from you.

Tim: Oh yeah. The chart thing. The old guy …

Personnel Director: Professor Swan.

Tim: Professor Swan gave me all these columns of numbers to enter into a big chart in his database. It took forever. And, you know, all those rows of numbers can make you dizzy and stuff. So I accidentally put some of the figures on the wrong line or in the wrong column or something. He had a real problem with it.

Personnel Director: That's because he based hours of intense and difficult work on those numbers, and they turned out to be wrong! You didn't even check your work, did you?

Tim: Well, no. It was after 5:00, and I only work till 5:00, you know. Quittin' time—the best part of the day!

Personnel Director: Tim, I'm sorry I have to tell you this, but you are no longer eligible to work for the college. Your lack of attention to detail and your attitude about your work has led to this unfortunate decision. Professor Swan has requested that we look for another student whose skills more closely match the job and I have to agree. I'm sorry.

Page 113, Exercise 3

Woman: You shouldn't have run that red light!

Man: I had to. Otherwise, the guy behind me wouldn't have been able to stop in time.

Woman: Yes, but you shouldn't have had to stop so suddenly. You should have seen that guy behind you, and you should have just slowed down.

Man: I suppose you're right. If the police had seen me, I'm sure they would have given me a ticket.

Unit 12: Wishful Thinking

Page 117, Exercise 2

Narrator: Conversation 1
Ann: That new guy in our biology class is really cute!
Bea: You aren't kidding. He's gorgeous! And he has the most beautiful green eyes!
Ann: Yeah, I've talked to him and he seems to be really friendly, too. I'd love to have green eyes like his.

Narrator: Conversation 2
Al: Aren't you coming to the party on Friday? Dorothy'll be there. You could ask her to dance.
Bob: I'd like to impress Dorothy, but I can't. She only goes out with the best dancers, but I have two left feet. If I'd learned to dance when I was young, I'd be OK, but it's too late now.
Al: Oh, don't be so hard on yourself. Dorothy'll understand.

Narrator: Conversation 3
Mr. Allen: Lucy, I know you're a good student, but you never ask any questions in class. Why is that?
Lucy: Oh, Mr. Allen, I'm too shy! I get really embarrassed when you call on me. I can't help it. I just don't like to talk in front of people. I'm afraid I'll make a mistake and everyone'll laugh at me.
Mr. Allen: Lucy, everyone feels shy at times, but you should participate more. You're one of the best students in the class, and if you participated, your grades would probably be even better.

Page 122, Exercise 2

Narrator: Conversation 1
Woman: I wish you hadn't admitted that you were the criminal's roommate!
Man: But you told me to answer **all** the questions the other lawyers asked me.
Woman: I know, but now you'll be called as a witness in the trial.

Narrator: Conversation 2
Ann: Oh, Cathy, I'd give anything if John would ask me to the dance on Saturday.
Cathy: Do you want me to mention it to him at school tomorrow?
Ann: Great idea! Tell him I wish he'd call me.

Narrator: Conversation 3
Greg: Gee, Ms. Simms, I wish you had asked me to work late last night instead of tonight. I've already made plans for this evening.
Ms. Simms: Well, I'll see if Gloria can stay later. Maybe she can type this report.
Greg: I'm sure she won't mind. And I'd really appreciate it!

Narrator: Conversation 4
Daughter: But this party is really important! Everybody'll be there. I just have to have a new dress!
Mother: I'm sorry, Honey, but it's the end of the month and we're short of cash. I wish you could understand. We just don't have the money for a new dress right now.
Daughter: And I wish you could understand how important this is to me. Everyone'll be looking at me.

Narrator: Conversation 5
Woman: You know, I wish the city would put more streetlights on our block.
Man: Yeah, everyone's always complaining about how dark and dangerous it is at night, but nobody's done anything to get it changed.
Woman: I think it's time we all go and complain to the neighborhood association.
Man: Great! I'll get the people next door to me to go, too. Let's start calling up the neighbors!

Page 123, Exercise 4

A: I wish we had taken the main road.
B: But I thought you wanted to take a long walk.
A: I did. If only we'd get to the waterfalls already.
B: On Golden State Highway, you wouldn't have been able to see tall trees, green grass, or blue birds. And look at that beautiful blue sky and those aspen trees.
A: Well, I'm tired and hungry. I wish we had brought fresh fruit or chips or something. You can't eat tall trees, green grass, or a nice view.

Workbook Audioscript

UNIT 1: Making Progress

Practice 8

Advisor: Thank you for being on time, Andrea. I have a lot of students to see today. Since you're in your last year at the university, I need to know which required courses you haven't taken yet. You'll have to take them to graduate at the end of the year.

Andrea: Well, I've already taken most of them, I think. I only need two or three more.

Advisor: Can you be more specific? Have you taken biology?

Andrea: Yes, I took it my first year here.

Advisor: What about the foreign language requirement?

Andrea: I'm taking a Spanish course this semester.

Advisor: Good. What history courses have you taken so far?

Andrea: None, I'm afraid. I still haven't studied world history. I'll have to do it next semester.

Advisor: Yes, you have to have all the requirements. What about chemistry and math?

Andrea: I've already taken chemistry. I had it last semester. And I'm taking a math course now.

Advisor: Have you taken geography yet?

Andrea: No, I still haven't taken it. I'll have to take it next semester.

Advisor: And what about physical education?

Andrea: I took swimming my third year.

Advisor: One more question. You've already taken literature, haven't you?

Andrea: Yes, in my second year. It's been my favorite course so far!

Advisor: Well, that finishes up the list of required courses. Let's see. You've got to register for world history and geography. Here are the forms. Why don't you fill them out now while you're here?

Practice 9B

1. amazed
2. answered
3. achieved
4. baked
5. damaged
6. failed
7. finished
8. hugged
9. hummed
10. laughed
11. listened
12. practiced

UNIT 2: Whodunit?

Practice 9A, B

Albert: Well, that's great, Ken. Teaching can be a good profession. What kind of teacher do you want to be?

Ken: I'm sure I want to be a teacher, but I don't know. I could be a math or a chemistry teacher. I really like both subjects, and I could be happy teaching either one. Luckily I still have time to decide.

Albert: What about you, Ruth? You study so hard that you must want to be a teacher, too!

Ruth: Well, I study hard because I'll need a scholarship for law school. It's expensive, and I need all the money I can get. But with my grades being so high, I think I may get a scholarship, and then my dream of being a lawyer will come true at last. What's your dream, Albert?

Albert: You might not believe this, but I may become an artist.

Ken: But you're a great football player! You should go into professional football!

Albert: I know that's what everybody thinks I should do, and I know I'll make a lot of money if I do. But I just might surprise everybody and be an artist.

June: I believe you, Albert. You could become a famous artist. You're strong and sensitive.

Mario: Give me a break, June. I'm strong and sensitive, too.

June: You may be both, Mario, but you aren't planning to be an artist or even a football player as far as I know.

Mario: Of course not. Everybody knows I'll be a cook in my father's Italian restaurant. I love cooking, and I know I'll be a good cook for sure. I'll be a better cook than you!

June: That's fine with me, Mario. Pilots don't have to be good cooks. I'll get all my gourmet meals on airplanes!

Ken: You want to be a pilot? You're kidding!

June: I certainly am not kidding! I've wanted to pilot planes and helicopters ever since my uncle took me up in his plane. And I might get a chance at it, if I can convince my uncle to give me a job at the airport.

Practice 10B

A: Gee, you sure know a lot of English now! How in the world did you increase your vocabulary so fast?

B: I needed to progress very quickly for my new job.

A: Well, how did you produce such fast results?

B: Easy. My parents gave me a birthday present.

A: What did they present you with?

B: A magic record in English.

A: Magic? I suspect you're joking, right?

B: No, I'm not kidding. Just look at my progress!

Unit 3: Because I Told You To!

Practice 8

Announcer: Good evening and welcome to our show. Our guest today on *Money Talk* is Mr. Charles Chou.

Mr. Chou: Good evening.

Announcer: Mr. Chou, you are the world's most influential businessman. Could you tell us how you got where you are today?

Mr. Chou: I owe all my success to good advice.

Announcer: Many people gave you advice, didn't they? For example, I understand your grandfather wanted you to be an artist.

Mr. Chou: That's right. He told me to go to a good art school. He even wanted to give me money to go. He encouraged me because he knew I loved art.

Announcer: But you're a businessman. Did he ask you to study business, too?

Mr. Chou: No, he let me do exactly what I wanted. He wanted me to be happy.

Announcer: Did your parents force you to study business?

Mr. Chou: Well, they didn't force me to. They always let me make the final decision, but they sure encouraged me to study business, and encouraged me, and encouraged me more …

Announcer: Parents are like that, all right.

Mr. Chou: Yes, They wanted me to follow their advice, but so did a lot of other people! My best friend wanted me to open a restaurant with him, and my girlfriend asked me to get married.

Announcer: And you finally went into the family business, right?

Mr. Chou: Yes, I didn't want to at first, but I changed my mind later.

Announcer: Who made you change your mind?

Mr. Chou: Well, you see …

Announcer: Oh, I get it! You took everyone's advice and now you're one of the most successful businessmen on Wall Street.

Mr. Chou: No, no, no. I just took one person's advice—Miss Robinson, my first grade teacher.

Announcer: Really?

Mr. Chou: Yeah, she's been giving me advice since I was six years old! I let her make all my career and business decisions.

Announcer: What's the best advice she ever gave you?

Mr. Chou: She told me not to listen to anybody else's advice.

Practice 9B

A: Harold hates his new school. He says it's like a prison.

B: Well, his brother didn't go there. Why are they making him go there?

A: Because they want him to have a better education.

B: Then, why does Harold hate it so much? What do they make him do?

A: Well, they force him and his friends to obey the rules.

B: Do the teachers expect them to get up early, make their beds, be on time, and all those things?

A: Yes, and they won't let them do anything that's fun!

B: Now tell me about Jessica. Why are they forcing her to go there, too? She has always been good in school.

A: They wanted her to do better, too.

B: Gee, how did their parents persuade them to go to that school?

A: It was easy! They gave them both brand new cars.

UNIT 4: Child's Play

Practice 9

Lecturer: Child prodigy Ruth Lawrence never went to school as a young child. Her parents were her teachers. Her father, Harry Lawrence, was a computer consultant, but when he realized how talented Ruth was, he gave up his job to become her teacher. By the time she was four, Ruth had already learned to read. And by the time she was five, she had already begun to study academic subjects.

Ruth loved to study all kinds of math, but she also enjoyed English literature, history, geography, and piano. According to her father, Ruth didn't work harder than other children her age. She simply spent more time concentrating on what she enjoyed, especially math. As a result, by the time she was ten, she had won first place in a higher math test and had entered Oxford University. Ruth hopes to become a math professor when she finishes her education.

Practice 10B

A: So, did Mom drag you to go see an opera with her in Paris?

B: No, by the time she arrived, I'd already seen one.

A: Which one?

B: *The Tales of Hoffmann.*

A: What did you say?

B: I said *The Tales of Hoffmann*. And I really loved it!

A: You loved it?

B: Yes, you know I like opera.

A: Really?

B: Really.

A: I'd have never guessed.

Unit 5: The Real You?

Practice 11A

Frank: Good evening … ah … Miss Barbara Logan?

Barbara: Hi. That's me. Are you my blind date?

Frank: Uh … yeah, I guess I am. I'm John's friend, Frank Blair. He and your friend, Mary, arranged for us to go out together tonight.

Barbara: I know. Wasn't it a fantastic idea? I just love meeting new people!

Frank: I can tell you do.

Barbara: Well, come on in, Frank, and meet my family.

Frank: Gee, I don't know. Being around people's parents really makes me feel nervous.

Barbara: Oh, come on. You can talk about sports with my dad. He loves talking about football and basketball.

Frank: But I hate talking about sports. Uh, I mean … um … I just don't know anything about them.

Barbara: Really? I play on a basketball team. And I enjoy tennis and swimming, too.

Frank: Oh, well, I like going to the beach, but I don't like to swim. I like collecting different kinds of shells.

Barbara: I see. Well, if you don't feel like meeting my parents, we'd better leave. The movie starts at eight.

Frank: Movie? Gee, movies are pretty expensive. Wouldn't you like to go to a concert? They're playing Bach and Handel at the concert hall tonight, and I have free tickets.

Barbara: To tell you the truth, Frank, I don't enjoy listening to classical music very much, but I'll go if you really want to.

Frank: No, no. We can do something else.

Barbara: How about bowling? Do you like doing that?

Frank: I've never gone bowling in my life! I'd probably be just awful! Everybody would die laughing at me.

Barbara: Gee, you don't have much confidence in yourself, do you? Well, OK, we won't go bowling. But what do you want to do?

Frank: What if we just take a walk in the park? It's really nice out.

Barbara: OK, Frank. That sounds just fine to me. I like taking walks … and they're free!

UNIT 6: If I Had My Way

Practice 9A

Mary: Hello,

Jake: Hi, Mary. Do you have a minute?

Mary: What's the matter, Jake? You sound upset.

Jake: I really need to talk to a friend, Mary, and I know you'll understand.

Mary: What's wrong? Is it something at work?

Jake: Well, kind of …

Mary: Does it have to do with Katherine?

Jake: Yeah, You know, when she got a job in the same company as me, I thought it was a great idea. I thought we'd see each other more, have more to share with each other, and become even closer. But it hasn't turned out that way at all.

Mary: Are you upset because she got that promotion?

Jake: No, not at all. I'm proud of her. But I feel like she's ignoring me at work because her job is more important than mine. I don't feel that she respects me anymore. Especially now that she goes to the executive dining room with the big bosses. She never has lunch with me.

Mary: But that's expected of her! A lot of work gets done at those power lunches. Now, come on, you know she'd rather be with you.

Jake: Well, if I talked to her about it, I know she'd think I was jealous of her new job.

Mary: Jake, if I were you, I'd bring it up tonight as soon as you get home. You need to tell Katherine how you really feel.

Jake: If I did, she'd laugh at me!

Mary: No, she wouldn't. If you told her how you felt, she'd realize how important this was to you. Then you could find a way to solve the problem together. Really. Tell her how you feel.

Jake: I just don't think I can. I don't know if I'm an important part of her life anymore. Why did she ever take this stupid job with my company? If she were back in her old job, we wouldn't have this problem.

Mary: Stop worrying about it, Jake. Be frank with Katherine and tell her your feelings. Believe me, it really is the best thing to do.

Practice 10C

There once was a critic named Brook
Who wanted to talk with the cook.
    She looked at her dish
    Said that can't be fish.
So the cook was sautéed in her book.

Unit 7: What's So Funny?

Practice 8A

Narrator: Joke 1

Teller: What did one light say to another light?

Narrator: Joke 2

Teller: Which animals can jump higher than a house?

Narrator: Joke 3

Teller: Where does Thursday come before Wednesday?

Narrator: Joke 4

Teller: What is black when it's clean and white when it's dirty?

Narrator: Joke 5

Teller: Why do birds fly south for the winter?

Practice 9B

Conversation 1

A: Did you say you had difficulty understanding British humor?

B: No, I said I had a hard time understanding American humor.

Conversation 2

A: What did your doctor say was good for pain?

B: He said that laughter could help reduce pain.

Conversation 3

A: When do babies usually begin to smile?

B: They say babies start to smile during their second month.

Conversation 4

A: Did he say that people from all cultures laugh at the same things?

B: No, he said that people from different cultures laugh at different things.

Unit 8: So That's How … !

Practice 8

Joan: Hi, Jack.

Jack: Hi Joan. Did you hear that Eileen was promoted?

Joan: No kidding! When?

Jack: This morning. We were all told as soon as we got to the office. Can you believe it?

Joan: Well, that was quick! As I recall, she was just promoted six months ago, too.

Jack: That's right. Back then she was moved up to manager, and now she's been promoted to vice-president!

Joan: Well, she must be doing something right.

Jack: Yeah. She's a hard worker, that's for sure. Her projects are always developed before anybody else's. She always takes work home with her. Her briefcase is always stuffed with papers and plans.

Joan: Is she getting a new office?

Jack: She sure is. She's moving to the corner office with the big window!

Joan: Well, good for her! I'm happy for her.

Jack: Yeah, she deserved it. Nothing succeeds like good hard work!

Practice 9C

Limerick 1

A: There was an Old Man with a beard,
B: Who said, "It is just as I feared!—
A: Two Owls and a Hen,
B: Four Larks and a Wren,
A: Have all built their nests in my beard!"

Limerick 2

A: There was an Old Man in a tree,
B: Who was horribly bored by a bee;
A: When they said, "Does it buzz?"
B: He replied, "Yes it does!
A: It's a regular brute of a bee!"

Unit 9: Home Sweet Home

Practice 9

Announcer: Some people complain of having to live in a small house. "It's like living in a box," they say. But at least one person really did live in a box. The Englishman Alexander Wortley lived in a box until his death in 1980 at the age of 80. His "home sweet home" was a green box only one meter wide, a meter and a half deep, and a little more than a meter and a half tall. Inside the box, he could neither lie down full length nor stand up completely.

The box itself was made of wood; the arched roof was made of metal. Wortley could move the box wherever he wanted because it had four small wheels. Inside, he installed an old seat from a bus and a few shelves for his food and his clothes.

While most people see the disadvantages of living in a box, such as no electricity and little comfort, Wortley saw several distinct advantages. For one thing, he never had to pay rent. Also, he could move whenever he wanted. For Wortley, these considerations were more important than having a fixed address.

Unit 10: Mysteries of Science

Practice 8A

Mr. Diaz: Most people have heard about the lost land of Atlantis, but few realize that it was first mentioned by Plato, a Greek philosopher, in 335 B.C. He described it as a sophisticated civilization with richly decorated buildings, an ideal political system, and a strong army. When Atlantis tried to dominate the Mediterranean, however, its army was defeated by the army of Athens, Greece. Shortly afterward, a huge earthquake caused Atlantis to sink into the ocean. (pause) Yes, Hiroshi, do you have a question?
Hiroshi: Who did you say first described Atlantis?
Mr. Diaz: It was the Greek philosopher Plato.
Hiroshi: Thank you.
Mr. Diaz: Ever since Plato's time, people the world over have had theories about the location of Atlantis. After Europeans reached the Americas in 1492, for example, some scholars thought that America must have been Atlantis. Other thinkers of that time speculated that Atlantis might have been an island between Europe and America.

Then, in the 1920s, some experts felt that Atlantis could have been located at Tartessus in southwest Spain. Ancient legends said that this place was so rich that sailors made anchors for their boats out of silver. Some artifacts were in fact located there, but they date from later civilizations. Yes, Eva.
Eva: I'm sorry. I missed the name of the town in Spain.
Mr. Diaz: That was Tartessus, and it's spelled T-A-R-T-E-S-S-U-S. (pause) Later this century, the Greek scientist Galanopoulos decided that the island of Crete may have been the home of Atlantis. And in fact, excavations on Thera, a small island near Crete, showed a city dating from after 1500 B.C. that had been covered under volcanic material. Still later in 1972, a Frenchman and an American discovered huge walls made from 16 foot blocks of stone under the water near the island of Bimini in the Bahamas. Experts have dated these walls, which spread over 38 square miles, to between 7000 and 10,000 B.C., even before the building of the pyramids in Egypt.
Linda: Excuse me, Mr. Diaz. I have a question. There are so many places Atlantis could have been, but where was it really located?
Mr. Diaz: That's for you to decide!

Unit 11: Sadder but Wiser

Practice 10A,B

Narrator: Conversation 1
Ann: Hi, Bob! You should have come to the party last night. It was really fun!
Bob: I wanted to, but I had to study.

Narrator: Conversation 2
Mrs. Hill: Keith, I've told you to clean your room at least ten times this week!
Keith: Oh, Mom, I would have done it if I hadn't had basketball practice every night.

Narrator: Conversation 3
Ed: Well, Sue, in my opinion, you shouldn't have talked to the director.
Sue: But the director took care of everything. If I'd taken your advice, the problem would never have been solved.

Narrator: Conversation 4
(two little boys)
Billy: Look, Timmy. I'm in a lot of trouble with my parents because yesterday you told me to go to your house instead of having supper with my family! So just leave me alone for a while, OK?
Timmy: But, Billy, won't you come out and play with me?
Billy: I can't. My parents are making me stay in all weekend. If I hadn't listened to you, they wouldn't be so angry now.

Narrator: Conversation 5
Rita: Hi, Jane. I didn't expect to see you working through lunch. You should have stayed late last night and finished that report.
Jane: Well, I couldn't stay because I had a ticket to the opera. Oh well, maybe a quick lunch'll give me some energy. Let's go.

UNIT 12: Wishful Thinking

Practice 6

Narrator: Conversation A

Lisa: Gee, Mom, I wish you'd drive a little faster. We're going to be late for the movie.

Mom: No, we won't, Lisa. We're doing fine. Stop worrying.

Mark: Wow! Look how fast that motorcycle is going! I wish I had a motorcycle like that!

Mom: Well, I think motorcycles are dangerous. I wish the government would ban motorcycle riding altogether.

Lisa: Yeah, Mark. Cars are a lot safer … and more comfortable, too.

Narrator: Conversation B

Mr. Thorn: Oh, Ms. Warren, I wish the boss had told us about this meeting earlier. I didn't have time to finish my report.

Ms. Warren: I know what you mean, Mr. Thorn. I wish I'd had the time to check these pollution regulations before the meeting, too. She's going to be furious with us.

Mr. Thorn: I just hope she's in a good mood today.

Practice 7B

A: Wasn't the last lecture in our environment class fascinating?

B: It was a real eye-opener. Air pollution, water pollution, population growth, species extinction. What are we doing to the planet?

A: And how about the greenhouse effect and how it's caused the global temperature to rise by one degree centigrade just within the last century.

B: I know. The teacher said that this could cause sea levels to rise.

A: And then there would be coastal flooding, severe hurricanes and devastating droughts.

B: I didn't know the global temperature was only 2.2 degrees cooler during the last ice age.

A: Well, I know it's wishful thinking, but I wish our governments would stop being so greedy and start making our environment a top priority.

B: I do, too. If only the international community could agree to develop tough environmental laws to protect us and to exercise damage control.

A: They have to agree to enforce the laws, too.

B: You're right. What can we do?

Workbook Answer Key

UNIT 1: Making Progress

Practice 1

Answers will vary.

Practice 2

1. c
2. a
3. d
4. e
5. b
6. f

Practice 3

Dialogues will vary. Sample dialogue:

A: Have you taken biology yet?

B: Yes, I have./No, I haven't taken it yet. Have you taken physics yet?

A: Yes, I took it last semester.

Practice 4

A. 1. put, put, put
   2. send, sent, sent; spend, spent, spent; deal, dealt, dealt
   3. speak, spoke, spoken; steal, stole, stolen
   4. leave, left, left
   5. drive, drove, driven
   6. begin, began, begun; swim, swam, swum; sink, sank, sunk
   7. teach, taught, taught; think, thought, thought
   8. fly, flew, flown; throw, threw, thrown

Practice 5

1. has been
2. have you been
3. has already graduated
4. has changed
5. has gotten
6. Have you finished
7. still haven't shown
8. have begun
9. still haven't forgotten
10. have you seen
11. haven't had
12. has learned

Practice 6

Answers will vary.

Practice 7

1. have been working
2. haven't finished
3. Have you sent/Did you send
4. sent
5. have you looked at/did you look at
6. have already done/already did
7. have gone/went
8. have taken/took
9. haven't gotten
10. Has (the secretary) told
11. have been trying
12. have had/have been having

Practice 8

Biology—past; Chemistry—past; Geography—next; World history—next; Math—present; Physical education—past; Foreign language—past and present

Practice 9

A. 1. /zd/
   2. /rd/
   3. /vd/
   4. /kt/
   5. /jd/
   6. /ld/
   7. /st/
   8. /gd/
   9. /md/
   10. /ft/
   11. /nd/
   12. /st/

C. 1. /ɪd/
   2. /st/
   3. /kt/

Practice 10

Answers will vary.

Practice 11

4, 14, 2, 15, 1, 13, 3, 12, 5, 8, 6, 7, 11, 9, 10

Check Your Knowledge

Vocabulary Check

1. communicate
2. be aware of
3. take advantage of
4. characteristics
5. strategies
6. make progress

Check Your Understanding

1. has given
2. has traveled
3. hasn't visited
4. hasn't finished
5. has accepted

UNIT 2: Whodunit?

Practice 1

Answers will vary.

Practice 2

A. 1. lawyer
   2. housekeeper
   3. accountants
   4. widow
   5. suspects
   6. fiancé
   7. assistants
   8. victim

B. whodunit

Practice 3

Dialogues will vary.

Practice 4

1. He couldn't be the thief.
2. She must be worried. Do you think she must be worried?
3. They may lie in court. Do you think they may lie in court?

Practice 5

1. must
2. can/may/might
3. could/may/might
4. must
5. could/may/might
6. could/may/might

Practice 6

Answers will vary.

Practice 7

1. could/may/might
2. could/may/might
3. could/may/might
4. must
5. could/may/might

Practice 8

B. a. 4
   b. 1
   c. 3
   d. 2

Practice 9

A. 1. lawyer
   2. artist
   3. cook
   4. pilot

B. Answers will vary.

Practice 10

A. 1. increase
   2. progress
   3. produce

T166

4. present
5. present
6. record
7. suspect
8. progress

Practice 11

B. A: The Smiths definitely live in house 5 because their house has an apple tree.
   B: The Vitellos can't live in house 4 because their house had a pine tree next to it. They must live in either house 2 or 3.
1. Krolls
2. Garcías
3. Vitellos
4. Wongs
5. Smiths

Practice 12

Narratives will vary.

Check Your Knowledge

Vocabulary Check
1. familiar with
2. According to
3. valuable
4. come up with
5. motive
6. thief

Check Your Understanding
1. could/might
2. could/might
3. could/might
4. could/might
5. Could
6. must

UNIT 3: Because I Told You To!

Practice 1

Answers will vary.

Practice 2

Answers will vary.

Practice 3

Dialogues will vary.

Practice 4

1. My boss did not tell his assistant not to turn off the computer.
2. Did my boss tell his assistant to turn off the computer?
3. My boss told his assistant to turn off the computer.
4. Does her commander usually ask her to fly the plane?
5. Her commander usually asks her not to fly the plane.

Practice 5

1. my boss to give
2. me to ask
3. me to go
4. me have
5. me to fill out
6. me to get
7. me to be
8. me to wait
9. us take
10. us to take
11. us to move
12. us wait
13. us leave
14. us to stay

Practice 6

1. Eve's son asked her to give him more milk.
2. Eve's boss expected her to finish a report before she left.
3. Eve asked the assistant to type up the report in a half hour.
4. Eve reminded her husband not to forget the hot dogs.
5. Eve ordered her daughter not to have ice cream until after dinner.
6. Eve warned her son and daughter not to forget to do their math homework.

Practice 7

Answers will vary.

Practice 8

1. grandfather
2. study business
3. open restaurant
4. girlfriend
5. don't listen to anybody else's advice, first grade teacher

Practice 9

Circled: 1. his 3. him 5. him
6. him 7. his 10. her 11. her
13. them
Crossed out: 2. his 4. him 8. them 9. them 12. them

Practice 10

1. Gina asked John to help her take out the garbage.
2. John told Gina to take it out herself.
3. Gina warned John not to be so mean.
4. John asked Gina to let him borrow her car tonight.
5. Gina forced John to help her clean the house first.
6. John expected Gina to lend him some money to go out.
7. Gina said she might if John would start being nicer to her.

Practice 11

Letters will vary.

Check Your Knowledge

Vocabulary Check
1. flexible
2. colleague
3. appreciate
4. frustrating
5. role

Check Your Understanding
1. advised her
2. warned her not
3. did you ask her
4. made her
5. encouraged her
6. expected her
7. let you

UNIT 4: Child's Play

Practice 1

Answers will vary.

Practice 2

Across
1. exceptionally
5. measures
7. ability
8. levels

Down
2. chess
3. admire
4. prodigy
6. talented

Practice 3

Dialogues will vary.

Practice 4

1. Had I hurried?
2. You'd known. You hadn't known.
3. He'd succeeded. Had he succeeded?
4. She hadn't stopped over. Had she stopped over?
5. It had taken off. Had it taken off?
6. We'd quit. We hadn't quit.
7. They hadn't given up. Had they given up?

Practice 5

1. By the time she was fifteen, Ginetta La Bianca had already sung in her first opera in Velletri, Italy.
2. By the time she was sixteen, Margo Feiden had already produced her first musical, *Peter Pan*.

3. By the time he was twelve, Marcus Hooper had already swum the English Channel.

4. By the time he was nine, Cody A. Locke had already flown a small 150 Cessna plane.

5. By the time he was eighteen, Avi Ben-Abraham had already received an medical degree from the University of Perugia in Italy.

Practice 6

1. arrived
2. had already been living/were already living
3. spoke
4. had already formed
5. were already using
6. had already erected
7. had already constructed
8. had been using
9. had laid
10. had developed
11. had been using

Practice 7

Possible answers.
1. had gone through
2. had been using
3. had opened
4. had taken
5. had stolen
6. hadn't looked

Practice 8

Conversations will vary.

Practice 9

Name: Ruth Lawrence
Education: taught at home by parents
Achievement at age 4: had learned to read
Achievement at age 5: had begun studying math and other academic subjects
Achievement at age 10: had won math test and had entered Oxford University
Future plans: wants to become a math professor

Practice 10

A.
1. question mark
2. period
3. question mark
4. period
5. question mark
6. period
7. period
8. question mark
9. period
10. question mark
11. period
12. period

Practice 11

A.
1. a
2. 16
3. a and e
B. Answers will vary.

Practice 12

Letters will vary.

Check Your Knowledge

Vocabulary Check
1. field
2. challenge
3. gifted
4. publish
5. average

Check Your Understanding
1. had already learned
2. didn't learn
3. had published
4. had only begun
5. had already finished
6. always needed
7. had already been developing
8. decided
9. worked
10. had won

UNIT 5: The Real You?

Practice 1

Descriptions will vary.

Practice 2

1. enjoy
2. looking forward to
3. avoid
4. invest
5. insist on

Practice 3

Dialogues will vary.

Practice 4

1. My friend wasn't criticized for using the computer.
2. Was my friend criticized for using the computer?
3. Mark missed eating in restaurants.
4. Mark missed not eating in restaurants.
5. Did Mark miss eating in restaurants?

Practice 5

1. to
2. in
3. about
4. on
5. about
6. for
7. on
8. of

Practice 6

A. Possible answers.
1. Yes, he thanked me for inviting him.
2. Well, he usually put off washing the dishes.
3. No, he always insisted on paying for them himself.
4. No, he had trouble seeing everything.
5. Yes, but he apologized for breaking it.
6. Sure, but he was criticized for his bad manners.
7. Sure. I look forward to him coming back.

Practice 7

Questions and interviews will vary.

Practice 8

1. liked getting up/liked to get up
2. looked forward to sleeping
3. enjoyed going
4. wanted to do
5. wanted to read
6. loved going out/loved to go out
7. couldn't stand being/couldn't stand to be
8. agreed to go
9. insisted on coming
10. began changing/began to change
11. thought about sitting
12. became interested in going

Practice 9

1. avoid, can't help, criticize for, deny, enjoy, finish, imagine, insist on, look forward to, miss, plan on, put off
2. ask, choose, decide, expect, need, refuse
3. continue, dislike, hate, like

Practice 10

Questions will vary.

Practice 11

A. **Barbara likes:** playing basketball, swimming, playing tennis, watching baseball, talking walks
Barbara dislikes: listening to classical music
Frank likes: going to the beach, collecting seashells, listening to classical music, taking walks

Frank dislikes: being around people's parents, taking about sports, swimming, spending money, trying new sports

B. 1. F
2. B
3. F
4. B
5. B
6. F
7. F
8. B

Practice 12

Student A's sentences:

I think Kay's really tired of /əv/ being a lawyer.

Did she apply for one of /ə/ your jobs?

Was she critical of /əv/ her present boss?

Student B's sentences:

She's seriously thinking of /əv/ another career.

Yes, and she asked a lot of /ə/ questions.

No, but she told us a lot of /əv/ interesting things.

Practice 13

Paragraphs will vary.

Check Your Knowledge

Vocabulary Check

1. traits
2. interpret
3. avoid
4. insist on
5. daydream

Check Your Understanding

1. understanding
2. studying
3. working
4. exercising
5. thinking
6. doing
7. to do
8. preparing/to prepare

UNIT 6: If I Had My Way

Practice 1

Descriptions will vary.

Practice 2

1. restless
2. formula
3. go along with
4. propose
5. increase

6. change his mind
7. approve of

Practice 3

Dialogues will vary.

Practice 4

1. e
2. h
3. f
4. d, h
5. i
6. c
7. b, g
8. d, h
9. j
10. a, j

Practice 5

A. 1. were
2. would you change
3. would try
4. would make
5. would you do
6. would hire
7. would make
8. committed
9. would go
10. would you make
11. would work
12. would improve
13. wouldn't let
14. did
15. would have
16. wouldn't pay
17. would advise

B. Answers will vary.

Practice 6

A. 1. improbable
2. impossible
3. improbable
4. improbable
5. impossible
6. impossible
7. improbable
8. impossible

B. Sentences will vary.

Practice 7

A. Sentences will vary.

Practice 8

Dialogues will vary.

Practice 9

A. 1. F; Jake telephoned Mary.
2. T
3. F; Katherine got a promotion.
4. T
5. T
6. T

B. Answers will vary.

Practice 10

A. There <u>once</u> was a <u>critic</u> named <u>Brook</u>
Who <u>wanted</u> to <u>talk</u> with the <u>cook</u>.
She <u>looked</u> at her <u>dish</u>
Said <u>that</u> can't be <u>fish</u>.
So the <u>cook</u> was sautéed in her <u>book</u>.

Practice 11

Sentences will vary.

Practice 12

Answers and paragraphs will vary.

Check Your Knowledge

Vocabulary Check

1. brings it up
2. approved of
3. go along with
4. change her mind
5. last

Check Your Understanding

1. lived
2. would see
3. appears
4. wouldn't need
5. would be
6. were
7. could get
8. would not die
9. would have
10. chose
11. could travel
12. wanted
13. would be able
14. wouldn't need
15. would have
16. would spend

UNIT 7: What's So Funny?

Practice 1

Answers will vary.

Practice 2

1. a
2. b
3. f
4. k
5. c
6. e
7. d
8. l
9. h
10. j
11. i
12. g

Practice 3

Dialogues will vary.

Practice 4

1. worked
2. worked, had worked
3. was working
4. had been working
5. would work
6. could work
7. had worked

Practice 5

1. I took it back but the clerk said that <u>they couldn't give me my money back.</u>
2. I said that <u>I wanted to speak to the manager.</u>
3. The clerk said that <u>the manager was out of town.</u>
4. Well, I asked him (the clerk) <u>when the manager would come back.</u>
5. So then I I told him to (please) <u>get the assistant manager.</u>
6. The clerk said that <u>she was working at another store.</u>
7. When she came out, I asked if <u>I could (please) exchange the coat for a different one.</u>
8. No, she said <u>that she would be happy to.</u>

Practice 6

1. He said that experience is the name everyone gives to his mistakes.
2. He said that one can always be kind to people about whom one cares nothing.
3. He said that he had put all his genius into his life; he had put only his talent into his works.
4. He said that a cynic is a man who knows the price of everything and the value of nothing.

Practice 7

1. I asked a policeman if he thought we would find my parents. He said he didn't know. He said there were so many places they could hide.
2. I told my father that nobody liked me. He told me not to say that. He said that everybody hadn't met me yet.
3. I asked my father to let me go on the roller coaster. I told him it was safe. He said he knew. He told me to try the parachute jump.

Practice 8

1. f
2. b
3. a
4. e
5. c

Practice 9

1. **A:** British; **B:** American
2. **A:** What; **B:** laughter
3. **A:** When; **B:** second month
4. **A:** all, same; **B:** different, different

Practice 10

1. He said that a verbal contract isn't worth the paper it's written on.
2. He said that anybody who goes to see a psychiatrist ought to have his head examined.
3. He said that if Roosevelt were alive today, he would turn over in his grave.
4. He said that a Goldwyn comedy is not to be laughed at.
5. He said to include him out. (He said that he didn't want to be included.)
6. He asked why you named your baby John when every Tom, Dick, and Harry is named John.

Practice 11

Sayings will vary.

Practice 12

Paragraphs will vary.

Check Your Knowledge

Vocabulary Check

1. confidence
2. allowance
3. raise
4. hilarious
5. attributes

Check Your Understanding

1. An elephant went into a restaurant and said it wanted something to drink.
2. The waiter asked what it wanted.
3. The elephant replied that it would like a chocolate milk shake.
4. The waiter said that it would be $200.
5. The waiter commented that he didn't get many elephants there (in the restaurant)
6. The waiter added that it was the first elephant he had ever served.
7. The elephant exclaimed that at those prices it wasn't surprised.

UNIT 8: So That's How ... !

Practice 1

Paragraphs will vary. (There are several ways to put a model ship into a bottle. In the past, people actually assembled ships inside small-mouthed bottles with special long, thin tools. People also had bottles made around already-built ships, or put ships inside pairs of half-bottles, which they glued together. Another way is to insert a completely built ship with sails down into a bottle with a large mouth, and then raise the sails by pulling a string.)

Practice 2

Possible pairs of words: apply/pressure; paste/force; paste/pressure; paste/tube; squeeze/paste; squeeze/tube; crawl/box; crawl/compartment; get into/box; help out of/box; help out of/compartment; get into/compartment; holes/box; expose/holes.
Sentences will vary.

Practice 3

Dialogues will vary.

Practice 4

1. The auditorium isn't reserved. Is the auditorium reserved?
2. The program is typed up. Is the program typed up?
3. The equipment was tested. The equipment wasn't tested.
4. The comedians won't be registered free. Will the comedians be registered free?
5. The hotel has been paid for. Has the hotel been paid for?
6. The invitations were mailed. The invitations weren't mailed.
7. The conference dinner isn't being planned. Is the conference dinner being planned?
8. A live band was being considered. A live band wasn't being considered.

Practice 5

1. are prepared
2. are picked
3. are taken
4. are separated
5. are put
6. are covered
7. is needed
8. is washed
9. are treated
10. are heated

Practice 6

1. Plans for a bridge connecting Gibraltar and Tangiers were discussed.
2. A $10,000 reward was given to a child for saving a kitten.
3. A 2,000-year-old olive tree was found in Greece.
4. A new English alphabet was proposed to the British government.

Practice 7

1. The church of Hagia Sophia in Constantinople was built by the Byzantine emperor Justinian during the sixth century.
2. The church was designed by Anthemius of Tralles and Isidorus of Miletus.
3. The church was begun in A.D. 532 and was finished in A.D. 537.
4. In 1204, Constantinople was attacked by Christian Crusaders and the church was robbed of many of its treasures.
5. Later, the church was changed into a mosque by Sultan Mehmet II.
6. The building was repaired and strengthened by Mehmet II and a tall minaret was added.
7. Five centuries later, in 1935, the mosque was converted into a museum by the Turkish government.
8. Today, the Hagia Sophia is thought of as a monument to two great religions and 1,400 years of history.

Practice 8

1. T
2. F; Eileen was promoted.
3. F; They were informed this morning.
4. T
5. T
6. F; Her projects were turned in early
7. T
8. F, Eileen is moving to a corner office.

Practice 9

Limerick 1

A: There **was** an Old **Man** with a **beard**,
B: Who **said**, "It is **just** as I **feared**!—
A: Two **Owls** and a **Hen**,
B: Four **Larks** and a **Wren**,
A: Have **all** built their **nests** in my **beard**!"

Limerick 2

A: There **was** an Old **Man** in a **tree**,
B: Who was **horribly bored** by a **bee**;
A: When they **said**, "Does it **buzz**?"
B: He re**plied**, "Yes it **does**!
A: It's a **regular brute** of a **bee**!"

Practice 10

Topics and opinions will vary.

Practice 11

Before the performance, a pair of nail cutters were hidden on Houdini's body. Once he was inside the crate, the trick handcuffs were opened by Houdini with a secret spring. Next, the nail cutters were used by Houdini to take several nails out of the top of the crate. The top was moved aside by Houdini. Then he crawled out, and the top was put back in place. He then sat on top of the crate as it was pulled out of the water. Then, out of sight of the audience, the broken nails were removed by Houdini's assistant. New nails were secretly hammered in by Houdini's assistant before the boat got back to shore. As a result, an undamaged crate was inspected by the audience.

Practice 12

Paragraphs will vary.

Check Your Knowledge

Vocabulary Check

1. pressure
2. hammer
3. trick
4. undamaged
5. shore

Check Your Understanding

1. Instant coffee is measured (put) into a cup.
2. Boiling water is poured into the cup.
3. Sugar is put into the cup.
4. Milk is poured into the cup.
5. The coffee is stirred.

UNIT 9: Home Sweet Home

Practice 1

Answers and preferences will vary.

Practice 2

1. carpenter
2. roofer
3. painter
4. bricklayer
5. gardener
6. plumber
7. electrician
8. architect
9. metalworker
10. interior decorator

Practice 3

Dialogues will vary.

Practice 4

Conversations will vary.

Practice 5

1. to wear
2. eat
3. decorated
4. flooded
5. to make
6. brought in
7. built
8. prepare
9. dress
10. to sing

Practice 6

1. Sadi is having his motorcycle tuned up.
2. Ali is having rose bushes planted in his backyard.
3. Grace is having her basement checked for mice.
4. Ann is getting a new memory installed in her computer..
5. Keiko is getting a garbage disposal installed in her kitchen sink.

Practice 7

Conversations will vary.

Practice 8

Answers will vary.

Practice 9

Date of death: 1980
Nationality: English/British
Kind of house: box
Walls made of: wood
Roof made of: metal
Furniture: old seat from a bus, a few shelves
Number of wheels: 4
Two advantages: no rent, can move when you want
Two disadvantages: no electricity, little comfort

Practice 10

Conversation A: eat, seat, he's, rich

Conversation B: it, leave, been, ship, cheap

Practice 11

Tasks and explanations will vary.

Practice 12

Paragraphs will vary.

Check Your Knowledge

Vocabulary Check

1. replace
2. estimates
3. convert
4. remodeling
5. plumbing
6. install

Check Your Understanding

1. fix
2. (in order) to
3. checked
4. so (that)
5. repaired
6. so (that)
7. cleaned
8. to install
9. wash
10. so (that)

UNIT 10: Mysteries of Science

Practice 1

1. botanist
2. anthropologist
3. geologist
4. astronomer
5. zoologist
6. archaeologist

Practice 2

Answers will vary.

Practice 3

Dialogues will vary.

Practice 4

Possible answers.

1. She might have gone to the doctor's office. She might not have wanted to come.
2. The delivery person might be sick. The delivery person might not have delivered it to our house.
3. They might have decided to go somewhere else. They might not have wanted to spend their money.

4. He might have felt sick. He might not have liked the food.

Practice 5

Possible answers.

1. It could/might have been Mike.
2. He could/might have gotten a promotion.
3. I think it could/might have been Tony.
4. I know. It must have been Gary.

Practice 6

1. must have been
2. must have rained
3. must have been
4. must not have had (taken)/ must have forgotten
5. must not have had

Practice 7

1. could have been
2. could have used
3. could have survived
4. must have hunted
5. must have developed
6. could have conquered
7. could have led
8. could have been
9. could have killed

Practice 8

First mentioned: by Plato, in 335 B.C.

Atlantean civilization: sophisticated, with richly decorated buildings, an ideal political system, and a strong army

Why it disappeared: An earthquake caused it to sink into the ocean.

Practice 9

1. must have
2. couldn't have
3. might have
4. Could
5. could have
6. could have
7. may have
8. could have
9. must have

Practice 10

Answers will vary.

Practice 11

Letters will vary.

Check Your Knowledge

Vocabulary Check

1. purposes

2. theory
3. lake
4. sophisticated
5. carve
6. transported
7. locate

Check Your Understanding

Sentences will vary.

UNIT 11: Sadder but Wiser

Practice 1

1. b
2. g
3. d
4. a
5. h
6. e
7. f
8. c

Practice 2

1. dependable
2. admit
3. sprained
4. surgery
5. wreck

Practice 3

Dialogues will vary.

Practice 4

1. shouldn't have tried
2. should have gotten
3. should have known
4. should have sent
5. shouldn't have escaped
6. should have planned

Practice 5

Possible sentences:

1. They ought to have turned the alarm on and closed the safe.
2. The security guard ought to have been awake.
3. The guard ought to have put the keys somewhere safe.
4. Someone ought to have closed the window and locked the back door.
5. The teller ought to have put all the money in the safe.

Practice 6

1. to have
2. should
3. ought to have/should have
4. should
5. have

Practice 7

Conversations will vary.

Practice 8

Possible sentences:

1. If the train hadn't been delayed, I would have arrived on time for the appointment.
2. If I hadn't insisted on fixing my own roof, I wouldn't have gotten hurt.
3. If I had looked more carefully at my ticket before going to the airport, I wouldn't have missed my flight.
4. If I had followed my doctor's advice, I wouldn't need to have surgery now.

Practice 9

Answers will vary.

Practice 10

A. 1. no
   2. no
   3. no
   4. yes
   5. no

B. 1. Bob studied.
   2. Jane went to the opera last night.

Practice 11

1. should have
2. should have
3. shouldn't have
4. should have
5. should have
6. should have
7. shouldn't have
8. shouldn't have
9. should have
10. should have
11. should have
12. shouldn't have

Practice 12

Answers and paragraphs will vary.

Check Your Knowledge

Vocabulary Check

1. condition
2. admit
3. surgery
4. ulcer
5. dependable
6. wreck
7. windshield
8. tire
9. headlights
10. stuck

Check Your Understanding

Possible sentences:

1. If Jan hadn't taken her father's car, she would be able to go to the party.
2. If Steve hadn't forgotten to take his passport to the airport, he wouldn't miss his plane.
3. If Mario and Ali hadn't moved to France, they would still have their good jobs in Italy.
4. If I hadn't forgotten to tell Teresa I wanted to buy her computer, she wouldn't have sold it to Carol.
5. If Dan hadn't bought a new car, he would have enough money to pay his bills.

UNIT 12: Wishful Thinking

Practice 1

Answers will vary.

Practice 2

A. Answers may include any of these words: killing, planet, polluting, pollution, air, chemicals, rivers, oceans, disposal, toxic waste, technology, nature, rain forests, destroyed, oxygen, plants, animals, extinct, conserve

Practice 3

Dialogues will vary.

Practice 4

1. knew
2. were
3. had moved
4. had

Practice 5

1. had won
2. would start
3. had thought
4. would do
5. would do
6. would double
7. had paid

Practice 6

Conversation A

Lisa: wishes that her mother would drive faster

Mark: wishes that he had a motorcycle like the one he saw

Mom: wishes that the government would ban motorcycle riding

Conversation B

Mr. Thorn: wishes the boss had told them about the meeting earlier

Ms. Warren: wishes that she had the time to check the pollution regulations before the meeting

Practice 7

A: environment class

B: eye-opener. Air pollution, water pollution, population growth, species extinction

A: greenhouse effect , global temperature

B: sea levels

A: coastal flooding, severe hurricanes, devastating droughts

B: global temperature, ice age.

A: wishful thinking, top priority.

B: international community, environmental laws, damage control

Practice 8

Letters will vary.

Check Your Knowledge

Vocabulary Check

1. Disposal
2. voluntary
3. regulations
4. weapons
5. extinction
6. benefit

Check Your Understanding

Answers (wishes) will vary.